COLLECTIONS OF REFORMED

PAST PAPERS

ACT Math
Practice Book

authored by

act test official website

Thanks to K.H, Lee and M.G, Kim

Table of Contents

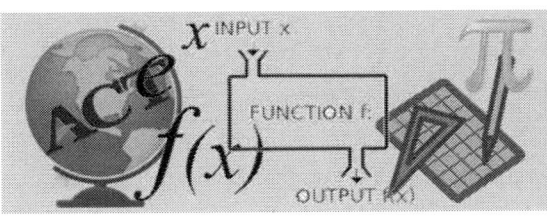 
The Processes of Reforming Real ACT Math Past Papers

Analyzing Information of *REAL ACT Math Test*

- ▶ Key math concept for ACT
- ▶ Analyzing questions category

Gathering Information of *REAL ACT Math Test*

- ▶ Gathering all REAL ACT Math test
- ▶ Gathering all preparing ACT Math test
- ▶ Gathering all prep-ACT Math book

Finding Rule of *REAL ACT Math Test*

- ▶ Matching math concept to question
- ▶ Classifying each question
- ▶ Finding the distribution of questions

Reforming Questions of *REAL ACT Math Test*

- ▶ Brief summary of the key concepts
- ▶ Provide representative questions
- ▶ Intuitive problem-solving strategies
- ▶ Provide detailed answers

Making Concept-Map of *REAL ACT Math Test*

- ▶ Finding relation between questions
- ▶ Making concept map

Examples of Re-Formed Past Paper Questions

ACT-72E Math Question Reforming

As shown in the figure below, the graph of $f(x)$, dashed line, and $g(x)$, solid line, are shown in the standard (x,y) coordinate plane. Which of the following expressions represents $g(x)$ in term of $f(x)$?

A. $-2(x+4)+5$

B. $-2(x-4)+5$

C. $2(x-4)+5$

D. $-\dfrac{1}{2}(x+4)+5$

E. $-\dfrac{1}{2}(x-4)+5$

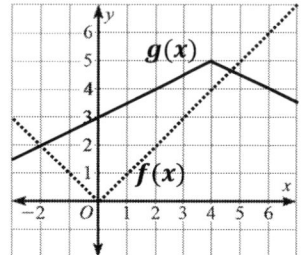

ACT-72G Math Question Reforming

On the map below, Beatrice is standing on a sailing boat at point B on the north side of the island. As measured by line of sight, she is 60 miles from a light house at W, and 100 miles from another light house at E. Suppose that Beatrice, B, west light house, W, and east light house, E, are all same elevation, and the measure of $\angle W$ is 32°. What is the equation for the measure of $\angle E$?

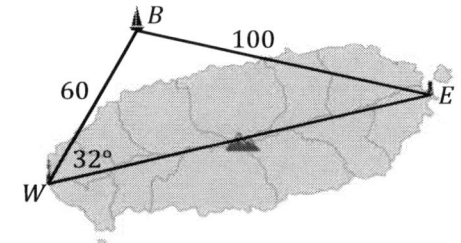

F. $\dfrac{\sin E}{160} = \dfrac{\sin 32°}{40}$

G. $\dfrac{\sin E}{60} = \dfrac{\sin 32°}{100}$

H. $\dfrac{\sin E}{100} = \dfrac{\sin 32°}{60}$

J. $\dfrac{\sin E}{\sin 32°} = \dfrac{60}{100}$

K. $\dfrac{\sin E}{60} = \dfrac{\sin 32°}{40}$

ACT-71C Math Question Reforming

The side lengths of the flat, trapezoidal backyard of a house are given in the figure below. Miny will lay the entire backyard with artificial grass, the artificial grass that has a price of $32 per box and is sold only by the full box. Each box of artificial grass lays an area of 15 square feet. What is the total price of the artificial grass that Miny needs to buy?

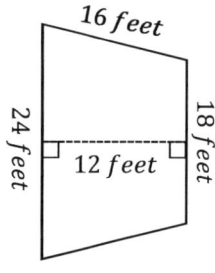

F. $512

G. $544

H. $567

J. $602

K. $632

Composition of Collections of reformed Past Papers ACT Math

12 Key Concepts for ACT Math

63 Subdivided Item Types

Hunting Past Papers **ACT Math**

11. Trigonometric Functions

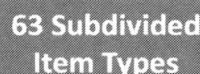 Type 056. *Trigonometric Ratio*

① Six trigonometric functions

$$\sin\theta = \frac{O}{H}, \qquad \csc\theta = \frac{1}{\sin\theta} = \frac{H}{O}$$

$$\cos\theta = \frac{A}{H}, \qquad \sec\theta = \frac{1}{\cos\theta} = \frac{H}{A}$$

$$\tan\theta = \frac{O}{A}, \qquad \cot\theta = \frac{1}{\tan\theta} = \frac{A}{O}$$

② Inverse trigonometric functions

$$\theta = \frac{O}{H}, \qquad \theta = \cos^{-1}\left(\frac{A}{H}\right), \qquad \theta = \tan^{-1}\left(\frac{O}{A}\right)$$

163.
As shown below, Cyma is loading a cargo truck by using a ramp. The ramp connecting the ground to a loading platform 3 feet above the ground. The ramp measures 10 feet from the ground to the top of the loading platform. Which of the following expression is the angle of elevation formed by the ramp the ground?

A. $\arccos\left(\frac{10}{3}\right)$

B. $\arccos\left(\frac{3}{10}\right)$

C. $\arccos\left(\frac{7}{10}\right)$

Concise Explanation for Concept

Concise Explanation for Concept

12 Reformed Past Papers Practice Tests

Hunting Past Papers **ACT Math**

2 △ △ △ △ △ △ △ △ △ △ 2

Reformed Past Paper MATH TEST 05

60 Questions – 60 Minutes

DIRECTIONS:
Solve each problem, choose the correct answer, and then fill in the corresponding oval on your answer in the grid on the answer sheet.
Do not linger over problems that take too much time. Solve as many as you can; then return to the others in the time you have left.
You are permitted to use a calculator on this test.

This test has reformed the REAL ACT Mathematics Test

Note: Unless otherwise stated, all of the following should be assumed.

1. ... to scale unless ...
2. All figures lie in a plane unless otherwise indicated.
3. All variables and expressions used represent real numbers unless otherwise indicated.

01.
Which of the following numbers is *not* a factor of 196?

A. 6
B. 7

05.

Intuitive Problem-Solving Strategies

Answer Explanations

Hunting Past Papers **ACT Math**

Answer explanations

01. Answer **(A)**
The number, which is represented by scientific notation, consists of a integer part and a power part. And time is the quotient of distance and speed.

Converting to scientific notation:
$$300{,}000{,}000 m/s = 3 \times 100{,}000{,}000 = 3 \times 10^8 m/s$$
$$150{,}000{,}000{,}000 m = 1.5 \times 100{,}000{,}000{,}000 = 1.5 \times 10^{11} m$$

Calculating time:
$$time = \frac{distance}{speed} = \frac{1.5 \times 10^{11}}{3 \times 10^8} = \frac{1.5}{3} \times \frac{10^{11}}{10^8} = 0.5 \times 10^3$$
$$= 5 \times 10^{-1} \times 10^3 = 5 \times 10^2$$

02. Answer **(H)**
This problem is just multiplication.

Multiplication:
$$0.00524 \times 1000 = 5.24$$

03. Answer **(A)**
"A number is divisible by 5" means that it is multiple of 5.

The smallest 4-digit number is a multiple of LCM of 3 and 5. And the LCM of 3 and 5 is 15.
The correct answer is $15 \times 67 = 1005$.

07. Answer **(B)**
"no less than" means ≥.

Convert to algebraic expression:
"5 less than twice a number x": → $2x - 5$
"no less than 12": → ≥ 12
Thus, the inequality is $2x - 5 \geq 12$.

08. Answer **(H)**
Let a be less than 1 and greater than 0. $b = ac$ → $c > b$.

Find the relationship between x and y;
Divide by 4 on both sides;
$$3x = 4y \rightarrow \frac{3x}{4} = \frac{4y}{4} \rightarrow y = \frac{3}{4}x \rightarrow x > y \ (\because \frac{3}{4} < 1)$$

Find the relationship between y and z;
Multiply by 6 on both sides;
$$\frac{1}{2}y = \frac{1}{3}z \rightarrow 6 \times \frac{1}{2}y = 6 \times \frac{1}{3}z \rightarrow 3y = 2z$$
Divide by 3 on both sides;
$$3y = 2z \rightarrow \frac{3y}{3} = \frac{2z}{3} \rightarrow y = \frac{2}{3}z \rightarrow z > y \ (\because \frac{2}{3} < 1)$$

Find the relationship between x and z;
Substitute $\frac{3}{4}x$ for y;
$$\frac{1}{2}y = \frac{1}{3}z \rightarrow \frac{1}{2}\left(\frac{3}{4}x\right) = \frac{1}{3}z \rightarrow \frac{3}{8}x = \frac{1}{3}z$$

Multiply by $\frac{8}{3}$ on both sides;
$$\frac{3}{8}x = \frac{1}{3}z \rightarrow \frac{8}{3} \times \frac{3}{8}x = \frac{8}{3} \times \frac{1}{3}z \rightarrow x = \frac{8}{9}z \rightarrow z > x \ \left(\because \frac{8}{9} < 1\right)$$
Thus, the relationship is $z > x > y$.

Detailed Explanations

WHAT IS ... **ACT** Mathematics Test

Only tenth-, eleventh-, and twelfth-grade students attend Washington High School. The ratio of tenth graders to the school's total student population is 86:255, and the ratio of eleventh graders to the school's total student population is 18:51. If 1 student is chosen at random from the entire school, which grade is that student most likely to be in?

A. Tenth
B. Eleventh
C. Twelfth
D. All grades are equally likely.
E. Cannot be determined from the given information

ACT-1572CPRE

1. **60**-question, **60**-minute test.
2. **Multiple-choice** questions.
3. Most questions are self-contained.
4. Some questions may belong to a **set** of several questions.
5. Total raw score is 60 and **total scale score is 36**.

TIP **Tips for Taking the ACT Mathematics Test**

Pace yourself.
- average of 1 minute per question
- spend less time on each question
- use the remaining time allowed to review

Use the calculator wisely.
- some of the problems are best done without a calculator.
- all of the mathematics problems can be solved without using a calculator

Do not using mental calculation.
- could not be sure of your mental math
- you will usually solve problem in the space provided in the test booklet.

The answer is ALWAYS in the choices.
- If your answer is not included among the choices, carefully reread the problem to see whether you missed important information.
- Pay careful attention to the question being asked.

Check your solving problem.
- An incorrect solution is by making common errors in the problem-solving process.
- Check your answers to make sure they are correct.

12 Reformed ACT *past-paper* Full Tests

PRIMUS INTER PARES

K·DEAN

Reformed Past Paper ACT MATH TEST 01

60 Questions – 60 Minutes

DIRECTIONS:
Solve each problem, choose the correct answer, and then fill in the corresponding oval on your answer in the grid on the answer sheet.

Do not linger over problems that take too much time. Do as many as you can, then return to the others in the time you have left for the test.

You are permitted to use a calculator on this test.

Note: Unless otherwise stated, all of the following should be assumed.

1. Figures are not necessarily drawn to scale unless otherwise indicated.

2. All figures lie in a plane unless otherwise indicated.

3. All variables and expressions used represent real numbers unless otherwise indicated.

This test has reformed the REAL ACT Mathematics Test

01.

The speed of light in a vacuum is estimated to be 300,000,000 metes per second. How many seconds would it take to reach the sun with distance 150,000,000,000 meters from earth ?

A. 5×10^2

B. 2×10^3

C. 5×10^3

D. 2×10^4

E. 5×10^4

02.

If 0.00524 times 1000, what is the result ?

F. 0.0524

G. 0.524

H. 5.24

J. 52.4

K. 524

03.

What is the smallest 4 -digit number that is a multiple of 3 and is divisible by 5 ?

A. 1005

B. 1015

C. 1020

D. 1025

E. 1045

04.

If an operation ★, is defined on ordered pairs of integers as follows $(a, b) \star (c, d) = \frac{ad+cb}{bd-ac}$, then what is the value of $(1,2) \star (3,4)$?

F. $-\frac{1}{4}$

G. $-\frac{3}{4}$

H. -1

J. 1

K. 2

05.

The expression
$(2x - 3) + (x^2 - 2x + 4) + (x - 2) - (2x - 3x - 4x)$ is
equivalent to ?

A. $x^2 - 10x - 5$

B. $x^2 + 10x - 5$

C. $x^2 + 6x - 5$

D. $x^2 - 6x + 5$

E. $x^2 - 6x - 5$

06.

Doctors measure the cholesterol in human blood to
see if they are at risk for heart disease. The formula
below gives their total cholesterol level, C, is
$C = L + \frac{4H+T}{5}$ in terms of L, low density cholesterol,
H, high density cholesterol, and T, triglycerides.
Which of the following expressions gives H in terms
of C, L and T ?

F. $\frac{C - L}{4} - 5T$

G. $\frac{5C - 5L}{4} + T$

H. $\frac{5C - 5L}{4} - T$

J. $\frac{5C - 5L - T}{4}$

K. $\frac{5C + 5L + T}{4}$

07.

Which of the following inequalities is equivalent to
the statements below ?

5 less than twice a number x is no less than 12

A. $2x - 5 \geq -12$

B. $2x - 5 \geq 12$

C. $2x - 5 < -12$

D. $2x - 5 > -12$

E. $2x - 5 \leq 12$

08.

If $3x = 4y$ and $\frac{1}{2}y = \frac{1}{3}z$ for $x > 0$, $y > 0$ and $z > 0$
which of the following inequalities represents the
relation x, y, and z ?

F. $x > y > z$

G. $x > z > y$

H. $z > x > y$

J. $z > y > x$

K. $y > x > z$

09.

Several coins are in a box, which value is $4.28. In
the box, there are 2 less quarters ($0.25) than dimes
($0.10), 2 more nickels ($0.05) than dimes, and 13
more pennies ($0.01) than dimes. What is the sum
of all the coins in the box ?

A. 61

B. 60

C. 59

D. 58

E. 57

10.

Which of the following expressions is equal to $-x(3 - 2x) + 4(x - 5)$ for real value of x ?

F. $-2x^2 + 7x - 20$

G. $2x^2 + x - 20$

H. $2x^2 - x + 20$

J. $-2x^2 - x - 20$

K. $2x^2 - x - 20$

11.

What is the value of $g(-2)$ when $g(x) = -(2x - 5)^3$?

F. -81

G. 132

H. -132

J. 729

K. -729

12.

What is the slope of the line of the equation $-2x + 3y = 9$?

A. -2

B. $\dfrac{2}{3}$

C. $-\dfrac{2}{3}$

D. -3

E. 3

13.

Some providers of high-speed internet service offer a choice of two plans A and B. The table below gives the total charge to use a internet service from the two plans for various numbers of months. For what number of months would the total charge for using a internet service from plan A's be equal to the total charge for using a internet service from plan B's ?

(Note: There is a linear relationship between the number of months and the total charge for both plan A's and B's)

Number of months	Total charge	
	plan A's	plan B's
1	$32	$10
2	$35	$15
3	$38	$20
4	$41	$25
5	$44	$30

F. 18

G. 16

H. 14

J. 12

K. 10

14.

Which of the following graphs shows the solution set for the system of linear inequalities $-2x + 3 < 7$ and $3x < 6$?

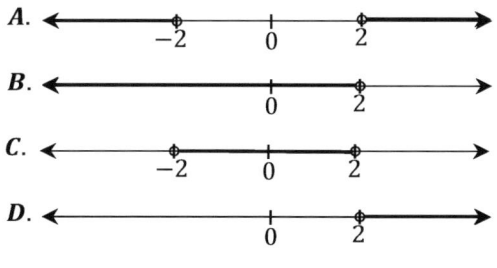

15.

The absolute value of which of the following numbers is the smallest ?

F.   0.004

G.   −0.5

H.   0.025

J.   0.003

K.   −0.011

16.

The graph of $y = g(x)$ is shown in the standard (x, y) coordinate plane below. Which of the following sets is the range of the function $g(x)$?

F. $\{-2, -1, 0, 1, 2, 3\}$

G. $\{-2, -1, 0, 1, 2, 3, 4\}$

H. $\{0, 1\}$

J. $\{x \mid -2 \leq x < 4\}$

K. $\{y \mid 0 \leq y < 1\}$

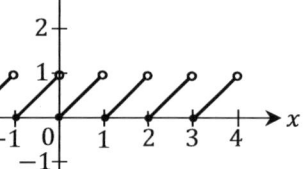

17.

If an equation of the line is $-6x + 5y = 96$, what is the slope of the line that is perpendicular to the line ?

A. $\dfrac{96}{5}$

B. $-\dfrac{6}{5}$

C. $\dfrac{6}{5}$

D. $\dfrac{5}{6}$

E. $-\dfrac{5}{6}$

18.

The four distinct points $X, Y, W,$ and Z are collinear, and Y is between X and W. For Z to be between X and W such that $XZ + ZY + YW = XW$, which of statements below must be true?

I . $XZ = ZY$
II. $XY = WZ$
III. Z is between X and Y

A.   I only

B.   II only

C.   III only

D.   II and III

E.   I, II, and III

19.

The figure below shows a combination of two rectangles and its dimensions are in centimeters. What is the area, in square centimeters, of shaded region?

F. $6x^2 + 280$

G. $x^2 - 41x + 140$

H. $x^2 + 41x + 140$

J. $6x^2 - 82x + 280$

K. $6x^2 + 82x + 280$

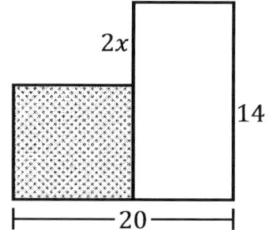

2 △ △ △ △ △ △ △ △ △ **2**

Use the following information to answer questions 20 - 22.

Lauren is converting a 45-foot-by-60-foot rooftop in her house to a roof garden. Lauren will lay down in grass herself but will have Green Landscaping Firm build and install the flowerbeds. The scale drawing shown below displays the location of the flowerbeds in the roof garden. (0.2 inch represents 3 feet)

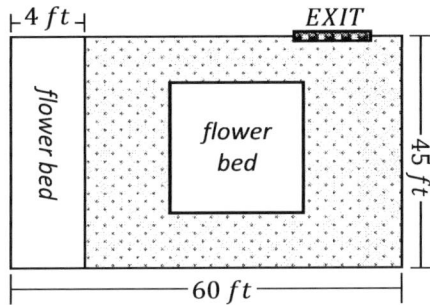

Flower beds will be installed along one of the 45-foot walls, and a square flowerbed with 10 feet in side length will be installed in the middle of the rooftop. Green Landscaping Firm has given Lauren an estimate of $3,250.00 for building and installing the flower beds.

20.

Lauren will lay down in grass on the portion of the rooftop that will NOT be covered by flowerbeds. What is the area, in square feet, of the portion of the rooftop that will NOT be covered by flowerbeds?

A. 2240

B. 2280

C. 2320

D. 2420

E. 2460

21.

A 60-foot wall is how many inches long in the scale drawing ?

A. 3.6

B. 3.8

C. 4.0

D. 4.4

E. 4.8

22.

Green Landscaping Firm's estimate consists of a $730.00 charge for labor, plus a fixed charge per square feet of the flowerbeds. The labor charge and the charge per square feet of the flowerbeds remain the same for any area of flowerbeds built and installed. Green Landscaping Firm would give Lauren what estimate if the rooftop were to have twice as many flowerbeds as Lauren is planning to have?

F. $5,670.00

G. $5,670.25

H. $5,760.75

J. $5,770.00

K. $5,775.25

23.

A swimming pool in the shape of a right cylinder has radius 10 feet. If the volume of water in the pool is 1,560 cubic feet, what is the depth, to the nearest tenth, of the water in the pool?

A. 4.1

B. 4.4

C. 4.7

D. 5.0

E. 5.3

24.

In the figure below, a right rectangular prism is intersected by a plane that is **not** parallel to the base and does not intersect the base. One of the following figures shows the shape of the intersection. Which figure is it?

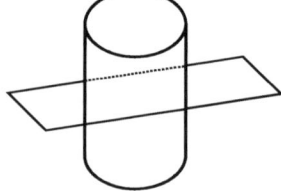

F.
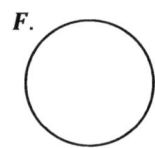

G.
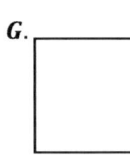

H.
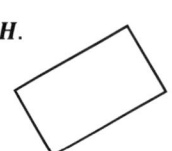

J.

K.
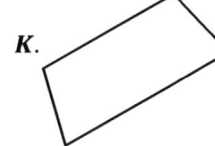

25.

The volume of a sphere with radius r is $\frac{4}{3}\pi r^3$. If a sphere has a volume of 36 cubic centimeters, what is the value of radius, in centimeters, of the sphere?

A. $\dfrac{\pi}{\sqrt[3]{3}}$

B. $\sqrt[3]{\dfrac{144}{3\pi}}$

C. $\dfrac{3}{\sqrt[3]{\pi}}$

D. $\dfrac{27}{\pi}$

E. $\dfrac{144}{\pi^2}$

26.

Hexahedrons, cubes, having a edge length of 2 inches are put together to form a right rectangular prism with 3 layer. If each layer has 8 cubes, what is the volume, in cubic inches, of the right rectangular prism?

F. 24

G. 48

H. 64

J. 160

K. 192

27.

If the diameter of a circle is 8cm, what is the area, in square centimeters, of the circle?

A. 64π

B. 36π

C. 24π

D. 16π

E. 12π

28.

In the figure below, four non-overlapping circles, each with radius r feet, are inscribed in a square. What is the area, in square feet, of the shaded region?

F. $4\pi r^2$

G. $4r^2 - 4\pi r^2$

H. $16r^2 - 4\pi r^2$

J. $64r^2 - 4\pi r^2$

K. $64r^2 + 4\pi r^2$

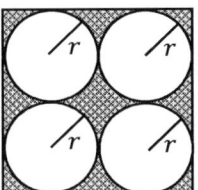

29.

The baseball coach, Gregory, has $200 available to buy balls to train for his team members. Each baseball has a $5, and he will pay a sales tax of 5% of the total price of the balls. What is the maximum number of baseballs Gregory can buy ?

A. 35

B. 36

C. 37

D. 38

E. 39

30.

In the figure below, the graph of $f(x) = -\dfrac{3}{2}x - 5$ and $g(x) = -(x+2)^2 - 1$ are in the standard (x,y) coordinate plane. Which of following is **true** ?

A. $g(f(-2)) = -1$

B. $g(x) \geq -1$

C. $f(0) < g(0)$

D. $g(x) = |g(x)|$

E. $f(x) = -|f(x)|$

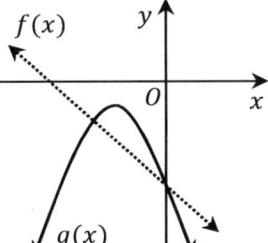

31.

The height above the ground of a placekicked football t seconds after being kicked from the ground is given by $h(t) = -3t^2 + 12t + 36$. Which of following statements is **true** from the equation?

F. Reaches the ground after 2 seconds.

G. Maximum height reaching time is 4 seconds.

H. Starts at a point 12 units off the ground.

J. Maximum height of ball is 48 units.

K. Maximum height of ball is 36 units.

32.

Which of the following expressions is a factor of the polynomial $5x^2 - 17x + 6$?

A. $x - 2$

B. $5x - 3$

C. $5x + 2$

D. $x + 3$

E. $5x - 2$

33.

The expression $x^2 + 2x + 1$ is equivalent to;

F. $(x + 1)(x - 1)$

G. $(x + 4)\left(x - \dfrac{1}{4}\right)$

H. $(x - 4)\left(x + \dfrac{1}{4}\right)$

J. $(x + 1)^2$

K. $(x - 1)^2$

34.

The product of a complex number $2a + bi$, for a and b are nonzero real numbers, and which of the following complex numbers is a real number ?

F. $a + 2bi$

G. $a - 2bi$

H. $2a + bi$

J. $2a - bi$

K. i

35.

Which of the following expression is equivalent to $(2x - 4)(x + 2)$?

A. $2x^2 + 8$

B. $2x^2 - 8$

C. $2x^2 - 8x + 8$

D. $2x^2 + 8x + 8$

E. $2x^2 - 8x - 8$

36.

When an account earns interest compounded annually, the balance A is given by the formula

$$A = P\left(1 + \frac{r}{100}\right)^t$$

where P is the principal, r is the annual interest rate (written as a percent), and t is the time in years.

Delphine is saving to make a down payment on a car. With an initial deposit of $1,000$, she have opened an account that compounds interest at an annual rate 6.5%. Which of the following expressions is the value, in dollars, of the account 3 years after the initial deposit?

A. $1,000(1 + 3 \times 0.065)$

B. $1,000(1 + 3 \times 6.5)$

C. $1,000(1.065)^3$

D. $1,000(1.65)^3$

E. $1,000(7.5)^3$

37.

For what positive real number of n is the equation $(a^4)^2(a^3)^5 = a^n$ **true** ?

A. 12

B. 14

C. 16

D. 20

E. 23

38.

Which of the following expressions is equivalent to $(2a^2b^3)(5a^6b^2)$, for all nonzero real numbers a and b ?

F. $7a^8b^5$

G. $7a^6b^{10}$

H. $10a^5b^7$

J. $10a^8b^5$

K. $10a^6b^{10}$

39.

If $a = \sqrt{7}$ and $b = \sqrt{13}$, then what is the value of $\sqrt{a^2 + b^2}$?

A. 2

B. $\sqrt{6}$

C. $2\sqrt{5}$

D. 20

E. $\sqrt{218}$

40.

Let $h(x) = x - 3$ and $r(x) = 3 - x^2$. What is the value of $h(r(-3))$?

A. -18

B. -12

C. -9

D. 9

E. 12

41.

A climbing expedition ascended Mt. Everest, which is 8,848 meters high. They started from a base camp at 2,000 meters. The points on the graph below show the climbing expedition's cumulative height climbed at the end of each day.

After the climbing expedition began their climbing, they climbed the *greatest* number of meters on which of these 5 days?

F. Day 1

G. Day 2

H. Day 3

J. Day 4

K. Day 5

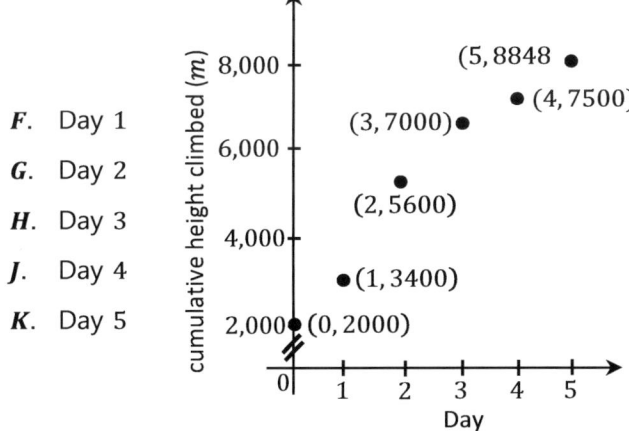

42.

As shown figure below, a spinner is divided into 8 equal sections. Bessie spins the spinner, and it will point one of the sectors in the spinner. What is the probability that the sector the pointer points is both a multiple of 2 and a multiple of 3 ?

A. $\dfrac{1}{8}$

B. $\dfrac{1}{4}$

C. $\dfrac{3}{8}$

D. $\dfrac{1}{2}$

E. $\dfrac{5}{8}$

43.

The figure below is 3 different views of the same cubic dice. Each face of the dice has 1 design drawn on it. If the cubic dice will be drawn once, what is the probability of that a face showing a letter C will be top?

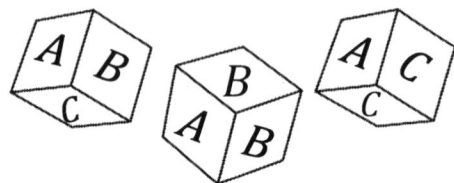

F. $\dfrac{1}{6}$

G. $\dfrac{1}{3}$

H. $\dfrac{1}{2}$

J. $\dfrac{1}{4}$

K. $\dfrac{2}{3}$

44.

The table below shows the number of drivers caught speeding in each month last year. What is the median of the data in the table?

Month	Number of drivers
January	72
February	63
March	60
April	88
May	55
June	78
July	42
August	34
September	51
October	62
November	57
December	81

A. 57

B. 58.5

C. 60

D. 60.5

E. 61

45.

Which of the following data sets has the least standard deviation ?

F. $3, 3, 3, 3, 3, 3, 3, 3, 3$

G. $1, 2, 3, 4, 5$

H. $6, 7, 8, 9, 10, 11$

J. $-5, -2, 0, 2, 5$

K. $-3, -1, 0, 1, 3$

46.

A triangular number counts objects arranged in an equilateral triangle, as in the figure in the below. The nth triangular number, t_n, is the number of dots in the triangular arrangement with n dots on a side. What is the value of t_{36}?

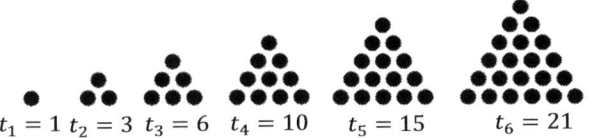

$t_1 = 1$ $t_2 = 3$ $t_3 = 6$ $t_4 = 10$ $t_5 = 15$ $t_6 = 21$

A. 448

B. 576

C. 666

D. 728

E. 816

47.

Which of the following equations is the equation of the ellipse that is graphed in the standard (x, y) coordinate plane below?

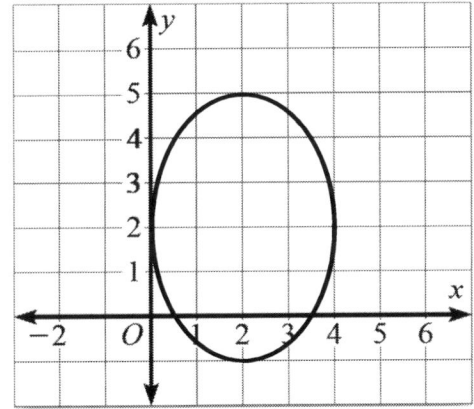

A. $\dfrac{(x-2)^2}{3} - \dfrac{(y-2)^2}{2} = 1$

B. $\dfrac{(x+2)^2}{2} + \dfrac{(y+2)^2}{3} = 1$

C. $\dfrac{(x-2)^2}{4} + \dfrac{(y-2)^2}{9} = 1$

D. $\dfrac{(x+2)^2}{9} + \dfrac{(y+2)^2}{4} = 1$

E. $\dfrac{(x-2)^2}{4} - \dfrac{(y-2)^2}{9} = 1$

48.

As shown in the standard (x, y) coordinate plane below, which of the values is the length, in coordinate units, of the altitude from R to $\overline{PQ}$ in $\triangle PQR$?

A. 4

B. 5

C. $5\sqrt{2}$

D. 6

E. $6\sqrt{3}$

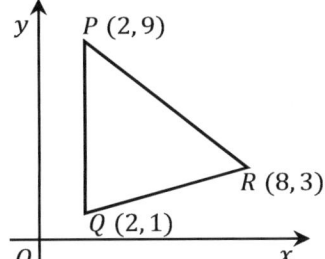

49.

Suppose that the coordinates of the midpoint of $\overline{AB}$ are $(3, -2)$ and the coordinates of A are $(-10, 10)$. What are the coordinates of B?

A. $(14, -10)$

B. $(16, -12)$

C. $(18, -14)$

D. $(-12, 14)$

E. $(-14, 16)$

Use the following information to answer questions *50 - 52.*

In the standard (x, y) coordinate, a map of Hanahill, Duri City, and Sezi Town is shown below, where 1 coordinate unit is 1 kilometer. The coordinates of Hanahill and Sezi Town are given, and Duri City is located along a straight line exactly halfway between Hanahill and Sezi Town. Road 12 from Hanahill to Sezi Town is 250 kilometers along and Road 15 from Duri City to Sezi Town is 130 kilometers along.

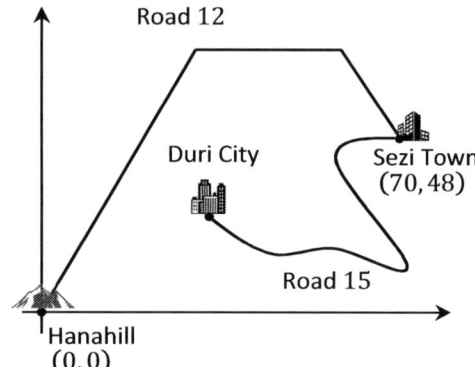

50.

What are the coordinates of Duri City?

A. $(24, 16)$

B. $(27, 18)$

C. $(30, 20)$

D. $(32, 22)$

E. $(35, 24)$

51.

Dave's car travels an average of 52 kilometers per gallon of gasoline used, and he pays an average $3.75 per gallon of gasoline. Dave will drive his car along Road 15 from Duri City to Sezi Town, and then drives along Road 12 to Hanahill. Which of the following costs, in dollars, is closest to the total cost of gasoline that his car uses for the drive?

A. $21.05

B. $23.72

C. $25.68

D. $27.40

E. $29.52

52.

Which of the following values is closest to the straight-line distance, in kilometers, from Hanahill to Sezi Town?

F. 76.8

G. 78.6

H. 80.5

J. 82.3

K. 84.9

53.

As shown the figure below, The radius of circle, O, is 8 cm and length of chord $\overline{PR}$ is 12 cm. What is the length, in centimeters, from O, the center of the circle, to Q, the midpoint of $\overline{PR}$?

A. $2\sqrt{5}$

B. $2\sqrt{7}$

C. 5

D. 6

E. $6\sqrt{2}$

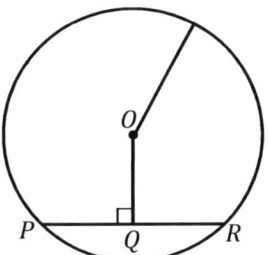

54.

For all x, which of the following is the simplified form of the expression $\sin x + \cos x \cot x$?

F. $\cos x$

G. $\sin x$

H. $\sec x$

J. $\csc x$

K. $\tan x$

55.

A wind pump is a type of windmill which is used for pumping water. On the day when the wind is very weak, the wind pump wheel rotates at a constant speed and complete 1 rotation in 2 minutes. How many degrees does the wind pump wheel rotates in 20 seconds?

A. 15°

B. 30°

C. 45°

D. 60°

E. 72°

56.

In the figure below, the shaded sector of the circle is bounded by two radii and minor arc. The length of the radius is 2 feet, and the area of the shaded sector is $\frac{4}{3}\pi$ square feet. Which of the following degree measures is the angle of θ?

F. 60°

G. 90°

H. 100°

J. 120°

K. 135°

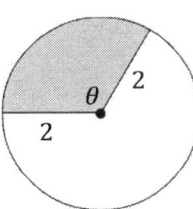

57.

On the map below, electrical engineers are installing a straight high-voltage line from a power plant at P to Moon City located at M on a straight stretch of highway. The distance from the power plant to the city is 65 miles, and the distance from the power plant to the highway is 43 miles. What is the expression of the angle formed by the high-voltage line and the highway?

A. $\cos^{-1}\left(\dfrac{43}{65}\right)$

B. $\cos^{-1}\left(\dfrac{65}{43}\right)$

C. $\sin^{-1}\left(\dfrac{43}{65}\right)$

D. $\tan^{-1}\left(\dfrac{43}{65}\right)$

E. $\tan^{-1}\left(\dfrac{65}{43}\right)$

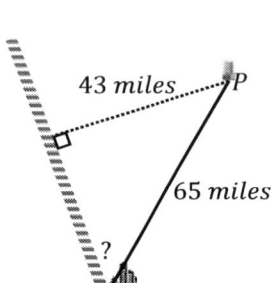

43 miles ⋯⋯ P

65 miles

? M

58.

As shown figure below, Caley is standing in a river bank looking up his friend Charlie. Charlie is standing in a bungee jump dock looking at Caley. Which of the following expressions is the angle of elevation of Caley's line of sight?

F. $\arctan\left(\dfrac{27}{7}\right)$

G. $\arcsin\left(\dfrac{27}{7}\right)$

H. $\text{arccot}\left(\dfrac{7}{27}\right)$

J. $\arctan\left(\dfrac{7}{27}\right)$

K. $\arctan\left(\dfrac{27}{7}\right)$

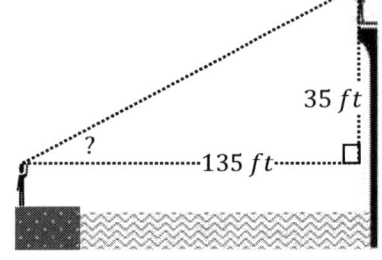

35 ft

? ⋯⋯135 ft⋯⋯

59.

In the standard (x, y) coordinate plane, the graph of $f(x) = 2 - 3\cos(x + \pi)$ is shown below. What is the range of $f(x)$?

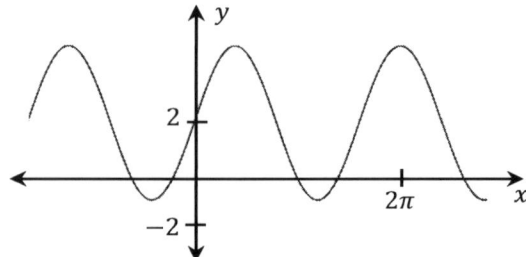

A. $-1 \le y \le 2$

B. $-3 \le y \le 3$

C. $-1 \le y \le 5$

D. $0 \le x \le 2\pi$

E. $0 \le x \le \dfrac{3\pi}{2}$

60.

The core of the revised South Korea election law is as follows:

"If people are 18 years of age, then the people could vote."

Which of the following statements is logically equivalent to the core of the revised election law?

F. All-18-years-olds could not vote.

G. Being able to vote is not necessary for people to be 18.

H. If people could vote, then the people are 18 years of age.

J. If people are not 18 years of age, then the people could not vote.

K. If people could not vote, then the people are not 18 years of age.

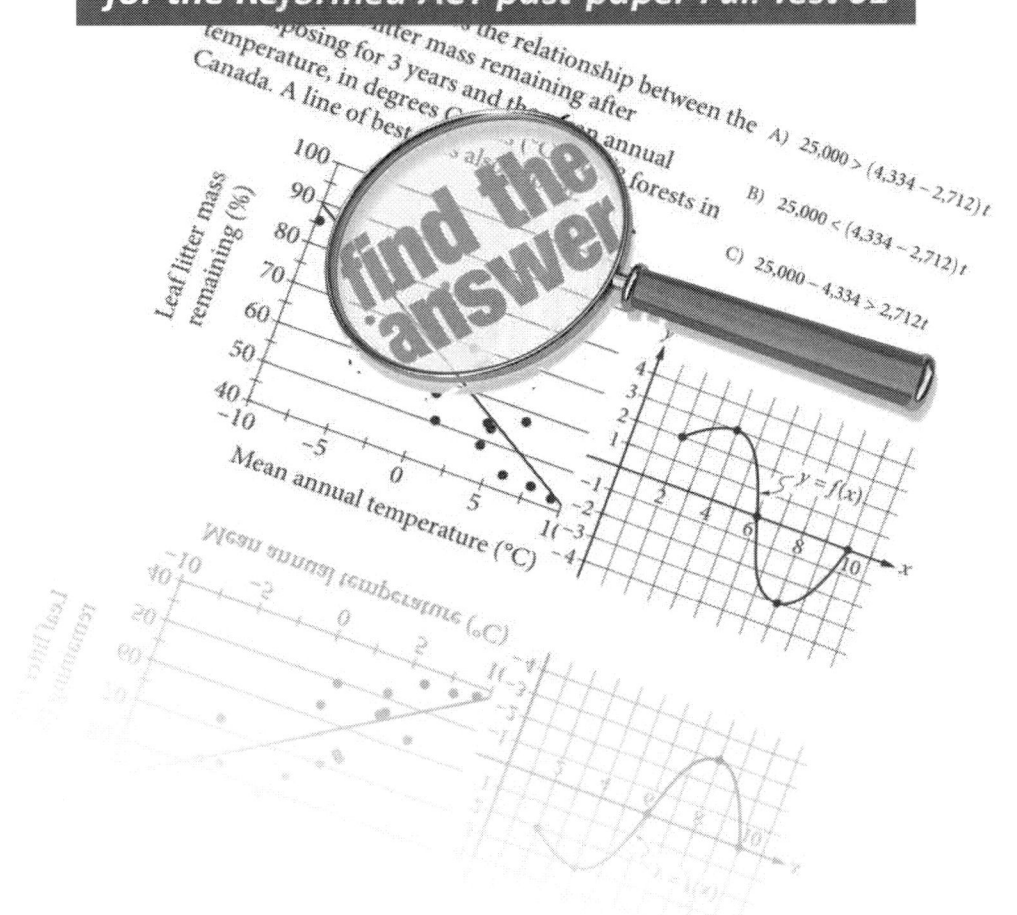

...posing ...lter mass ... the relationship between the
temperature for 3 years and th... ...annual
Canada. A line of best... ...forests in

A) $25,000 > (4,334 - 2,712)t$

B) $25,000 < (4,334 - 2,712)t$

C) $25,000 - 4,334 > 2,712t$

Obtain Scale Scores from Raw Scores

Scale Score	Raw Score	Scale Score	Raw Score	Scale Score	Raw Score
36	60	24	36-37	12	7
35	58-59	23	34-35	11	5-6
34	57	22	32-33	10	4
33	55-56	21	30-31	9	-
32	54	20	29	8	3
31	52-53	19	27-28	7	-
30	50-51	18	24-26	6	2
29	48-49	17	21-23	5	-
28	45-47	16	17-20	4	1
27	43-44	15	13-16	3	-
26	40-42	14	11-12	2	-
25	38-39	13	8-10	1	0

1. Scoring Key

Key		Question Category	Y/N
01.	A	Number Theory	
02.	H	Number Theory	
03.	A	Number Theory	
04.	K	Expression and Linear Equation	
05.	C	Expression and Linear Equation	
06.	J	Expression and Linear Equation	
07.	B	Expression and Linear Equation	
08.	H	Expression and Linear Equation	
09.	A	Expression and Linear Equation	
10.	G	Expression and Linear Equation	
11.	J	Linear Function inequality	
12.	B	Linear Function inequality	
13.	J	Linear Function inequality	
14.	C	Linear Function inequality	
15.	J	Linear Function inequality	
16.	K	Linear Function inequality	
17.	E	Linear Function inequality	
18.	C	Basic Geometry	
19.	J	Basic Geometry	
20.	D	Arithmetic Topic and Ratio	
21.	C	Arithmetic Topic and Ratio	
22.	J	Arithmetic Topic and Ratio	
23.	D	Basic Geometry	
24.	J	Basic Geometry	
25.	C	Basic Geometry	
26.	K	Basic Geometry	
27.	D	Basic Geometry	
28.	H	Basic Geometry	
29.	D	Arithmetic Topic and Ratio	
30.	A	Quadratic and Polynomial Function	

Key		Question Category	Y/N
31.	J	Quadratic and Polynomial Function	
32.	E	Quadratic and Polynomial Function	
33.	J	Quadratic and Polynomial Function	
34.	J	Quadratic and Polynomial Function	
35.	B	Quadratic and Polynomial Function	
36.	C	Further Equations and Functions	
37.	E	Further Equations and Functions	
38.	J	Further Equations and Functions	
39.	C	Further Equations and Functions	
40.	C	Further Equations and Functions	
41.	G	Statistics and Probability	
42.	D	Statistics and Probability	
43.	G	Statistics and Probability	
44.	E	Statistics and Probability	
45.	F	Statistics and Probability	
46.	C	Sequence and Series	
47.	C	Analytic Geometry and Conic Section	
48.	D	Analytic Geometry and Conic Section	
49.	B	Analytic Geometry and Conic Section	
50.	E	Analytic Geometry and Conic Section	
51.	D	Analytic Geometry and Conic Section	
52.	K	Analytic Geometry and Conic Section	
53.	B	Analytic Geometry and Conic Section	
54.	J	Trigonometric Functions	
55.	D	Trigonometric Functions	
56.	J	Trigonometric Functions	
57.	C	Trigonometric Functions	
58.	J	Trigonometric Functions	
59.	C	Trigonometric Functions	
60.	K	Intermediate Algebra	

2. Answer Explanations

---

01. Answer **(A)**

The number, which is represented by scientific notation, consists of a integer part and a power part. And time is the quotient of distance and speed.

Converting to scientific notation;
$$300,000,000 m/s = 3 \times 100,000,000 = 3 \times 10^8 m/s$$
$$150,000,000,000 m = 1.5 \times 100,000,000,000 = 1.5 \times 10^{11} m$$

Calculating time;
$$time = \frac{distance}{speed} = \frac{1.5 \times 10^{11}}{3 \times 10^8} = \frac{1.5}{3} \times \frac{10^{11}}{10^8} = 0.5 \times 10^3$$
$$= 5 \times 10^{-1} \times 10^3 = 5 \times 10^2$$

---

02. Answer **(H)**

This problem is just multiplication .

Multiplication;
$$0.00524 \times 1000 = 5.24$$

---

03. Answer **(A)**

"A number is divisible by 5 "means that it is multiple of 5.

The smallest 4-digit number is a multiple of LCM of 3 and 5. And the LCM of 3 and 5 is 15.

The correct answer is $15 \times 67 = 1005$.

---

04. Answer **(K)**

Substitute the integers for the variables and then evaluate .

Substitute 1 for a, 2 for b, 3 for c and 4 for d;
$$(1,2) \star (3,4) = \frac{1 \times 4 + 3 \times 2}{2 \times 4 - 1 \times 3} = \frac{4 + 6}{8 - 3} = \frac{10}{5} = 2$$
Thus, the value is 2.

---

05. Answer **(C)**

Expanding the polynomial by using the distributive property.

Expanding the polynomial
$$(2x - 3) + (x^2 - 2x + 4) + (x - 2) - (2x - 3x - 4x)$$
$$= 2x - 3 + x^2 - 2x + 4 + x - 2 - (-5x)$$
$$= 2x - 3 + x^2 - 2x + 4 + x - 2 + 5x$$
Combing the like terms;
$$\rightarrow x^2 + (2x - 2x + x + 5x) - 3 - 2$$
$$= x^2 + 6x - 5$$
Thus, the equivalent expression is $x^2 + 6x - 5$.

---

06. Answer **(J)**

Solving for H.

Substracting L on both sides;
$$C = L + \frac{(4H + T)}{5} \rightarrow C - L = \frac{4H + T}{5}$$
Multiplying 5 on both sides;
$$C - L = \frac{4H + T}{5} \rightarrow 4H + T = 5(C - L)$$
Substracting T on both sides;
$$4H + T = 5(C - L) \rightarrow 4H = 5C - 5L - T$$
Dividing by 4 on both sides;
$$4H = 5C - 5L - T \rightarrow H = \frac{5C - 5L - T}{4}$$
Thus, the expression is $\frac{5C-5L-T}{4}$.

---

07. Answer **(B)**

"no less than" means $\geq$.

Convert to algebraic expressions;
"5 less than twice an number x"; $\rightarrow$ $2x - 5$
"no less than 12"; $\rightarrow \geq 12$

Thus, the inequality is $2x - 5 \geq 12$.

---

08. Answer **(H)**

Let a be less than 1 and greater than 0. b=ac $\rightarrow$ c>b.

Find the relationship between x and y;
Divide by 4 on both sides;
$$3x = 4y \rightarrow \frac{3x}{4} = \frac{4y}{4} \rightarrow y = \frac{3}{4}x \rightarrow x > y \ (\because \frac{3}{4} < 1)$$

Find the relationship between y and z;
Multiply by 6 on both sides;
$$\frac{1}{2}y = \frac{1}{3}z \rightarrow 6 \times \frac{1}{2}y = 6 \times \frac{1}{3}z \rightarrow 3y = 2z$$
Divide by 3 on both sides;
$$3y = 2z \rightarrow \frac{3y}{3} = \frac{2z}{3} \rightarrow y = \frac{2}{3}z \rightarrow z > y \ (\because \frac{2}{3} < 1)$$
Find the relationship between x and z;
Substitute $\frac{3}{4}x$ for y;
$$\frac{1}{2}y = \frac{1}{3}z \rightarrow \frac{1}{2}\left(\frac{3}{4}x\right) = \frac{1}{3}z \rightarrow \frac{3}{8}x = \frac{1}{3}z$$
Multiply by $\frac{8}{3}$ on both sides;
$$\frac{3}{8}x = \frac{1}{3}z \rightarrow \frac{8}{3} \times \frac{3}{8}x = \frac{8}{3} \times \frac{1}{3}z \rightarrow x = \frac{8}{9}z \rightarrow z > x \left(\because \frac{8}{9} < 1\right)$$
Thus, the relationship is $z > x > y$.

---

09. Answer **(A)**

Convert number of other coins to number of dimes.

If the number of quarters is Q, dimes is D, nickels is N, and pennies is P then,
"2 less quarters than dimes" $\rightarrow$ $Q = D - 2$
"2 more nickels than dimes" $\rightarrow$ $N = D + 2$
"13 more pennies than dimes" $\rightarrow$ $P = D + 13$.

The value of coins is \$4.65.
$$0.25Q + 0.1D + 0.05N + 0.01P = 4.65$$
Substituting expression represented by dimes;
$$0.25(D - 2) + 0.1D + 0.05(D + 2) + 0.01(D + 13) = 4.65$$
Expanding by the distributive property;
$$0.25D - 0.5 + 0.1D + 0.05D + 0.1 + 0.01D + 0.13 = 4.65$$
$$\rightarrow 0.41D - 0.27 = 4.65$$
Adding 0.27 to both sides;
$$0.41D - 0.27 = 4.65 \rightarrow 0.41D - 0.27 + 0.27 = 4.65 + 0.27$$
$$\rightarrow 0.41D = 4.92$$
Dividing both sides by 0.41;
$$0.41D = 4.92 \rightarrow \frac{0.41D}{0.41} = \frac{4.92}{0.41} \rightarrow D = 12$$
Substituting 12 for D;
$$Q = D - 2 \rightarrow Q = 12 - 2 \rightarrow Q = 10$$
$$N = D + 2 \rightarrow N = 12 + 2 \rightarrow N = 14$$
$$P = D + 13 \rightarrow P = 12 + 13 \rightarrow P = 25$$
Thus, the sum of the coins in the box is;
$$Q + D + N + P = 10 + 12 + 14 + 25 = 61.$$

---

10. Answer **(G)**

Distributive property: $A(B + C) = AB + AC$.

Rewrite by using distributive property;
$$-x(3 - 2x) + 4(x - 5) = -3x + 2x^2 + 4x - 20$$
Combining like terms;
$$2x^2 - 3x + 4x - 20 = 2x^2 + x - 20$$

11. Answer **(J)**

Substitute each value and then evaluate.

Substituting -2 for x;
$$g(x) = -(2x - 5)^3 \quad \rightarrow \quad g(-2) = -(2 \times (-2) - 5)^3 = -(-9)^3 = 729$$
Thus, the value of $g(-2)$ is 729.

12. Answer **(B)**

Convert the equation to the slope intercept form.

Convert the given equation to slope-intercept form by;
adding $2x$ to both sides;
$$-2x + 3y = 9 \quad \rightarrow \quad -2x + 3y + 2x = 9 + 2x \quad \rightarrow \quad 3y = 9 + 2x$$
dividing both sides by 3;
$$3y = 2x + 9 \quad \rightarrow \quad \frac{3y}{3} = \frac{2x + 9}{3} \quad \rightarrow \quad y = \frac{2}{3}x + 3$$
Thus, the slope of the equation is $\frac{2}{3}$.

13. Answer **(J)**

Calculate the input value when the output values are equal.

If the number of months is input, x, and the total charge is, y, then it could make the two linear equations.

1st, plan A:
· increase charge \$3 per month so, rate, slope m, is 3
Therefore, the linear equation for plan A is $y = 3x + b$
· substitute a data, $(1, 32)$, for the equation;
$$y = 3x + b \quad \rightarrow \quad 32 = 3(1) + b \quad \rightarrow \quad b = 29$$
Thus, the linear equation for plan A is $y = 3x + 29$ ------ ①

2nd, plan B:
· increase charge \$5 per month so, rate, slope m, is 3
Therefore, the linear equation for plan A is $y = 5x + b$
· substitute a data, $(1, 10)$, for the equation;
$$y = 5x + b \quad \rightarrow \quad 10 = 5(1) + b \quad \rightarrow \quad b = 5$$
Thus, the linear equation for plan B is $y = 5x + 5$ ------- ②

3rd, solving system of linear equation ① and ② by substitution;
$$② = ① \quad \rightarrow \quad 5x + 5 = 3x + 29 \quad \rightarrow \quad 2x = 24 \quad \rightarrow \quad x = 12$$
Thus, the total charge of 12 months is same.

14. Answer **(C)**

Solving inequality by using inverse operation.

A inequality, subtracting 3 from both sides;
$$-2x + 3 < 7 \quad \rightarrow \quad -2x + 3 - 3 < 7 - 3 \quad \rightarrow \quad -2x < 4$$
Dividing both sides by -2;
$$-2x < 4 \quad \rightarrow \quad \frac{-2x}{-2} < \frac{4}{-2} \quad \rightarrow \quad x > -2$$
Other inequality, dividing both sides by 3;
$$3x < 6 \quad \rightarrow \quad \frac{3x}{3} < \frac{6}{3} \quad \rightarrow \quad x < 2$$
So, solution is '$x > -2$ and $x < 2$' $\rightarrow \quad -2 < x < 2$
Thus, the correct answer is

$$c. \quad \xleftarrow{\quad\quad} \underset{-2 \quad\quad 0 \quad\quad 2}{\bullet\!-\!-\!-\!-\!\bullet}$$

15. Answer **(J)**

Absolute value is never negative.

Evaluate absolute value for each number;
$$|0.004| = 0.004, \quad |-0.5| = 0.5, \quad |0.025| = 0.025,$$
$$|0.003| = 0.003, \quad |-0.011| = 0.011$$
Thus, the smallest absolute value is 0.003.

16. Answer **(K)**

The range of function is the set of y-values.

The y-values, range, for whole x-values, domain, are $0 \leq y < 1$.

Thus, the correct answer is **K**.

17. Answer **(E)**

Two lines are perpendicular if and only if their slopes are negative reciprocals of each other.

Convert the equation to slope-intercept form;
add $6x$ to both sides;
$$-6x + 5y = 96 \quad \rightarrow \quad -6x + 5y + 6x = 96 + 6x \quad \rightarrow \quad 5y = 96 + 6x$$
divide both sides by 5;
$$5y = 6x + 96 \quad \rightarrow \quad \frac{5y}{5} = \frac{6x + 96}{5} \quad \rightarrow \quad y = \frac{6}{5}x + \frac{96}{5}$$
So, the slope, m', of the perpendicular line is;
$$m' = -\frac{1}{\frac{6}{5}} = -\frac{5}{6}$$
Thus, the slope is $-\frac{5}{6}$.

18. Answer **(C)**

Let's draw a picture of the situation given in the problem.

$XZ + ZY + YW = XW$, Y is between X and W, and Z to be between X and W. So, the position of the four points are;

Thus, the only III is correct.

19. Answer **(J)**

The area of a rectangle is a product of width and length.

The width of the shaded region is $(14 - 2x)$ and the length of the region is $(20 - 3x)$. Therefore, the area is;
$$area = width \times length = (14 - 2x) \times (20 - 3x)$$
Using the distributive property;
$$(14 - 2x) \times (20 - 3x) = 280 - 42x - 40x + 6x^2 = 6x^2 - 82x + 280$$
Thus, the area is $6x^2 - 82x + 280$.

20. Answer **(D)**

Find area of each portion.

The total area of rooftop is $45ft \times 60ft = 2700ft^2$.
The area of flowerbeds are;
A square flowerbed is $10ft \times 10ft = 100ft^2$ and a rectangular flowerbeds is $4ft \times 45ft = 180ft^2$.
so, the area of two flowerbeds are $100 + 180 = 280ft^2$.

Thus, the portion is;
$$2700 - 280 = 2420.$$

21. Answer **(C)**

Using proportion.

If x is the scale drawing length, use the proportion;
$$\frac{0.2\,inch}{3\,feet} = \frac{x\,inch}{65\,feet} \quad \rightarrow \quad 3x = 0.2 \times 60 \quad \rightarrow \quad 3x = 12 \quad \rightarrow \quad x = 4$$

Thus, 60 feet is 4 inches in scale drawing.

---

22. Answer **(J)**

The charge for labor is not changed.

The charge for flowerbeds is;
$$total\ chare - labor\ charge = \$3,250.00 - \$730.00 = \$2,520$$
The charge per square feet of the flowerbeds is:
$$\frac{charge\ for\ flowerbeds}{area\ of\ flowerbeds} = \frac{\$2,520}{4ft \times 95ft + 10ft \times 10ft} = \frac{\$2,520}{280ft^2}$$
$$= \frac{\$9}{ft^2}$$

The charge for twice flowerbeds is
$$\frac{\$9}{ft^2} \times (2 \times 280ft^2) = \$5,040.$$

Thus, the total charge is $\$730 + \$5,040 = \$5,770.00$

---

23. Answer **(D)**

Using the formula.

From the formula of cylinder;
$$V = \pi r^2 h \quad \to \quad 1,560 = \pi(10)^2 h \quad \to \quad h = \frac{1,560}{100\pi} \approx 4.9656\ ....$$

Thus, the depth of the water is 5.0 ft.

---

24. Answer **(J)**

Prism has round lateral face.

Because prism has a round lateral face,
the cross section is not polygon.
And the plane is not parallel to base so,
the cross section is not circle.

Thus, the correct answer is *J*. ellipse.

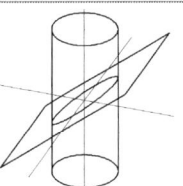

---

25. Answer **(C)**

Using the formula.

From the formula of the sphere's volume;
$$V = \frac{4}{3}\pi r^3 \to 36 = \frac{4}{3}\pi r^3 \to \frac{3}{4\pi} \times \frac{4}{3}\pi r^3 = \frac{3}{4\pi} \times 36 \to r^3 = \frac{27}{\pi}$$
Take cubic root on both sides;
$$\sqrt[3]{r^3} = \sqrt[3]{\frac{27}{\pi}} \to r = \frac{3}{\sqrt[3]{\pi}} \to r = \frac{3}{\sqrt[3]{\pi}}$$

Thus, the radius of the sphere is $\dfrac{3}{\sqrt[3]{\pi}}$

---

26. Answer **(K)**

Finding the total number of cubes.

The volume of a cube is;
$$V = s^3 = (2)^3 = 8$$
The number of cubes for the prism is;
$$3 \times 8 = 24$$

Thus, the volume of the right rectangular prism is $8 \times 24 = 192in^3$.

---

27. Answer **(D)**

The area of circle is πr^2.

Because the diameter of the circle is 8cm, the radius of circle is
4cm. From the formula of circle area;
$$A = \pi r^2 \to A = \pi(4)^2 = 16\pi$$

Thus, the area of the circle is 16π.

---

28. Answer **(H)**

Finding the side length of the square.

Because the radius of the circle is r, the side length is twice of
the diameter, $2r$, of the circle.
So, the area of the shaded region is;
$$shaded\ area = square\ area - 4 \times circle\ area$$
$$= (4r)^2 - 4 \times \pi r^2 = 16r^2 - 4\pi r^2$$

Thus, the area of the shaded region is $16r^2 - 4\pi r^2$.

---

29. Answer **(D)**

Making the inequality for prices.

Let n be the number of his purchasing balls. The total payment is;
$$price + sales\ tax = 5 \times n + 0.05 \times 5 \times n = 5n + 0.25n = 5.25n$$
So, the maximum number of baseballs is;
$$5.25n \le 200 \quad \to \quad \frac{5.25n}{5.25} \le \frac{200}{5.25} \quad \to \quad n \le 38.0952\ ....$$
Thus, maximum number of purchasing balls is 38.

---

30. Answer **(A)**

f(x) is a linear function and g(x) is a quadratic function.

A. correct
$$f(-2) = -\frac{3}{2}(-2) - 5 = 3 - 5 = -2 \quad \to \quad g(f(-2)) = g(-2) = -1$$
B. not correct
Because the leading coefficient ($a = -1$) of $g(x)$ is less than 0,
$-1 > 0, y = -1$ is maximum of $g(x)$. → $g(x) \le -1$.
C. not correct
The y-intercept of two functions, $f(x)$ and $g(x)$, are same $y = -5$.
→ $f(0) = g(0) = -5$
D. not correct
Because the value of $|g(x)|$ is always positive, $g(x) \ne |g(x)|$. For
example, $g(-2) = -1 \ne |g(x)| = 1$.
E. not correct
Because the value of $-|f(x)|$ is always negative, $f(x) \ne -|f(x)|$.
For example, $f(-6) = 4 \ne -|f(-6)| = -4$.

---

31. Answer **(J)**

The given equation is a standard form.

From the standard form
$y = ax^2 + bx + c \quad \to \quad h(t) = -3t^2 + 12t + 36$
vertex is;
$$\left(-\frac{b}{2a}, c - \frac{b^2}{4a}\right) = \left(-\frac{12}{2(-3)}, 36 - \frac{12^2}{4(-3)}\right) = (2, 48)$$
so, maximum time is 2 seconds and
maximum height is 48 units.
y-intercept is; $y = c \quad \to \quad y = 36$ so, starting point is 36 units.
Intercept form is $y = a(x - p)(x - q) \to y = -3(x + 2)(x - 6)$ so,
x-intercepts are $x = -2$ and $x = 6$ and ground reaching time is 6
seconds.

Thus, the correct answer is *J*.

---

32. Answer **(E)**

Trial and error.

If $5x^2 - 17x + 6 = (ax + p)(bx + q)$, a, b are factors of 5, and p, q
are factors of 6.

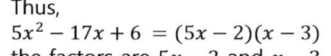
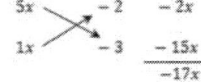

Thus,
$5x^2 - 17x + 6 = (5x - 2)(x - 3)$
the factors are $5x - 2$ and $x - 3$.

33. Answer (J)

Square of a binomial pattern.

Square of a binomial pattern;
$$x^2 + 2x + 1 = (x+1)^2$$
Thus, the correct answer is **J**.

34. Answer (J)

The product of complex conjugates is a real number.

The product of complex conjugates is a real number. So,
$$(2a + bi)(2a - bi) = (2a)^2 - (bi)^2 = 4a^2 - b^2 i^2.$$
Because $i^2 = -1$
$$4a^2 - b^2 i^2 = 4a^2 + b^2 \rightarrow real\ number$$
Thus, the complex number is $2a - bi$.

35. Answer (B)

Using FOIL pattern.

Using formula;
$$(2x - 4)(x + 2) = 2x^2 + 4x - 4x - 8 = 2x^2 - 8$$
Thus, the expression is $2x^2 - 8$.

36. Answer (C)

Substituting the values for variables.

From the given formula;
$$A = P\left(1 + \frac{r}{100}\right)^t = 1{,}000\left(1 + \frac{6.5}{100}\right)^3 = 1{,}000(1.065)^3$$
Thus, the correct answer is **C**.

37. Answer (E)

Using the properties of exponential.

Using the properties of exponential;
$$(a^4)^2(a^3)^5 = (a^{4\times2}) \times (a^{3\times5}) = a^8 \times a^{15} = a^{8+15} = a^{23}$$
Thus, the value of n is 23.

38. Answer (J)

Using the properties of exponential.

Using the properties of exponential;
$$(2a^2b^3)(5a^6b^2) = 2 \times 5 \times a^2 \times a^6 \times b^3 \times b^2 = 10a^{2+6}b^{3+2} = 10a^8b^5$$
Thus, the correct answer is **J**.

39. Answer (C)

For all real x, $\left(\sqrt{x}\right)^2 = |x|$.

Substitute $\sqrt{7}$ for a and $\sqrt{13}$ for b;
$$\sqrt{a^2 + b^2} = \sqrt{\left(\sqrt{7}\right)^2 + \left(\sqrt{13}\right)^2} = \sqrt{7 + 13} = \sqrt{20} = \sqrt{4 \times 5} = 2\sqrt{5}$$
Thus, the value is $2\sqrt{5}$.

40. Answer (C)

Using the concept of composition of function.

1st Method; substituting
Finding $r(-3)$;
$$r(x) = 3 - x^2 \rightarrow r(-3) = 3 - (-3)^2 = 3 - 9 = -6.$$
Substituting -6 for $r(-3)$ on $h(r(-3))$;
$$h(r(-3)) = h(-6) \rightarrow h(-6) = (-6) - 3 = -9$$

2nd Method; composition function
Finding $h(r(x))$;
$$h(r(x)) = r(x) - 3 = (3 - x^2) - 3 \rightarrow h(r(x)) = -x^2$$
Substituting -3 for x;
$$h(r(-3)) = -(-3)^2 = -9$$
Thus, the value of $h(r(-3))$ is -9.

41. Answer (G)

Find the difference of heights.

Day 2, the difference of heights is $5{,}600 - 3{,}400 = 2{,}200$.

Thus, the correct answer is **G**.

42. Answer (D)

Both a multiple of 2 and a multiple of 3 is a multiple of 6.

Both a multiple of 2 and a multiple of 3 is a multiple of 6, the numbers are $36, 72, 18, 6$. So, the probability is;
$$P = \frac{4}{8} = \frac{1}{2}$$
Thus, the correct answer is **D**.

43. Answer (G)

Re-drawing the cubic dice.

Re-drawing the dice,
there are 2 A's, 2 B's, and 2 C's.
So, the probability is:
$$P = \frac{2}{6} = \frac{1}{3}$$
Thus, the correct answer is **G**.

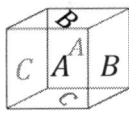

44. Answer (E)

The median is the middle of data set.

Rewritten data in order;
$$34, 42, 51, 55, 57, 60, 62, 63, 72, 78, 81, 88$$
And because the number of data is 12, the median is between 6th (60) and 7th (62) data. The median is the average of 60 and 62;
$$median = \frac{60 + 62}{2} = \frac{122}{2} = 61.$$
Thus, the median of data is 61.

45. Answer (F)

Do not calculate.

The standard deviation is measure of distance between mean and each data. So, at **F**, the distance is zero.

Thus, the correct answer is **F**.

46. Answer (C)

Finding the pattern of the numbers.

$t_1 = 1$
$t_2 = 1 + 2 = 3$
$t_3 = 1 + 2 + 3 = 6$
$t_4 = 1 + 2 + 3 + 4 = 10$
$t_5 = 1 + 2 + 3 + 4 + 5 = 10$
....

So, the triangular number is an arithmetic series, its first term is 1 and its common difference is also 1.
From the formula;

$$S_n = \frac{n \times (2a_1 + (n-1)d)}{2}$$

$$\to \quad S_{36} = t_{36} = \frac{36 \times (2 \times 1 + (36 - 1) \times 1)}{2} = 666$$

Thus, the t_{36} is 666.

47. Answer (C)

Drawing auxiliary lines.

Because the major axis is vertical, the equation has this form;
$$\frac{(x-h)^2}{b^2} + \frac{(y-k)^2}{a^2} = 1$$
The vertices are $(2,5)$ and $(2,-1)$,
so the center of the ellipse is midpoint of two vertices.

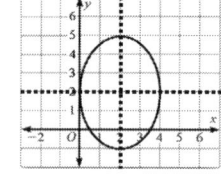

$$(h,k) = \left(\frac{2+2}{2}, \frac{-1+5}{2}\right) = (2,2)$$
$$\to \quad \frac{(x-2)^2}{b^2} + \frac{(y-2)^2}{a^2} = 1$$
The value of b is distance a co-vertex, $(0,2)$ or $(4,2)$, and the center $(2,2)$, so $b = |4 - 2| = 2$. And the value of a is distance a vertex, $(2,5)$ or $(2,-1)$, and the center $(2,2)$, so $a = |5 - 2| = 3$.

Thus, the equation is $\frac{(x-2)^2}{2^2} + \frac{(y-2)^2}{3^2} = 1$
$$\to \quad \frac{(x-2)^2}{4} + \frac{(y-2)^2}{9} = 1.$$

48. Answer (D)

The altitude is parallel to x-axis.

Drawing perpendicular line from R to $\overline{PO}$ and its intersecting point is S.
The perpendicular line is the altitude of $\triangle PQR$ and it is parallel to x-axis
so, it has same y-coordinate of R.
Therefore, the coordinates of S are $(2,3)$ and using the distance formula;
$$d = \sqrt{(x_2 - x_1)^2 + (y_2 - y_1)^2} = \sqrt{(8-2)^2 + (3-3)^2} = 6$$

Thus, the correct answer is **D**.

49. Answer (B)

Using the formula of the midpoint.

Let (x, y) be the coordinates of B and using the formula of the midpoint;
$$M = \left(\frac{x_1 + x_2}{2}, \frac{y_1 + y_2}{2}\right) = \left(\frac{x + (-10)}{2}, \frac{y + 10}{2}\right) = (3, -2)$$

So,

$$\frac{x - 10}{2} = 3 \quad \to \quad x - 10 = 6 \quad \to \quad x = 16$$
$$\frac{y + 10}{2} = -2 \quad \to \quad y + 10 = -2 \quad \to \quad y = -12$$

Thus, the coordinates are $(16, -12)$.

50. Answer (E)

Using the midpoint formula.

Halfway means that the midpoint so, using the midpoint formula;
$$M = \left(\frac{x_1 + x_2}{2}, \frac{y_2 + y_1}{2}\right) = \left(\frac{0 + 70}{2}, \frac{0 + 48}{2}\right) = (35, 24)$$

Thus, the coordinates are $(35, 24)$.

51. Answer (D)

Using unit analysis.

The total amount of using gasoline is;
$$amount\ of\ gasoline = total\ distance \div using\ rate$$
$$= (250 + 130)km \div 52km\ per\ gal$$
$$= \frac{95}{13}\ gal$$
The total cost of gasoline is;
$$cost\ of\ gasoline = amount\ of\ gasoline \times unit\ cost\ of\ gasoline$$
$$= \frac{95}{13}\ gal \times \$3.75\ per\ gal = \$\frac{1425}{52} \approx \$27.40$$

Thus, the correct answer is **D**.

52. Answer (K)

Using the distance formula

From the formula of distance;
$$d = \sqrt{(x_2 - x_1)^2 + (y_2 - y_1)^2} = \sqrt{(70 - 0)^2 + (48 - 0)^2} \approx 84.876....$$

Thus, the distance is 84.9 km.

53. Answer (B)

Drawing the auxiliary line.

Drawing the auxiliary line, making a right triangle, $\triangle OPQ$.
Using the Pythagorean theorem;

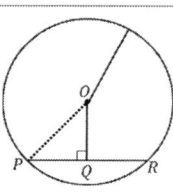

$$\overline{OP}^2 = \overline{OQ}^2 + \overline{PQ}^2 \quad \to \quad 8^2 = \overline{OQ}^2 + 6^2$$
$$(\because \overline{OP}\ is\ radius\ and\ Q\ is\ midpoint\ of\ \overline{PR})$$
$$\overline{OQ}^2 = 8^2 - 6^2 \quad \to \quad \overline{OQ} = \sqrt{8^2 - 6^2} = 2\sqrt{7}$$

Thus, the length is $2\sqrt{7}$ centimeters.

54. Answer (J)

Being expressed as sine or cosine.

Using trigonometric identities;
$$\sin x + \cos x \times \frac{\cos x}{\sin x} \to \frac{\sin^2 x}{\sin x} + \frac{\cos^2 x}{\sin x} \to \frac{\sin^2 x + \cos^2 x}{\sin x} \to \frac{1}{\sin x} = \csc x$$

Thus, the correct answer is **J**.

55. Answer (D)

2 minutes is 120 seconds.

Let x be the degree, and using proportional;
$$\frac{360°}{120} = \frac{x}{20} \quad \to \quad 120x = 7200 \quad \to \quad x = 60°$$

Thus, the correct answer is **D**.

56. `Answer` **(J)**

Finding central angle of the sector.

Using sector area formula;

$$sector\ area = circle\ area \times \frac{central\ angle}{360°}$$

$$\frac{4}{3}\pi = 4\pi \times \frac{\theta}{360°} \quad \rightarrow \quad \frac{1}{3} = \frac{\theta}{360°} \quad \rightarrow \quad \theta = 120°$$

Thus, the correct answer is **J**.

57. `Answer` **(C)**

Using the inverse trigonometric function.

In view of ?, 65 is hypotenuse and 43 is opposite side, so

$$? = \sin^{-1}\left(\frac{43}{65}\right)$$

Thus, the correct answer is **C**.

58. `Answer` **(J)**

Using the inverse trigonometric function.

Let θ be the angle;

$$\theta = \tan^{-1}\left(\frac{35}{135}\right) = \tan^{-1}\left(\frac{7}{27}\right) = \arctan\left(\frac{7}{27}\right)$$

Thus, the correct answer is **J**.

59. `Answer` **(C)**

Check amplitude and vertical translation.

From the standard form, $y = a\cos b(x - h) + k$, the range is
$$-a + k \le y \le a + k.$$
Rewrite the function;
$$f(x) = -3\cos(x + \pi) + 2.$$
So, the range is;
$$-3 + 2 \le y \le 3 + 2 \quad \rightarrow \quad -1 \le y \le 5$$

Thus, the correct answer is **C**.

60. `Answer` **(K)**

The given statement is a conditional statement.

F. and **G**. are not equivalent, because,
F. All-18-years-olds **could not** vote.
    → All-18-years-olds **could** vote.
G. Being able to vote **is not** necessary for people to be 18.
    → Being able to vote **is** necessary for people to be 18.

The hypothesis, p, is *'people are 18 years of age'* and the conclusion, q, is *'the people could vote'*.
Let $p \to q$ be the conditional statement;
H. is $q \to p$, so it is converse and is not equivalent to $p \to q$.
J. is $\sim p \to \sim q$, so it is inverse and is not equivalent to $p \to q$.
K. is $\sim q \to \sim p$, so it is contrapositive and is equivalent to $p \to q$.

Thus, the correct answer is **K**.

BLANK PAGE   *by K·DEAN*

Reformed Past Paper ACT MATH TEST 02

60 Questions – 60 Minutes

DIRECTIONS:

Solve each problem, choose the correct answer, and then fill in the corresponding oval on your answer in the grid on the answer sheet.

Do not linger over problems that take too much time as many as you can, then return to others in the time you have left for this test.

You are permitted to use a calculator on this test.

Note: Unless otherwise stated, all of the following should be assumed.

1. Figures are drawn to scale unless otherwise indicated.

2. All figures lie in a plane unless otherwise indicated.

3. All variables and expressions used represent real numbers unless otherwise indicated.

This test has reformed the REAL ACT Mathematics Test

01.

There are two main stages in the production of ice cream. First, the ice cream mixture is heated to sterilize at 92^oC. Second, the temperature of the mixture is cooled down for aging and storage at -7^oC. What is the change of the temperature between the two stages ?

A. -99^oC

B. -85^oC

C. -22^oC

D. 85^oC

E. 99^oC

02.

If p is a positive odd integer and pq^5 is a negative odd integer, which of the following sentences is true about integer q ?

F. q is a positive even integer.

G. q is a positive odd integer.

H. q is a negative even integer.

J. q is a negative odd integer.

K. Could not be determined.

03.

At Travel Agency, counselor interviewed whether the 400 customers had visited three countries: China, Korea, Japan. Of these 400 customers, 15% visited all three countries, and 30% visited exactly two countries. And 196 customers visited exactly one country. What percent of the customers did not visit above these three countries ?

A. 6%

B. 7%

C. 8%

D. 8.5%

E. 9%

04.

If $x = 2$ and $y = -2$, then what is the value of $-2x^2 + y^2 + 2x - 3$?

F. 4

G. 2

H. 0

J. −1

K. −3

05.

Which of the following is equivalent to $3 - 2(4x + 1)$?

A. $-8x + 1$

B. $8x - 1$

C. $8x - 5$

D. $-8x - 5$

E. $-8x + 5$

06.

If $x = -2$ and $y = 3$, then what is the value of $xy^3 + x^2y^2 - 8y$?

F. −4

G. −2

H. 0

J. 3

K. 6

07.

The width of a rectangle is $2cm$ less than half of the length of the rectangle. The perimeter of the rectangle is $23cm$. What is the length of the rectangle, in centimeters?

A. 5

B. 6

C. 7

D. 8

E. 9

08.

Lucy is making a flowers fence along 3 side of a rectangle, leaving 1 of the long sides unfenced. The fence is planting to rose trees and apple trees and the dimension of the rectangle is 24 feet by 36 feet. Apple trees are planted 6 feet apart, and there are 10 rose trees between each pair of apple trees. Apple trees are planted at both ends of the fence. How many rose trees will Lucy plant for the fence ?

F. 120

G. 130

H. 140

J. 150

K. 160

09.

Gardening company have just planted a rectangular flower bed in a city park. As shown in the figure below, the city park is 40 yards long, and the rectangular flower bed is 6 yards wide and 12 yards long. The left edge of the bed will be x yards from the left edge of the park, the right edge of the bed will be x yards from the right edge of the park. What is the value of x, in yards ?

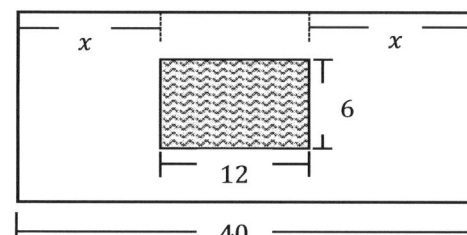

A. 10.5

B. 11.25

C. 12

D. 13.75

E. 14

10.

Jessica plants 62 flowers that are either roses, marigolds, or pansies. There are 20 more roses than marigold and 8 less marigolds than pansy. How many marigolds does she plant ?

F. 17

G. 16

H. 15

J. 14

K. 13

11.

If a function f is defined by $f(x) = -3x^2 + 4x$. What is the value of $f(-2)$?

A. −40

B. −20

C. 0

D. 10

E. 30

12.

In the standard (x, y) coordinate plane, what is the y-intercept of the line with equation $-4x = 3y - 12$?

F. 0

G. −3

H. 3

J. −4

K. 4

Use the following information to answer questions
13 - 15.

Hanni's Sweet Coffee Shop and Geony's Plentiful Coffee Shop both sells coffee beans in ounces. The table below lists the price (included tax) of each box of coffee beans sold at the shops. For each shop, there is a linear relationship between the price of a box of coffee beans and the weight (in ounces) of coffee beans in that box. These are the only weights of coffee beans that can be purchased at the shops.

Weight (oz) per box	Hanni's Sweet Coffee Shop	Geony's Plentiful Coffee Shop
3	$3.35	$3.15
6	$3.85	$3.75
9	$4.35	$4.35
12	$4.85	$4.95
15	$5.35	$5.45

13.

Which of the following equations represents the relationship between the price in dollars, p, and the weight, w, in a box of coffee beans at Geony's Plentiful Coffee Shop ?

A. $p = 0.2w$

B. $p = 0.2w + 2.55$

C. $p = 1.05w$

D. $p = 1.05w + 0.2$

E. $p = 1.05w + 2.55$

14.

At Hanni's Sweet Coffee Shop, what is unit cost in a box of 12, to the nearest $0.01 ?

A. 0.28

B. 0.39

C. 0.40

D. 0.51

E. 0.62

15.

Miny has $5.00 in nickels to spend on coffee bean. What is the number of nickels she would have left after paying for a box of 9 coffee beans at Hanni's Sweet Coffee Shop ?

(Note: Each nickel is worth $0.05)

F. 9

G. 10

H. 11

J. 12

K. 13

16.

When the two lines $x = -4$ and $y = x + 7$ are graphed in standard (x, y) coordinate plane, what is intersecting point of the two lines in the plane ?

- **A.** $(-4, 11)$
- **B.** $(7, -4)$
- **C.** $(-4, 3)$
- **D.** $(3, -4)$
- **E.** $(-4, 7)$

17.

Physical education teacher, Darby will order boxes of valley balls and basketballs for his school. The table below gives the number of balls in each box and price per box.

Type of balls	Number in each box	Price per box
Valley ball	8	$142
Basket ball	6	$113

He will order a total 8 boxes of both balls for a total price of $1,049. Which of the following system of linear equation gives a relationship between the v boxes of valley balls and b boxes of basket balls ?

- **F.** $v + b = 8$
  $8v + 6b = 1,049$
- **G.** $8v + 6b = 8$
  $142v + 113b = 1,049$
- **H.** $8v + 6b = 1,049$
  $142v + 113b = 8$
- **J.** $v + b = 8$
  $142v + 113b = 1,049$
- **K.** $v + b = 1,049$
  $8v + 6b = 8$

18.

A student council consists only junior and senior students. To raise money for disaster relief fund, the students sold pencil cases. Pencil cases sales averaged $30 for each junior and $40 for each senior. If the ratio of juniors to seniors in the student council was $2:3$, pencil cases sales averaged how many dollars per student ?

- **A.** $35.00
- **B.** $35.50
- **C.** $36.00
- **D.** $36.50
- **E.** $37.00

19.

Leslie drove from Salt Sea City to Frovo, a distance of 120 kilometers. From Frovo he drove on to Samdy, and then drove back to Salt Sea City. The ratio of Leslie's driving times on the first, second, and third segments of the trip, respectively, was $5:4:3$, and he drove at the same average speed on each segment. What was Leslie's total driving distance, in kilometers, for the 3 segments of the trip?

- **F.** 168
- **G.** 240
- **H.** 288
- **J.** 292
- **K.** 306

20.

The shipping rate for SME(small and medium-sized enterprises) customers of Bimazon.com consists of a fee per box and a price per kilogram for each box for SME customers shipping boxes of various weights.

Weight of box (kilograms)	Fee	Price per kilogram
Less than 3	$ 2.00	$1.00
3~10	$10.00	$0.50
More than 10	$25.00	$0.30

A SME, *e*-mart, wants Bimazon.com to ship 2 boxes that one box weighs 6 kilograms and the other box weighs 12 kilograms. What is the shipping costs for the two boxes?

A. $39.24

B. $40.42

C. $41.60

D. $42.00

E. $43.18

21.

Helen makes pretzels and donuts for 6 hours every Friday for the homeless. It takes her 12 minutes to make a pretzel and 8 minutes to make a donut. This Friday, Helen will make three times as many donuts as pretzels. How many of the donuts will she make this Friday?

F. 28

G. 30

H. 32

J. 34

K. 36

22.

In the figure below, $\overline{AC}$ and $\overline{BD}$ intersect at a point C, $\overline{AB}$ and $\overline{CD}$ are parallel, and 2 angle measures are given. What is the measure of $\angle COD$?

A. 140°

B. 100°

C. 75°

D. 80°

E. 85°

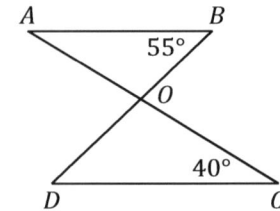

23.

In the figure below, $\overline{AB} \parallel \overline{DE}$, the measure of $\angle ACD$ is 124°, and the measure of $\angle CDE$ is 35°. What is the measure of $x°$?

F. 35°

G. 91°

H. 56°

J. 124°

K. 86°

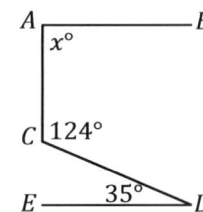

24.

Which of the following sets of numbers could be the side length, in centimeters, of a triangle?

F. $\{2, 6, 8\}$

G. $\{3, 7, 11\}$

H. $\{4, 9, 12\}$

J. $\{5, 10, 15\}$

K. $\{6, 11, 18\}$

25.

In $\triangle PQR$ below, $\overline{XY}$ is parallel to $\overline{QR}$, X lies on $\overline{PQ}$, and Y lies on $\overline{PR}$. If the length of $\overline{PX}$ is $\frac{3}{4}$ of $\overline{PQ}$, what is the ratio of the area of $\triangle PXY$ to the area of $\triangle PQR$?

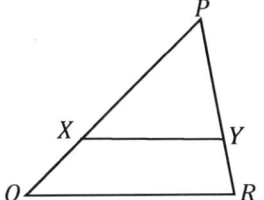

A. $1:4$

B. $2:3$

C. $3:4$

D. $6:8$

E. $9:16$

26.

Bob and Walter carefully place wooden stakes to measure the width of Muddy Pond, represented by $\overline{CD}$ in the figure below. They place stakes at point $A, B, C, D,$ and O so that O is intersecting point of $\overline{AD}$ and $\overline{BC}$ and so that $\overline{AB}$ is parallel to $\overline{CD}$. The distance between certain stakes are shown in the figure. What is the width of the pond, in feet?

F. 148.4

G. 152.9

H. 163.2

J. 176.4

K. 182.5

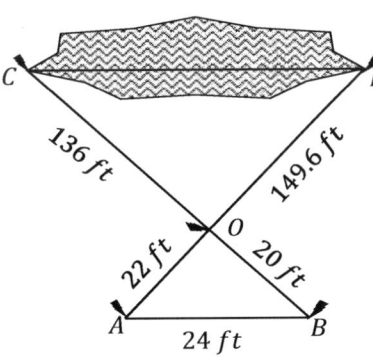

27.

Assume that $\triangle PQR$ and $\triangle XYZ$ are similar to each other and the scale factor of $\triangle PQR$ to $\triangle XYZ$ is $\frac{3}{4}$. If the perimeter of $\triangle PQR$ is 45 inches, what is the perimeter of $\triangle XYZ$, in inches?

A. 120

B. 106

C. 100

D. 80

E. 60

28.

As shown in the figure below, two circular gears with centers 9 feet apart are connected with a tight belt. The belt winds $\frac{3}{4}$ of the circumference around the larger gear, which has a diameter of 6 feet, and $\frac{1}{4}$ of the circumference around the smaller gear, which has a diameter of 2 feet. What is the exact length of the belt, in feet?

F. $5\pi + 2\sqrt{77}$

G. $5\pi + \sqrt{77}$

H. $10\pi + \sqrt{77}$

J. $10\pi + 2\sqrt{77}$

K. $10\pi + \dfrac{\sqrt{77}}{2}$

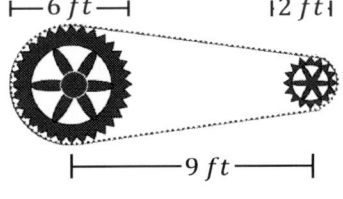

29.

As shown in the figure below, the solid is composed of right circular cylinder and a hemisphere with base diameter and height given in inches. The hemisphere and the cylinder have equal base diameters. What is the volume, in cubic inches, of the solid?

(Note: The volume of a sphere with radius r is $\frac{4}{3}\pi r^3$.)

A. 168π

B. 284π

C. 426π

D. 648π

E. 762π

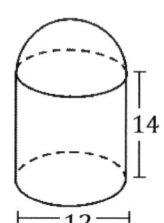

30.

If $(x - 3)$ and $(x + 1)$ are two factors of the quadratic expression below, what is the value of p and q?

$$x^2 + (p - q)x + 3 + p$$

	p	q
F.	-8	-8
G.	-8	-6
H.	-4	-6
J.	-2	0
K.	1	3

31.

If $x^2 - 5 = 11$, then $x^2 + 5 =$?

A. 2

B. 4

C. 9

D. 16

E. 21

32.

If a real solution of the equation $(x + 3)(x - 4) = p$ is $x = -2$, then what is the value of p?

F. 1

G. -12

H. 12

J. -6

K. 6

33.

Which of the following numbers is a real solution of an equation $-x^2 - 4 = 5x$?

A. -3

B. -2

C. -1

D. 2

E. 4

34.

Each of the following standard (x,y) coordinate planes is the graph of a quadratic function. If one of the graphs of the functions has two real distinct zeros , which one?

A.

B.
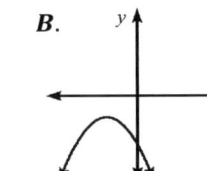

C.
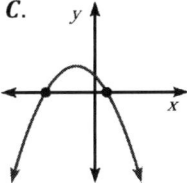

D.
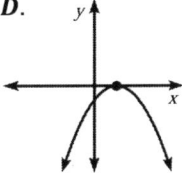

E.
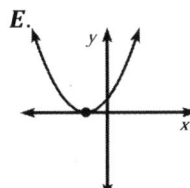

35.

The point X $(-2,-5)$ is lied on the standard (x,y) coordinate plane. If the point X will be reflected over y-axis , what will be the coordinates of the image of X?

F. $(-2,5)$

G. $(2,-5)$

H. $(2,5)$

J. $(5,-2)$

K. $(5,2)$

36.

If $x^{2a} = 4$, for rational positive numbers x and a, then what is the value of x^{5a} ?

A. 8

B. 16

C. 32

D. 64

E. 128

37.

Whenever x and y are nonzero real numbers, which of the following expressions is equivalent to $\dfrac{\left(5x^2\right)^2}{x^6}$?

F. $\dfrac{5}{x^2}$

G. $\dfrac{10}{x^2}$

H. $\dfrac{25}{x^2}$

J. $\dfrac{10}{x^4}$

K. $\dfrac{25}{x^4}$

38.

The solution set of the equation of $3^{2x^2+4} = 1$ contain:

A. One imaginary number.

B. Two imaginary numbers.

C. One real number and one imaginary number.

D. One real number.

E. Two real numbers.

39.

A formula to estimate monthly installment plan, D dollars, on an air-conditioner is

$$D = \frac{\frac{1}{2}Irt + \frac{3}{4}I}{12t}$$

where I dollars is the amount of a monthly payment, r is the annual interest rate expressed as decimal, and t years is the period of the installment. If I is doubled, what is effect on D?

A. D is multiplied by 0.5

B. D is multiplied by 1.5

C. D is multiplied by 2

D. D is multiplied by 2.5

E. D is multiplied by 3

40.

If $a > 1$, $0 < b < 1$, and $x > 1$, which of the following statements expresses the function f defined by $f(x) = a \cdot (b)^{-x}$?

F. $f(x)$ is a constant function.

G. $f(x)$ is a linear function with positive slope.

H. $f(x)$ is an open down parabola function.

J. $f(x)$ is increasing for all x.

K. $f(x)$ is decreasing for all x.

41.

The table below shows the shipping charges for shipping a single product from an online shopping mall. The shipping charges depend on the weight of the product.

Weight in kilograms	Shipping charge
$0 < w \le 2$	$0 (free)
$2 < w \le 4$	$2
$4 < w \le 6$	$5
$6 < w$	$10

Which of the following graphs best represents this table?

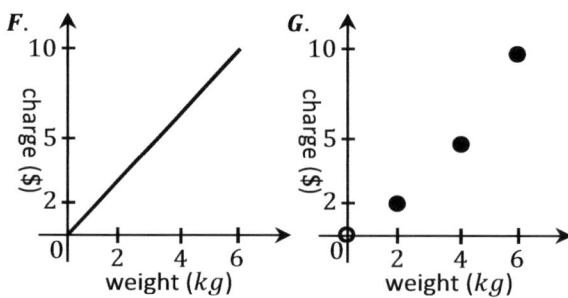

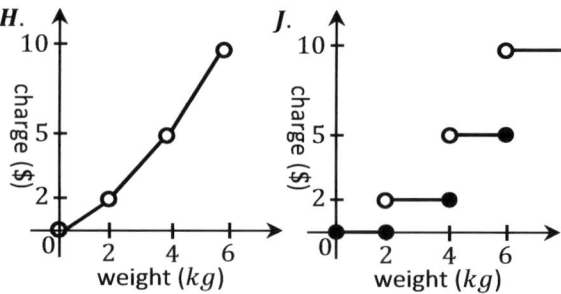

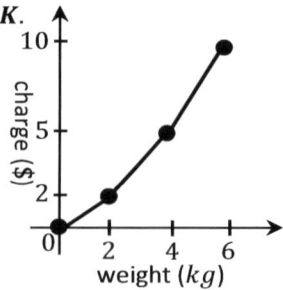

Use the following information to answer questions 42 - 45.

Benjamin conducted a survey of the friends to determine which of 6 types of movie were the most popular. Each friend who responded to the survey selected 1 movie type as his or her favorite. The circle graph below shows the number of friends who selected each of the 6 types of movie. A total of 30 friends responded to the survey.

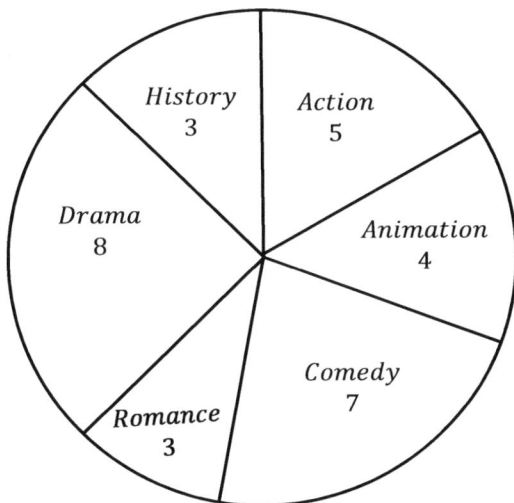

42.

In this survey, what is the ratio of the number of friends who selected Action to the number if friends who selected Comedy?

A. 5 : 7

B. 5 : 12

C. 7 : 5

D. 7 : 12

E. 7 : 30

43.

To the nearest 0.01%, what percent of the friends who responded to the survey selected Animation?

A. 12.25%

B. 13.33%

C. 14.77%

D. 15.23%

E. 16.67%

44.

In the circle graph, what is the measure of the central angle of the sector that illustrates the number of friends who responded to the survey who selected Romance ?

F. 36°

G. 39°

H. 42°

J. 45°

K. 48°

45.

Each of 20 students who own mobile phones was used to collect data on the amount of time, whole number hour, they spent per day using their phones. The median of the time was 4 hours. None of the students used their phones for 4 hours, and 25% of the students used their phones for 7 hours or above. How many students used their phones for 5 hours or 6 hours?

F. Could not be determined

G. 2

H. 3

J. 4

K. 5

46.

Assume that the first term is 4 in the geometric sequence $3, -6, 12, -24, ...$. What is the eighth term of the geometric sequence?

F. 384

G. −384

H. −768

J. 768

K. −128

Use the following information to answer questions 47 - 48.

As shown below, rectangle $ABCD$ is a soccer field and point O is midpoint of $\overline{AD}$.

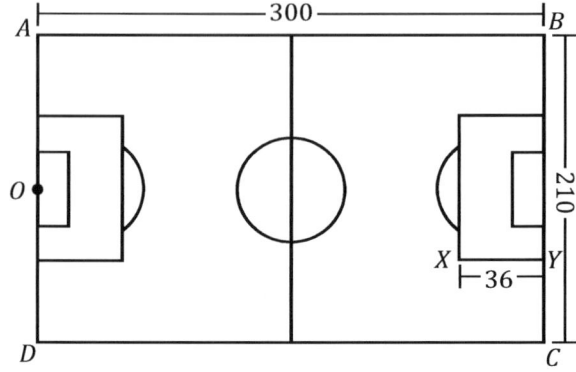

47.

The length of $\overline{XY}$ is what percent of the length $\overline{BC}$?

A. 10.9%

B. 13.2%

C. 17.1%

D. 19.5%

E. 21.4%

48.

What is the length of $\overline{OC}$?

F. 310

G. $15\sqrt{449}$

H. $15\sqrt{467}$

J. $16\sqrt{467}$

K. 335

49.

As shown in standard (x,y) coordinate below, the coordinates of three vertices of an equilateral triangle $\triangle OPQ$ are $O(0,0)$, $P(\alpha, \beta)$, and $Q(0, 2\gamma)$. What is the β, in term of γ ?

A. γ

B. $\dfrac{3}{2}\gamma$

C. 2γ

D. $\dfrac{5}{2}\gamma$

E. 3γ

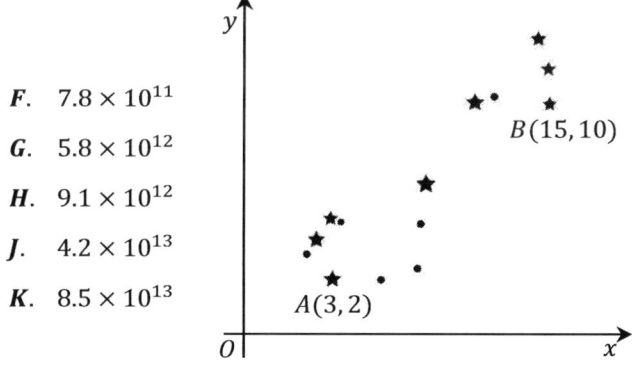

50.

In the figure below, the stars of Sagittarius is placed standard (x,y) coordinate plane. If a coordinate unit is 1 light-year, 1 light-year$\approx 5.88 \times 10^{12}$ miles, what is the distance, in miles, between star A and star B?

F. 7.8×10^{11}

G. 5.8×10^{12}

H. 9.1×10^{12}

J. 4.2×10^{13}

K. 8.5×10^{13}

$B(15, 10)$

$A(3, 2)$

51.

As shown below, suppose that the length of the hypotenuse of an isosceles right triangle is $7\sqrt{2}$ centimeters. What is the perimeter, in centimeters, of the isosceles right triangle?

A. $7 + 7\sqrt{2}$

B. $14 + 7\sqrt{2}$

C. $14 - 7\sqrt{2}$

D. $14 + 14\sqrt{2}$

E. $7\sqrt{2} - 14$

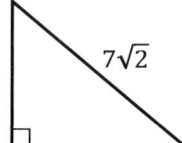

52.

A mountain infantry arrived at a point that is designated on the tactical map (-3, 4) and is 3 kilometers west and 4 kilometers north of the headquarters of a battalion. From the point, the mountain infantry moves 5 kilometers due east, 5 kilometers due south and then 7 kilometers due west, where the mountain infantry builds a strongpoint. Which of the following is closest to the straight line distance, in kilometers, the mountain infantry is from the headquarters of a battalion?

F. 5.1

G. 9.6

H. 14.7

J. 21.3

K. 26.0

53.

As shown below, a right square pyramid with equilateral lateral faces is shown in the figure. The length of slant height is $5\sqrt{3}$ centimeters. What is the total length, in centimeters, of all 8 edges of the pyramid?

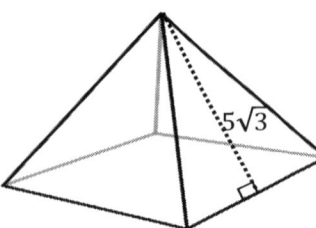

A. 40

B. $40\sqrt{2}$

C. $40\sqrt{3}$

D. $40\sqrt{5}$

E. 80

54.

A drone takes off from the ground with a constant vertical speed 10 feet per second. After 20 seconds the angle of elevation from Ashley to the drone is 60°. Ashley is 6 feet tall. How far is the drone from the Ashely's head at this time?

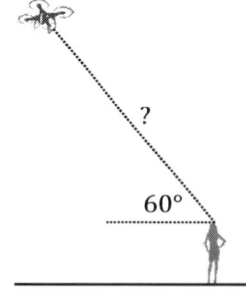

F. 117.9

G. 224.0

H. 232.5

J. 247.2

K. 252.8

55.

Suppose that the area of trapezoid $\square ABCD$ is $\frac{21\sqrt{3}}{2}$ square inches. Which of the following values of the length, in inches, of $\overline{CD}$?

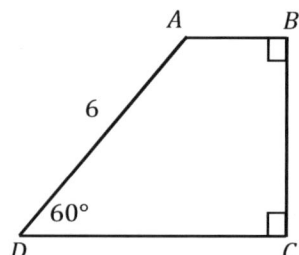

A. $3+\sqrt{3}$

B. 4

C. $4+\sqrt{3}$

D. 5

E. $5+\sqrt{3}$

56.

In the figure below, the base of a wheelchair access ramp in a school is 35 feet horizontal run and 4 feet vertical rise. Which of the following expressions is the angle of gradient between the base of the ramp and the ground level?

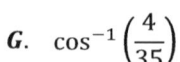

F. $\cos^{-1}\left(\frac{35}{4}\right)$

G. $\cos^{-1}\left(\frac{4}{35}\right)$

H. $\tan^{-1}\left(\frac{4}{35}\right)$

J. $\tan^{-1}\left(\frac{35}{4}\right)$

K. $\sin^{-1}\left(\frac{4}{35}\right)$

57.

Armadillo Camp and Bear Camp are placed on opposite side of Colorado River. As shown on the map below, campers are standing 500 meters from Armadillo Camp and estimated the angle between the three positions. Using these estimates, what is the expression of the distance, in meters, between Armadillo Camp and Bear Camp?

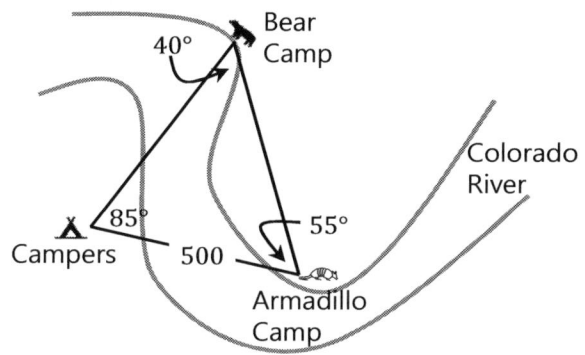

A. $500 \times \dfrac{\sin 85°}{\sin 40°}$

B. $500 \times \dfrac{\sin 40°}{\sin 85°}$

C. $\dfrac{\sin 85°}{500 \times \sin 40°}$

D. $\dfrac{\sin 40°}{500 \times \sin 85°}$

E. $500 \times \sin 45°$

58.

In the triangle $\triangle ABC$ below, the length of $\overline{PQ}$ is 8 inches, the length of $\overline{QR}$ is 12 inches, and the measure of $\angle Q$ is 42°. What is the approximate length, in inches, of $\overline{PR}$?

F. 8.1

G. 9.8

H. 10.3

J. 11.4

K. 12.5

59.

As shown below, the length of $\overline{OP}$ is 1 coordinate unit, Q is placed on the positive x-axis, and the measure of $\angle POQ$ is 120°. Which of the following coordinates is the coordinates of point P?

A. $\left(-\dfrac{1}{2}, \dfrac{\sqrt{3}}{2}\right)$

B. $\left(\dfrac{1}{2}, -\dfrac{\sqrt{3}}{2}\right)$

C. $\left(-\dfrac{\sqrt{3}}{2}, \dfrac{1}{2}\right)$

D. $\left(\dfrac{\sqrt{3}}{2}, -\dfrac{1}{2}\right)$

E. $\left(-\dfrac{\sqrt{3}}{2}, -\dfrac{1}{2}\right)$

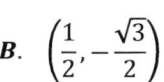

60.

Suppose that $k\begin{bmatrix} 2 & 4 \\ 8 & -6 \end{bmatrix} = \begin{bmatrix} a & b \\ 24 & c \end{bmatrix}$, what is the value of $a + b + c$?

F. 0

G. −4

H. 8

J. −12

K. 24

BLANK PAGE   *by K·DEAN*

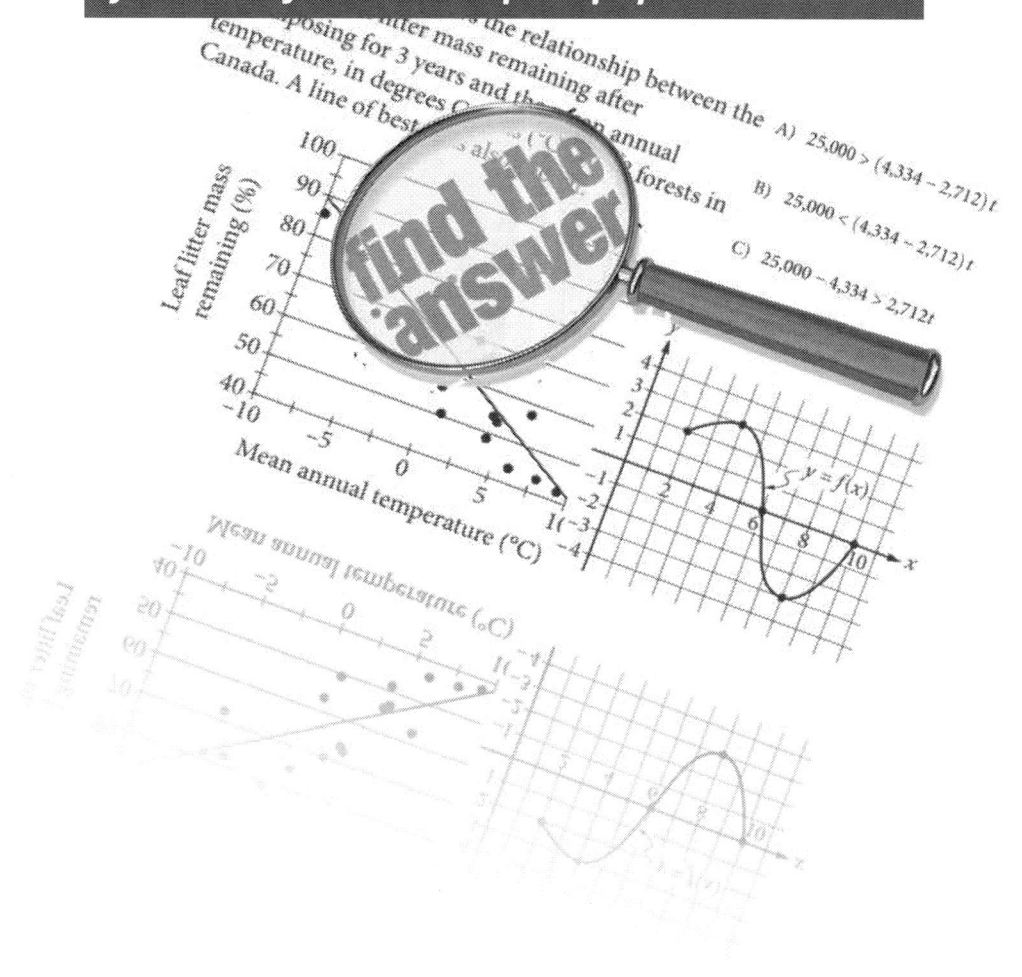

Obtain Scale Scores from Raw Scores

Scale Score	Raw Score	Scale Score	Raw Score	Scale Score	Raw Score
36	60	24	36-37	12	7
35	58-59	23	34-35	11	5-6
34	57	22	32-33	10	4
33	55-56	21	30-31	9	-
32	54	20	29	8	3
31	52-53	19	27-28	7	-
30	50-51	18	24-26	6	2
29	48-49	17	21-23	5	-
28	45-47	16	17-20	4	1
27	43-44	15	13-16	3	-
26	40-42	14	11-12	2	-
25	38-39	13	8-10	1	0

1. Scoring Key

Key		Question Category	Y/N
01.	A	Number Theory	
02.	J	Number Theory	
03.	A	Number Theory	
04.	K	Expression and Linear Equation	
05.	D	Expression and Linear Equation	
06.	G	Expression and Linear Equation	
07.	E	Expression and Linear Equation	
08.	H	Expression and Linear Equation	
09.	E	Expression and Linear Equation	
10.	J	Expression and Linear Equation	
11.	B	Linear Function inequality	
12.	K	Linear Function inequality	
13.	B	Linear Function inequality	
14.	C	Linear Function inequality	
15.	K	Linear Function inequality	
16.	C	Linear Function inequality	
17.	J	Linear Function inequality	
18.	C	Arithmetic Topic and Ratio	
19.	H	Arithmetic Topic and Ratio	
20.	C	Arithmetic Topic and Ratio	
21.	G	Arithmetic Topic and Ratio	
22.	E	Basic Geometry	
23.	G	Basic Geometry	
24.	H	Basic Geometry	
25.	E	Basic Geometry	
26.	H	Basic Geometry	
27.	E	Basic Geometry	
28.	F	Basic Geometry	
29.	D	Arithmetic Topic and Ratio	
30.	G	Quadratic and Polynomial Function	

Key		Question Category	Y/N
31.	E	Quadratic and Polynomial Function	
32.	J	Quadratic and Polynomial Function	
33.	C	Quadratic and Polynomial Function	
34.	C	Quadratic and Polynomial Function	
35.	G	Quadratic and Polynomial Function	
36.	C	Further Equations and Functions	
37.	H	Further Equations and Functions	
38.	B	Further Equations and Functions	
39.	C	Further Equations and Functions	
40.	J	Further Equations and Functions	
41.	J	Statistics and Probability	
42.	A	Statistics and Probability	
43.	B	Statistics and Probability	
44.	F	Statistics and Probability	
45.	K	Statistics and Probability	
46.	G	Sequence and Series	
47.	C	Analytic Geometry and Conic Section	
48.	G	Analytic Geometry and Conic Section	
49.	A	Analytic Geometry and Conic Section	
50.	K	Analytic Geometry and Conic Section	
51.	B	Analytic Geometry and Conic Section	
52.	F	Analytic Geometry and Conic Section	
53.	E	Analytic Geometry and Conic Section	
54.	G	Trigonometric Functions	
55.	D	Trigonometric Functions	
56.	H	Trigonometric Functions	
57.	A	Trigonometric Functions	
58.	F	Trigonometric Functions	
59.	A	Trigonometric Functions	
60.		Intermediate Algebra	

2. Answer Explanations

01. Answer (A)

Calculating change is subtracting initial from final value.

By definition of evaluating change;
$$change = -7 - 92 = -99^\circ C$$

02. Answer (J)

(odd)×(odd) is an odd integer and (positive)×(negative)=is a negative integer.

p is a positive integer and pq^5 is a negative integer so, q^5 must be a negative integer. And p is an odd integer and pq^5 is also an odd integer so, q^5 must be an odd integer.
Therefore q^5 is a negative odd integer.

The negative integer to the odd natural number power $(negative^{odd})$ is always a negative integer [ex: $(-5)^3 = -125$]. and the odd integer to the any natural number is always an odd integer.

Thus, q is a negative odd integer.

03. Answer (A)

The percent data convert to number.

Draw the Venn diagram;
visited 3 countries is $a = 0.15 \times 400 = 60$
visited exactly 2 countries is
$$x + y + z = 0.3 \times 400 = 120$$
visited exactly 1 countries is
$$c + k + j = 196.$$

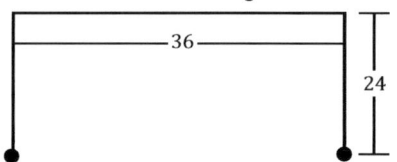

So, the number of customers did not visited these 3 countries is;
$$400 - (a + x + y + z + c + k + j) = 400 - (60 + 120 + 196) = 24.$$

Thus, the percent of customers is;
$$\frac{24}{400} \times 100 = 6\%.$$

04. Answer (K)

Substitute 2 for x and −2 for y and then simplify.

Substitute 2 for x and -2 for y;
$$-2x^2 + y^2 + 2x - 3 = -2(2)^2 + (-2)^2 + 2(2) - 3$$
$$= -8 + 4 + 4 - 3 = -3$$

05. Answer (A)

Expanding the polynomial by using the distributive property.

Expanding the polynomial and then simplifying;
$$3 - 2(4x + 1) = 3 - 8x - 2 = -8x + 1$$
Thus, the equivalent expression is $-8x + 1$.

06. Answer (G)

Substitute the values for each variables.

Substitute -2 for x and 3 for y;
$$xy^3 + x^2y^2 - 8x = (-2)(3)^3 - (-2)^2(3)^2 - 8(-2)$$
Evaluate the expression;
$$-54 + 36 + 16 = -2$$
Thus, the value is -2.

07. Answer (E)

Let x be the length of the rectangle.

Let x be the length of the rectangle. And the perimeter is twice the sum of width and length. So,
$$23 = 2 \times \left(x + \frac{1}{2}x - 2\right) \rightarrow 23 = 2 \cdot \left(\frac{3}{2}x - 2\right) \rightarrow 23 = 3x - 4$$
Add 4 to both sides;
$$3x - 4 = 23 \rightarrow 3x - 4 + 4 = 23 + 4 \rightarrow 3x = 27$$
Divide by 3 on both sides;
$$\frac{3x}{3} = \frac{27}{3} \rightarrow x = 9$$
Thus, the length of the rectangle is $9cm$.

08. Answer (H)

It is also a good idea to draw a figure appropriate to the situation.

The fence has one side of 36 ft length and two sides of 24 ft length;

24 feet side is equally divided by 6 feet, and there are 4 intervals and 36 feet side is equally divided by 6 feet, and there are 6 intervals. So, there are $4 + 6 + 4 = 14$ intervals.
Thus, Lucy plant $14 \times 10 = 140$ roses for the fence.

09. Answer (E)

Set up a linear equation to suit the situation..

Making a linear equation;
$$x + 12 + x = 40 \rightarrow 2x + 12 = 40$$
Subtracting 12 from both sides;
$$2x + 12 = 40 \rightarrow 2x + 12 - 12 = 40 - 12 \rightarrow 2x = 28$$
Dividing by 2 on both sides;
$$2x = 28 \rightarrow \frac{2x}{2} = \frac{28}{2} \rightarrow x = 14$$
Thus, the value of x is 14.

10. Answer (J)

Convert number of other flowers to number of marigolds.

If the number of roses is R, marigolds is M, and pansies is P then;
"20 more roses than marigold" $\rightarrow R = M + 12$
"8 less marigolds than pansy" $\rightarrow M = P - 8 \rightarrow P = M + 8$.

Because the total number of flowers is 62;
$$R + M + P = 62$$
Substituting expression represented by M;
$$R + M + P = 62 \rightarrow (M + 12) + M + (M + 8) = 62$$
$$\rightarrow 3M + 20 = 62$$
Subtracting 20 form both sides;
$$3M + 20 = 62 \rightarrow 3M + 20 - 20 = 62 - 20 \rightarrow 3M = 42$$
Dividing the both sides by 3;
$$3M = 42 \rightarrow \frac{3M}{3} = \frac{42}{3} \rightarrow M = 14$$
Thus, the number of marigolds is 14.

11. Answer (B)

Substitute each value and then evaluate.

Substitute -2 for x;
$$f(x) = -3x^2 + 4x \quad \rightarrow \quad f(-2) = -3(-2)^2 + 4(-2) = -20$$
Thus, the value of $f(-2)$ is -20.

12. Answer (K)

Convert the equation to slope-intercept form.

Convert the standard form to slope-intercept form by;
adding $4x$ to both sides;
$$-4x = 3y - 12 \quad \rightarrow \quad -4x + 4x = 3y - 12 + 4x \quad \rightarrow \quad 0 = 3y - 12 + 4x$$
subtracting $3y$ from both sides;
$$0 = 3y - 12 + 4x \quad \rightarrow \quad 0 - 3y = 3y - 12 + 4x - 3y$$
$$\rightarrow \quad -3y = -12 + 4x$$
dividing both sides by -3;
$$-3y = 4x - 12 \quad \rightarrow \quad \frac{-3y}{-3} = \frac{4x - 12}{-3} \quad \rightarrow \quad y = -\frac{4}{3}x + 4$$
Thus, the y-intercept of the given equation is 4.

13. Answer (B)

Using slope-intercept form.

At the shop, the price of $3oz$ is $3.15 and $6oz$ is $3.75. This means that the line of the relationship passes through $(3, 3.15), (6, 3.75)$.
So, the slope is;
$$m = \frac{y_2 - y_1}{x_2 - x_1} = \frac{3.75 - 3.15}{6 - 3} = \frac{0.6}{3} = 0.2$$
Therefore $y = mx + b \quad \rightarrow \quad y = 0.2x + b$, and substitute a point for $y = 0.2x + b$;
$$y = 0.2x + b \quad \rightarrow \quad 3.15 = 0.2(3) + b \quad \rightarrow \quad 3.15 = 0.6 + b \quad \rightarrow \quad b = 2.55$$
Thus, the relationship is $y = 0.2x + 2.55 \quad \rightarrow \quad p = 0.2w + 2.55$

14. Answer (C)

The unit cost is price per weight.

Unit cost is;
$$unit\ cost = \frac{price}{weight} = \frac{\$4.85}{12\ oz} = 0.4041666\ldots.$$
Thus, the unit cost is $0.40 per oz.

15. Answer (K)

It is a question of change.

The change of her buying coffee beans is;
$$\$5.00 - \$4.35 = \$0.65$$
The number of nickels for $0.65 is;
$$\$0.65 \div \$0.05 = 13$$

16. Answer (C)

Substitute -4 for x.

Substitute -4 for $y = x + 7$;
$$y = x + 7 \quad \rightarrow \quad y = -4 + 7 \quad \rightarrow \quad y = 3$$
Thus, the intersecting point is $(-4, 3)$.

17. Answer (J)

The total number of both boxes is 8 and the total price of both boxes is $1,049.

The sum of total boxes is 8, so;
$$v + b = 8$$
The price of a valley balls box is $142, a basket ball box is $113, and the total price is $1,049, therefore;
$$142v + 113b = 1,049$$
Thus, the system of linear equation is;
$v + b = 8$ and $142v + 113b = 1,049$.

18. Answer (C)

Average is the quotient total money and total students.

If the total number of students in the council is n, then the number of junior is $\frac{2}{5}n$ and senior is $\frac{3}{5}n$.
So, the total raising money of junior is $\frac{2}{5}n \times \$30 = \$12n$ and the total raising money of junior is $\frac{3}{5}n \times \$40 = \$24n$. Therefore, the average is calculated by;
$$average = \frac{raising\ money}{total\ number\ of\ students} = \frac{\$12n + \$24n}{n} = \frac{\$36n}{n} = \$36$$
Thus, the averaged raising money is $36.

19. Answer (H)

The average speed on each segment is same.

Suppose that the time of each segment is $5t, 4t$ and $3t$ and the sum of second and third is d. And because average speed on each segment is same;
$$\frac{120}{5t} = \frac{d}{4t + 3t} \quad \rightarrow \quad \frac{24}{t} = \frac{d}{7t}$$
Using cross product;
$$dt = 7t \times 24 \quad \rightarrow \quad dt = 168t$$
Dividing both sides by t;
$$dt = 168t \quad \rightarrow \quad \frac{dt}{t} = \frac{168t}{t} \quad \rightarrow \quad d = 168$$
Thus, the total distance is $120 + 168 = 288$.

20. Answer (C)

The shipping costs is sum of fee and price.

For 6 kg box;
$$\$10 + 6 \times \$0.5 = \$10 + \$3 = \$13$$
For 12 kg box;
$$\$25 + 12 \times \$0.3 = \$25 + \$3.6 = \$28.6$$
Thus, the total shipping cost is $13 + $28.6 = $41.6.

21. Answer (G)

Making a system of linear equation and 6 hours are 360 minutes

If the number of pretzels is p and the number of donuts is d, then;
"make three times as many donuts as pretzels" $\rightarrow \quad d = 3p \quad - \quad ①$
and "It takes her 12 minutes to make a pretzel and 8 minutes to make a donut." $\rightarrow \quad 12p + 8d = 360 \quad - \quad ②$.
Substitute ① for ②;
$$12p + 8d = 360 \quad \rightarrow \quad 12p + 8(3p) = 360 \quad \rightarrow \quad 12p + 24p = 360$$
$$\rightarrow \quad 36p = 360 \quad \rightarrow \quad p = 10$$
Thus, the number of donuts are $d = 3p \quad \rightarrow \quad d = 30$.

22. `Answer` **(E)**

Angle sum of a triangle is 180°

$\overline{AB} \parallel \overline{CD}$ and $\overline{BD}$ is transversal so, $\angle ABO \cong \angle CDO = 55°$ ($\because$alternate interior angle). Because the angle sum of $\triangle COD$ is $180°$;
$\angle COD + 40° + 55° = 180° \rightarrow \angle COD + 95° = 180° \rightarrow \angle COD = 85°$

Thus, the measure of $\angle COD$ is $85°$.

23. `Answer` **(G)**

Draw an auxiliary line .

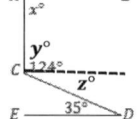

Drawing an auxiliary line parallel to $\overline{AB}$ and $\overline{DE}$.
$z°$ and $\angle CDE$ are alternate interior angles so,
$$z = 35$$
And $124° = z° + y° \rightarrow 124° = 35° + y° \rightarrow y° = 89°$.
Because $x°$ and $y°$ are Co-interior angles,
$x° + y° = 180° \rightarrow x° + 89° = 180 \rightarrow x° = 91°$.

Thus, the measure of $x°$ is $91°$.

24. `Answer` **(H)**

Using the inequalities in a triangle.

The inequalities in a triangle;
  sum of two smaller sides length is greater than largest side length
$$4 + 9 > 12 \rightarrow 13 > 12$$

Thus, the correct answer is **H**.

25. `Answer` **(E)**

Area is 2-Dimensional.

If the ratio of the side length of similar two figures is $\frac{a}{b}$, then

$$Area\ ratio \rightarrow \frac{a^2}{b^2}, \qquad Volume\ ratio \rightarrow \frac{a^3}{b^3}$$

$\triangle PXY \backsim \triangle PQR$($\because$ AA similarity)   and the side length ratio is $3:4$, so, the ratio of area of two triangle is $9:16$.

Thus, the ratio of the area of $\triangle PXY$ to the area of $\triangle PQR$ is $9:16$.

26. `Answer` **(H)**

Be careful corresponding parts.

$\triangle AOB \backsim \triangle DOC$ ($\because$ angle-angle (AA) similarity). Using triangle similarity;
$$\frac{\overline{CO}}{\overline{BO}} = \frac{\overline{CD}}{\overline{BA}} \rightarrow \frac{136}{20} = \frac{\overline{CD}}{24} \rightarrow 20 \times \overline{CD} = 24 \times 136$$
$$\rightarrow \overline{CD} = 163.2$$

Thus, the width of the pond $\overline{CD}$ is 163.2.

27. `Answer` **(E)**

The scale factor is the ratio of the side length.

If the ratio of the side length of similar two figures is $\frac{a}{b}$, then

$$Perimeter\ ratio \rightarrow \frac{a}{b} \quad Area\ ratio \rightarrow \frac{a^2}{b^2}, \quad Volume\ ratio \rightarrow \frac{a^3}{b^3}$$

The scale factor, the ratio of the side length is $\frac{3}{4}$ and the ratio of the perimeter is also, $\frac{3}{4}$.

$$\frac{perimeter\ of\ \triangle PQR}{perimeter\ of\ \triangle XYZ, P} = \frac{3}{4} \rightarrow \frac{45}{P} = \frac{3}{4} \rightarrow 3P = 180 \rightarrow P = 60$$

Thus, the perimeter of $\triangle XYZ$ is 60.

28. `Answer` **(F)**

The Pythagorean theorem is always useful.

The winding belt length is;
  larger gear $\rightarrow \frac{3}{4} \times \pi(6) \rightarrow \frac{9}{2}\pi$,
  smaller gear $\rightarrow \frac{1}{4} \times \pi(2) \rightarrow \frac{1}{2}\pi$
so, the winding length is
$$\frac{9}{2}\pi + \frac{1}{2}\pi = \frac{10}{2}\pi = 5\pi.$$

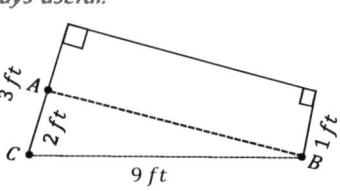

If B is a center of smaller gear and C is a center of larger center, $\triangle ABC$ is a right triangle. So, using the Pythagorean theorem;
$$\overline{BC}^2 = \overline{AB}^2 + \overline{AC}^2 \rightarrow \overline{AB} = \sqrt{\overline{BC}^2 - \overline{AC}^2} = \sqrt{81 - 4} = \sqrt{77}$$
Therefore, the length of the belt is;
$$5\pi + 2 \times \sqrt{77} = 5\pi + 2\sqrt{77}$$

Thus, the exact length of the belt is $5\pi + 2\sqrt{77}$.

29. `Answer` **(D)**

Using the formula.

Because the diameter of hemisphere is 12, the radius is 6. From the formula of the hemisphere's volume;
$$V = \frac{1}{2} \times \left(\frac{4}{3}\pi r^3\right) = \frac{1}{2} \times \left(\frac{4}{3}\pi(6)^3\right) = 144\pi$$
The volume of the cylinder is;
$$V = \pi r^2 h = \pi(6)^2(14) = 504\pi$$

Thus, the volume of the solid is $144\pi + 504\pi = 648\pi$.

30. `Answer` **(G)**

The quadratic expression is the product of two factors.

The quadratic expression is the product of two factors so,
$$x^2 + (p - q)x + 3 + q = (x - 3)(x + 1)$$
$$= x^2 + x - 3x - 3$$
$$= x^2 - 2x - 3$$
Therefore, $p - q = -2$ and $3 + q = -3 \rightarrow q = -6$.
Substitute -6 for q; $p - q = -2 \rightarrow p - (-6) = -2$
$$p + 6 = -2 \rightarrow p = -8$$

Thus, $p = -8$ and $q = -6$.

31. `Answer` **(E)**

Think simple.

Adding 5 to the both sides;
$$x^2 - 5 = 11 \rightarrow x^2 - 5 + 5 = 11 + 5 \rightarrow x^2 = 16$$
Thus, the value of $x^2 + 5 = 16 + 5 = 21$.

32. `Answer` **(J)**

Substitute -2 for x.

Substitute -2 for x and then solve for p;
$$(x + 3)(x - 3) = p \rightarrow (-2 + 3)(-2 - 4) = p \rightarrow (1)(-6) = p$$
Thus, the value of p is -6.

33. `Answer` **(C)**

Multiplying both sides by -1.

Rewriting the equation and then multiplying by -1;
$$-x^2 - 4 - 5x = 0 \rightarrow -x^2 - 5x - 4 = 0 \rightarrow x^2 + 5x + 4 = 0$$
The product of two roots is 4 and the sum of two roots is -5 so, using factoring;
$$x^2 + 5x + 4 = 0 \rightarrow (x + 4)(x + 1) = 0$$
So, $x + 4 = 0$ or $x + 1 = 0 \rightarrow x = -4$ or $x = -1$.

Thus, the solution is -1 or -4.

34. `Answer` **(C)**

Two real distinct zeros → Two x-intercepts

If a graph has two x-intercepts, the equation has two distinct real zeros, roots, and solutions.

Thus, the correct answer is **C**.

---

35. `Answer` **(G)**

Reflection on y-axis: (x,y) → (-x, y).

A figure is reflected in y-axis;
$$(x, y) \rightarrow (-x, y) \quad (-2, -5) \rightarrow (2, -5)$$

Thus, the correct answer is **G**.

---

36. `Answer` **(C)**

4 is 2^2.

Rewrite;
$$x^{5a} = (x^{2a})^{\frac{5}{2}} = (4)^{\frac{5}{2}} = (2^2)^{\frac{5}{2}} = 2^5 = 32$$

Thus, the value of $x^{5a} = 32$.

---

37. `Answer` **(H)**

Using the properties of exponential.

Using the properties of exponential;
$$\frac{(5x^2)^2}{x^6} = \frac{25x^4}{x^6} = 25x^{4-6} = 25x^{-2} = \frac{25}{x^2}$$

Thus, the correct answer is **H**.

---

38. `Answer` **(B)**

$\sqrt{-1} = i$ and $1 = 3^0$.

Using the properties of exponential;
$$3^{2x^2+4} = 1 \quad \rightarrow \quad 3^{2x^2+4} = 3^0 \quad \rightarrow \quad 2x^2 + 4 = 0$$
So, $2x^2 + 4 = 0 \quad \rightarrow \quad 2x^2 = -4 \quad \rightarrow \quad x^2 = -2 \quad \rightarrow \quad x = \pm\sqrt{-2}$
$$\rightarrow \quad x = \pm\sqrt{2}i \quad \rightarrow \quad x = \sqrt{2}i \text{ or } -\sqrt{2}i$$

Thus, the correct answer is **B**.

---

39. `Answer` **(C)**

There are two I's.

Let I' be new I and D' be new D, so;
$$D = \frac{\frac{1}{2}Irt + \frac{3}{4}I}{12t} \quad \rightarrow \quad D' = \frac{\frac{1}{2}I'rt + \frac{3}{4}I'}{12t}$$
Substitute $2I$ for I';
$$D' = \frac{\frac{1}{2}(2I)rt + \frac{3}{4}(2I)}{12t} = \frac{2 \times \left(\frac{1}{2}Irt + \frac{3}{4}I\right)}{12t} = 2 \times D$$

Thus, the correct answer is **C**.

---

40. `Answer` **(J)**

If you substitute appropriate numbers for given variables, it is easy to understand.

Using exponential properties;
$$b^{-x} = (b^{-1})^x = \left(\frac{1}{b}\right)^x \quad \leftarrow \frac{1}{b} > 1 (\because 0 < b < 1)$$

so, the $f(x)$ is exponential growth function.

Or, let 3 be a and $\frac{1}{2}$ be b;

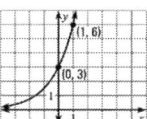

$$f(x) = 3 \cdot \left(\frac{1}{2}\right)^{-x} = 3 \cdot (2^{-1})^{-x} \quad \rightarrow \quad f(x) = 3 \cdot 2^x$$

And this function is exponential growth function so, as shown in the figure, $f(x)$ is increasing for all x.

Thus, the correct answer is **J**.

---

41. `Answer` **(J)**

The shipping charges are constant at each weight interval..

The shipping charges are constant at each weight interval.

Thus, the correct answer is **J**.

---

42. `Answer` **(A)**

The ratio of a to b is a:b.

The number of friends who selected Action to the number if friends who selected Comedy is 5 to 7, it is $5:7$.

Thus, the correct answer is **A**.

---

43. `Answer` **(B)**

The quotient of Animation and total.

The percent is
$$percent = \frac{4}{30} \times 100 = 13.3333 \dots \%$$

Thus, the percent is 13.33%.

---

44. `Answer` **(F)**

The central angle and ratio of budget vary directly.

The central angle is determined by the ratio of types of movie. So,
$$central\ angle = \frac{3}{30} \times 360° = 36°$$

Thus, the measure of central angle is 36°.

---

45. `Answer` **(K)**

The median is the middle of data set. .

Because the number of total students is 20, the middle is between 10th and 11th . And 5 (25%) students used their phones for 7 hours or above.($\because 0.25 \times 20 = 5$)
So, drawing diagram

Order	10th	Median	11th~15th	16th~20th
Time	3 or below	4	5 or 6	7 or above

Thus, 5 (11th~15th) of the students used their phones for 5 or 6 hours.

46. **Answer** **(G)**

Finding the common ratio.

The common ratio, r, is;
$$-\frac{6}{3} = \frac{12}{-6} = -\frac{24}{12} = -2$$
From the formula of geometric sequence;
$$a_n = a_1 r^{n-1} \rightarrow a_8 = 3(-2)^{8-1} = 3(-2)^7 = -384$$
Thus, the eighth term is -384.

47. **Answer** **(C)**

Percent is a ratio whose denominator is 100.

From the definition of percent, let p be percent;
$$\frac{\overline{XY}}{\overline{BC}} = \frac{p}{100} \rightarrow \frac{36}{210} = \frac{p}{100}$$
Using cross product;
$$210 \times p = 36 \times 100 \rightarrow p = \frac{36}{210} \times 100 = 17.14285 \ldots \%$$
Thus, the percent is 17.1%.

48. **Answer** **(G)**

Using the Pythagorean theorem.

ΔODC is a right triangle ($\because \square ABCD$ is a rectangle) and the length of $\overline{OD}$ is 105.($\because$ point O is midpoint of $\overline{AD}$)
Using the Pythagorean theorem;
$$\overline{OC}^2 = \overline{OD}^2 + \overline{DC}^2 \rightarrow \overline{OC} = \sqrt{105^2 + 300^2} = 15\sqrt{449}$$
Thus, the correct answer is **G**.

49. **Answer** **(A)**

An equilateral triangle is also an isosceles triangle.

Drawing perpendicular line from vertex P to base side and let Q be intersecting point.

The point Q is midpoint of $\overline{OR}$ and have same y-coordinate of P. So, the coordinate of Q is $(0, r) = (0, \beta)$.

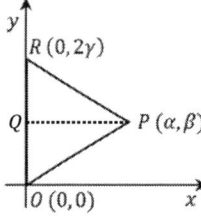

Thus, $\beta = \gamma$.

50. **Answer** **(K)**

Using the formula of distance.

Using the formula of distance;
$$d = \sqrt{(x_2 - x_1)^2 + (y_2 - y_1)^2} = \sqrt{(15 - 3)^2 + (10 - 2)^2}$$
$$= \sqrt{12^2 + 8^2} = 4\sqrt{13} \text{ light years.}$$
Thus, the distance, in miles, is $4\sqrt{13} \times 5.88 \times 10^{12} \approx 8.5 \times 10^{13}$.

51. **Answer** **(B)**

Using the Pythagorean theorem.

Let x be the two legs of the right triangle, and then using the Pythagorean theorem;

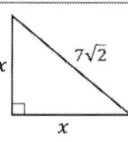

$$(7\sqrt{2})^2 = x^2 + x^2 \rightarrow 2x^2 = 7^2(\sqrt{2})^2$$
$$\rightarrow 2x^2 = 98 \rightarrow x^2 = \frac{98}{2} = 49$$
Take square root on both sides;
$$\sqrt{x^2} = \sqrt{49} \rightarrow x = 7$$
Thus, the perimeter of the triangle is $7 + 7 + 7\sqrt{2} = 14 + 7\sqrt{2}$.

52. **Answer** **(F)**

From the headquarters of a battalion not previous point.

The coordinate of the headquarters of a battalion is $(0,0)$ and east direction is $+x$, west direction is $-x$, north direction is $+y$, and south direction is $-y$.
Apply their distance on the point coordinate;
$$(-3, 4) - 5 \, east \rightarrow (2, 4) - 5 \, south \rightarrow (2, -1)$$
$$-7 \, west \rightarrow (-5, -1)$$
So, final coordinate is $(-5, -1)$ and using the distance formula;
$$d = \sqrt{(x_2 - x_1)^2 + (y_2 - y_1)^2} = \sqrt{(-5 - 0)^2 + (-1 - 0)^2} = \sqrt{26}$$
Thus, the distance is $\sqrt{26} \approx 5.1$.

53. **Answer** **(E)**

Using the Pythagorean theorem.

A lateral face of the pyramid is an equilateral triangle, and let x be the length of a side the lateral face.
So, using the Pythagorean theorem;
$$x^2 = \left(\frac{1}{2}x\right)^2 + (5\sqrt{3})^2 \rightarrow x^2 = \frac{1}{4}x^2 + 75$$
$$\rightarrow \frac{3}{4}x^2 = 75 \rightarrow x^2 = 75 \times \frac{4}{3} = 100 \rightarrow x = \sqrt{100} = 10$$

All edges have same length of side,
Thus, the total length of 8 edges is $8 \times 10 = 80$.

54. **Answer** **(G)**

Distance is speed $\times$ time.

The altitude of the drone is;
$$\frac{10ft}{s} \times 20s = 200ft$$
So, the vertical distance of the drone from her head is $200 - 6 = 194ft$.
Using $\sin 60°$;

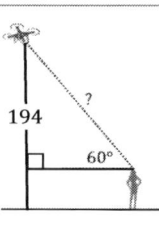

$$\sin 60° = \frac{O}{H} = \frac{194}{?} = \frac{\sqrt{3}}{2}$$
$$\rightarrow ? = 194 \times \frac{2}{\sqrt{3}} = 224.0119044 \ldots ft.$$

Thus, the distance is 224.0.

55. **Answer** **(D)**

Using the trigonometric ratio.

The area of □$ABCD$ is;
$$area = \frac{1}{2}(\overline{AB} + \overline{CD}) \times \overline{AX}.$$

Using the trigonometric ratio;
$$\sin 60° = \frac{O}{H} = \frac{\overline{AX}}{6} \rightarrow \overline{AX} = 6 \times \sin 60° = 3\sqrt{3}.$$
$$\cos 60° = \frac{A}{H} = \frac{\overline{DX}}{6} \rightarrow \overline{DX} = 6 \times \cos 60° = 3.$$

Let x be the length of $\overline{AB} = \overline{CX}$.
$$area = \frac{1}{2}(\overline{AB} + \overline{CD}) \times \overline{AX} = \frac{1}{2} \times (x + x + 3) \times 3\sqrt{3}$$
$$= \frac{1}{2} \times (2x + 3) \times 3\sqrt{3} = \frac{21\sqrt{3}}{2} \rightarrow (2x + 3) \times 3\sqrt{3} = 21\sqrt{3}$$
$$\rightarrow (2x + 3) = 7 \rightarrow 2x = 4 \rightarrow x = 2$$

Thus, the length of $\overline{CD}$ is 5.

56. **Answer** **(H)**

Using the inverse trigonometric function.

Let θ be the angle and using trigonometry;
$$\tan \theta = \frac{O}{H} \rightarrow \theta = \tan^{-1}\left(\frac{O}{H}\right) = \tan^{-1}\left(\frac{4}{35}\right)$$

Thus, the correct answer is **H**.

57. **Answer** **(A)**

One side and three angles.

Because the question is given one side length and three angles, using sine law and let c be the distance;
$$\frac{b}{\sin B} = \frac{c}{\sin C} \rightarrow \frac{500}{\sin 40°} = \frac{c}{\sin 85°} \rightarrow c \times \sin 40° = 500 \times \sin 85°$$
$$\rightarrow c = 500 \times \frac{\sin 85°}{\sin 40°}$$

Thus, the correct answer is **A**.

58. **Answer** **(F)**

One angle and two sides.

The given values are two sides lengths and one included angle, so using cosine law;
$$\overline{PR}^2 = \overline{PQ}^2 + \overline{QR}^2 - 2 \times \overline{PQ} \times \overline{QR} \times \cos Q$$
$$\rightarrow \overline{PR}^2 = 8^2 + 12^2 - 2 \times 8 \times 12 \times \cos 42°$$
$$\rightarrow \overline{PR}^2 = 65.31619....$$

Thus, the length of $\overline{PQ} = \sqrt{65.31629...} \approx 8.0818... \approx 8.1,$

59. **Answer** **(A)**

Cosine is x and Sine is y.

Using unit circle and trigonometric ratio;
$$\cos \theta = \frac{x}{r} \rightarrow \cos 120° = \frac{x}{1} = -\frac{1}{2}$$
$$\sin \theta = \frac{y}{r} \rightarrow \sin 120° = \frac{y}{1} = \frac{\sqrt{3}}{2}$$

Thus, the coordinates are $(-\frac{1}{2}, \frac{\sqrt{3}}{2})$.

60. **Answer** **(F)**

Finding corresponding elements.

Using scalar multiplication;
$$k\begin{bmatrix} 2 & 4 \\ 8 & -6 \end{bmatrix} = \begin{bmatrix} 2k & 4k \\ 8k & -6k \end{bmatrix} = \begin{bmatrix} a & b \\ 24 & c \end{bmatrix} \rightarrow 8k = 24 \rightarrow k = 3$$
So,
$$2 \times 3 = a \rightarrow a = 6, \quad 4 \times 3 = b \rightarrow b = 12,$$
$$-6 \times 3 = c \rightarrow c = -18$$

Thus, the value of $a + b + c = 6 + 12 + (-18) = 0$.

BLANK PAGE   *by K·DEAN*

Reformed Past Paper ACT MATH TEST 03

60 Questions – 60 Minutes

DIRECTIONS:
Solve each problem, choose the correct answer, and then fill in the corresponding oval on your answer in the grid on the answer sheet.

Do not linger over problems that take too much time as many as you can; then return ... ... in the time you have left for this test.

You are permitted to use a calculator on this test.

Note: Unless otherwise stated, all of the following should be assumed.

1. Figures ... ... are drawn to scale unless ... ... indicated.

2. All figures lie in a plane unless otherwise indicated.

3. All variables and expressions used represent real numbers unless otherwise indicated.

This test has reformed the REAL ACT Mathematics Test

01.

The diameter of the Mars is about 4.2×10^3 mi and the diameter of the Mercury is about 3.0×10^3 mi. Which of the following is the sum of the diameter of the Mars and the diameter of the Mercury ?

A. 7.2×10^6

B. 7.2×10^5

C. 7.2×10^4

D. 7.2×10^3

E. 7.2×10^2

02.

Which of the following is equivalent to $\frac{12}{11}$?

F. 1.09

G. $1.\overline{09}$

H. 1.091

J. $1.09\overline{9}$

K. 1.090909

03.

Suppose that $0 < A < 1$, and N is a negative integer. Which of the following expressions about the range of A^N **must** be true ?

A. $-1 < A^N < 1$

B. $A^N < 0$

C. $0 < A^N < 1$

D. $A^N > 0$

E. $A^N > 1$

04.

Which of the following expressions is equivalent to $\frac{1}{3}a(-9b^2 - 3a^2 + 12b^2 + 3a^2)$ for all real number a and b?

F. ab^2

G. $4ab^2$

H. $-3ab^2 + a^3$

J. $4ab^2 - 2a^3$

K. $2x^2 - x - 20$

05.

At online shopping mall, the price of 1 DVD is $6 and the price of 1 pair of socks $4. Melissa spent $76 to buy 16 items – a combination of DVDs and pairs of socks. How many DVDs did she buy ?

A. 5

B. 6

C. 7

D. 8

E. 9

06.

$$y = -2x + 6$$
$$y = -x + 8$$

A system of equations is given above. What is the value of x in the (x, y) solution to the system?

F. 4

G. 2

H. −2

J. −4

K. −6

07.

A sport equipment store was having a sale on volleyballs and basketballs. The volleyballs sold for $12 each, and the basketballs sold for $16 each. Last month, the store sold 363 balls in volleyballs and basketballs. And the amount of money they received from the sales of the basketballs was twice the amount of money they received from the sales of the volleyballs. How many basketballs did they sell last month ?

A. 108

B. 84

C. 132

D. 99

E. 264

08.

A circle with center O is shown below. Points A, B, C, and D lie on the circle. The measure of the angle ∠AOC is 95°, the measure of the angle ∠BOD is 93°, and the measure of the angle ∠AOD is 160°. What is the measure of the angle ∠BOC?

F. 24

G. 28

H. 33

J. 37

K. 41

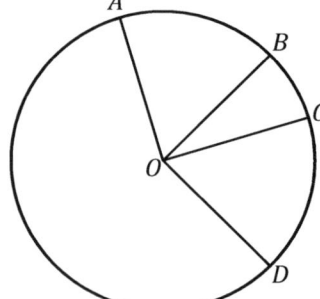

09.

Ruby, Eva, and Freya own shares of stock in the Well-Relax Hotel. Ruby owns 160 shares, Eva owns 250 shares, and Freya own 170 shares. Today, the value of 1 share of the hotel is $11.5. What is the total value of Ruby's, Eva's, and Freya's shares of Well-Relax Hotel stock ?

A.　$6,670

B.　$6,780

C.　$6,870

D.　$6,960

E.　$7,070

10.

Kay played 3 games for his basket ball team. In first game, he scored 6 points more than in the second game; in the second game, he scored 3 points less than in the third game. His average score was 18 points for the 3 games. How many points did he score in first game ?

F.　12

G.　15

H.　18

J.　21

K.　24

11.

A function is defined by $h(x) = 3x - 12$, and its domain is the set of integers from 0 to 20, inclusive. For how many values of x is $h(x)$ positive ?

A.　13

B.　14

C.　15

D.　16

E.　17

12.

Mike and Agnes rode a car 24 miles at a constant speed, from home to wildlife park. After arrival, they took a rest and ate lunch for 1 hour. Sketch a graph to show the distance from their home compared to time. The shape of the graph could best be described as a:

F.
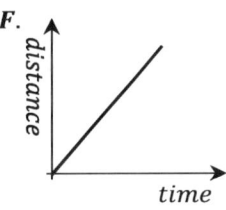

J.
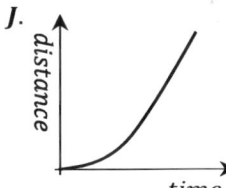

G.
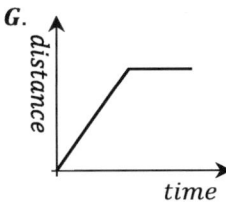

K.
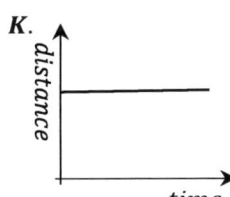

H.
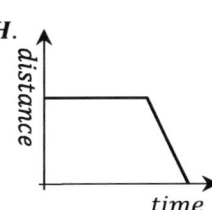

13.

In a coordinate plane, line l contains the two points $(3, -2)$ and $(1, -5)$, and line m contains the two points $(0, -2)$ and $(0, 6)$. At what point does line l intersect line m ?

A. $\left(\dfrac{3}{2}, 0\right)$

B. $\left(-\dfrac{4}{5}, \dfrac{3}{2}\right)$

C. $\left(0, -\dfrac{13}{2}\right)$

D. $(4, -8)$

E. $\left(\dfrac{7}{2}, -7\right)$

14.

If any line that passes through the two point $(-6, 2)$ and $(a, 2)$ will be horizontal in the standard (x, y) coordinate plane, what are all real value of a ?

F. -6

G. 2

H. a is all real numbers expect -6.

J. a is all real numbers.

K. There is no real number that satisfies the given condition.

15.

The cost of car washing for total 40 buses of a city bus company is $800. To encourage use of the gas station operated by the car wash, the cost of car washing is reduced by $100 for each group of 5 buses filled up the bus with gas through the gas station. All 5 buses in a group must be filled up with gas for each reduction in the cost of car washing. Which of the following graphs is expressed as the cost of car washing when 0 to 40 buses are filled up with gas ?

A.
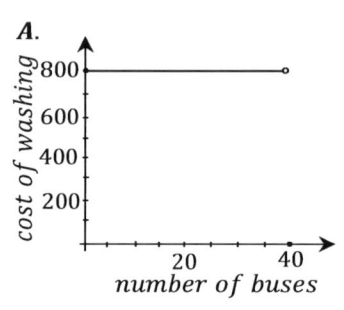

B.
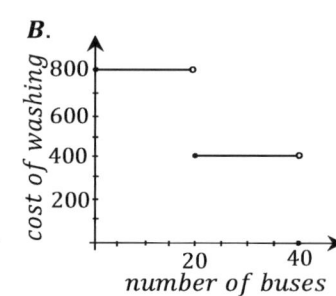

C.
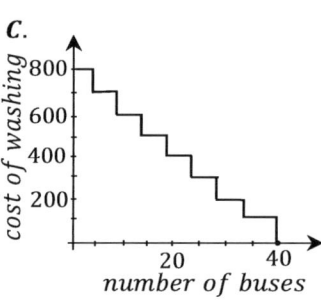

D.
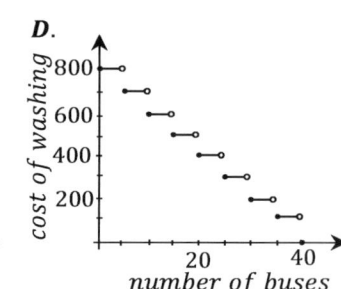

E.
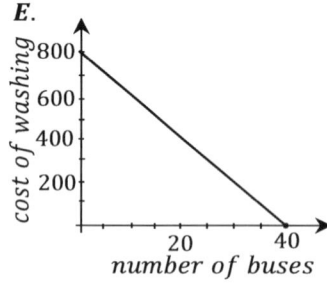

2 △ △ △ △ △ △ △ △ △ 2

16.

The total cost of repairing a car is the sum of the amount paid for parts and the amount paid for labor. Steven took his car in the car repairing shop and he paid $86 for parts, plus $40 for each hour of labor. When he got his car back, Steven was a given a bill of $252. He checked time in hours of his car being repaired and thought that the bill was in error-specifically, that the bill was $46 more than it should have been. If Steven was correct, how many hours of his car being repaired ?

A. 2

B. 2.5

C. 3

D. 3.5

E. 4

17.

Which of the following graphs shows the solution set for the inequality $2x + 3 \le 5$?

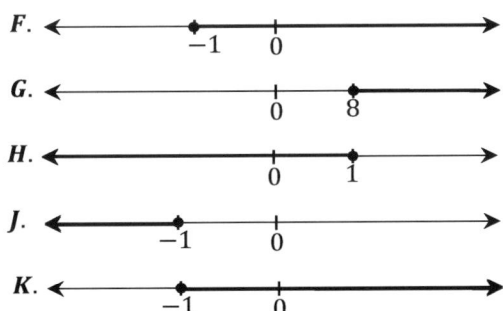

F.
G.
H.
J.
K.

18.

At Superior Computer store, monthly revenue for next month will be $10\frac{3}{4}\%$ less than this month's revenue. If this month's revenue is $5,300, then what will be revenue next month ?

A. $4,728.00

B. $4,728.25

C. $4,730.25

D. $4,735.25

E. $4,735.75

19.

In chemistry lab, Esther mixes 120 milliliters of aqueous solution A with 80 milliliters of aqueous solution B. Aqueous solution A has a 30% sodium hydroxide concentration and aqueous solution B has an unknown sodium hydroxide concentration. If the resulting 200 milliliters solution has a 20% sodium hydroxide concentration, what is the sodium hydroxide concentration of aqueous solution B?

F. 3%

G. 5%

H. 8%

J. 10%

K. 12%

2   **2**

20.

Rebecca and Veronica are contributing a total of $1,337 per month for their monthly rent. Each month, Rebecca contributes $\frac{3}{4}$ of the amount Veronica contributes. What is the amount, in dollars, Veronica will contribute over a period of 6 months?

A. $3,020

B. $3,438

C. $4,028

D. $4,584

E. $5,028

21.

The killer whale (*Orcinus orca*) has triangular teeth. The table below gives the length of a side of a tooth and the body length for each of five great killer whales. If the length of body varies directly with the length of tooth, based on the below data, which of the following values is closest to constant of variation?

Length of Tooth x, (inches)	Length of Body y, (feet)
4.6	25.2
3.8	20.8
3.9	21.3
6.4	35.0
8.2	44.9

F. 4.98

G. 5.02

H. 5.47

J. 5.85

K. 6.10

22.

Daniel is buying tiles for his trapezoidal shaped bathroom floor shown below. If each tile will cover 1.25 square feet, which of the following is closest to the number of tiles Daniel will need for his bathroom?

A. 111

B. 115

C. 119

D. 121

E. 125

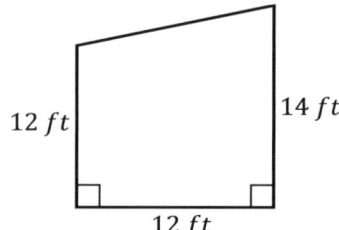

23.

In the figure below, the empty container is a right rectangular prism with dimensions given in feet. How many cubic feet of goods are needed to fill the container to 70% of its capacity?

F. 2,395

G. 2,475

H. 2,555

J. 2,625

K. 2,735

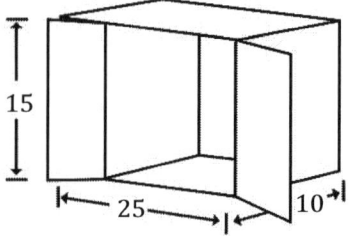

2 △ △ △ △ △ △ △ △ △ **2**

Use the following information to answer questions 24 - 26.

In the figure below, Kenneth will have a tile patio constructed beside his grocery store. The patio will have a width of 3 meters, and the top surface area of the patio will have an area 195 square meters. The patio will be constructed so that two sides of the patio is against two sides of the store.

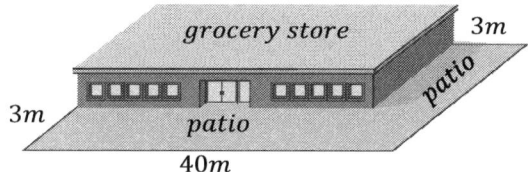

24.

If the thickness of a tile is 1.5cm, what will be the total volume, in cubic meters, of the entire tile on the patio?

A. 2.157

B. 2.852

C. 2.925

D. 292.5

E. 315.7

25.

One of patio tiling company, Strong Ceramic Tiling, proposes estimated cost that be used formula $C = 5.8S + 250$, C dollars, to tile a patio, where S square meters is the surface area of the patio, to him. What will be the estimated cost for tiling Kenneth's patio?

A. $1,272

B. $1,381

C. $1,453

D. $1,512

E. $1,673

26.

Kenneth will stand signboards for no-parking along the portion of the perimeter of the patio that is not against his store. What is the length, in meters, of that portion?

F. 69

G. 71

H. 74

J. 108

K. 136

27.

In the figure below, the radius of a circle is 6 inches. What is the circle's circumference, in inches?

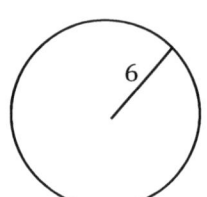

A. 3π

B. 18π

C. 6π

D. 36π

E. 12π

28.

The circumference of a circle is 40 inches. What is the length, in inches, of the radius of the circle?

F. 20

G. $\dfrac{20}{\pi}$

H. 20π

J. $\dfrac{40}{\pi}$

K. 40π

29.

As shown in the figure below, all angles are right angles, and the side lengths given are in feet. What is the area, in square feet, of the figure?

A. 18

B. 20

C. 40

D. 62

E. 80

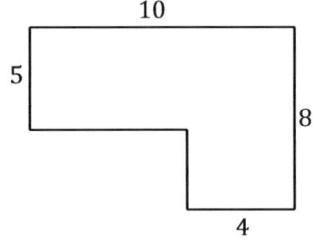

30.

As shown in the figure, the height of the cuboid is twice the length. The length and the width are the same. If the volume of the cuboid is 250 cubic centimeters, what is the width, in centimeters, of the cuboid?

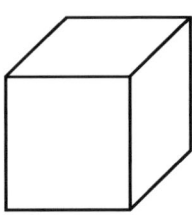

F. 3

G. 4

H. 5

J. 6

K. 7

31.

Which of the following absolute value functions is graphed in the standard (x,y) coordinate plane below?

A. $y = -|x - 3| - 5$

B. $y = -|x + 3| + 5$

C. $y = -|x - 3| + 5$

D. $y = |x + 3| + 5$

E. $y = |x - 3| - 5$

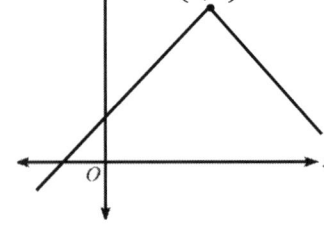

Use the following information to answer questions 32 - 34.

A rectangular region of stained glass is 10 inches wide by 15 inches long and has an area of 150 square inches. A glassmaker produced a 3-inch-wide wooden border along all four sides of this region of stained glass, as shown below. The outer edge of the wooden boarder is 21 inches long and 16 inches wide.

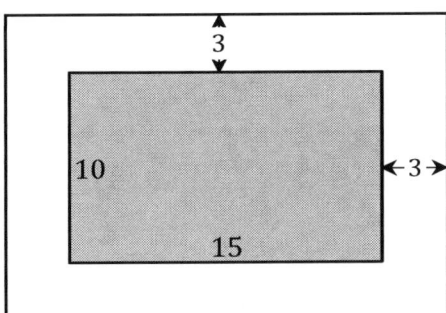

32.

The glassmaker plans to preprocess the region of stained glass. The glassmaker can buy only full cans of mineral dyes and will use at least 1 can per 28 square inches of the glass. What is the minimum number of cans of mineral dyes the glassmaker needs to buy?

A. 3

B. 4

C. 5

D. 6

E. 7

33.

How many inches of metallic banding would be needed to enclose the wooden border along its outer edge?

A. 50

B. 62

C. 74

D. 86

E. 98

34.

An acrylic pedestal will be added along one of the longest sides of the wooden border and will be equal in length to that side. The top of pedestal will be a rectangle with a width of 5 inches, and will be $2\frac{1}{2}$ inches thick. What is the volume, in cubic inches, of the acrylic pedestal?

F. 233.5

G. 243.5

H. 256.5

J. 262.5

K. 278.5

35.

What number(s) when multiplied by its reciprocal, multiplicative inverse, has a result of 1?

A. -1

B. 1

C. $1 \ or \ -1$

D. All real numbers. (But it is not zero)

E. No solution.

36.

The two functions $f(x)$ and $g(x)$ are defined by $f(x) = 2x - 3$ and $g(x) = x + 2$. What is the value of $g(f(2))$?

F. 1

G. 2

H. 3

J. 4

K. 5

37.

The domain of $g(x) = \dfrac{x-3}{x^3-4x}$ is the set of all real numbers EXCEPT:

A. 3

B. 0

C. $-2, 0, and \ 2$

D. $-2, 0, and \ 3$

E. $-2, 0, 2, and \ 3$

38.

What is the horizontal asymptote of the graph of $y = \dfrac{-3x+6}{-x-1}$ in the standard (x, y) coordinate plane?

A. $x = 2$

B. $x = -1$

C. $y = 3$

D. $y = 6$

E. $y = -3x + 6$

39.

For what real value of a, if any, is $\log_{27} a = -\dfrac{2}{3}$?

F. $\dfrac{1}{9}$

G. $-\dfrac{1}{9}$

H. $\dfrac{9}{27}$

J. $-\dfrac{9}{27}$

K. $\dfrac{1}{27}$

40.

Consider $h(x) = \sqrt[3]{2x - 3}$. Which of the following expressions is the inverse function of $h(x)$ for all real numbers x ?

A. $h^{-1}(x) = \dfrac{x^3 - 3}{2}$

B. $h^{-1}(x) = \dfrac{x^3 + 3}{2}$

C. $h^{-1}(x) = \sqrt[3]{2x - 3}$

D. $h^{-1}(x) = \sqrt[3]{2x + 3}$

E. $h^{-1}(x) = \sqrt[3]{\dfrac{x - 3}{2}}$

41.

In the figure below, Lawrence drew the circle graph that is described classmates' favorite subjects. His friend, Madison said that the numbers of classmates listed were correct, but that the central angle measures for the sector were not correct. What should be the central angle measure for language sector?

F. 54°

G. 68°

H. 72°

J. 84°

K. 90°

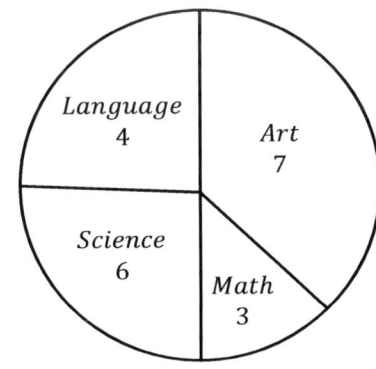

42.

The stem-and –leaf plot below shows the distance of a long jump in physical education class. What is the median distance of a long jump?

A. 2.7

B. 2.8

C. 2.9

D. 3.0

E. 3.1

Stem	Leaf
1	3 4 4 5 5 6 7
2	2 4 5 6 6 6 8 9 9
3	0 0 1 3 3 4 4 4 5 7 7
4	0 1 2 5 9
5	1

Key: 2 | 3 = 2.3

43.

In the figure below, the bell-shaped curve represents the normal distribution. The percent of the data that falls within each standard deviation from the mean is given to the nearest 0.1%.

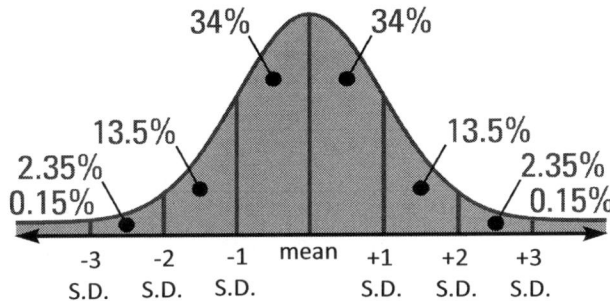

Suppose that the blood cholesterol concentration of men in a certain population are normally distributed with a mean of $170 mg/dL$ and a standard deviation of $15 mg/dL$. To the nearest 0.1%, what percent of men in the population are at least $155 mg/dL$?

F. 13.5%

G. 16.0%

H. 34.0%

J. 68.0%

K. 84.0%

44.

As shown the figure below, a circular spinner has 5 section (white, black, blue, red, and yellow) whose areas are in the ratio of $2:3:5:6:7$, respectively. Harold spins the spinner, and it will point one of the sectors in the spinner. What is the probability that the sector the pointer points is **not** the yellow sector?

A. $\dfrac{7}{23}$

B. $\dfrac{10}{23}$

C. $\dfrac{16}{23}$

D. $\dfrac{17}{23}$

E. $\dfrac{20}{23}$

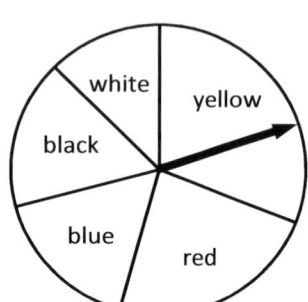

45.

Two events are independent if the occurrence of one has no effect on the occurrence of the other. Which of the following statements does **not** describe independent events?

F. Elsa rolls an even number on a number cube, and then she rolls the number cube again and roll an even number.

G. Eric chooses a member of a baseball team to be the pitcher, and then he chooses a different member of the team to be the catcher.

H. Jackson randomly draws a name from a box, then he put it back in the box and randomly draws a second name from the box.

J. A coin lands tail up, then another coin lands head up.

K. A queen card is drawn from a standard deck of cards, then with replacing the card, a 5 is drawn.

46.

The first 2 isosceles triangles of a sequence of isosceles triangles are shown below. The first triangle has three sides 2, 2, and 3centimeters. The dimension of second isosceles triangle, and of each successive isosceles triangle after the second, are determined by continuing the following pattern; the length of two leg sides is 2 centimeters longer than the length of two leg sides of the previous triangle, and the length of base side is 3 centimeters longer than the length of base side of the previous triangle. What is the perimeter, in centimeters, of the 5th isosceles triangle in the sequence?

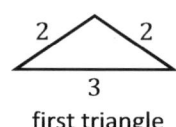 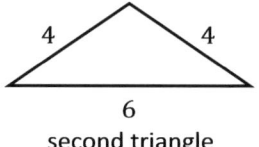

first triangle   second triangle

A. 26

B. 28

C. 33

D. 35

E. 42

47.

The vertices of $\square EFGH$ are the midpoints of the sides of $\square OPQR$. The dimensions of $\square OPQR$ are 18 inches by 24 inches. What is the perimeter, in inches, of $\square EFGH$?

F. 30

G. 40

H. 56

J. 60

K. 120

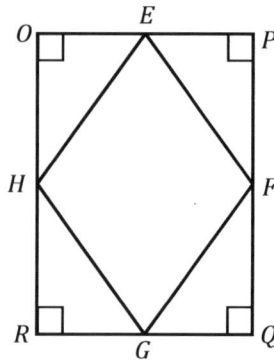

Use the following information to answer questions
48 - 49.

As shown in the figure below, □*PQRS* is a square
and it has side length 16 inches. The square is
divided into 16 nonoverlapping congruent squares.
Point *O* is the center of □*PQRS*.

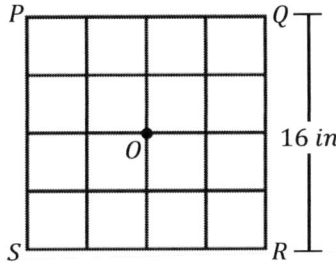

48.

What is the length, in inches, of $\overline{QS}$?

A. 18

B. 16

C. $18\sqrt{2}$

D. $16\sqrt{2}$

E. 32

49.

What is the area, in square inches, of 1 of the 16
congruent squares?

F. 8

G. 10

H. 12

J. 16

K. 24

50.

The floor plan of Juliet's living room is shown in the
diagram below; the given dimensions are in meters.
Juliet will install LED Lamp along the top of each wall
(shown by bold-solid lines in the floor plan).
According to the floor plan, which of the following
numbers is the perimeter, in meters, of Juliet's living
room?

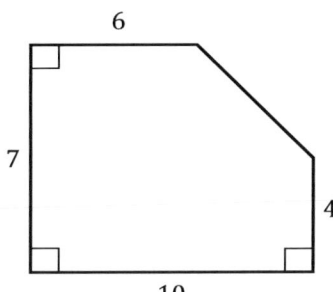

A. 30

B. 31

C. 32

D. 33

E. 34

51.

The length of the two legs of a right triangle are 7
inches and 9 inches, respectively. Which of the
following lengths, in inches, is closest to the length
of the hypotenuse of the right triangle?

F. 9.8

G. 10.7

H. 11.4

J. 13.5

K. 16.0

52.

A student council will be selected from a group of 68 junior students and 72 senior students. The council will consist of 4 junior students and 6 senior students. Which of the following expressions gives the number of different councils that could be selected from these 140 students?

A. $_{140}C_{10}$

B. $_{140}P_{10}$

C. $(_{68}C_4)(_{72}C_6)$

D. $(_{68}C_4) + (_{72}C_6)$

E. $(_{68}P_4) + (_{72}P_6)$

53.

As shown below, Olivia plans to make a triangular shelf on the corner of her bathroom wall that forms a right angle. The corner shelf and the lengths, in inches, of 2 of its sides are shown in the figure. The corner shelf will be enclosed by a finishing plastic material that is covered along its entire perimeter. To the nearest inch, how many inches of finishing plastic material will enclose the corner shelf?

F. 31

G. 34

H. 37

J. 40

K. 42

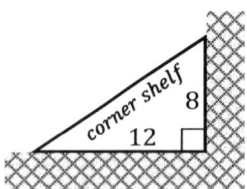

54.

The trigonometric function $y = 2\sin 3(x - \pi)$ is graphed below. Which of the following values is the period of the trigonometric function?

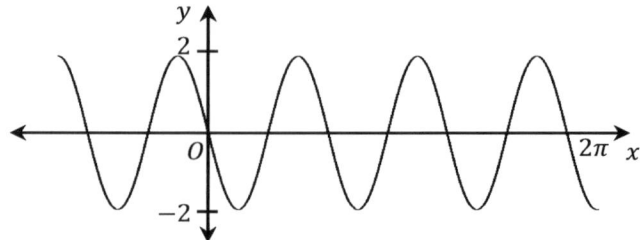

A. $\dfrac{\pi}{3}$

B. $\dfrac{2\pi}{3}$

C. π

D. 2π

E. 6π

55.

Suppose that angle α measures $\dfrac{21}{4}\pi$ radians from its initial side to its terminal side and angle β has the same initial side and terminal side as angle α. Which of the following degrees could be that of the angle β?

F. 45°

G. 60°

H. 135°

J. 205°

K. 225°

56.

As shown below, θ is the radian measure of any angle in the standard position with the point (a, b) on the terminal side in the standard (x, y) coordinate plane. Which of the following points is on the terminal side of the angle in standard position having radian measure $\pi + \theta$?

A. (a, b)

B. $(-a, b)$

C. $(b, -a)$

D. (b, a)

E. $(-a, -b)$

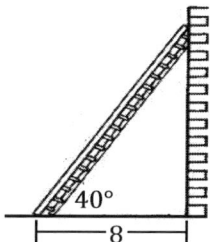

57.

As shown figure below, an electrical installation company will bury one end of a support wire 10 meters from the base of a power transmission tower and the other end of the support wire is holding at a point on the tower 30 meter above ground. When the wire is stretched tight, the length of the wire will be $10\sqrt{10}$ meters. What is the expression of the angle the wire will make with the level ground?

F. $\cos^{-1}\left(\dfrac{3}{\sqrt{10}}\right)$

G. $\cos^{-1}\left(\dfrac{1}{3}\right)$

H. $\tan^{-1}\left(\dfrac{1}{\sqrt{10}}\right)$

J. $\tan^{-1}\left(\dfrac{1}{3}\right)$

K. $\tan^{-1}(3)$

58.

As shown below, a ladder is placed against a wall . The base of the ladder is 8 feet from the wall and makes 40° angle with the level ground. To the nearest foot how far up the wall does the ladder reach?

(Note: $\sin 40° \approx 0.64, \cos 40° \approx 0.77, \tan 40° \approx 0.84$)

A. 5

B. 6

C. 7

D. 8

E. 9

59.

In the figure below, $\overline{QS}$ divides parallelogram $PRST$ into one trapezoid and one right triangle. The measure of $\angle RSQ$ is 30° and the lengths $\overline{PQ}$ and $\overline{RS}$ are given in inches. Which of the following values is the area, in square inches, of parallelogram $PRST$?

F. 40

G. $40\sqrt{3}$

H. 48

J. $48\sqrt{3}$

K. 56

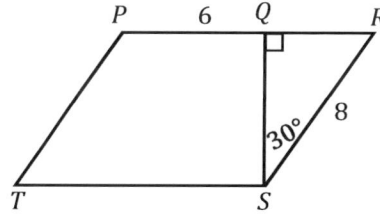

60.

If two vectors are $\mathbf{p} = \langle -1, 3 \rangle$ and $\mathbf{q} = \langle -2, -3 \rangle$, then what is the value of $|\mathbf{p} - \mathbf{q}|$?

A. 5

B. $\sqrt{7}$

C. 7

D. $\sqrt{37}$

E. $\sqrt{41}$

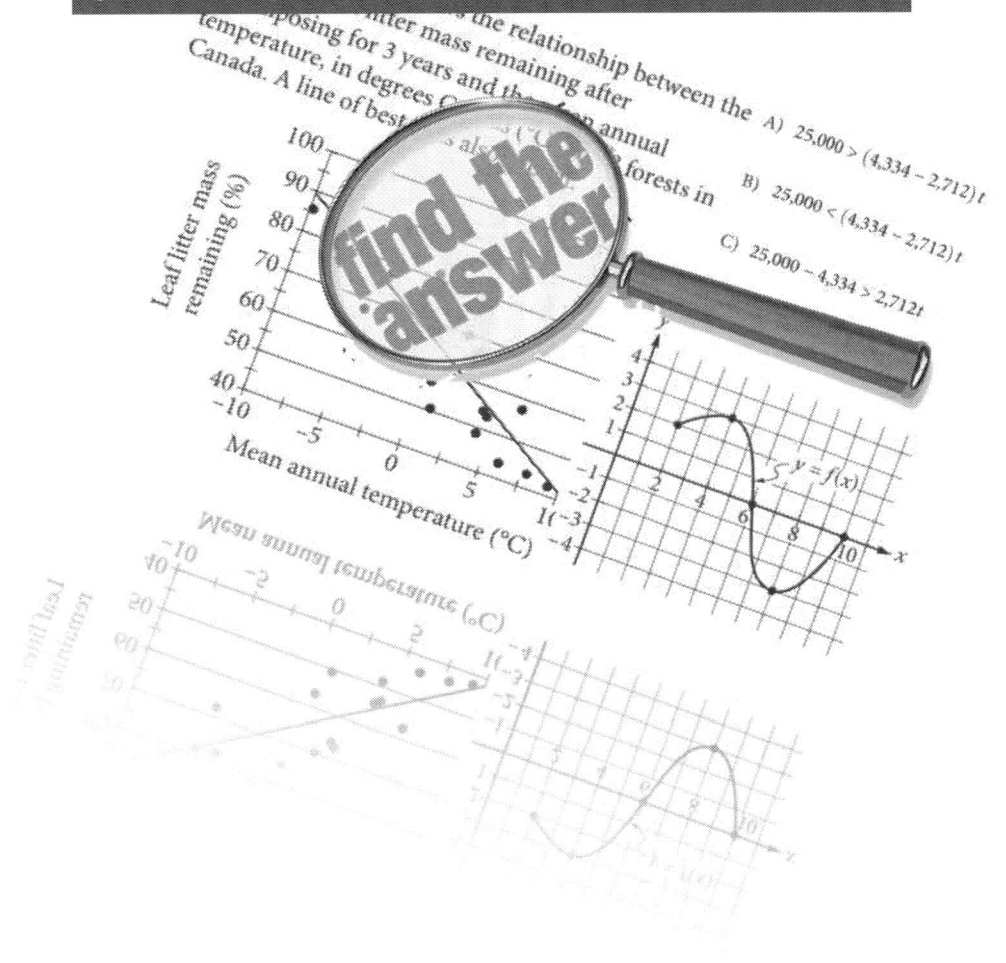

Obtain Scale Scores from Raw Scores

Scale Score	Raw Score	Scale Score	Raw Score	Scale Score	Raw Score
36	60	24	36-37	12	7
35	58-59	23	34-35	11	5-6
34	57	22	32-33	10	4
33	55-56	21	30-31	9	-
32	54	20	29	8	3
31	52-53	19	27-28	7	-
30	50-51	18	24-26	6	2
29	48-49	17	21-23	5	-
28	45-47	16	17-20	4	1
27	43-44	15	13-16	3	-
26	40-42	14	11-12	2	-
25	38-39	13	8-10	1	0

1. Scoring Key

Key		Question Category	Y/N
01.	D	Number Theory	
02.	G	Number Theory	
03.	E	Number Theory	
04.	F	Expression and Linear Equation	
05.	B	Expression and Linear Equation	
06.	H	Expression and Linear Equation	
07.	D	Expression and Linear Equation	
08.	G	Expression and Linear Equation	
09.	A	Expression and Linear Equation	
10.	J	Expression and Linear Equation	
11.	D	Linear Function inequality	
12.	G	Linear Function inequality	
13.	C	Linear Function inequality	
14.	H	Linear Function inequality	
15.	D	Linear Function inequality	
16.	C	Linear Function inequality	
17.	H	Linear Function inequality	
18.	C	Arithmetic Topic and Ratio	
19.	G	Arithmetic Topic and Ratio	
20.	D	Arithmetic Topic and Ratio	
21.	H	Arithmetic Topic and Ratio	
22.	E	Basic Geometry	
23.	J	Basic Geometry	
24.	C	Basic Geometry	
25.	B	Basic Geometry	
26.	H	Basic Geometry	
27.	E	Basic Geometry	
28.	G	Basic Geometry	
29.	D	Arithmetic Topic and Ratio	
30.	H	Quadratic and Polynomial Function	

Key		Question Category	Y/N
31.	C	Quadratic and Polynomial Function	
32.	D	Quadratic and Polynomial Function	
33.	C	Quadratic and Polynomial Function	
34.	J	Quadratic and Polynomial Function	
35.	D	Quadratic and Polynomial Function	
36.	H	Further Equations and Functions	
37.	C	Further Equations and Functions	
38.	C	Further Equations and Functions	
39.	F	Further Equations and Functions	
40.	B	Further Equations and Functions	
41.	H	Statistics and Probability	
42.	D	Statistics and Probability	
43.	K	Statistics and Probability	
44.	C	Statistics and Probability	
45.	G	Statistics and Probability	
46.	D	Sequence and Series	
47.	J	Analytic Geometry and Conic Section	
48.	D	Analytic Geometry and Conic Section	
49.	J	Analytic Geometry and Conic Section	
50.	C	Analytic Geometry and Conic Section	
51.	H	Analytic Geometry and Conic Section	
52.	C	Analytic Geometry and Conic Section	
53.	G	Analytic Geometry and Conic Section	
54.	B	Trigonometric Functions	
55.	K	Trigonometric Functions	
56.	E	Trigonometric Functions	
57.	K	Trigonometric Functions	
58.	C	Trigonometric Functions	
59.	G	Trigonometric Functions	
60.	D	Intermediate Algebra	

2. Answer Explanations

01. Answer (D)

The given problem is just adding problem. The number of operations represented by the scientific notation could be calculated more easily by using distributive property $AB+CB=(A+C)B$.

Adding process using distributive property;
$$4.2 \times 10^3 + 3.0 \times 10^3 = (4.2 + 3) \times 10^3 = 7.2 \times 10^3$$

02. Answer (G)

To find the decimal equivalent of a fraction; the numerator divide by the denominator.

Division;
$$12 \div 11 = 1.09090909\ldots = 1.\overline{09}$$

03. Answer (E)

For any nonzero number a and any integer n, $a^{-n} = \dfrac{1}{a^n}$.

Because $0 < A < 1$,
$\dfrac{1}{A} = A^{-1} = B$ and $B > 1$, B is positive. (ex: $A = \dfrac{1}{5} \rightarrow \dfrac{1}{A} = A^{-1} = 5$).
And because $N < 0$, $N = -M$, and M is positive integer.
Thus,

$A^N = A^{-M} = (A^{-1})^M = \left(\dfrac{1}{A}\right)^M = B^M$ for $B > 1$ and M is positive

integer. So, $A^N = B^M > 1$.
For example,

If $A = \dfrac{1}{5}$ and $N = -2$, $A^N = \left(\dfrac{1}{5}\right)^{-2} = (5^{-1})^{-2} = 5^2 = 25$.

04. Answer (F)

Distributive property: $A(B + C) = AB + AC$.

Rewrite the expression;
$$\frac{1}{3}a(-9b^2 - 3a^2 + 12b^2 + 3a^2) = \frac{1}{3}a(-3a^2 + 3a^2 - 9b^2 + 12b^2)$$
Using distributive property;
$$\frac{1}{3}a(3b^2) = ab^2$$

05. Answer (B)

Convert word expression to variable expression.

Equation 1: Number of total items

Number of DVDs	+	Number of pairs of socks	=	Number of total items
x	+	y	=	16

Equation 2: Total prices

Number of DVDs	×	Price of a DVD	+	Number of pairs of socks	×	Price of a pair of socks	=	Total price
→ 6	×	x	+	4	×	y	=	\$76

Thus, the equation 2 is $6x + 4y = 76$.

Multiplying 1st equation by 4 and then subtracting;
$$\begin{array}{r} x + y = 16 \quad -\times 4 \rightarrow \quad 4x + 4y = 64 \\ 6x + 4y = 76 \\ \hline -2x \quad = -12 \end{array}$$
Dividing both sides by -2;
$$-2x = -12 \quad \rightarrow \quad \frac{-2x}{-2} = \frac{-12}{-2} \quad \rightarrow \quad x = 6$$
Thus, the number of DVDs is 6.

06. Answer (H)

Substitute $-2x+6$ for y.

Substituting $-2x + 6$ for y on other equation $y = -x + 8$;
$$y = -x + 8 \quad \rightarrow \quad -2x + 6 = -x + 8$$
Subtracting 6 from both sides;
$$-2x + 6 = -x + 8 \quad \rightarrow \quad -2x + 6 - 6 = -x + 8 - 6$$
$$\rightarrow \quad -2x = -x + 2$$
Adding x to both sides;
$$-2x = -x + 2 \quad \rightarrow \quad -2x + x = -x + x + 2 \quad \rightarrow \quad -x = 2$$
Multiplying both sides by -1;
$$-x = 2 \quad \rightarrow \quad -x \times (-1) = 2 \times (-1) \quad \rightarrow \quad x = -2$$
Thus, the value of x is -2.

07. Answer (D)

Solve for one variable and then substitute the value for other equation.

If b is the number of sold basketballs and v is the number of sold volleyballs, then;
"the store sold 363 balls in volleyballs and basketballs"
$$\rightarrow \quad b + v = 363$$
"~ basketballs was twice the amount of money~"
$$\rightarrow \quad 2 \times (16b) = 12v$$
So, $b + v = 363$ and $32b = 12v$.
Dividing both sides by 12;
$$12v = 32b \quad \rightarrow \quad \frac{12v}{12} = \frac{32b}{12} \quad \rightarrow \quad v = \frac{8}{3}b$$
Substituting $\dfrac{8}{3}b$ for v;
$$b + v = 363 \quad \rightarrow \quad b + \frac{8}{3}b = 363 \quad \rightarrow \quad \frac{11}{3}b = 363$$
Multiplying both sides by $\dfrac{3}{11}$;
$$\frac{11}{3}b = 363 \quad \rightarrow \quad \frac{3}{11} \times \frac{11}{3}b = 363 \times \frac{3}{11} \quad \rightarrow \quad b = 99$$
Thus, the number of sold basketballs is 99.

08. Answer (G)

Using angle sum property.

Let the measure of $\angle BOC$ be $x°$ and using angle sum property;
$$\angle AOD = \angle AOB + \angle BOC + \angle COD$$
$$= \angle AOB + \angle BOC + \angle COD + \angle BOC - \angle BOC$$
$$= \angle AOB + \angle BOC + \angle BOC + \angle COD - \angle BOC$$
$$\angle AOD = \angle AOC + \angle BOD - \angle BOC$$
So, substitute each value for each angle;
$$160° = 95° + 93° - x° \quad \rightarrow \quad 160 = 188 - x$$
Subtracting 188 from both sides;
$$188 - x = 160 \quad \rightarrow \quad 188 - x - 188 = 160 - 188 \quad \rightarrow \quad -x = -28$$
Multiplying by (-1) on both sides;
$$-x = -28 \quad \rightarrow \quad -x \times (-1) = -28 \times (-1) \quad \rightarrow \quad x = 28$$
Thus, the measure of the angle $\angle BOC$ is $28°$.

09. Answer (A)

Total value is product of number of shares and value of 1 share.

The total number of shares;
$$160 + 250 + 170 = 580 \ shares$$
The total value of shares;
$$580 \times 11.5 = 6,670$$
Thus, the total value of the shares is \$ 6,670.

10. **Answer** **(J)**

Averages is calculated by the quotient of score's sum and the number of games.

Let x be the scored point of the third game.
In the second game, he scored 3 less than x so, the scored points of the second game is $x - 3$.
And in first game, he scored 6 points more than in the second game; so, the scored first game is $(x - 3) + 6 = x + 3$.
Therefore, from the formula of average;
$$18 = \frac{x + 3 + x - 3 + x}{3} \quad \rightarrow \quad 18 = \frac{3x}{3} \quad \rightarrow \quad x = 18$$
Thus, the scored point of the first game is $x + 3 = 18 + 3 = 21$.

11. **Answer** **(D)**

Evaluating each value of x or using inequality

1st: Using inequality
$0 \le x \le 20$
and $h(x) > 0$
$\rightarrow 3x - 12 > 0$
Adding 12 to both sides;
$\rightarrow 3x - 12 + 12 > 12$
$\rightarrow 3x > 12$
Dividing both sides by 3;
$\rightarrow \frac{3x}{3} > \frac{12}{3} \rightarrow x > 4$
Thus, the solution of
$0 \le x \le 20$ and $x > 4$ is
$4 < x \le 20$
So,
x is $5, 6, 7, \sim, 20$.
there are 16 integers.

2nd: Evaluating each value of x

x	$3x - 12$	$h(x)$
0	$3 \times 0 - 12$	-12
1	$3 \times 1 - 12$	-9
:	:	:
4	$3 \times 4 - 12$	0
5	$3 \times 5 - 12$	3
:	:	:
:	:	:
20	$3 \times 20 - 12$	48

12. **Answer** **(G)**

For 1 hour, is the slope is zero.

The slope is the rate of change in real situation so, "constant speed" means constant positive slope.
And "rest state" is not change of distance so, the slope is zero.

Thus, the graph has a positive constant slope and zero slope, the correct answer is G.

13. **Answer** **(C)**

The coordinates of x-axis are $(a, 0)$ and the coordinates of y-axis are $(0, b)$.

The line passes through the two point $(0, -2)$ and $(0, 6)$ is y-axis, $x = 0$. Therefore this question is finding y-intercept of the line which contains the two points $(3, -2)$ and $(1, -5)$.

Finding the slope of the line;
$$m = \frac{y_2 - y_1}{x_2 - x_1} = \frac{-5 - (-2)}{1 - 3} = \frac{-3}{-2} = \frac{3}{2}$$
Finding y-intercept of the line by using slope intercept form;
$$y = mx + b \quad - \left(m = \frac{3}{2}\right) \rightarrow \quad y = \frac{3}{2}x + b$$
Substitute $(3, -2)$ for $y = \frac{3}{2}x + b$;
$$y = \frac{3}{2}x + b \quad \rightarrow \quad -2 = \frac{3}{2}(3) + b \quad \rightarrow \quad -2 = \frac{9}{2} + b$$
Subtract $\frac{9}{2}$ from both sides;
$$\frac{9}{2} + b = -2 \quad \rightarrow \quad \frac{9}{2} - \frac{9}{2} + b = -2 - \frac{9}{2} \quad \rightarrow \quad b = -\frac{13}{2}$$
Thus, y-intercept of the line is $-\frac{13}{2}$ and intersecting point is $\left(0, -\frac{13}{2}\right)$.

14. **Answer** **(H)**

At least two points are required for a line to be determined.

The standard form of a horizontal line that passes through (a, b) is $y = b$. And at the given point $(a, 2)$, if $a = -6$, then in fact, the given two points are a single point. So, it could not be determined a line.

Thus, the value a is all real numbers expect -6, and the horizontal line equation is $y = 2$.

15. **Answer** **(D)**

The number of buses to reduce the cost of car wash increases by 5.

Because every five buses are filled up with gas, the cost of car wash is reduced by $50, the number of buses that is filled up with gas is;
$5 \rightarrow$ reduction is $100 and the total cost of car washing is $700
$10 \rightarrow$ reduction is $200 and the total cost of car washing is $600
$15 \rightarrow$ reduction is $300 and the total cost of car washing is $500
... ...

Thus, the correct graph is D.

16. **Answer** **(C)**

The correct cost is $206 .

The total correct cost is $252 - \$46 = \$206$. And if the total repaired cost is C, the total repaired time in hours is t, then;
$$C = 40t + 86$$
Substitute 206 for C and then solve the equation for t;
$$C = 40t + 86 \quad \rightarrow \quad 206 = 40t + 86 \quad \rightarrow \quad 40t = 120 \quad \rightarrow \quad t = 3$$
Thus, the repaired time is 3 hours.

17. **Answer** **(H)**

Solving inequality by using inverse operation.

Subtracting 3 from both sides;
$$2x + 3 \le 5 \quad \rightarrow \quad 2x + 3 - 3 \le 5 - 3 \quad \rightarrow \quad 2x \le 2$$
Dividing both sides by 2;
$$2x \le 2 \quad \rightarrow \quad \frac{2x}{2} \le \frac{2}{2} \quad \rightarrow \quad x \le 1$$
Thus, the correct answer is
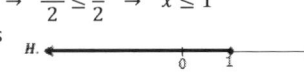
H.

18. **Answer** **(C)**

The percent converts to decimal and fraction.

$10\frac{3}{4}\%$ is $\frac{43}{4}\% = 10.75\%$ So, its value is 0.1075.
Therefore, the revenue of next month is;
$$5,300 - 5,300 \times 0.1075 = 5,300 - 569.75 = 4730.25$$
Thus, the revenue is $4730.25.

19. **Answer** **(G)**

The amount of solute, sodium hydroxide, is not changed.

The total amount of solute, sodium hydroxide, is $0.2 \times 200 = 40$ and the amount of solute in solution A is $0.3 \times 120 = 36$. So, the amount of solute in solution B is 4. ($\because 40 = 36 + 4$)

Thus, the sodium hydroxide concentration of aqueous solution B is;
$$\frac{4}{80} \times 100 = 5 \quad \rightarrow \quad 5\%.$$

20. **Answer** **(D)**

The total amount of 6 months is 1337×6.

Let Veronica's contribute be x;

$$x + \frac{3}{4}x = 6 \times \$1,337 \quad \rightarrow \quad \frac{7}{4}x = 8,022 \quad \rightarrow \quad x = 8,022 \times \frac{4}{7} = 4,584$$

Thus, the amount is \$4,584.

21. **Answer** **(H)**

Finding the ratio of two data.

"the length of body varies directly with the length of tooth" so, finding the ratio of y to x;

$$\frac{y}{x} = \frac{25.2}{4.6} \approx 5.478, \quad \frac{20.8}{3.8} \approx 5.474, \quad \frac{21.3}{3.9} \approx 5.462$$
$$\frac{35.0}{6.4} \approx 5.469, \quad \frac{44.9}{8.2} \approx 5.476$$

Thus, the constant of variation is about 5.47.

22. **Answer** **(E)**

Using the formula.

The area of trapezoid is;

$$A = \frac{1}{2}(b_1 + b_2)h = \frac{1}{2}(12 + 14)(12) = 156 \, ft^2$$

Thus, the number of tiles is $156 \div 1.25 = 124.8 \rightarrow 125$.

23. **Answer** **(J)**

Using the formula.

The volume of the container is;

$$V = w \times l \times h = 10 \times 25 \times 15 = 3750 \, in^3$$

So, 70% of its capacity is $0.7 \times V = 0.7 \times 3750 = 2625 \, in^3$

Thus, the 70% of its capacity is $2625 in^3$.

24. **Answer** **(C)**

The volume is the product of base area and height.

Converting 1.5cm to meter;

$$1.5cm \times \frac{1 \, m}{100 \, cm} = 0.015 \, m$$

and, the thickness is the height. So the volume is;

$$V = base \, area \times height = 195m^2 \times 0.015m = 2.925 \, m^3$$

Thus, the total volume is $2.925m^3$.

25. **Answer** **(B)**

Substitute proper value for variable.

Substitute 195 for S;

$$C = 5.8S + 250 \quad \rightarrow \quad C = 5.8(195) + 250 = 1381$$

Thus, the estimated cost is \$1,381.

26. **Answer** **(H)**

Using the surface area.

The surface area of the patio is $195 \, m^2$.

$$195 = 3 \times 40 + 3 \times x \quad \rightarrow \quad 195 = 120 + 3x \quad \rightarrow \quad x = 25 \, m$$

Therefore that perimeter is;

$$3 + 40 + 3 + 25 + 3 = 74 \, m$$

Thus, the length of that portion is 74.

27. **Answer** **(E)**

The circumference is πd or $2\pi r$.

From the formula of the circumference of the circle;

$$C = 2\pi r = \pi d \quad \rightarrow \quad C = 2\pi r \quad \rightarrow \quad C = 2\pi(6) = 12\pi$$

Thus, the circumference of the circle is 12π inches.

28. **Answer** **(G)**

The circumference is $2\pi r$ or πd.

From the formula of the circumference of circle;

$$C = \pi d = 2\pi r \quad \rightarrow \quad 40 = 2\pi r \quad \rightarrow \quad r = \frac{40}{2\pi} = \frac{20}{\pi}$$

Thus, the radius of the circle is $\frac{20}{\pi}$.

29. **Answer** **(D)**

drawing two auxiliary lines.

Drawing two auxiliary lines;
The area is difference of total area and shaded region so,

$$10 \times 8 - 6 \times 3 = 80 - 18 = 62 \, ft^2$$

Thus, the area is 62.

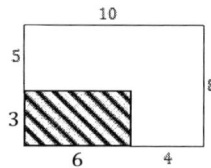

30. **Answer** **(H)**

The volume is the product of width, length and height.

Let x be the width of the cuboid, the length is also x and the height is $2x$ so, the volume is;

$$V = w \times l \times h \quad \rightarrow \quad x \times x \times 2x = 250 \quad \rightarrow \quad 2x^3 = 250 \quad \rightarrow \quad x^3 = 125$$

Take both sides by cubic root;

$$\sqrt[3]{x^3} = \sqrt[3]{125} \quad \rightarrow \quad x = \sqrt[3]{5^3} = 5$$

Thus, the width is 5 cm.

31. **Answer** **(C)**

The vertex is (3,5).

Let y be $a|x - h| + k$;
the vertex is moved to $(3, 5)$ so, $h = 3$ and $k = 5$ and the graph is reflected so, $a < 0$.

Thus, the correct answer is C.

32. **Answer** **(D)**

The given problem is about rate.

From analyzing unit, the number of cans is the product of total area and rate so,

$$number \, of \, cans = 150 \, in^2 \times \frac{1 \, can}{28 \, in^2} = 5.35714 \dots$$

Thus, the minimum number of cans is 6.

33. **Answer** **(C)**

The given problem is about a perimeter.

The perimeter of the wooden border is;

$$Perimeter = 2 \times width + 2 \times length = 2 \times 16 + 2 \times 21 = 74$$

Thus, the length of metallic banding is 74 inches.

34. Answer (*J*)

The volume is the product of width, length and height.

The volume of the pedestal is;
$$V = 5 \times 21 \times 2\frac{1}{2} = 262.5 \ in^3$$
The correct answer is *J*.

35. Answer (*D*)

The reciprocal of $\frac{a}{b}$ is $\frac{b}{a}$.

If x is a number, then its reciprocal is $\frac{1}{x}$.
$$x \times \frac{1}{x} = 1$$
Thus, the numbers are all real numbers.

36. Answer (*H*)

Using the concept of composition of function.

1st Method; substituting
  Finding $f(2)$;
$$f(x) = 2x - 3 \ \rightarrow \ f(2) = 2(2) - 3 = 4 - 3 = 1.$$
  Substituting 1 for $f(2)$ on $g(f(2))$;
$$g(f(2)) = g(1) \ \rightarrow \ g(1) = 1 + 2 = 3$$

2nd Method; composition function
  Finding $g(f(x))$;
$$g(f(x)) = f(x) + 2 \ \rightarrow \ g(f(x)) = 2x - 3 + 2 = 2x - 1$$
  Substituting 2 for x;
$$g(f(2)) = 2(2) - 1 = 4 - 1 = 3$$

Thus, the value of $g(f(2))$ is 3.

37. Answer (*C*)

The domain does not contain vertical asymptotes.

The vertical asymptotes are real zeros of denominator equation so,
$$x^3 - 4x = 0 \ \rightarrow \ x(x^2 - 4) = 0 \ \rightarrow \ x(x + 2)(x - 2) = 0$$
$$\rightarrow \ x = 0 \ or \ x + 2 = 0 \ or \ x - 2 = 0 \ \rightarrow \ x = 0 \ or \ x = -2 \ or \ x = 2$$

Thus, the correct answer is *C*.

38. Answer (*C*)

A horizontal asymptote is $y = \frac{a}{c}$.

A horizontal asymptote is $y = \frac{a}{c}$ for $y = \frac{ax+b}{cx+d}$.
So, horizontal asymptote is
$$y = 3 \ for \ y = \frac{-3x+6}{-x-1}$$
Or using GDC.

Thus, the horizontal asymptote is $y = 3$.

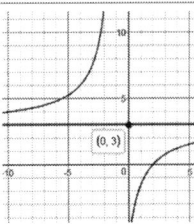
(0, 3)

39. Answer (*F*)

Using the properties of logarithm.

Using the properties of logarithm, $b^{\log_b x} = x$, so, take 27th power on both sides;
$$\log_{27} a = -\frac{2}{3} \ \rightarrow \ 27^{\log_{27} a} = (27)^{-\frac{2}{3}} \ \rightarrow \ a = (3^3)^{-\frac{2}{3}} = 3^{-2} = \frac{1}{9}$$

Thus. the real value of a is $\frac{1}{9}$.

40. Answer (*B*)

Switch x and y.

Switch x and y;
$$h(x) = \sqrt[3]{2x - 3} \ \rightarrow \ y = \sqrt[3]{2x - 3} \ \rightarrow \ x = \sqrt[3]{2y - 3}$$
Solve for y;
  taking cubed on both sides;
$$x = \sqrt[3]{2y - 3} \ \rightarrow \ x^3 = (\sqrt[3]{2y - 3})^3 \ \rightarrow \ 2y - 3 = x^3$$
  adding both sides to 3;
$$2y - 3 = x^3 \ \rightarrow \ 2y = x^3 + 3$$
  dividing both sides by 2;
$$2y = x^3 + 3 \ \rightarrow \ y = \frac{x^3 + 3}{2}$$

Thus, the inverse function $h^{-1}(x) = \frac{x^3+3}{2}$.

41. Answer (*H*)

The central angle and ratio of budget vary directly.

The central angle is determined by the ratio of language sector. So,
$$central \ angle = \frac{4}{20} \times 360° = 72°$$
Thus, the measure of central angle is 72°.

42. Answer (*D*)

The median is the middle of data set.

Because the number of data is 33, the median is 17th (3.0).

Thus, the correct answer is *D*.

43. Answer (*K*)

155=170-15.

$155(x) = 170(\bar{x}) - 15(\sigma)$ so, from the curve, $x \leq \bar{x} - \sigma$ is $34 + 34 + 13.5 + 2.35 + 0.15 = 84\%$.

Thus, the percent is 84%.

44. Answer (*C*)

Geometric probability is the ratio of desired area to total area.

The probability is;
$$P = \frac{2 + 3 + 5 + 6}{2 + 3 + 5 + 6 + 7} = \frac{16}{23} \ \ or \ \ 1 - \frac{7}{23} = \frac{16}{23}$$

Thus, the correct answer is *C*.

45. Answer (*G*)

Two events are dependent event if the occurrence of one event does affect the probability of the occurrence of the other event.

The pitcher can not be a catcher.

Thus, the correct answer is *G*.

---

46. **Answer** **(D)**

The sequence is arithmetic sequence.

For the length of the two leg sides,
first term, a_1, is 2 and common difference, d, is 2. So, using arithmetic sequence rule;
$$a_n = a_1 + (n-1)d \quad \rightarrow \quad a_n = 2 + (n-1) \times 2$$
$$\rightarrow \quad a_n = 2 + 2n - 2 \quad \rightarrow \quad a_n = 2n \quad \rightarrow \quad a_5 = 2 \times 5 = 10$$
For the length of the base side,
first term, a_1, is 3 and common difference, d, is 3. So, using arithmetic sequence rule;
$$a_n = a_1 + (n-1)d \quad \rightarrow \quad a_n = 3 + (n-1) \times 3$$
$$\rightarrow \quad a_n = 3 + 3n - 3 \quad \rightarrow \quad a_n = 3n \quad \rightarrow \quad a_5 = 3 \times 5 = 15$$
Therefore, the dimension of 5th isosceles triangle is, two 10 centimeters leg sides and one 15 centimeters base side.

Thus, the perimeter is $10 + 10 + 15 = 35$ centimeters.

---

47. **Answer** **(J)**

The 4 angles are right angle.

The 4 interior angles of $\square OPQR$ is 90° so, $\triangle OEH, \triangle PEF, \triangle QFG$, and $\triangle RGH$ are congruent right triangle. And E and H are midpoints so, $\overline{EO} = 9\ in$ and $\overline{HO} = 12\ in$.
Using the Pythagorean theorem;
$$\overline{EH}^2 = \overline{EO}^2 + \overline{HO}^2 \quad \rightarrow \quad \overline{EH} = \sqrt{9^2 + 12^2} = 15$$
Because 4 right triangle are congruent, $\overline{EH} = \overline{HG} = \overline{GF} = \overline{FE} = 15$.

Thus, the perimeter is $15 + 15 + 15 + 15 = 4 \times 15 = 60$ inches.

---

48. **Answer** **(D)**

Using the Pythagorean theorem.

The line segment of $\overline{QS}$ is a diagonal of the square so, using the Pythagorean theorem;
$$\overline{QS}^2 = \overline{QR}^2 + \overline{RS}^2 \quad \rightarrow \quad \overline{QR} = \sqrt{16^2 + 16^2} = 16\sqrt{2}$$
Thus, the length is $16\sqrt{2}$ inches.

---

49. **Answer** **(J)**

The side length of the small squares is 4 inches.

The side length of the small congruent squares is $16 \div 4 = 4$ inches. So, the area is;
$$s^2 = 4 \times 4 = 16$$
Thus, the area is $16\ in^2$.

---

50. **Answer** **(C)**

Drawing the auxiliary line.

Drawing the auxiliary line, making a right triangle.
$$7 = a + 4 \quad \rightarrow \quad a = 3 \text{ and}$$
$$10 = b + 6 \quad \rightarrow \quad b = 4$$
Using the Pythagorean theorem;
$$c^2 = a^2 + b^2 \quad \rightarrow \quad c = \sqrt{3^2 + 4^2} = 5$$
Thus, the perimeter is $6 + 7 + 10 + 4 + c(=5) = 32$.

---

51. **Answer** **(H)**

Using the Pythagorean theorem.

Let x be the length of the hypotenuse of the right triangle, using the Pythagorean theorem;
$$x^2 = 7^2 + 9^2 \quad \rightarrow \quad x = \sqrt{7^2 + 9^2} = 11.40175425\ldots.$$
Thus, the length of the hypotenuse is 11.4 inches.

---

52. **Answer** **(C)**

10 representatives are equal.

The representatives of student council are equal so, the given situation is combination and the selections are and event.
So, 4 from 68 is $_{68}C_4$ and 6 from 72 is $_{72}C_6$ and total is
$$(_{68}C_4)(_{72}C_6)$$
Thus, the correct answer is **C**.

---

53. **Answer** **(G)**

Using the Pythagorean theorem.

Let x be the length of the hypotenuse of the triangular corner shelf, and then using the Pythagorean theorem;
$$x^2 = 12^2 + 8^2 \quad \rightarrow \quad x = \sqrt{12^2 + 8^2} = 4\sqrt{13}$$
So, the perimeter of the shelf is;
$$12 + 8 + 4\sqrt{13} = 20 + 4\sqrt{13} \approx 34.4222051\ldots. \approx 34$$
Thus, the correct answer is **G**.

---

54. **Answer** **(B)**

Finding b value.

The period of the trigonometric function $y = a \sin b(x - h) + k$ is;
$$period = \frac{2\pi}{|b|} = \frac{2\pi}{|3|} = \frac{2\pi}{3}$$
Thus, the correct answer is **B**.

---

55. **Answer** **(K)**

Finding coterminal angle.

Convert $\frac{21}{4}\pi$ to degrees;
$$\frac{21}{4}\pi \times \frac{180°}{\pi} = 945° \quad \rightarrow \quad 2 \times 365° + 225°$$
This means that $\frac{21}{4}\pi$ and 945° are same angles, 945° and 225° are coterminal angles, so are same angles.

Thus, the correct answer is **K**.

---

56. **Answer** **(E)**

The two positions have same r.

The two positions have same r and the position is placed on quadrant III.

Thus, the correct answer is **E**.

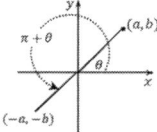

---

57. **Answer** (K)

Using the inverse trigonometric function.

Let θ be the angle;
$$\theta = \sin^{-1}(\frac{30}{10\sqrt{10}}) = \sin^{-1}\left(\frac{3}{\sqrt{10}}\right)$$
$$= \cos^{-1}\left(\frac{10}{10\sqrt{10}}\right) = \cos^{-1}\left(\frac{1}{\sqrt{10}}\right)$$
$$= \tan^{-1}\left(\frac{30}{10}\right) = \tan^{-1}(3)$$

Thus, the correct answer is K.

58. **Answer** (C)

Using the trigonometric ratio.

Let x be the height and using trigonometric ratio;
$$\tan 40° = \frac{O}{A} \approx 0.84 = \frac{x}{8} \quad \rightarrow \quad x = 0.84 \times 8 = 6.72$$

Thus, the correct answer is C.

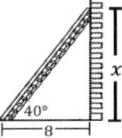

59. **Answer** (G)

The area of parallelogram is the product of base and height.

Using the trigonometric ratio;
$$\sin 30° = \frac{1}{2} = \frac{\overline{QR}}{8} \quad \rightarrow \quad 2 \times \overline{QR} = 1 \times 8 \quad \rightarrow \quad \overline{QR} = 4.$$
$$\cos 30° = \frac{\sqrt{3}}{2} = \frac{\overline{QS}}{8} \quad \rightarrow \quad 2 \times \overline{QS} = 8 \times \sqrt{3} \quad \rightarrow \quad \overline{QS} = 4\sqrt{3}.$$

So, the area is;
$$area = height \times base = \overline{QS} \times (\overline{PQ} + \overline{QR}) = 4\sqrt{3} \times 10 = 40\sqrt{3}.$$

Thus, the area is $40\sqrt{3}$.

60. **Answer** (D)

Subtracting each components.

Subtracting each components;
$$\langle -1, 3 \rangle - \langle -2, -3 \rangle = \langle -1 - (-2), 3 - (-3) \rangle = \langle 1, 6 \rangle$$

So,
$$|\mathbf{p} - \mathbf{q}| = \sqrt{1^2 + 6^2} = \sqrt{37}$$

Thus, the correct answer is D.

BLANK PAGE _by K·DEAN_

Reformed Past Paper ACT MATH TEST 04

60 Questions – 60 Minutes

DIRECTIONS:
Solve each problem, choose the correct answer, and then fill in the corresponding oval on your answer in the grid on the answer sheet.

Do not linger over problems that take too much time as many as you can; then return to the others in the time you have left for this test.

You are permitted to use a calculator on this test.

Note: Unless otherwise stated, all of the following should be assumed.

1. Figures ~~are drawn to scale unless~~ ~~indicated.~~

2. All figures lie in a plane unless otherwise indicated.

3. All variables and expressions used represent real numbers unless otherwise indicated.

This test has reformed the REAL ACT Mathematics Test

01.

An computer store sells about 80 of a new model of laptop computer per month at a price of $750 each. For each $20 increases in the $750 price per each, about 10 less laptop computers per month are sold. Let n be the number of $20 increases in the price per each. Which of the followings best represents the dollar amount of the store's monthly sales of laptop computers ?

A. $(750 + 20n)(60)$

B. $(770)(80 - 20n)$

C. $(750 + 10n)(80 - 20n)$

D. $(750 + 20n)(80 - 10n)$

E. $(750 - 20n)(80 + 10n)$

02.

Geony deposits $ 75 in a bank. When a bank teller records the savings in his bankbook, she accidentally subtract $ 75 from his balance instead of adding $ 75, which cause discrepancy between what his bankbook shows and what it should show. Since the teller made a mistake, Geony's bankbook shows;

A. $ 150 more than it should show

B. $ 75 more than it should show

C. $ 37.5 less than it should show

D. $ 75 less than it should show

E. $ 150 less than it should show

03.

If $\dfrac{2}{x} = 6$ and $\dfrac{y}{x} = 3$, what is the value of y ?

F. 1

G. 2

H. $\dfrac{3}{2}$

J. 3

K. $\dfrac{3}{4}$

Use the following information to answer questions
04 - 06.

Each of the 300 students in a random sample of the 1,800 students at the stationery store was asked which, if any, of the following type of stationery items they buys. All 300 students answered the question. The results are summarized in the diagram below as percentages.

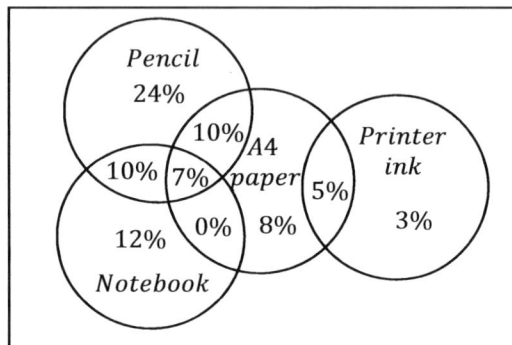

04.

What estimate does this diagram for the number of students at the store who buys exactly one item among all the students ?

A. 141

B. 329

C. 651

D. 846

E. 1,800

05.

What percent of the students do not buy the items in the diagram ?

A. 15%

B. 21%

C. 34%

D. 42%

E. 55%

06.

Let 30 additional students at random be asked the questions. And the answers are; 12 buys pencil only, 8 buys notebook and pencil only, 10 buys ball pen and note book. Among all 330 students surveyed, what fraction of students who buy pencil but none of the 3 types of items ?

F. $\dfrac{14}{55}$

G. $\dfrac{17}{65}$

H. $\dfrac{83}{110}$

J. $\dfrac{97}{300}$

K. $\dfrac{101}{330}$

 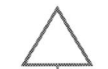

07.

On a mathematics competition, 30 problems are given. 10 points are given for each correct answer and 5 points are deducted for each incorrect answer. Ronald scored 195 points. how many correct answers did he get? ?

A. 24

B. 23

C. 22

D. 21

E. 20

08.

The dimension of rectangle $\square ABCD$ are given in inches in the figure below. What is the value of b ?

F. 1.4

G. 1.5

H. 1.6

J. 1.7

K. 1.8

```
        A    −3a + 4    B
         ┌─────────────┐
 2b − 5  │             │ a − 3
         └─────────────┘
        D    4b − 8     C
```

09.

If the system of equations are $-2x - 5y = 9$ and $3x + 11y = 4$, what is the value of $y - x$?

A. −1

B. 12

C. −12

D. 22

E. −22

10.

Let the lengths of the three sides of a triangle be in $4:7:8$. The perimeter of the triangle is 114 inches. What is the length, in inches, of the shortest side of the triangle ?

F. 36

G. 32

H. 28

J. 24

K. 20

11.

If $X = YZ^2$, $X = 24$, and $Z = -4$, what is the value of Y ?

A. −2

B. $-\dfrac{1}{2}$

C. $\dfrac{3}{2}$

D. 2

E. $\dfrac{7}{4}$

12.

Anthony leaves home and drives to the beach. He stays at the beach all day before driving back home.

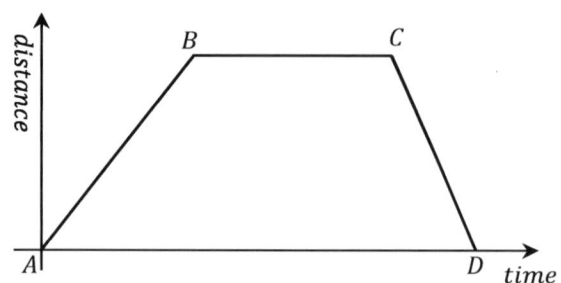

Which of the following statements could describe what Anthony did during the time interval covered by the line segment $\overline{CD}$?

A. He drives to the beach.

B. He stays at the beach.

C. He returns to his home.

D. He is resting

E. He drives to the beach at a slower speed.

13.

Which of the following graphs best represents the system of inequalities below ?

$$-4 \leq x \leq 4$$
$$-3 \leq y \leq 3$$

F.

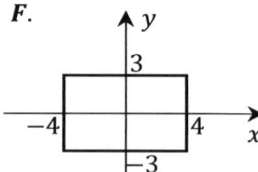

G.

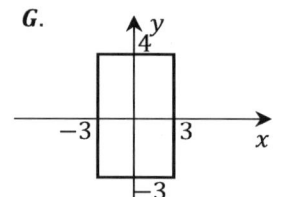

H.

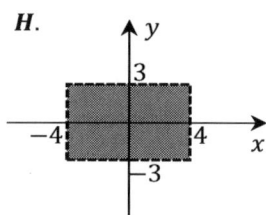

J.

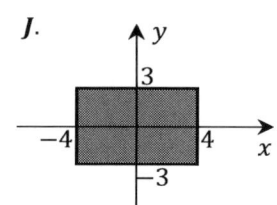

K.

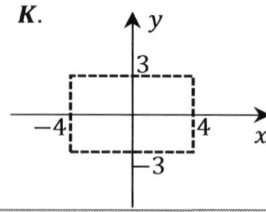

14.

What is the value of $|6 - 3| - |5 - 8| = $?

A. -6

B. 6

C. 0

D. 12

E. -12

15.

Which of the following inequalities is the solution set to inequality $2|x - 3| + 1 \geq 7$?

F. $x \leq 0 \ or \ x \geq 6$

G. $0 \leq x \leq 6$

H. $x \leq -6 \ or \ x \geq 0$

J. $-6 \leq x \leq 0$

K. $-6 \leq x \leq 6$

16.

In the standard (x, y) coordinate plane, the three line with equation $y = -2x$, $y = 12$, and $x = 6$ bound a triangular region. What is the area of the triangular region (1 coordinate unit is 1 in.)?

A. $36 \ in^2$

B. $72 \ in^2$

C. $108 \ in^2$

D. $132 \ in^2$

E. $144 \ in^2$

17.

In the standard (x, y) coordinate plane, which of the following is an equation of the line that contains the two points $(-5, 3)$ and $(3, -4)$?

A. $y = \frac{11}{3}x - \frac{8}{3}$

B. $y = \frac{7}{8}x + \frac{8}{3}$

C. $y = \frac{7}{2}x - \frac{8}{3}$

D. $y = -\frac{7}{8}x - \frac{11}{3}$

E. $y = -\frac{7}{2}x + \frac{11}{3}$

18.

Let k be a constant of variation and $x, y, z,$ and w be real number variables. In which of the following equations does the variable z vary jointly with x and y and inversely with the square of w?

F. $z = \frac{kxy}{w^2}$

G. $z = kxyw$

H. $z = kxyw^2$

J. $z = \frac{kw^2}{xy}$

K. $z = \frac{kw}{xy}$

19.

Madison and 9 of her friends are having dinner. Each of the ten people will pay for their own restaurant meal, but they agree to divide the tip equally among themselves. The total for the 10 dinners is $140, and the group will add a tip of 12% of the total. Each person's portion of the tip will be how much ?

A. $1.48

B. $1.58

C. $1.68

D. $15.68

E. $16.68

20.

Zenia is making a rainbow cake with chocolate frosting. The recipe calls for $\frac{3}{4}$ cup of chocolate powder for the cake and $\frac{3}{8}$ cup of chocolate powder for the frosting. To make 3 rainbow cakes with frosting by trebling this recipe, how many teaspoons of chocolate powder does Zenia need?

F. $3\frac{1}{8}$

G. $3\frac{3}{8}$

H. $3\frac{1}{2}$

J. $3\frac{7}{8}$

K. $4\frac{1}{8}$

21.

A toy train travels at a constant speed of 8 feet every 15 seconds. At this speed, which of the following is closest to the number of inches the train travels in 1 minute?

A. 32

B. 125

C. 267

D. 384

E. 408

22.

For all rectangles with an area of 64 square feet, what is the minimum value for the perimeter, in feet?

F. 16

G. 32

H. 68

J. 130

K. Cannot be determined from the given information

23.

As shown in the figure below, the side lengths and the length of an height of quadrilateral $PQRS$ are given in inches. What is the area, in square inches, of $\square PQRS$?

A. 40

B. 60

C. 96

D. 100

E. 120

24.

As shown in the figure below, three points $A, B,$ and C lie on the circumference of the circle whose center is O, and the measure of $\angle ABC$ is 50°. What is the sum of the measures of $\angle BAO$ and $\angle BCO$?

F. 40°

G. 45°

H. 50°

J. 55°

K. 60°

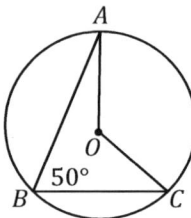

25.

As shown in the figure below, $\overline{DE}$ is parallel to $\overline{BC}$, which of the following proportional equations involving the length of $\overline{DE}$, must be true?

F. $\dfrac{DE}{6} = \dfrac{9}{10}$

G. $\dfrac{DE}{6} = \dfrac{10}{9}$

H. $\dfrac{DE}{10} = \dfrac{6}{9}$

J. $\dfrac{DE}{10} = \dfrac{6}{15}$

K. $\dfrac{DE}{15} = \dfrac{6}{10}$

26.

The two distinct line segments $\overline{AB}$ and $\overline{CD}$ intersect at a point, forming 4 pairs of adjacent angles. Which of the following statements must be always **true** about these 4 pairs of adjacent angles?

A. The sum of a pair of adjacent angles is 180°.

B. The sum of a pair of adjacent angles is less than 180°.

C. The difference of a pair of adjacent angles is 90°.

D. The difference of a pair of adjacent angles is less than 90°.

E. The difference of each pair of adjacent angles is 45°.

27.

As shown in the figure below, two lines m and n are parallel. And two lines s and t intersect line m at a point. What is the value of θ?

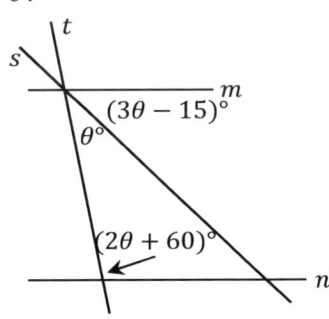

F. 22

G. 25

H. 27

J. 45

K. 48

28.

In the figure below, the two lines $\overleftrightarrow{PQ}$ and $\overleftrightarrow{RS}$ are parallel, and other two lines $\overrightarrow{PS}$ and $\overleftrightarrow{QR}$ intersect at a point O. If the $\triangle OPQ$ is an equilateral triangle, what is the value of θ?

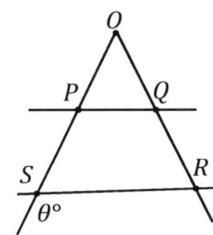

A. 60

B. 90

C. 120

D. 140

E. 160

29.

A toy company ships Magic Cubes in rectangular cardboard boxes that each have inside dimensions measuring 24 inches long, 18 inches wide, and 12 inches tall. Each Magic Cube is in the shape of a cube with an edge length of 2 inches. What is the maximum number of Magic Cubes that will fit in one box?

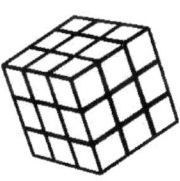

F. 372

G. 426

H. 648

J. 1,248

K. 5,184

30.

As shown in the figure below, the dimensions of the rectangle are given in centimeters. Which of the following expressions is the area, in cm^2, of the rectangle?

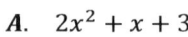

A. $2x^2 + x + 3$

B. $2x^2 - x - 3$

C. $2x^2 - 5x - 3$

D. $2x^2 + 5x - 3$

E. $2x^2 - 5x + 3$

$x + 1$

$2x - 3$

31.

As shown in the figure, three line segments are graphed in the standard (x, y) coordinate plane. A line segment $\overline{PQ}$ has two endpoints $P(0, 1)$ and $Q(0, 5)$, $\overline{P'Q'}$ is the image of $\overline{PQ}$ after a rotation clockwise by $150°$ about the origin $(0, 0)$, and $\overline{P''Q''}$ is projected on y-axis. What is the length of $\overline{P''Q''}$?

F. $\dfrac{4\sqrt{2}}{3}$

G. 4

H. $\dfrac{8\sqrt{3}}{3}$

J. $2\sqrt{3}$

K. Could not be determined.

32.

As shown in the figure below, the function $f(x) = -\dfrac{1}{2}|x| + 3$ is graphed in the standard (x, y) coordinate plane.

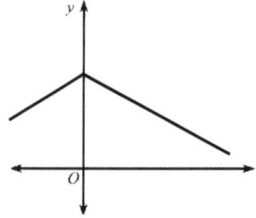

Which of the following graphs shows the result of translating the function right 2 units?

A.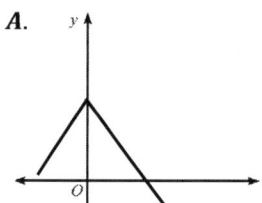

B.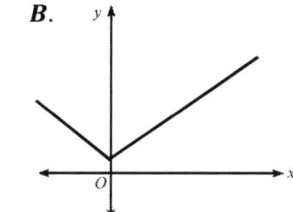

C.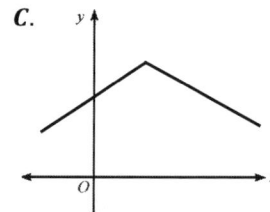

D.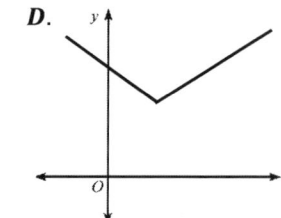

E.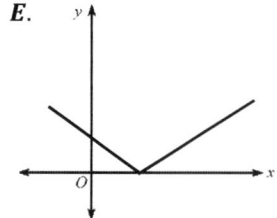

33.

Consider the transformation of the standard (x, y) coordinate plane that maps each point (a, b) to the image point (ka, kb) for scale factor, k. In particular, this transformation maps $(4, 8)$ to $(1, 2)$. This transformation maps $(28, -32)$ to which of the following points?

A. $(112, -128)$

B. $(-112, 128)$

C. $(7, 8)$

D. $(7, -8)$

E. $(-7, 8)$

34.

A point, P, has coordinate $(5, -4)$, the point P is translated 3 units to the lefts and 8 units up and the image is P'. What are the coordinates of P'?

F. $(-3, 8)$

G. $(2, 4)$

H. $(2, -4)$

J. $(8, -12)$

K. $(-8, 12)$

35.

If $f(x) = 3x^2 + 5x - 12$, then what is the value of $f(-4)$?

A. -8

B. 16

C. -24

D. 36

E. -48

36.

The rational function $f(x) = \dfrac{x+2}{-x^2+1}$ is graphed in the standard (x, y) coordinate plane below. What value(s) of x is undefined?

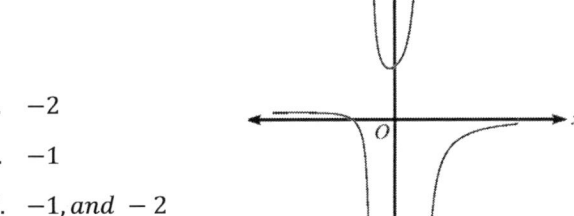

F. -2

G. -1

H. $-1, and -2$

J. $-1, and 1$

K. $-1, 1, and -2$

37.

Consider $f(x) = 2x^3 + 1$. Which of the following expressions is the inverse function of $f(x)$ for all real numbers x ?

A. $f^{-1}(x) = \sqrt[3]{\dfrac{x+1}{2}}$

B. $f^{-1}(x) = \sqrt[3]{\dfrac{x-1}{2}}$

C. $f^{-1}(x) = 2x^3 - 1$

D. $f^{-1}(x) = 2x^3 + 1$

E. $f^{-1}(x) = \dfrac{x^3 - 1}{2}$

Use the following information to answer questions *38 - 40.*

At an art auction, the value of a picture can be modeled by the formula $P = P_0(1 + r)^t$, where P_0 is the picture's purchase price, in dollars, r is the picture's constant annual rate of increase in value, expressed as decimal, and P is the picture's price after t years.

38.

When the given formula is solved for t, which of the following equation shows the result ?

A. $t = \dfrac{P}{P_0(1 + r)}$

B. $t = \dfrac{P}{P_0} - 1 - r$

C. $t = \sqrt{\dfrac{\left(\frac{P}{P_0}\right)}{(1 + r)}}$

D. $t = \log(1 + r) - \log\dfrac{P}{P_0}$

E. $t = \dfrac{\left(\log\frac{P}{P_0}\right)}{\log(1 + r)}$

39.

A picture with a purchase price of $1,500 has a constant annual rate of increase in value of 8.5%. According to the given model, what is the price of the picture, to the nearest dollar, after 5 years?

A. $1,995

B. $2,085

C. $2,135

D. $2,255

E. $2,555

40.

From 2013 to 2017, the value of another picture that has a purchase price of $2,000 increased to $4,000. If the picture's annual rate of increase, r, is constant, what is the value of r, expressed as percent?

F. 17.53%

G. 18.92%

H. 19.37%

J. 20.01%

K. 21.46%

41.

In the figure below, let points that are shown in the standard (x, y) coordinate plane be represented for some data. Which of the following numbers is the slope of best fit for the points?

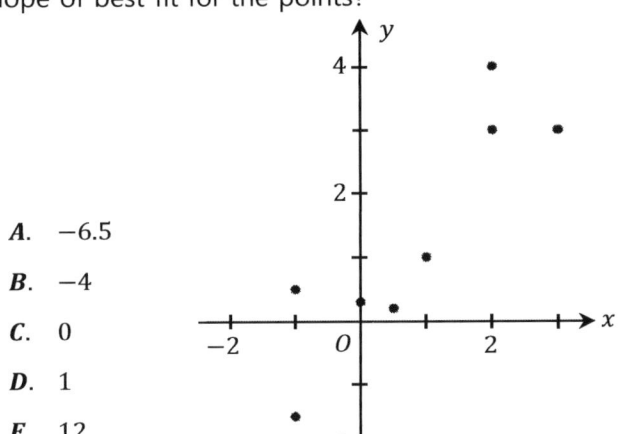

A. -6.5

B. -4

C. 0

D. 1

E. 12

42.

The elevation of the top of a volcano relative to sea level is called the summit elevation. The highest summit elevation of volcano in Jeju is 1,950 meters and the lowest summit elevation of volcano in Jeju is -320 meters, it is located at the underwater.

Which of the statements below is necessarily true about the summit elevations of volcanoes in Jeju?

I. The range of summit elevations is 1,630 meters.
II. The median of summit elevations is 815 meters.
III. The range of summit elevations is 2,270 meters.

A. I only

B. II only

C. III only

D. I and II only

E. II and III only

43.

An experiment consisted of rolling a 4-sided regular tetrahedral dice with the letters A, B, C, and D on its faces, 1 letter per face. The regular tetrahedral dice was rolled 40 times, and after each roll, the letter appearing on the top face was recorded. The number of times each letter was recorded is represented in the bar graph shown below. In what percent of the total number of rolls did a B appear on the top face of the dice?

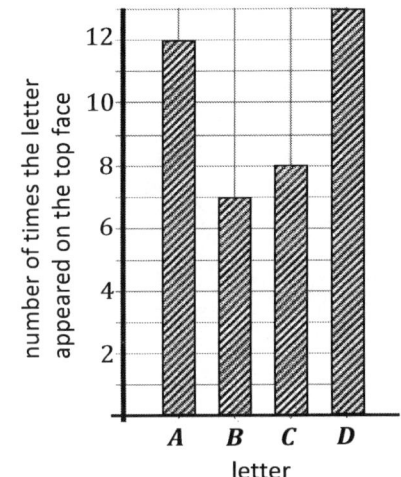

F. 7%

G. $13\frac{1}{2}\%$

H. 15%

J. $17\frac{1}{2}\%$

K. 25%

44.

A jar contains 9 identically shape, size, and being unchanged color balls. Two balls are blue, three are white, and four are black. A ball is picked up at random and replaced to the jar, then second ball is picked up at random. What is the probability that the first ball is blue and the second ball is white?

A. $\frac{1}{12}$

B. $\frac{2}{27}$

C. $\frac{1}{24}$

D. $\frac{5}{72}$

E. $\frac{5}{9}$

45.

In winter, car tires are important for safe driving. A batch of 200 defective car tires consisting of 2 types (A and B) and manufactured by 2 companies (Goodtime and Tecem) was selected, and it was determined how many of each type of tire was made by each company. The results are given in the table below.

Type of tire	Number of chips made by company	
	Goodtime	Tecem
A	67	52
B	46	35

What is the probability, in percent, that a randomly selected tire from this batch of 200 is Type B and made by Company Tecem ?

- **A.** 17.5%
- **B.** 23.0%
- **C.** 26.0%
- **D.** 32.5%
- **E.** 35.0%

46.

Suppose that this month, Brittany has deposited $50, and her goal is to have a total of $350 deposited 10 months from now. After adding to her deposit next month, each month she will add $2 more than what she added the previous month. During the next 10 months, Brittany will not withdraw any money from what she has already deposited. What is the minimum amount of money she must add to her deposit next month so that she accomplishes her goal?

- **F.** $18
- **G.** $19
- **H.** $24
- **J.** $25
- **K.** $32

47.

As shown below, a circle has a diameter of 10 inches. Which of the following is the area, in square inches, of the square inscribed in the circle?

- **A.** 100
- **B.** 25
- **C.** 25π
- **D.** 50
- **E.** 50π

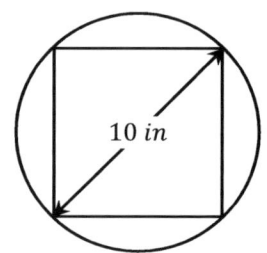

48.

In the standard (x, y) coordinate plane below, the center of an ellipse is $(0, 0)$, and six points $(-5, 0)$, $(p, 4)$, $(7, 0)$, $(q, 4)$, $(5, 0)$, and $(-7, 0)$ is placed in the ellipse. Which of the following values is closest to the distance, in coordinate units, from P to Q ?

- **F.** 9.0
- **G.** 8.2
- **H.** 7.4
- **J.** 5.8
- **K.** 4.1

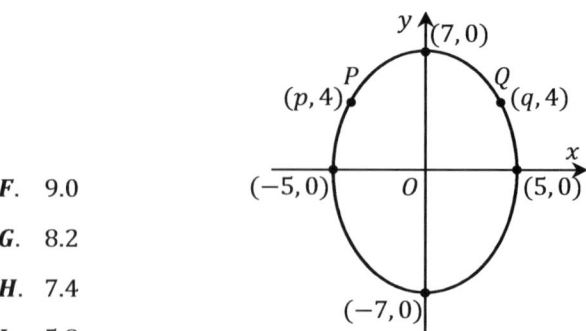

Use the following information to answer questions 49 - 50.

As shown the figure below, point A is located at $(-1, 1)$, point B is located at $(6, 1)$, and point C $(6, 6)$ to form a right triangle ΔABC.

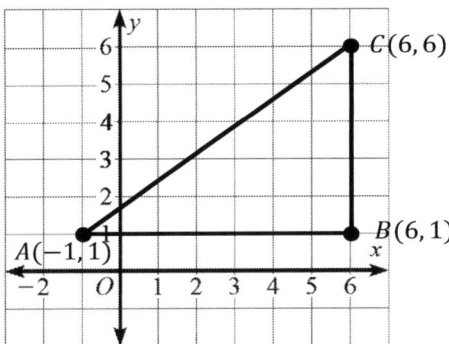

49.
What is the slope $\overline{AC}$?

A. $\dfrac{3}{4}$

B. $\dfrac{5}{6}$

C. $\dfrac{6}{7}$

D. $-\dfrac{7}{6}$

E. $-\dfrac{6}{5}$

50.
What is the midpoint of $\overline{AC}$?

F. $\left(2\dfrac{1}{2}, 2\dfrac{1}{2}\right)$

G. $\left(2\dfrac{1}{2}, 3\dfrac{1}{2}\right)$

H. $(3, 3)$

J. $\left(3\dfrac{1}{2}, 4\dfrac{1}{2}\right)$

K. $\left(3, 3\dfrac{1}{2}\right)$

51.
Suppose that the two endpoints of a line segment are $(3, 2)$ and $(-4, 7)$ in the standard (x, y) coordinate. What is the length, in coordinate units, of the line segment?

A. $6\sqrt{2}$

B. $\sqrt{74}$

C. 8

D. $\sqrt{78}$

E. 9

52.
The width of a rectangle is 3 inches and the length is 4 inches. If one vertex of the rectangle is at $(3, 5)$ on the standard (x, y) coordinate plane, a coordinate unit is 1 inch, which of the following coordinates can be another vertex of the rectangle ?

F. $(0, 5)$

G. $(1, 5)$

H. $(2, -5)$

J. $(3, 0)$

K. $(4, -8)$

53.
Which of the following sets of 3 numbers could be the side lengths, in inches, of a right triangle?

A. $1, 2, 3$

B. $3, 4, 6$

C. $13, 14, 15$

D. $12, 35, 47$

E. $11, 60, 61$

Use the following information to answer questions 54 - 56.

In the figure below, a triangle ΔPQR is a right triangle with the given dimensions in inches.

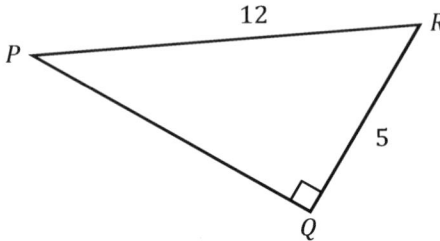

54.

Which of the following values is the length, in inches, of $\overline{PQ}$?

A. $\sqrt{119}$

B. 7

C. $7\sqrt{2}$

D. $8\sqrt{3}$

E. 13

55.

What is the trigonometric ratio of $\cos R$?

A. $\dfrac{5}{7}$

B. $\dfrac{5}{12}$

C. $\dfrac{\sqrt{119}}{12}$

D. $\dfrac{7\sqrt{2}}{12}$

E. $\dfrac{12}{13}$

56.

What is **not** a true statement about the measures of the interior angles in the right triangle ΔPQR?

F. $\angle P + \angle R < 90°$

G. $\angle P + \angle Q + \angle R = 180°$

H. $\angle P$ is an acute angle

J. $\angle R$ is an acute angle

K. $\angle P$ and $\angle R$ are complementary angles

57.

As shown figure below, a support wire is holding up a power transmission tower. The wire, which is fixated to the tower at a point 30 meters above the level ground, has an angle of elevation of 50°. What is the length, in meters, of the support wire?

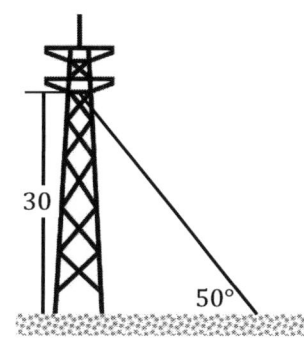

A. $\dfrac{30}{\cos 50°}$

B. $30 \cos 50°$

C. $\dfrac{30}{\sin 50°}$

D. $30 \sin 50°$

E. $30 \tan 50°$

58.

Which of the following values is the amplitude of the function $y = -3 \sin(0.5x - 0.4\pi) + 1$?

F. 2

G. −2

H. 3

J. −3

K. 4

59.

A water wheel is a machine for converting the energy of falling water into useful forms of power, often in a water mill. A water wheel is turning at a constant during its rotation. Let x be the time that has elapsed since wheel started rotating and y be the height of above water level of a certain point of the water wheel. The point is at its maximum height at $x = x_1$, and is at its minimum height at $x = x_2$. Which of the following graphs represents the relationship between time and height during this rotation?

A.
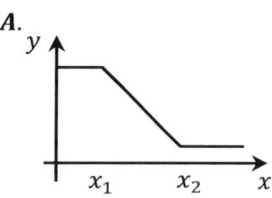

D.
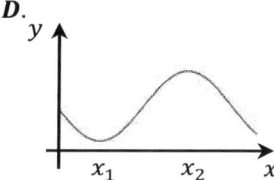

B.
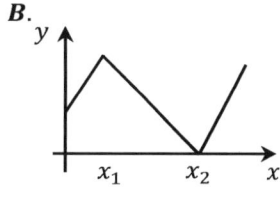

E.
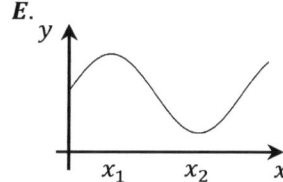

C.
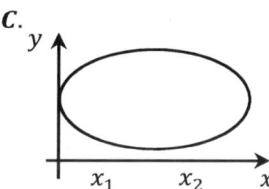

60.

Which of the following vectors is the result of adding of the three vectors $\langle -2, 3 \rangle$, $\langle -1, 4 \rangle$, and $\langle 2, -5 \rangle$

A. $\langle 1, 2 \rangle$

B. $\langle 1, -2 \rangle$

C. $\langle -1, 2 \rangle$

D. $\langle 4, -60 \rangle$

E. $\langle -4, 60 \rangle$

BLANK PAGE   *by K·DEAN*

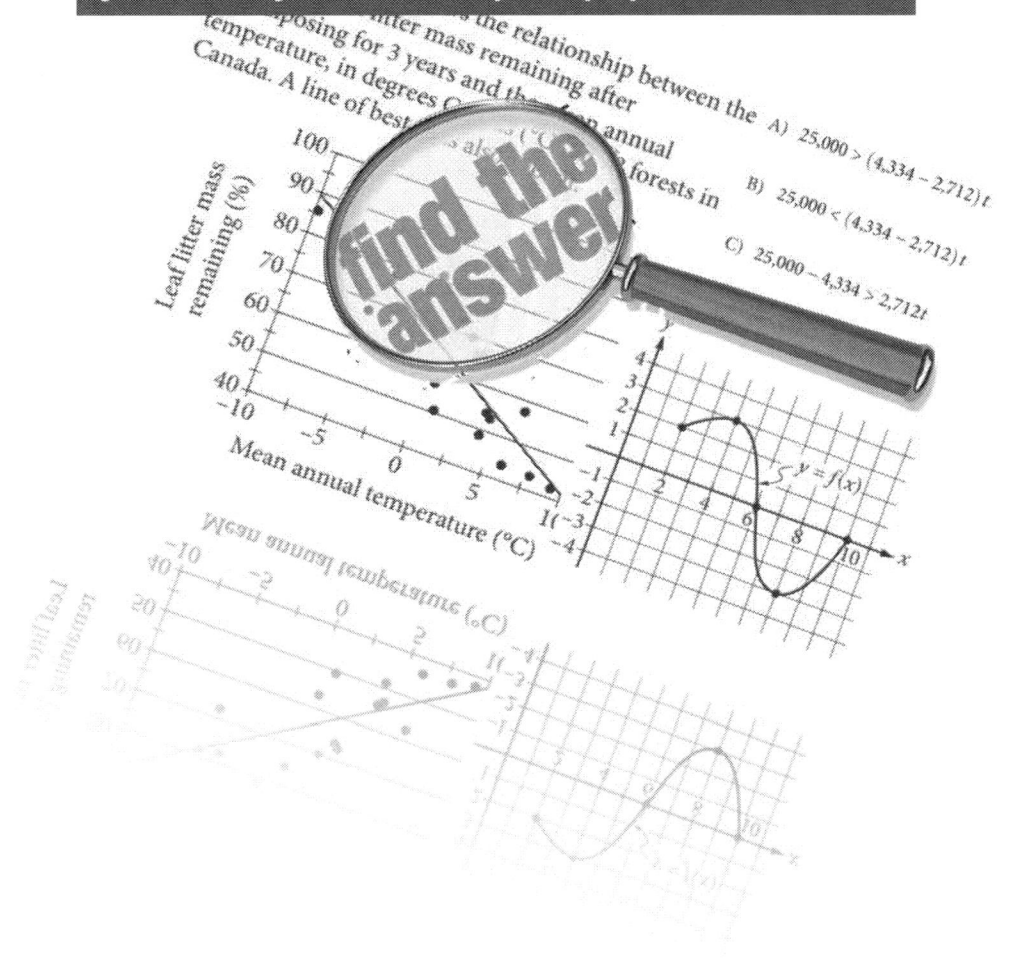

Obtain Scale Scores from Raw Scores

Scale Score	Raw Score	Scale Score	Raw Score	Scale Score	Raw Score
36	60	24	36-37	12	7
35	58-59	23	34-35	11	5-6
34	57	22	32-33	10	4
33	55-56	21	30-31	9	-
32	54	20	29	8	3
31	52-53	19	27-28	7	-
30	50-51	18	24-26	6	2
29	48-49	17	21-23	5	-
28	45-47	16	17-20	4	1
27	43-44	15	13-16	3	-
26	40-42	14	11-12	2	-
25	38-39	13	8-10	1	0

1. Scoring Key

Key		Question Category	Y/N
01.	D	Expression and Linear Equation	
02.	E	Expression and Linear Equation	
03.	F	Expression and Linear Equation	
04.	D	Number Theory	
05.	B	Number Theory	
06.	F	Number Theory	
07.	B	Expression and Linear Equation	
08.	K	Expression and Linear Equation	
09.	D	Expression and Linear Equation	
10.	J	Expression and Linear Equation	
11.	C	Linear Function inequality	
12.	C	Linear Function inequality	
13.	J	Linear Function inequality	
14.	C	Linear Function inequality	
15.	F	Linear Function inequality	
16.	E	Linear Function inequality	
17.	D	Linear Function inequality	
18.	F	Arithmetic Topic and Ratio	
19.	C	Arithmetic Topic and Ratio	
20.	G	Arithmetic Topic and Ratio	
21.	D	Arithmetic Topic and Ratio	
22.	G	Basic Geometry	
23.	C	Basic Geometry	
24.	H	Basic Geometry	
25.	J	Basic Geometry	
26.	A	Basic Geometry	
27.	H	Basic Geometry	
28.	C	Basic Geometry	
29.	H	Arithmetic Topic and Ratio	
30.	B	Quadratic and Polynomial Function	

Key		Question Category	Y/N
31.	J	Quadratic and Polynomial Function	
32.	C	Quadratic and Polynomial Function	
33.	D	Quadratic and Polynomial Function	
34.	G	Quadratic and Polynomial Function	
35.	B	Quadratic and Polynomial Function	
36.	J	Further Equations and Functions	
37.	B	Further Equations and Functions	
38.	E	Further Equations and Functions	
39.	D	Further Equations and Functions	
40.	G	Further Equations and Functions	
41.	D	Statistics and Probability	
42.	C	Statistics and Probability	
43.	J	Statistics and Probability	
44.	B	Statistics and Probability	
45.	A	Statistics and Probability	
46.	H	Sequence and Series	
47.	D	Analytic Geometry and Conic Section	
48.	G	Analytic Geometry and Conic Section	
49.	C	Analytic Geometry and Conic Section	
50.	G	Analytic Geometry and Conic Section	
51.	B	Analytic Geometry and Conic Section	
52.	F	Analytic Geometry and Conic Section	
53.	E	Analytic Geometry and Conic Section	
54.	A	Trigonometric Functions	
55.	B	Trigonometric Functions	
56.	F	Trigonometric Functions	
57.	C	Trigonometric Functions	
58.	H	Trigonometric Functions	
59.	E	Trigonometric Functions	
60.		Intermediate Algebra	

2. Answer Explanations

01. Answer (D)

The revenue is calculated by the product of price and sales.

Whenever the price increases by \$20, sales decrease by 10.
Therefore, if the price increases n times by \$20, the new price is \$$(750 + 20n)$ and the sales is $(80 - 10n)$.

Thus, the dollar amount of the store's monthly sales is;
$$(750 + 20n)(80 - 10n)$$

02. Answer (E)

Let the amount of savings before deposit is x.

If the amount of savings before deposit is x, then his bankbook shows $x - 75$ and it should show $x + 75$.
So, the difference is $(x + 75) - (x - 75) = x + 75 - x + 75 = 150$.
Thus,
the bankbook shows \$ 150 less than it should show.

03. Answer (F)

Solve the equation and then substitute the value of x for the other equation

Solving the equation;
multiply by x on both sides;
$$\frac{2}{x} = 6 \;\to\; x \cdot \frac{2}{x} = 6x \;\to\; 2 = 6x$$
divide by 6 on both sides;
$$6x = 2 \;\to\; \frac{6x}{6} = \frac{2}{6} \;\to\; x = \frac{1}{3}$$
Substituting $\frac{1}{3}$ for x of the expression;
$$\frac{y}{x} = 3 \;\to\; \frac{y}{\frac{1}{3}} = 3 \;\to\; 3y = 3 \;\to\; y = 1$$

04. Answer (D)

"all the students" means 1800 students.

The students who buys only pencil is 24%, only note book is 12%, only ball pen is 8%, and A4 paper is 3%. So, these sums are 47%.

Thus, approximate number of these students is
$$0.47 \times 1800 = 846$$

05. Answer (B)

Find percent of students who buys at least one item.

The percent of the students who buys at least one item is;
$$24 + 10 + 10 + 7 + 12 + 0 + 8 + 5 + 3 = 79\%$$
So, the percent of the students who does not buy the items is;
$$100 - 79 = 21\%.$$

06. Answer (F)

Find the number of students who buy only pencil.

Before additional survey, the number of students who buy only pencil (24%) is; $300 \times 0.24 = 72$. And, in additional survey, 12 students buy only pencil.
So, total number of students who buy pencil but none of the 3 types of items is $72 + 12 = 84$.

Thus, the fraction is;
$$\frac{84}{330} = \frac{14}{55}$$

07. Answer (B)

Let x be the number of correct answers

If the number of correct answers is x, then the number of incorrect answers is $30 - x$.
Therefore, because his score is 195;
$$10 \times x - 5 \times (30 - x) = 195 \;\to\; 10x - 150 + 5x = 195$$
$$\to\; 15x - 150 = 195$$
Adding 150 to the both sides;
$$15x - 150 = 195 \;\to\; 15x - 150 + 150 = 195 + 150 \;\to\; 15x = 345$$
Dividing the both sides by 15;
$$15x = 345 \;\to\; \frac{15x}{15} = \frac{345}{15} \;\to\; x = 23$$
Thus, the number of correct answers is 23.

08. Answer (K)

Opposite sides of rectangle are parallel and of equal length.

Equation about lengths; $-3a + 4 = 4b - 8$
Subtracting 4 from both sides;
$$-3a + 4 = 4b - 8 \;\to\; -3a + 4 - 4 = 4b - 8 - 4 \;\to\; -3a = 4b - 12$$
Subtracting $4b$ from both sides;
$$-3a = 4b - 12 \;\to\; -3a - 4b = 4b - 12 - 4b \;\to\; -3a - 4b = -12$$
Equation about widths; $a - 3 = 2b - 5$
Adding 3 to both sides;
$$a - 3 = 2b - 5 \;\to\; a - 3 + 3 = 2b - 5 + 3 \;\to\; a = 2b - 2$$
Subtracting $2b$ from both sides;
$$a = 2b - 2 \;\to\; a - 2b = 2b - 2 - 2b \;\to\; a - 2b = -2$$
Multiplying 2nd equation by 3 and then adding the two equation;
$$a - 2b = -2 \quad -\times 3 \to \quad \begin{array}{r} -3a - 4b = -12 \\ 3a - 6b = -6 \\ \hline -10b = -18 \end{array}$$
Dividing both sides by -10;
$$-10b = -18 \;\to\; \frac{-10b}{-10} = \frac{-18}{-10} \;\to\; b = 1.8$$
Thus, the value of b is 1.8.

09. Answer (D)

Solve for one variable and then substitute the value for other equation.

Multiplying $-2x - 5y = 9$ by 3 and multiplying $3x + 11y = 4$ by 2, then adding two equation;
$$\begin{array}{r} -2x - 5y = 9 \quad -\times 3 \to \quad -6x - 15y = 27 \\ 3x + 11y = 4 \quad -\times 2 \to \quad 6x + 22y = 8 \\ \hline 7y = 35 \end{array}$$
Dividing both sides by 7;
$$7y = 35 \;\to\; \frac{7y}{7} = \frac{35}{7} \;\to\; y = 5$$
Substituting 5 for y on the equation $-2x - 5y = 9$;
$$-2x - 5y = 9 \;\to\; -2x - 5(5) = 9 \;\to\; -2x - 25 = 9$$
Adding 25 to both sides;
$$-2x - 25 = 9 \;\to\; -2x - 25 + 25 = 9 + 25 \;\to\; -2x = 34$$
Dividing both sides by -2;
$$-2x = 34 \;\to\; \frac{-2x}{-2} = \frac{34}{-2} \;\to\; x = -17$$
Thus, $y - x = 5 - (-17) = 22$.

10. Answer (J)

Let the length of the shortest side be 4x.

If the length of the shortest side is $4x$, then other sides are $7x$, $8x$.
So, the perimeter is;
$$4x + 7x + 8x = 114 \;\to\; 19x = 114$$
Dividing by 19 on both sides;
$$19x = 114 \;\to\; \frac{19x}{19} = \frac{114}{19} \;\to\; x = 6$$
Thus, the shortest side $4x$ is $4 \times 6 = 24$ inches.

11. Answer (C)

Substitute each value and then solve the equation.

Substituting 24 for X, and -4 for Z;
$$X = YZ^2 \quad \rightarrow \quad 24 = Y(-4)^2 \quad \rightarrow \quad 24 = 16Y$$
Dividing both sides by 16;
$$16Y = 24 \quad \rightarrow \quad \frac{16Y}{16} = \frac{24}{16} \quad \rightarrow \quad Y = \frac{3}{2}$$
Thus, the value of Y is $\frac{3}{2}$.

12. Answer (C)

The sign of the slope is direction.

The interval $\overline{AB}$ has a positive slope, so he drives to beach at constant speed. The interval $\overline{BC}$ has zero slope, therefore he stays at beach. The interval $\overline{CD}$ has a negative slope, so he returns to his home at constant speed.

13. Answer (J)

The boundary lines are the solid line.

$-4 \le x \le 4$ is interior region between $x = -4$ and $x = 4$ and the boundary lines are $x = -4$ and $x = 4$ vertical solid lines.
$-3 \le x \le 3$ is interior region between $y = -3$ and $y = 3$ and the boundary lines are $y = -3$ and $y = 3$ horizontal solid lines.

Thus, the correct answer is *J*.

14. Answer (C)

Absolute value is never negative.

Evaluate;
$$|6 - 3| - |5 - 8| = |-3| - |-3| = 3 - 3 = 0$$
Thus, the value is 0.

15. Answer (F)

Absolute value is never negative.

Subtracting 1 from both sides;
$$2|x - 3| + 1 \ge 7 \quad \rightarrow \quad 2|x - 3| + 1 - 1 \ge 7 - 1 \quad \rightarrow \quad 2|x - 3| \ge 6$$
Dividing both sides by 2;
$$2|x - 3| \ge 6 \quad \rightarrow \quad \frac{2|x - 3|}{2} \ge \frac{6}{2} \quad \rightarrow \quad |x - 3| \ge 3$$
So, $x - 3 \le -3$ or $x - 3 \ge 3$.
Adding 3 to both sides;
$$x - 3 + 3 \le -3 + 3 \qquad x - 3 + 3 \ge 3 + 3$$
$$\rightarrow \quad x \le 0 \qquad \qquad \rightarrow \quad x \ge 6$$
Thus, the solution set is $x \le 0$ or $x \ge 6$.

16. Answer (E)

The triangle is a right triangle.

The triangle is a right triangle and the three intersecting points are;
$(-6, 12)$, $(6, 12)$, and $(6, -12)$.

So, the area is
$$\frac{1}{2} \times (6 - (-6)) \times (12 - (12)) = 144 \; in^2$$

Thus, the correct answer is *E*.

17. Answer (D)

Finding a slope and a y-intercept of the line.

Finding a slope of the line;
$$m = \frac{y_2 - y_1}{x_2 - x_1} = \frac{-4 - 3}{3 - (-5)} = \frac{-7}{8} = -\frac{7}{8}$$
Substitute $-\frac{7}{8}$ for m;
$$y = mx + b \quad \rightarrow \quad y = -\frac{7}{8}x + b$$
Substitute -5 for x and 3 for y;
$$y = -\frac{7}{8}x + b \quad \rightarrow \quad 3 = -\frac{7}{8}(-5) + b \quad \rightarrow \quad 3 = \frac{35}{8} + b$$
Subtract $\frac{35}{8}$ from both sides;
$$\frac{35}{8} + b = 3 \quad \rightarrow \quad \frac{35}{8} + b - \frac{35}{8} = 3 - \frac{35}{8} \quad \rightarrow \quad b = -\frac{11}{3}$$
Thus the equation of the line is;
$$y = -\frac{7}{8}x - \frac{11}{3}$$

18. Answer (F)

k is the constant of variation.

"z vary jointly with x and y" is; $z \propto xy$
and "inversely with the square of w" is; $z \propto \frac{1}{w^2}$
So, $z \propto \frac{xy}{w^2}$ and using constant variation is k;
Thus, the equation is;
$$z = \frac{kxy}{w^2}$$

19. Answer (C)

The question is about tip.

The tip is calculated by;
$$0.12 \times \$140 = \$16.8$$
Thus, each person's portion of the tip is;
$$\frac{\$16.8}{10} = \$1.68$$

20. Answer (G)

Multiplying the sum of chocolate powder by 3.

The teaspoons of chocolate powder for 1 rainbow cake is
$$\frac{3}{4} + \frac{3}{8} = \frac{6}{8} + \frac{3}{8} = \frac{9}{8}$$
Thus, the teaspoons of chocolate powder for 3 rainbow cake is
$$3 \times \frac{9}{8} = \frac{27}{8} = \frac{24 + 3}{8} = 3\frac{3}{8}.$$

21. Answer (D)

1 foot is 12 inches.

1 minutes have FOUR 15seconds ($\because 60 seconds = 4 \times 15 seconds$)
So, using proportion;
$$\frac{8 \, feet}{15 \, seconds} = \frac{distance, x}{4 \times 15 \, seconds} \quad \rightarrow \quad 15x = 8 \times 4 \times 15 \quad \rightarrow \quad x = 32 \, ft$$
Because 1 foot is 12 inches, thus 32 feet is $32 \times 12 = 384 \; inches$.

22. Answer (G)

A squares are also a rectangular.

When the areas are the same, the closer to the square, the smaller the perimeter. For example;
$$Area \; is \; 1 \times 64 = 64 \quad \rightarrow \quad Perimeter \; is \; 2 \times 1 + 2 \times 64 = 130$$
$$Area \; is \; 2 \times 32 = 64 \quad \rightarrow \quad Perimeter \; is \; 2 \times 2 + 2 \times 32 = 68$$
$$\dots .$$
$$Area \; is \; 8 \times 8 = 64 \quad \rightarrow \quad Perimeter \; is \; 2 \times 8 + 2 \times 8 = 32$$
Thus, the minimum value for the perimeter is 32.

23. Answer (C)

The area of a parallelogram is a product of base and height.

The two pairs of the opposite sides are same so, $\square PQRS$ is a parallelogram. Therefore the area is;
$$area = base \times height = 12 \times 8 = 96 \; in^2$$
Thus, the area of $\square PQRS$ is 96.

24. Answer (H)

The angle sum of quadrilateral is 360°.

$\angle AOC = 2\angle ABC = 2 \times 50 = 100^\circ$ and the exterior angle of $\angle AOC$ is $360 - 100 = 260^\circ$. Because angle sum of $\square ABCO$ is;
$$50^\circ + 260^\circ + \angle BAO + \angle BCO = 360^\circ$$
$$\rightarrow \quad \angle BAO + \angle BCO + 310^\circ = 360^\circ \quad \rightarrow \quad \angle BAO + \angle BCO = 50^\circ$$
Thus, the sum is 50°.

25. Answer (J)

The two triangle are similar to each other.

$\angle DAE \cong \angle BAC$ ($\because$ common angle) and $\angle ADE \cong \angle ABC$ ($\because \overline{DE} \parallel \overline{BC}$ and corresponding angles). $\triangle ADE \backsim \triangle ABC$ (angle-angle (AA) similarity. So, the proportion for DE is;
$$\frac{DE}{BC} = \frac{AE}{AC} \quad \rightarrow \quad \frac{DE}{10} = \frac{6}{15}$$
Thus, the correct answer is J.

26. Answer (A)

The pairs of adjacent angles are all linear pairs.

Draw a picture of the situation given in the problem.
There are 4 pairs of adjacent angles;
$$x + y, \qquad y + z, \qquad z + w, \qquad w + x$$
And all the 4 pairs are linear pair so, their sum is 180°. Thus, the correct answer is A.

27. Answer (H)

Using Alternate interior angles.

A and $(2\theta + 60)^\circ$ are alternate interior angles so, $A = (2\theta + 60)^\circ$.
Three angles lie on same line, m.
$$(2\theta + 60)^\circ + \theta^\circ + (3\theta - 15)^\circ = 180^\circ$$
$$\rightarrow \quad 5\theta + 45 = 180 \quad \rightarrow \quad 5\theta = 135 \quad \rightarrow \quad \theta = 27$$
Thus, the value of θ is 27.

28. Answer (C)

An interior angle of the equilateral triangle is 60°.

$\triangle OPQ$ is an equilateral triangle so, $\angle OPQ = 60^\circ$, $\angle SPQ$ and θ° are corresponding angles so, $\angle SPQ = \theta^\circ$.
And $\angle OPQ$ and $\angle SPQ$ are a linear pair so, $\angle OPQ + \angle SPQ = 180^\circ$.
Substitute 60° for $\angle OPQ$, and $\angle SPQ$ for θ°;
$$\angle OPQ + \angle SPQ = 180^\circ \quad \rightarrow \quad 60^\circ + \theta^\circ = 180^\circ \quad \rightarrow \quad \theta^\circ = 120^\circ$$
Thus the value of θ is 120.

29. Answer (H)

Volume is product of width, length and height.

The volume of the cardboard box is;
$$V = w \times l \times h = 18 \times 24 \times 12 = 5,184 \; in^3$$
The volume of one Magic Cube is;
$$V = 2^3 = 8 \; in^3$$

Thus, the maximum number of Magic Cubes is $\frac{5,184}{8} = 648$.

30. Answer (B)

Using FOIL pattern.

The area of the rectangle is $(x + 1)(2x - 3)$.
Expanding the expression;
$$(x + 1)(2x - 3) = 2x^2 - 3x + 2x - 3 = 2x^2 - x - 3$$
Thus, the area is $2x^2 - x - 3$.

31. Answer (J)

Using trigonometric ratio.

Translating $\overline{P'Q'}$ onto $\overline{P''Q''}$ to make right triangle. Because the rotation does not change the size and shape of figure, $\overline{P'Q'} = 4$. ($\because \overline{PQ} = 4$)

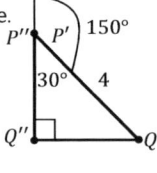

Using trigonometric ratio;
$$\cos 30^\circ = \frac{\sqrt{3}}{2} = \frac{\overline{P''Q''}}{\overline{P''Q'}} = \frac{\overline{P''Q''}}{4}$$
Using cross multiplying;
$$\frac{\sqrt{3}}{2} = \frac{\overline{P''Q''}}{4} \quad \rightarrow \quad 2\,\overline{P''Q''} = 4\sqrt{3} \quad \rightarrow \quad \overline{P''Q''} = 2\sqrt{3}$$
Thus, the length of $\overline{P''Q''}$ is $2\sqrt{3}$.

32. Answer (C)

The size and shape of graph or figure is not changed.

The graph is translated 2 unit right;
Thus, the correct answer is C.

33. Answer (D)

In dilation, $(x, y) \rightarrow (kx, ky)$, k is scale factor.

If a scale factor is k;
$$(x, y) \rightarrow (kx, ky), \qquad (4, 8) \rightarrow (k4, k8) = (1, 2)$$
So, $k = \frac{1}{4}$, $(28, -32) \rightarrow \left(\frac{1}{4} \times 28, \frac{1}{4} \times -32\right) = (7, -8)$
Thus, the correct answer is D.

34. Answer (G)

Translation; $(x, y) \rightarrow (x + h, y + k)$.

"is translated 3 units to the lefts and 8 units up" means $h = -3$ and $k = 8$. So,
$$(x, y) \rightarrow (x - 3, y + 8), \qquad (5, -4) \rightarrow (5 - 3, -4 + 8) = (2, 4)$$
Thus, the coordinates of P' are $(2, 4)$.

35. Answer (B)

Substitute −4 for x.

Substitute −4 for x;
$$f(-4) = 3(-4)^2 + 5(-4) - 12 = 16$$
Thus, the value of $f(-4) = 16$

36. Answer (J)

Finding the vertical asymptotes.

Because the undefined points are the vertical asymptotes and the points are the real zeros of denominator equation. So,
$$-x^2 + 1 = 0 \quad \rightarrow \quad -(x^2 - 1) = 0 \quad \rightarrow \quad -(x+1)(x-1) = 0$$
$$\rightarrow \quad x + 1 = 0 \text{ or } x - 1 = 0 \quad \rightarrow \quad x = -1 \text{ or } x = 1$$
Thus, the correct answer is J.

37. Answer (B)

Switch x and y.

Switch x and y;
$$f(x) = 2x^3 + 1 \quad \rightarrow \quad y = 2x^3 + 1 \quad \rightarrow \quad x = 2y^3 + 1$$
Solve for y;
subtract 1 from both sides;
$$x = 2y^3 + 1 \quad \rightarrow \quad 2y^3 = x - 1$$
divide both sides by 2 and then take cubic root on both sides;
$$y^3 = \frac{x-1}{2} \quad \rightarrow \quad y = \sqrt[3]{\frac{x-1}{2}}$$
Thus, the inverse function $f^{-1}(x) = \sqrt[3]{\frac{x-1}{2}}$.

38. Answer (E)

The exponential and the logarithm are invers relation each other.

Divide both sides by P_0;
$$P = P_0(1+r)^t \quad \rightarrow \quad (1+r)^t = \frac{P}{P_0}$$
Take natural logarithm on both sides and using the property of logarithm, $\log_b m^n = n\log_b m$, ;
$$\log(1+r)^t = \log\frac{P}{P_0} \quad \rightarrow \quad t \cdot \log(1+r) = \log\frac{P}{P_0}$$
Divide both sides by $\log(1+r)$;
$$t = \frac{\left(\log\frac{P}{P_0}\right)}{\log(1+r)}$$
Thus, the correct answer is E.

39. Answer (D)

Substitute the given values for variables.

Substitute 1500 for P_0, 0.085 for r, and 5 for t and then evaluate;
$$P = P_0(1+r)^t \quad \rightarrow \quad P = 1,500(1+0.085)^5 = 2,255.485 \dots$$
Thus, the price is $2,255.

40. Answer (G)

From 2013 to 2017 means t is 4 years.

Substitute 2,000 for P_0, 4,000 for P, and 3 for t;
$$P = P_0(1+r)^t \quad \rightarrow \quad 4,000 = 2,000(1+r)^4$$
Divide both sides by 2000 and then take 4th root on both sides;
$$(1+r)^4 = \frac{4000}{2000} \quad \rightarrow \quad 1+r = \sqrt[4]{2} = 1.189207$$
Subtracting 1 from both sides;
$$r = 1.189207 - 1 \quad \rightarrow \quad r = 0.189207$$
Thus, the value of r is 18.92%.

41. Answer (D)

Drawing a line that lies as close as possible to the data points.

1st Method; analyzing data
Because, in the data, if x-value increase, y-value also increase, the data is a positive correlation. This means that the best fit line has a positive slope. And there are $(1,1)/(3,3)/(-1,-1.5)$ points so, the slope is nearby 1.

2nd Method; using GDC

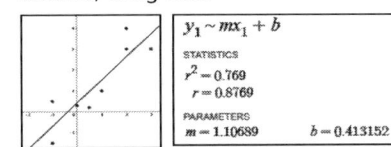

Thus, the slope is 1.

42. Answer (C)

The range is the difference between the greatest and least data value.

The range is $1,950 - (-320) = 2,270$ and the full data set is needed to find the median.

Thus, the correct answer is C.

43. Answer (J)

A percent is a ratio whose denominator is 100.

The probability is;
$$P = \frac{7}{40} \times 100 = \frac{35}{2}\% = 17\frac{1}{2}\%$$
Thus, the correct answer is J.

44. Answer (B)

"AND" event is the product of the two probabilities.

The first probability is $\frac{2}{9}$ and the second probability is $\frac{3}{9}$. The "AND" event is the product of two probabilities, so, the probability of the given two events is;
$$P = P(1st) \times P(2nd) = \frac{2}{9} \times \frac{3}{9} = \frac{2}{27}$$
Thus, the correct answer is B.

45. Answer (A)

The number of tire Type B and made by Company Tecem is 35.

The number of tire Type B and made by Company Tecem is 35. So, the probability is;
$$P = \frac{35}{200} \times 100\% = 17.5\%$$
Thus, the correct answer is A.

46. Answer (H)

She should deposit 350-50=$300.

The additional money she has to deposit is $350-$50=$300.
Let x be the minimum amount of money, it is a first term of an arithmetic sequence. And $2 is a common difference of the arithmetic sequence.
From the formula of the arithmetic series;
$$S_n = n\left(\frac{2a_1 + (n-1)d}{2}\right) \quad \rightarrow \quad S_{10} = 10 \times \left(\frac{2x + 9 \times 2}{2}\right) = 300$$
$$\rightarrow \quad 5(2x + 18) = 300 \quad \rightarrow \quad 2x + 18 = 60 \quad \rightarrow \quad 2x = 42$$
$$\rightarrow \quad x = 24$$
Thus, the minimum amount of money is $24.

47. **Answer** (**D**)

Finding a right triangle.

Let O be the center of the circle, P and Q be two points of the vertex of the square.

So, $\overline{OP}$ and $\overline{OQ}$ are radii of the circle and its length is 5 in and ΔOPQ is isosceles right triangle.

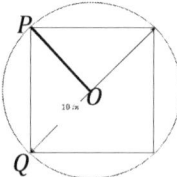

Using Pythagorean theorem;
$$\overline{PQ}^2 = \overline{OP}^2 + \overline{OQ}^2 = 5^2 + 5^2 = 50 \quad \rightarrow \quad \overline{PQ} = \sqrt{50}$$

Thus the area of the square is $\overline{PQ}^2 = 50 \ in^2$.

48. **Answer** (**G**)

The two points P and Q are sister points.

Because the vertex is on the y-axis and the co-vertex is on the x-axis, the major axis is vertical with $a = 7$, and the minor axis is horizontal with $b = 5$.
The equation of the parabola is;
$$\frac{x^2}{b^2} + \frac{y^2}{a^2} = 1 \quad \rightarrow \quad \frac{x^2}{5^2} + \frac{y^2}{7^2} = 1 \quad \rightarrow \quad \frac{x^2}{25} + \frac{y^2}{49} = 1.$$
Substitute $(p, 4)$ for (x, y);
$$\frac{p^2}{25} + \frac{4^2}{49} = 1 \quad \rightarrow \quad \frac{p^2}{25} = 1 - \frac{16}{49} = \frac{33}{49} \quad \rightarrow \quad \frac{p^2}{25} = \frac{33}{49} \quad \rightarrow \quad p^2 = \frac{825}{49}.$$
Take square root on both sides;
$$p = \pm\frac{5\sqrt{33}}{7} \approx \pm 4.1032590 \dots \approx \pm 4.1.$$

Thus, $p = -4.1$ and $q = 4.1$ and distance is $|4.1 - (-4.1)| = 8.2$.

49. **Answer** (**C**)

Using slope formula.

From the slope formula;
$$m = \frac{y_2 - y_1}{x_2 - x_1} = \frac{6 - 1}{6 - (-1)} = \frac{6}{7}$$

Thus, the correct answer is **C**.

50. **Answer** (**G**)

Using the formula of the midpoint.

Using the formula of the midpoint;
$$M = \left(\frac{x_1 + x_2}{2}, \frac{y_1 + y_2}{2}\right) = \left(\frac{6 + (-1)}{2}, \frac{6 + 1}{2}\right) = \left(\frac{5}{2}, \frac{7}{2}\right)$$

Thus, the midpoint is $\left(2\frac{1}{2}, 3\frac{1}{2}\right)$.

51. **Answer** (**B**)

Using the formula of distance.

From the distance formula;
$$d = \sqrt{(x_2 - x_1)^2 + (y_2 - y_1)^2} = \sqrt{(-4 - 3)^2 + (7 - 2)^2} = \sqrt{74}$$

Thus, the length is $\sqrt{74}$.

52. **Answer** (**F**)

A rectangle has 4 right angles.

The rectangle has 4 right angles so, one of the coordinates of $x-$ or y-coordinate is equal to the given coordinate. And the length is either 3 inches or 4 inches.

Thus, the correct answer is **F**.

53. **Answer** (**E**)

Using converse of the Pythagorean theorem.

If $c^2 = a^2 + b^2$, then the triangle is a right triangle.
So, $61^2 = 11^2 + 60^2 \quad \rightarrow \quad 3,721 = 121 + 3,600 = 3,721$.

Thus, the correct answer is **E**.

54. **Answer** (**A**)

Using the Pythagorean theorem.

Using the Pythagorean theorem;
$$\overline{PQ} = \sqrt{\overline{PR}^2 - \overline{QR}^2} = \sqrt{12^2 - 5^2} = \sqrt{119}$$

Thus, the length is $\sqrt{119}$.

55. **Answer** (**B**)

Using the Pythagorean theorem.

Using the Pythagorean theorem;
$$\cos R = \frac{A}{H} = \frac{5}{12}$$

Thus, the correct answer is **B**.

56. **Answer** (**F**)

Using the angle sum theorem.

From the angle sum theorem, $\angle P + \angle Q + \angle R = 180°$ and $\angle P + \angle R = 90° \quad \rightarrow \quad \angle P$ and $\angle R$ are complementary angles.
$\angle P$ and $\angle R$ are less than 90°, so the two angles are acute angles.

Thus, the correct answer is **F**.

57. **Answer** (**C**)

Using the Pythagorean theorem.

Let x the length of the wire and using the Pythagorean theorem;
$$\sin 50° = \frac{O}{H} = \frac{30}{x} \quad \rightarrow \quad x = \frac{30}{\sin 50°}$$

Thus, the correct answer is **C**.

58. **Answer** (**H**)

Amplitude is never negative.

In the function $y = a \sin b(x - h) + k$, the amplitude is $|a|$.
Thus, the amplitude is $|-3| = 3$.

---

59. **Answer** (**E**)

Circular motion.

The water wheel motion is a circular motion, so its graph is sine or cosine function.

Thus, the correct answer is **E**.

---

60. **Answer** (**C**)

Adding each components.

Adding each components;
$\langle -2, 3 \rangle + \langle -1, 4 \rangle + \langle 2, -5 \rangle = \langle -2 + (-1) + 2, 3 + 4 + (-5) \rangle = \langle -1, 2 \rangle$

Thus, the correct answer is **C**.

BLANK PAGE   *by K·DEAN*

Reformed Past Paper ACT MATH TEST 05

60 Questions – 60 Minutes

DIRECTIONS:
Solve each problem, choose the correct answer, and then fill in the corresponding oval on your answer in the grid on the answer sheet.

Do not linger over problems that take too much time as many as you can, then return to ~~in the time~~ you have left for the ~~test~~.

You are permitted to use a calculator on this test.

Note: Unless otherwise stated, all of the following should be assumed.

1. Figures ~~may~~ ~~are drawn~~ to scale unless ~~otherwise indicated.~~

2. All figures lie in a plane unless otherwise indicated.

3. All variables and expressions used represent real numbers unless otherwise indicated.

This test has reformed the REAL ACT Mathematics Test

01.

Which of the following numbers is **not** a factor of 196?

A. 6

B. 7

C. 49

D. 98

E. 196

02.

Suppose x and y be prime numbers. Which of the following numbers is **not** a factor of product x and y, xy ?

F. 1

G. x

H. y

J. $x + y$

K. xy

03.

What is the simplified form of $\dfrac{\sqrt{2}}{3-\sqrt{5}}$?

F. $-\dfrac{\sqrt{2}}{2}$

G. $\dfrac{\sqrt{2}}{3+\sqrt{5}}$

H. $\dfrac{-3\sqrt{2}+10}{2}$

J. $\dfrac{3\sqrt{2}-10}{4}$

K. $\dfrac{3\sqrt{2}+10}{4}$

Use the following information to answer questions
04 - 07.

Chavi's flower shop sells different styles of bouquets of roses. The sale price and number of roses per bouquet for 3 styles of bouquets are given in the table below.

Style of bouquet	Number of roses per bouquet	Sale price per bouquet
Bouquet A	25	$24.00
Bouquet B	12	$10.20
Bouquet C	6	$4.50

04.

Which of the following amount is the average sale price per rose for a bouquet A ?

A. $ 0.90

B. $ 0.92

C. $ 0.94

D. $ 0.96

E. $ 0.98

05.

The rose farmer is offering Chavi's a Bouquet D that has 25% less roses than Bouquet B has. How many roses does the Bouquet rose have ?

F. 14

G. 6

H. 10

J. 9

K. 8

06.

Last month, customers bought three times as many Bouquet B as Bouquet A, and customer bought four times as many Bouquet C as Bouquet A. Last month, customers bought 256 bouquets. What are the total revenues for 256 bouquets ?

A. $ 2,048.20

B. $ 2,096.40

C. $ 2,108.60

D. $ 2,224.00

E. $ 2,323.20

07.

A large basket contains 15 Bouquet A, 15 Bouquet B, and 15 Bouquet C. Clara will select 3 bouquets from the basket. How many different selections of 3 bouquets are possible ?
(The ordering does not matter.)

F. 27

G. 24

H. 12

J. 10

K. 3

08.

Gardening company have just planted a rectangular flower bed in a city park. As shown in the figure below, the city park is 25 yards long, and the rectangular flower bed is 6.5 yards wide and 8.5 yards long. The left edge of the bed will be x yards from the left edge of the park, the right edge of the bed will be x yards from the right edge of the park. What is the value of x, in yards ?

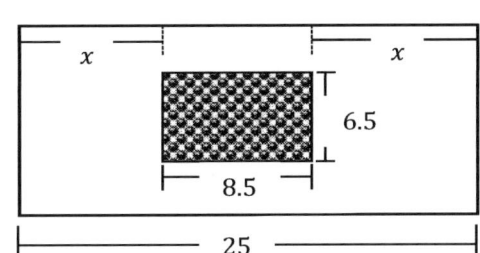

A. 6.75

B. 7.25

C. 7.5

D. 8.25

E. 8.5

09.

At fast food restaurant, Abigail spends \$9.53 on the purchase of 3 hamburgers and 4 tacos. The price of each hamburger is h dollars and the price of each taco is 1.5 times the price of a hamburger. Which system of equations can be used to find the price h (in dollars) of a hamburger and the price t (in dollars) of a taco at the restaurant ?

F. $\begin{array}{c} 2h + 4t = 9.53 \\ t = 2h \end{array}$

G. $\begin{array}{c} 2h + 3t = 9.53 \\ t = 2h \end{array}$

H. $\begin{array}{c} 3h + 4t = 9.53 \\ 2t = 3h \end{array}$

J. $\begin{array}{c} 3h + 2t = 9.53 \\ 2t = 3h \end{array}$

K. $\begin{array}{c} 3h + t = 9.53 \\ 2t = h \end{array}$

10.

Which of the following expressions is equivalent to $\dfrac{1+\dfrac{2}{x-2}}{\dfrac{3}{x-2}}$ for all real value of x ?

A. $\dfrac{2}{3}$

B. $-\dfrac{2}{3}$

C. $\dfrac{2}{x}$

D. $\dfrac{x}{3}$

E. $\dfrac{2}{(x-2)^2}$

11.

When a line passes through two points $(0,5)$ and $(3,1)$ in the standard (x,y) coordinate plane. Which of the following values is the slope of any line that is perpendicular to the line ?

F. $-\dfrac{4}{3}$

G. $\dfrac{4}{3}$

H. $\dfrac{3}{4}$

J. $-\dfrac{3}{4}$

K. -1

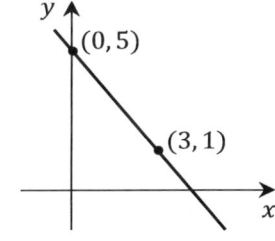

12.

If one of the following graphs in the standard (x, y) coordinate plane is the graph of $y \leq ax + b$ for negative real number a and positive real number b, then which one ?

A.
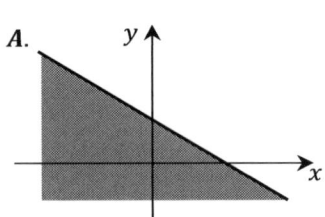

B.
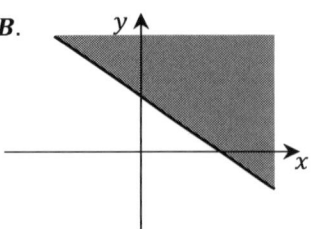

C.
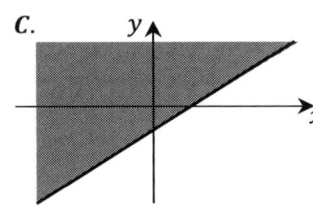

D.
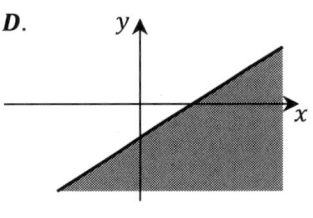

E.
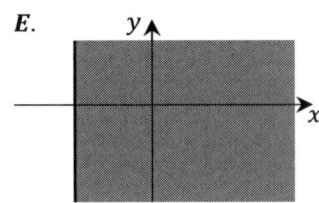

13.

Evaluate the numerical expression $|7(3) + 6(-5)|$?

F. 10

G. -51

H. 51

J. -9

K. 9

14.

A Semiconductor Factory calculates its profit by subtracting fixed manufacturing overhead cost from 53% of its total revenue. Which of the following equations expresses this relationship profit (P), total revenue (R), and fixed manufacturing overhead cost (C) of the factory ?

A. $P = R - C$

B. $P = 0.53(R - C)$

C. $P = 0.53R$

D. $P = 0.53R - C$

E. $P = C - 0.53R$

15.

The data of a experiment is represented in the xy coordinate plane by a scatterplot consisting of 7 point: $(0.5, 17.2), (2, 8.9), (4, 5.1), (6, 9.2), (7.5, 13.5),$ $(9, 30.2), (9.5, 35.5)$. If the all possible values of $p, q,$ and r are real numbers, then which of the following equation best fits the data ?

F. $x = r$

G. $y = (p - q)x$

H. $y = px^2 + qx + r$

J. $y = p(q)^x$

K. $y = p \ln x + q$

16.

For a tropical storm, the relationship between the amount of rainfall, y millimeters, and the time, x hours, was modeled by the linear equation;

$$-\frac{1}{2}x + 3y = 3$$

Which of the following graphs is the graph of the equation in the x, y coordinate ?

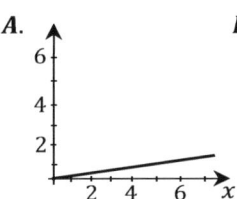
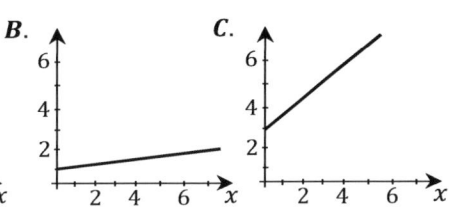

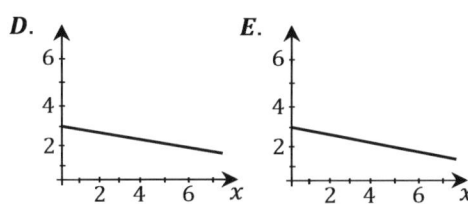

17.

In the standard (x, y) coordinate plane, an equation of line p is $-5x + 3y = 15$. If another line q has a slope that is -3 times the slope of p and has a y-intercept that is 2 more than the y-intercept of p, what is an equation of the line q ?

F. $y = 5x + 7$

G. $y = -5x + 7$

H. $y = 15x + 5$

J. $y = -15x - 5$

K. $y = -15x + 5$

18.

A car mechanic's labor costs are 15% higher this year than they had been when the basic repairing fee was \$80.00. If the basic repairing fee had increased by the same as the car mechanic's costs, what would the basic repairing fee be this year ?

A. \$90.75

B. \$92.00

C. \$92.75

D. \$94.25

E. \$96.00

19.

A sedan accelerated from 54 feet per second (fps) to 242 fps in exactly 5 seconds. What was the sedan's average acceleration, in feet per square second (ft/s^2), from 54 fps to 242 fps?

F. 37.2

G. 37.6

H. 38.0

J. 38.4

K. 38.8

20.

Given that $a = 4$ when $b = 18$ for proportion $\frac{a}{12} = \frac{p}{b}$, what is a when $b = 9$?

F. 14

G. 12

H. 10

J. 8

K. 6

21.

Sylvia is making sugar cookies, and the original recipe calls $1\frac{3}{4}$ teaspoons of white sugar and $3\frac{1}{2}$ cups of flour. Sylvia will use the entire contents of a packet that contains $2\frac{1}{2}$ teaspoons of white sugar and will use the same ratio of ingredient s called for in the original recipe. How many cups of flour will Sylvia use?

A. 4

B. $4\frac{1}{2}$

C. $4\frac{3}{4}$

D. 5

E. $5\frac{1}{2}$

22.

As shown in the figure below, C lies on both $\overline{AC}$ and $\overline{BD}$, and $\overline{AD}$ and $\overline{BC}$ are parallel. Which of following angles must have the same measure as $\angle DAO$?

F. $\angle AOD$

G. $\angle ADO$

H. $\angle BOC$

J. $\angle BCO$

K. $\angle CBO$

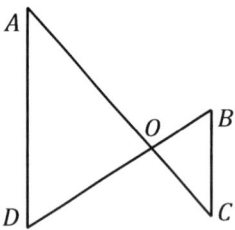

23.

In a plane, the distinct line segments $\overline{AB}$ and $\overline{CD}$ intersect at a point E, where E is between A and B, and between C and D. If the measure of $\angle BED$ is 56°, then what is the measure of $\angle AED$?

A. 56°

B. $(180 - 56)°$

C. $(90 + 56)°$

D. $(180 + 56)°$

E. $3 \times 56°$

24.

For trapezoid $XYWZ$ shown below, $\overline{XY} \parallel \overline{WZ}$, the measure of the interior angles are distinct, and the measure of $\angle X$ is $\theta°$. What is the degree measure of $\angle W$ in term of θ?

F. $(180 - \theta)°$

G. $(180 + \theta)°$

H. $(90 - \theta)°$

J. $(90 + \theta)°$

K. $2 \times \theta°$

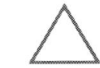  

25.

All lots shall maintain for safety vision purposes a triangular area formed by the lot lines adjoining the intersecting streets. The shaded lot is an isosceles right triangle having length of 24 feet, as shown in the figure below. What is the area, in square feet, of the lot?

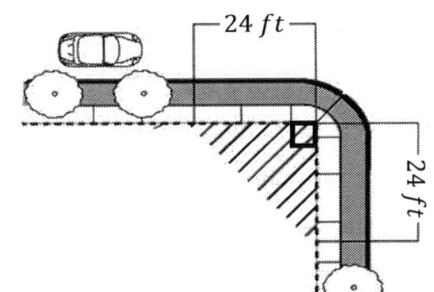

A. 100

B. 144

C. 186

D. 288

E. 576

26.

As shown in the figure below, $\overline{PT}$ is parallel to $\overline{RS}$, $\overline{PS}$ and $\overline{RT}$ intersect at a point Q, and the given lengths are in inches. What is the length , in inches, of $\overline{SQ}$?

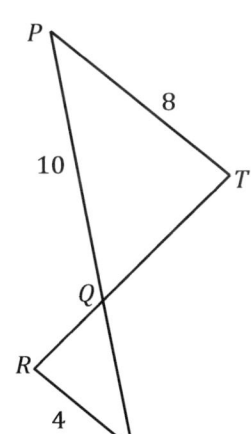

F. 5

G. 5.5

H. 6

J. 6.5

K. 7

27.

All of the following statements concern polygons that are congruent, similar, or both. Which statement is **TRUE**?

A. If the lengths of corresponding sides of two polygons are same, the two polygons are congruent to each other.

B. If the lengths of corresponding sides of two polygons are same, the two polygons are similar to each other.

C. All squares are congruent to each other.

D. All regular polygons are similar to each other.

E. Triangles that are similar to each other are always congruent to each other.

28.

In the figure below, six congruent quarter circles touch only at their corners. If the path from P to Q along the radii of the quarter circles is 72 feet long, how many feet long is path from Q back to P along the arcs of these quarter circles?

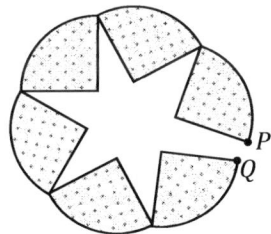

F. 12π

G. 18π

H. 20π

J. 24π

K. 36π

29.

Megan's family will have a oil tank installed in their farm. The interior of the tank is a right cylinder with a uniform depth of 3 meters and a diameter of 2 meters. The maximum volume of oil that can be in the tank is 80% of the volume of the tank. Which of the following values is the maximum number of cubic meters of oil that can be in the tank?

A. 1.6π

B. 2.4π

C. 3π

D. 3.6π

E. 8π

30.

Two students, Kiara and Jonathan, answered the examination question with different, yet equivalent, expressions. Kiara's expression was $(x - 2)^2 - 2x^2$ and Jonathan said his expression was a simplified form of Kiara's expression. Which of the following expressions could be the Kiara's expression?

F. $-x^2 - 4x + 4$

G. $-x^2 - 4x - 4$

H. $-x^2 + 4x - 4$

J. $4x + 4$

K. $-4x - 4$

31.

As shown in the figure below, the graph of the polynomial function with equation $y = x^3 + 2x^2 - 3x - 4$ is shown in the standard (x, y) coordinate plane. Which of the following graphs is the graph of the reflection of the polynomial function over x-axis?

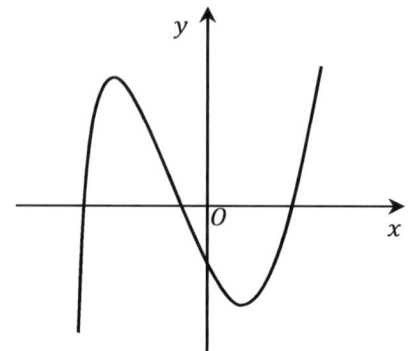

A.

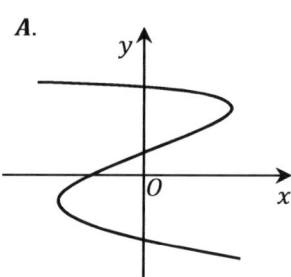

B.

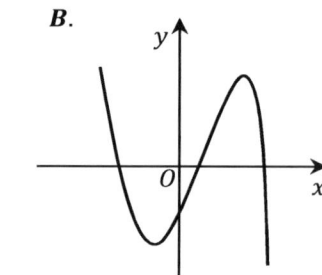

C.

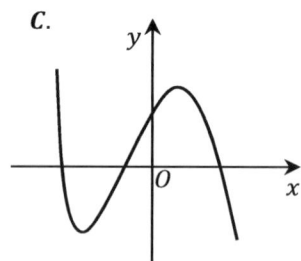

D.

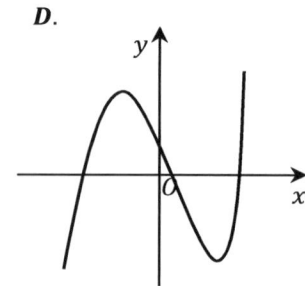

E.

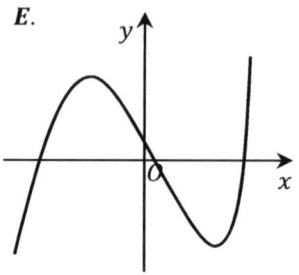

 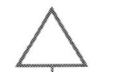

Use the following information to answer questions
32 - 34.

As shown in the figure below, a trapezoid PQRS is
graphed in standard (x, y) coordinate plane.

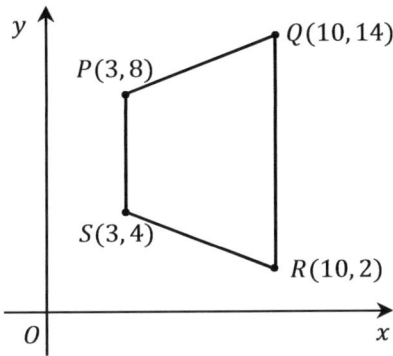

32.

What is the slope of $\overline{RS}$?

A. $-\dfrac{7}{2}$

B. $-\dfrac{2}{7}$

C. $-\dfrac{1}{7}$

D. $\dfrac{2}{7}$

E. $\dfrac{7}{2}$

33.

If $\square PQRS$ is reflected on x-axis to $\square P'Q'R'S'$, what
are the coordinates R'?

A. $(10, -2)$

B. $(-10, 2)$

C. $(-10, -2)$

D. $(2, -10)$

E. $(-2, 10)$

34.

Which of the following equations cuts $\square PQRS$ into 2
quadrilaterals with equal areas?

F. $y = 7$

G. $y = 6.5$

H. $y = 6$

J. $y = x + 6$

K. $y = x + 5$

35.

Which of the expressions below is a linear factor of the polynomial function $f(x) = -3x^3 + 12x^2 - 12x$?

I. x
II. $x - 2$
III. $x + 2$

A. I only

B. II only

C. III only

D. I and II

E. I, II, and III

36.

Which of the following expressions is equivalent to $-\dfrac{24x^5y^7}{(-2x^2y^3)^2}$ for nonzero real numbers of x and y?

A. $6xy$

B. $-6xy$

C. $12xy$

D. $-12xy$

E. $-12x^3y^4$

37.

If $-\sqrt{2x} + 7 = -1$, then what is the value of x?

F. 64

G. 32

H. $\sqrt{7}$

J. $4\sqrt{2}$

K. $2\sqrt{2}$

38.

The two functions $f(x)$ and $g(x)$ are defined by $f(x) = 3x - 2$ and $g(x) = 2x + p$, where p is a real number. If $f(g(x)) = g(f(x))$, then what is the value of p ?

F. 2

G. 1

H. 0

J. −1

K. −2

39.

Which of the following linear equations is the horizontal asymptote for the rational function graph of $f(x) = \dfrac{x-p}{2x+q}$, for $a \neq 0$ and $b \neq 0$, in the standard (x, y) coordinate plane?

A. $y = 2$

B. $y = \dfrac{1}{2}$

C. $x = p$

D. $x = -\dfrac{q}{2}$

E. $y = -\dfrac{p}{q}$

Use the following information to answer questions
40 - 43.

The data set below gives the original prices of nine
different tablet computers at an electronics store.

$360, $240, $120, $320, $280, $320, $180, $150, $140

40.

Which of the following bar graphs accurately
represents the data on the prices of nine different
tablet computers?

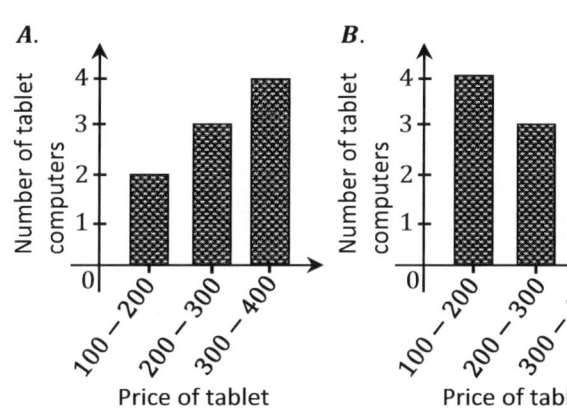

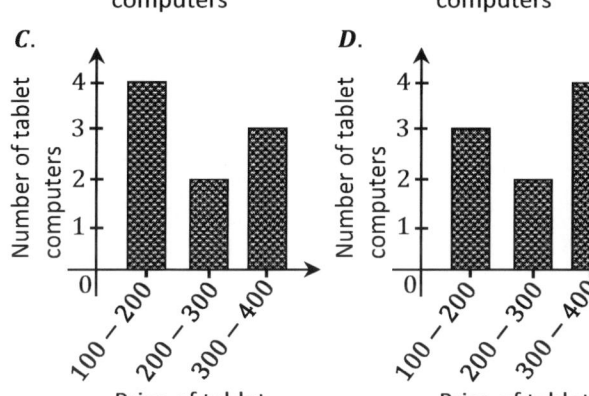

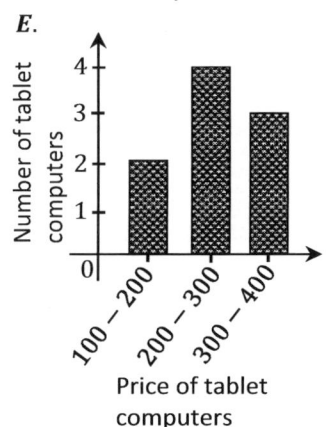

41.

Based on the data, what is the median price of tablet
computers at these nine tablet computer's prices?

F. $234

G. $240

H. $280

J. $320

K. $360

42.

The store is offering a promotion in which all tablet
computers ordered online are 25% off. If Smart
Esther bought her tablet computer online for $210,
what is the original price of the tablet computer?

A. $150

B. $180

C. $240

D. $280

E. $320

43.

The electronic store collects data from three
additional tablet computers and includes the new
data in the list. If three additional tablet computers
are priced $A, B,$ and C, respectively, which of the
following expressions is the mean of this larger of
prices?

F. $\dfrac{\$2,110 + A + B + C}{10}$

G. $\dfrac{\$2,110 + A + B + C}{11}$

H. $\dfrac{\$2,110 + A + B + C}{12}$

J. $\dfrac{\$2,110}{12}$

K. $\dfrac{A + B + C}{3}$

44.

If $\sqrt{a} = 2b$ and $b = 16$, what is the value of a ?

A. 4

B. $4\sqrt{2}$

C. 512

D. 1,024

E. 2,048

46.

In the geometric sequence, the ratio of any term to the previous term is constant. What is the 5th term in the geometric sequence with 3 terms 8, 12, and 18?

A. 24.5

B. 36

C. 40.5

D. 42

E. 56.5

45.

There are five stages in the production of ice cream. First, the mixture is pasteurized to sterilize bacteria. Next, the temperature of the mixture is lowered for first and second aging. Flavors are added and the temperature is lowered even more to harden the ice cream. Finally, the ice cream is stored in a freezer. The graph below shows the temperature at each stage. What is the mean temperature of five stage, to the nearest 0.1°C?

F. −1.4°C

G. 0°C

H. 1.6°C

J. 2.8°C

K. 3.2°C

Stage	Temperature
Pasteurization	75°C
First aging	4°C
Second aging	−5°C
Hardening	−50°C
Storage	−10°C

47.

On Friday night, the ship, Vasily Dincov, is anchored at Jeju Harbor. On Monday morning the ship sailed to the island 12 kilometers due south and 5 kilometers due west of Jeju Harbor. To the nearest 0.1 kilometer, what is the straight line distance from the Jeju Harbor to the island?

F. 11.7

G. 12.3

H. 13.0

J. 13.5

K. 14.1

Use the following information to answer questions 48 - 51.

A conservator-restorer will restore a right triangular sculpture to honor Pythagoras. The conservator-restorer has purchased the following material for restoring; 1 can of anti-corrosive agent at a price of $24.50, 40 hoop iron reinforcements at a price of $1.20 each, and 2 cans of oil coating agent at a price of $6.00 each. An 7% sales tax was added to the total price of these materials. The conservator-restorer will also install a LED Lighting that will be located an equal distance from the 3 vertices of the sculpture.

7 feet   4 feet

48.

The conservator-restorer calculated the area of the sculpture before purchasing these materials. What is the area, in square feet, of the triangle?

- **A.** 7
- **B.** 14
- **C.** 16
- **D.** 21
- **E.** 28

49.

What was the total cost, including sales tax, of the anti-corrosive agent, hoop iron reinforcements, and oil coating agent that the conservator-restorer purchased?

- **F.** $87.53
- **G.** $90.42
- **H.** $92.35
- **J.** $95.21
- **K.** $97.80

50.

A restoration drawing of the sculpture will be placed in the standard (x, y) coordinate plane so that the right angle is at the origin $(0, 0)$, and the other two vertices are at $(0, 4)$ and $(7, 0)$. What is the coordinate of the location of the LED Lighting?

- **A.** $(3, 2)$
- **B.** $(2, 3)$
- **C.** $(3.5, 2)$
- **D.** $(5.5, 5.5)$
- **E.** $(11, 11)$

51.

The conservator-restorer has decided to enclose the sculpture by installing a decorative plastic materials of uniform thickness along the sculpture's perimeter. Which of the following values is closest to the sculpture's perimeter?

- **F.** 15.6
- **G.** 17.8
- **H.** 19.1
- **J.** 21.3
- **K.** 23.5

52.

Suppose that two points $A\,(3,6)$ and $B\,(7,8)$ is placed in the standard (x,y) coordinate plane. What is the coordinates of the midpoint of $\overline{AB}$?

A. $(2,1)$

B. $(4,6)$

C. $(5,7)$

D. $(7,5)$

E. $(7,8)$

53.

Humphery's computer password has 3 capital letters followed by 6 digits. The 3 capital letters are K, A, Y. The followed 6 digits could be any digit 0 through 9, and digits may repeat. How many possible the computer passwords are there?

A. 60

B. 61

C. 10^6

D. $10^6 + 1$

E. $26^3 \times 10^6$

Use the following information to answer questions 54 - 55.

As shown below, $\square PQRS$ is composed of $\triangle PQS$ and $\triangle QRS$. The lengths are given in centimeters.

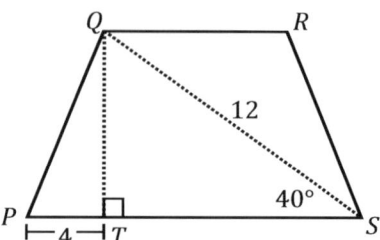

54.

Which of the following values is closest to the area, in square centimeters, of the $\triangle PQS$?

A. 44.2

B. 47.6

C. 50.8

D. 53.1

E. 56.0

55.

What is the ratio of $\sin P$?

F. $\dfrac{\overline{PT}}{\overline{PQ}}$

G. $\dfrac{\overline{PQ}}{\overline{PT}}$

H. $\dfrac{\overline{QT}}{\overline{PQ}}$

J. $\dfrac{\overline{PQ}}{\overline{QT}}$

K. $\dfrac{\overline{QT}}{\overline{PT}}$

56.

Assume that the angle of elevation from a place on level ground 35 feet from the base of a tree to the top of the tree is 50°. What is the height, in feet, of the tree?

A. 29.8

B. 32.7

C. 35.6

D. 38.3

E. 41.7

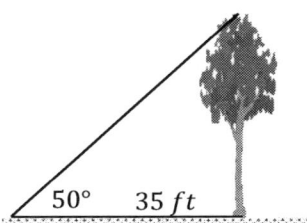

57.

A shown figure below, in a circle with center O, the length of radius is 8 inches, the length of $\overline{PR}$ is 7 inches. When the central angle $\angle POQ$ is expressed as radian, what is the area, in square inches, of sector OPR?

F. $64\pi \sin^{-1}\left(\frac{7}{8}\right)$

G. $\frac{8}{45}\sin^{-1}\left(\frac{7}{8}\right)$

H. $\frac{8\pi}{45}\sin^{-1}\left(\frac{7}{8}\right)$

J. $32\pi \sin^{-1}\left(\frac{7}{8}\right)$

K. $32\sin^{-1}\left(\frac{7}{8}\right)$

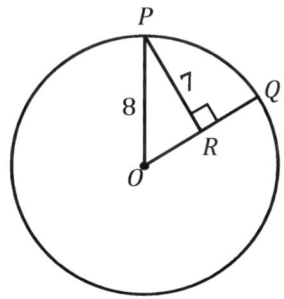

58.

The angle measures of ΔPQR and ΔPSR are shown below. What is the value of $\sin(\theta + \alpha)$?

A. $\frac{\sqrt{3}}{3}$

B. $\frac{1}{3}$

C. $\frac{1}{2}$

D. $\frac{\sqrt{3}}{2}$

E. $\frac{2\sqrt{3}}{3}$

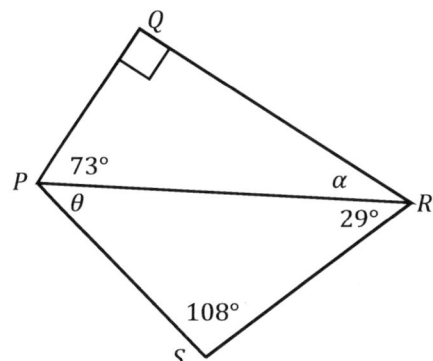

59.

The circle is divided into 5 congruent sectors to teach the geometrical probability. Which of the following degrees is the arc measure of each sector?

F. 30°

G. 60°

H. 72°

J. 108°

K. 120°

60.

What is the value of the matrices operation

$$(-2)\begin{bmatrix} 4 & -1 \\ -3 & -5 \end{bmatrix} + 3\begin{bmatrix} 2 & -2 \\ 0 & 6 \end{bmatrix} = ?$$

A. $\begin{bmatrix} 2 & 4 \\ 0 & -18 \end{bmatrix}$

B. $\begin{bmatrix} -28 & -4 \\ 6 & 2 \end{bmatrix}$

C. $\begin{bmatrix} -4 & -2 \\ 28 & 6 \end{bmatrix}$

D. $\begin{bmatrix} -2 & -4 \\ 6 & 28 \end{bmatrix}$

E. $\begin{bmatrix} -2 & -4 \\ 0 & 18 \end{bmatrix}$

BLANK PAGE *by K·DEAN*

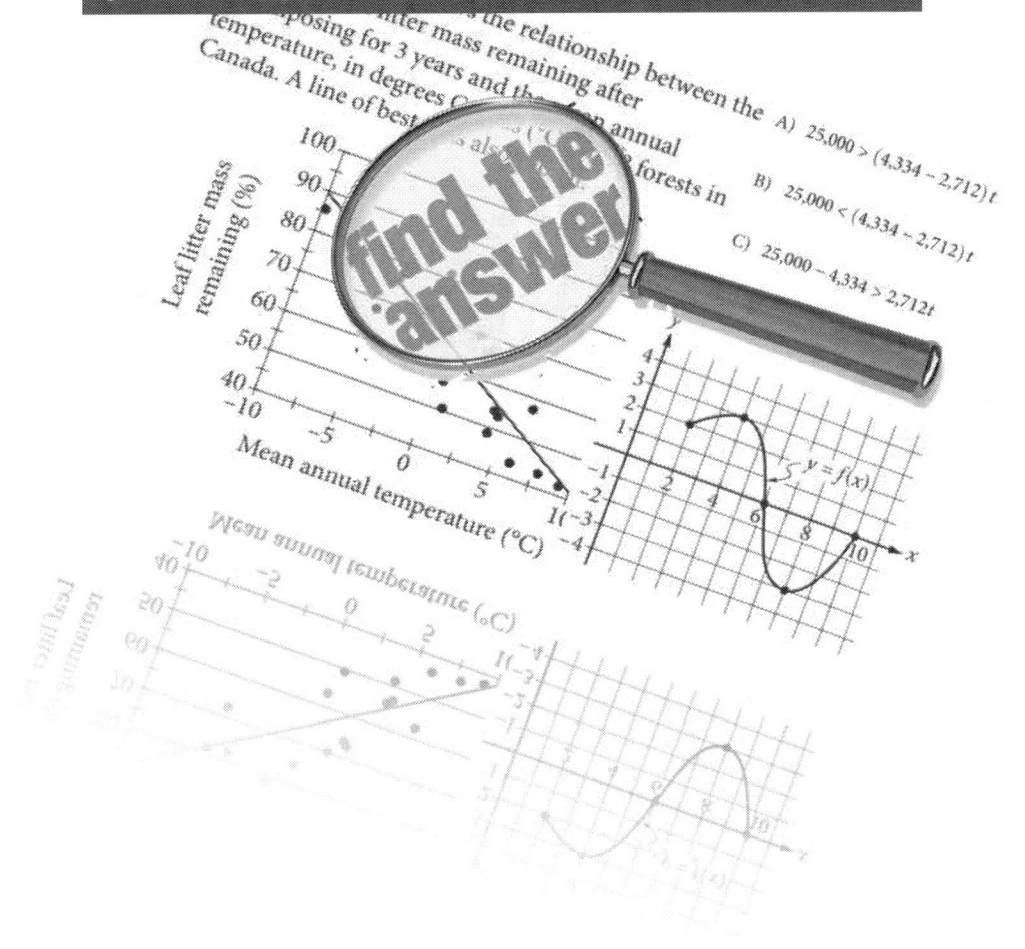

Obtain Scale Scores from Raw Scores					
Scale Score	Raw Score	Scale Score	Raw Score	Scale Score	Raw Score
36	60	24	36-37	12	7
35	58-59	23	34-35	11	5-6
34	57	22	32-33	10	4
33	55-56	21	30-31	9	-
32	54	20	29	8	3
31	52-53	19	27-28	7	-
30	50-51	18	24-26	6	2
29	48-49	17	21-23	5	-
28	45-47	16	17-20	4	1
27	43-44	15	13-16	3	-
26	40-42	14	11-12	2	-
25	38-39	13	8-10	1	0

1. Scoring Key

Key		Question Category	Y/N
01.	A	Number Theory	
02.	J	Number Theory	
03.	K	Number Theory	
04.	D	Expression and Linear Equation	
05.	J	Expression and Linear Equation	
06.	E	Expression and Linear Equation	
07.	J	Expression and Linear Equation	
08.	D	Expression and Linear Equation	
09.	H	Expression and Linear Equation	
10.	D	Expression and Linear Equation	
11.	H	Linear Function inequality	
12.	A	Linear Function inequality	
13.	K	Linear Function inequality	
14.	D	Linear Function inequality	
15.	H	Linear Function inequality	
16.	B	Linear Function inequality	
17.	G	Linear Function inequality	
18.	B	Arithmetic Topic and Ratio	
19.	G	Arithmetic Topic and Ratio	
20.	J	Arithmetic Topic and Ratio	
21.	D	Arithmetic Topic and Ratio	
22.	J	Basic Geometry	
23.	B	Basic Geometry	
24.	F	Basic Geometry	
25.	D	Basic Geometry	
26.	F	Basic Geometry	
27.	D	Basic Geometry	
28.	G	Basic Geometry	
29.	B	Arithmetic Topic and Ratio	
30.	F	Quadratic and Polynomial Function	

Key		Question Category	Y/N
31.	C	Quadratic and Polynomial Function	
32.	B	Quadratic and Polynomial Function	
33.	A	Quadratic and Polynomial Function	
34.	F	Quadratic and Polynomial Function	
35.	D	Quadratic and Polynomial Function	
36.	B	Further Equations and Functions	
37.	G	Further Equations and Functions	
38.	J	Further Equations and Functions	
39.	B	Further Equations and Functions	
40.	C	Statistics and Probability	
41.	G	Statistics and Probability	
42.	D	Statistics and Probability	
43.	H	Statistics and Probability	
44.	D	Further Equations and Functions	
45.	J	Statistics and Probability	
46.	C	Sequence and Series	
47.	H	Analytic Geometry and Conic Section	
48.	B	Analytic Geometry and Conic Section	
49.	G	Analytic Geometry and Conic Section	
50.	C	Analytic Geometry and Conic Section	
51.	H	Analytic Geometry and Conic Section	
52.	C	Analytic Geometry and Conic Section	
53.	C	Analytic Geometry and Conic Section	
54.	C	Trigonometric Functions	
55.	H	Trigonometric Functions	
56.	E	Trigonometric Functions	
57.	K	Trigonometric Functions	
58.	D	Trigonometric Functions	
59.	H	Trigonometric Functions	
60.	D	Intermediate Algebra	

2. Answer Explanations

---

01. **Answer** (A)

The factor of a number is product combination of its prime factors.

Prime factorization;
$$196 = 2 \times 2 \times 7 \times 7 = 2^2 \times 7^2$$

So, factors of 196 are product combination of its prime factors. That is; $1, 2, 4, 7, 14, 28, 49, 98, 196$.

---

02. **Answer** (J)

The factor of a number is product combination of its prime factors.

Prime factorization of product xy is; $xy = x \times y$ and number 1 is a factor of all numbers.
So, factors of xy are $1, x, y,$ and xy.

---

03. **Answer** (K)

No radical in a denominator.

Using conjugate for rationalizing the denominator;
$$\frac{\sqrt{2}}{3 - \sqrt{5}} \times \frac{3 + \sqrt{5}}{3 + \sqrt{5}} = \frac{3\sqrt{2} + \sqrt{10}}{3^2 - 5} = \frac{3\sqrt{2} + 10}{4}$$

Thus, the correct answer is K.

---

04. **Answer** (D)

An average is the quotient of sale price and number of roses .

The average sale price per rose for a bouquet A;
$$average\ sale\ price = \frac{sale\ price}{number\ of\ roses} = \frac{\$24.00}{25} = \$0.96$$

Thus, the price is $0.96.

---

05. **Answer** (J)

"less" means subtracting.

"a Bouquet D that has 25% less roses than Bouquet B has" means;
the amount of D= the amount of B-0.25× the amount of B
$$\rightarrow \quad D = 12 - 0.25 \times 12 = 9$$
Thus, the Bouquet D have 9 roses.

---

06. **Answer** (E)

Let the amount of A be x.

If the sale amount of Bouquet A is x, than;
"three times as many Bouquet B as Bouquet A" → B is $3x$ and
"four times as many Bouquet C as Bouquet A" → C is $4x$.
So, the total amount is;
$$x + 3x + 4x = 256 \quad \rightarrow \quad 8x = 256$$
Dividing by 8 on both sides;
$$8x = 256 \quad \rightarrow \quad \frac{8x}{8} = \frac{256}{8} \quad \rightarrow \quad x = 32$$
Therefore, A is 32, B is 96, and C is 128.
Thus, the total revenues is;
$$\$24 \times 32(A) + \$10.2 \times 96(B) + \$4.5 \times 128(C) = \$2,323.2$$

---

07. **Answer** (J)

The given problem about repeating .

Each selected case will be listed as follows;
AAA / AAB / AAC / ABB / ABC / ACC / BBB / BBC / BCC / CCC
Thus, there are 10 different selections.

---

08. **Answer** (D)

Set up a linear equation to suit the situation..

Making a linear equation;
$$x + 8.5 + x = 25 \quad \rightarrow \quad 2x + 8.5 = 25$$
Subtracting 8.5 from both sides;
$$2x + 8.5 = 25 \quad \rightarrow \quad 2x + 8.5 - 8.5 = 25 - 8.5 \quad \rightarrow \quad 2x = 16.5$$
Dividing by 2 on both sides;
$$2x = 16.5 \quad \rightarrow \quad \frac{2x}{2} = \frac{16.5}{2} \quad \rightarrow \quad x = 8.25$$
Thus, the value of x is 8.25.

---

09. **Answer** (H)

Convert word expression to variable expression.

Equation 1: Total price

Number of hamburgers	×	Price of a hamburger	+	Number of tacos	×	Price of a taco	=	Total price
→ 3	×	h	+	4	×	t	=	$9.53

Thus, the equation is $3h + 4t = 9.53$.

Equation 2: Relation of the two prices

Price of a taco = 1.5 × Price of a hamburger
$$\rightarrow \quad t \quad = 1.5 \times \quad h$$
Thus, the equation is $t = 1.5h$ and multiply both sides by 2;
$$\rightarrow 2t = 3h$$

---

10. **Answer** (D)

This problem about complex fraction.

Simplifying the numerator part;
$$1 + \frac{2}{x-2} = \frac{x-2}{x-2} + \frac{2}{x-2} = \frac{x}{x-2}$$
So,
$$\frac{1 + \frac{2}{x-2}}{\frac{3}{x-2}} = \frac{\frac{x}{x-2}}{\frac{3}{x-2}} = \frac{x}{x-2} \div \frac{3}{x-2} = \frac{x}{x-2} \times \frac{x-2}{3} = \frac{x}{3}$$

---

11. **Answer** (H)

Two lines are perpendicular if and only if their slopes are negative reciprocals of each other.

The slope of the line is;
$$m = \frac{y_2 - y_1}{x_2 - x_1} = \frac{1 - 5}{3 - 0} = \frac{-4}{3} = -\frac{4}{3}$$
So, the slope, m', of perpendicular line is;
$$m' = -\frac{1}{m} = -\left(\frac{1}{-\frac{4}{3}}\right) = \frac{3}{4}$$

---

12. **Answer** (A)

Interpreting y-intercept and x-intercept.

Interpreting the intercepts of the graph $y = ax + b$, $a < 0$, $b > 0$;
The y-intercept is positive, and calculating x-intercept;
$$y = ax + b \quad \rightarrow \quad 0 = ax + b \quad \rightarrow \quad ax = -b \quad \rightarrow \quad x = \frac{-b}{a} > 0$$
that is x-intercept is positive. → possible answers are A. and B.
Testing a point $(0,0)$; $\quad 0 \cdots a \times 0 + b \quad \rightarrow \quad 0 < b \ (\because b > 0)$

Thus, this means that $(0,0)$ is a solution that is correct answer is A.

---

13. Answer **(K)**

Absolute value is never negative.

Evaluate inside the expression;
$$7(3) + 6(-5) = 21 + (-30) = -9$$
Thus, $|7(3) + 6(-5)| = |-9| = 9$

---

14. Answer **(D)**

53% is 0.53 in numbers.

"53% of its total revenue (R)" is $0.53R$;

Thus, the profit (P) is;
$$P = 0.53R - C$$

---

15. Answer **(H)**

Finding the pattern of y-value as x-value increase.

From analyzing the data, as the values of x increase, the values of y increase and then decrease.
F. because $x = r$ is vertical line,
the x −value is not changed.
At $G. y = (p - q)x, J. y = p(q)^x$, and $K. y = p\ln x + q$,
as x-value increases, the pattern of y-value is not changed.
$H. y = px^2 + qx + r$ is parabola, its pattern of y-value is changed at the vertex. Or be plotted on graphic calculator.

Thus, the best fitting equation is H.

---

16. Answer **(B)**

Finding the slope and y-intercept of the equation

Convert the given equation to slope-intercept form by;
adding $\frac{1}{2}x$ to both sides;
$$-\frac{1}{2}x + 3y = 3 \quad \rightarrow \quad -\frac{1}{2}x + 3y + \frac{1}{2}x = 3 + \frac{1}{2}x \quad \rightarrow \quad 3y = \frac{1}{2}x + 3$$

dividing both sides by 3;
$$3y = \frac{1}{2}x + 3 \quad \rightarrow \quad \frac{3y}{3} = \frac{\left(\frac{1}{2}x + 3\right)}{3} \quad \rightarrow \quad y = \frac{1}{6}x + 1$$
The slope is $\frac{1}{6}$ and y-intercept is 1, thus the correct graph is B.

---

17. Answer **(G)**

Convert the line p to slope intercept form.

Finding slope and y-intercept of the line p;
$$-5x + 3y = 15 \quad \rightarrow \quad y = mx + b$$
Add $5x$ to both sides;
$$-5x + 3y = 15 \quad \rightarrow \quad -5x + 3y + 5x = 15 + 5x \quad \rightarrow \quad 3y = 5x + 15$$
Divide both sides by 3;
$$3y = 5x + 15 \quad \rightarrow \quad \frac{3y}{3} = \frac{5x + 15}{3} \quad \rightarrow \quad y = \frac{5}{3}x + 5$$
So, the slope of the line q is $\frac{5}{3} \times (-3) = -5$ and the y-intercept is $5 + 2 = 7$. Thus, the equation of the line q is $y = -5x + 7$.

---

18. Answer **(B)**

"higher than" means that add.

The new basic repairing fee is;
$$\$80 + 0.15 \times \$80 = \$80 + \$12 = \$92$$

---

19. Answer **(G)**

Acceleration is the quotient of change of speed and time.

The acceleration is;
$$acceleration = \frac{change\ of\ speed}{time} = \frac{(242 - 54)fps}{5sec} = 37.6ft/s^2$$

---

20. Answer **(J)**

Using cross product.

Substitute each value for a, b and then solving for p;
$$\frac{4}{12} = \frac{p}{18} \quad \rightarrow \quad 12p = 4 \times 18 \quad \rightarrow \quad 12p = 72 \quad \rightarrow \quad p = 6$$
So, make a new proportion;
$$\frac{a}{12} = \frac{6}{9} \quad \rightarrow \quad 9a = 6 \times 12 \quad \rightarrow \quad 9a = 72 \quad \rightarrow \quad a = 8$$
Thus, the value of a is 8.

---

21. Answer **(D)**

Using proportion.

Let x be the cups of flour, convert the mixed numbers to the improper fractions and then make a proportion;
$$1\frac{3}{4} = \frac{7}{4}, \qquad 3\frac{1}{2} = \frac{7}{2}, \qquad 2\frac{1}{2} = \frac{5}{2}$$
So,
$$\frac{white\ sugar}{flour} \rightarrow \frac{\frac{7}{4}}{\frac{7}{2}} = \frac{\frac{5}{2}}{x} \rightarrow \frac{7}{4}x = \frac{7}{2} \times \frac{5}{2} \rightarrow \frac{7}{4}x = \frac{35}{4} \rightarrow x = 5$$
Thus, the cups of flour are 5 cups

---

22. Answer **(J)**

Using Alternate interior angles.

$\overline{AD} \parallel \overline{BC}$ and $\overline{AC}$ is transversal so, $\angle DAO \cong \angle BCO$ (∵ alternate interior angle).

Thus, the angle is $\angle BCO$.

---

23. Answer **(B)**

Let's draw a picture of the situation given in the problem.

$\angle BED$ and $\angle AED$ are a linear pair so, their angle sum is 180°.
$\angle AED + \angle BED = 180° \quad \rightarrow \quad \angle AED + 56° = 180°$
$\rightarrow \quad \angle AED = (180 - 56)° = 124°$

Thus, the correct answer is B.

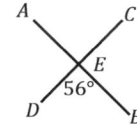

---

24. Answer **(F)**

Trapezoid is a quadrilateral with exactly 1 pair of parallel sides.

Because $\overline{XY} \parallel \overline{WZ}$, $\angle X$ and $\angle W$ are Co-interior angle. So,
$$\angle W + \angle X = 180° \quad \rightarrow \quad \angle W + \theta° = 180° \quad \rightarrow \quad \angle W = 180° - \theta°$$
Thus, the degree measure of $\angle W$ is $(180 - \theta)°$.

---

25. Answer **(D)**

Using the formula of triangle area.

Using the formula of triangle area;
$$area = \frac{1}{2}bh = \frac{1}{2} \times 24 \times 24 = 288ft^2$$
Thus, the area of the shaded lot is $288\ ft^2$

---

26. **Answer** (**F**)

Using the property of triangle similarity.

$\angle PQT \cong \angle SQR$ ($\because$ vertical angle) and $\overline{PT} \parallel \overline{SR}$ so, $\angle QSR \cong \angle QPT$ ($\because$ alternate interior angle).
Therefore $\triangle PQT \backsim \triangle SQR$ ($\because$ angle-angle (AA) similarity). Using triangle similarity;
$$\frac{\overline{PT}}{\overline{SR}} = \frac{\overline{PQ}}{\overline{SQ}} \rightarrow \frac{8}{4} = \frac{10}{\overline{SQ}} \rightarrow \overline{SQ} = 5$$

Thus, the length of $\overline{SQ}$ is 5.

---

27. **Answer** (**D**)

If the two figures are congruent to each other, the two figure are similar to each other.

A. and **B.** are not correct.
Two figures are similar if they have the same shape but not necessarily the same size For example;

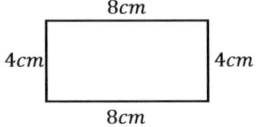 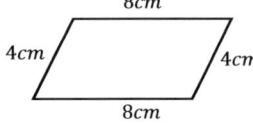

All regular polygons are always similar to each other. So, **C.** is not correct and **D. is correct**.
If the two figures are congruent to each other, the two figure are similar to each other, and the converse is not true in reverse. So, **E.** is not correct.

---

28. **Answer** (**G**)

Don't make a whole circle.

Because, the given figure has 12 congruent radii, r, the radius of the quarter circles is;
$$12r = 72 \rightarrow r = 6$$
The 6 quarter circles have 6 of $\frac{1}{4}$ of circle's circumference so,
$$length\ of\ arcs = 6 \times \frac{1}{4} \times 2\pi r = 6 \times \frac{1}{4} \times 2\pi(6) = 18\pi$$

Thus, the length of the arcs is 18π.

---

29. **Answer** (**B**)

The volume is product of base area and height.

From the formula of the cylinder's volume;
$$V = \pi r^2 h = \pi(1)^2(3) = 3\pi$$
So, 80% of the volume is $0.8(3\pi) = 2.4\pi$.

Thus, the maximum number of cubic meters of oil is 2.4π.

---

30. **Answer** (**F**)

Expanding and then simplifying.

Expanding by square of a binomial pattern and then simplifying;
$$(x - 2)^2 - 2x^2 = x^2 - 4x + 4 - 2x^2 = -x^2 - 4x + 4$$

Thus, the expression is $-x^2 - 4x + 4$.

---

31. **Answer** (**C**)

Reflection on x-axis; $y = f(x) \rightarrow y = -f(x)$, $(x,y) \rightarrow (x,-y)$.

The resulting of reflection on x-axis is $(x, y) \rightarrow (x, -y)$ and size and shape is not changed.

Thus, the correct answer is **C**.

---

32. **Answer** (**B**)

The slope is ratio of rise to run.

From the formula of slope;
$$m = \frac{y_2 - y_1}{x_2 - x_1} = \frac{2 - 4}{10 - 3} = \frac{-2}{7} = -\frac{2}{7}$$

Thus, the correct answer is **B**.

---

33. **Answer** (**A**)

Reflection on x-axis: (x,y) → (x, -y).

A figure is reflected in x-axis;
$$(x, y) \rightarrow (x, -y) \qquad (10, 2) \rightarrow (10, -2)$$

Thus, the correct answer is **A**.

---

34. **Answer** (**F**)

Finding the area of the original trapezoid.

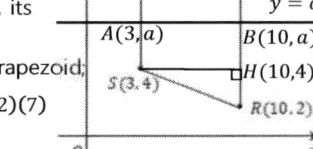

From S, drawing a line that is perpendicular to line $\overline{QR}$. So, H is (10,4) and $\overline{SH}$ is height of the trapezoid, its length is 7.

From the formula of area of the trapezoid;
$$A = \frac{1}{2}(b_1 + b_2)h \rightarrow A = \frac{1}{2}(4 + 12)(7)$$
$$\rightarrow A = 56$$

If the equation of cutting line is $y = a$ and intersecting points on each base sides are $A(3, a)$, $B(10, a)$;

the area of $\square ABRS$ is $\frac{1}{2} \times 56 = 28$ and the calculation is;
$$A = \frac{1}{2}(b_1 + b_2)h \rightarrow 28 = \frac{1}{2}((a - 4) + (a - 2))(7)$$
$$\rightarrow \frac{1}{2}(2a - 6)(7) = 28$$

Multiply both sides by $\frac{2}{7}$ and then add 6 to the sides;
$$\frac{2}{7} \times \frac{1}{2}(2a - 6)(7) = 28 \times \frac{2}{7} \rightarrow 2a - 6 = 8 \rightarrow 2a = 14$$
Divide both side by 2;
$$2a = 14 \rightarrow a = 7$$
Thus, the equation is $y = 7$.

---

35. **Answer** (**D**)

Grouping by common factors.

Grouping by common factors and then using square of a binomial pattern;
$$f(x) = -3x^3 + 12x^2 - 12x \rightarrow f(x) = -3x(x^2 - 4x + 4)$$
$$\rightarrow f(x) = -3x(x - 2)^2$$
Thus, the linear factors are x and $x - 2$.

---

36. **Answer** (**B**)

Using the properties of exponential.

From the properties of exponential;
$$-\frac{24x^5y^7}{(-2x^2y^3)^2} = -\frac{24x^5y^7}{4x^4y^6} = -\frac{24}{4}\frac{x^5}{x^4}\frac{y^7}{y^6} = -6xy$$

Thus, the equivalent expression is $-6xy$.

---

37. Answer (**G**)

For all real x, $\left(\sqrt{x}\right)^2 = |x|$.

Subtract 7 from both sides and then divide both sides by -1;
$$-\sqrt{2x} + 7 = -1 \;\;\rightarrow\;\; -\sqrt{2x} = -1 - 7 \;\;\rightarrow\;\; -\sqrt{2x} = -8$$
$$\rightarrow\;\; \sqrt{2x} = -8 \times (-1) \;\;\rightarrow\;\; \sqrt{2x} = 8$$
Take square on both sides;
$$\left(\sqrt{2x}\right)^2 = 8^2 \;\;\rightarrow\;\; 2x = 64$$
Divide both sides by 2;
$$x = \frac{64}{2} = 32$$

Thus, the value of x is 32.

38. Answer (**J**)

Using the concept of composition of function.

Expressing $f\big(g(x)\big)$ by substitute $g(x)$ for x;
$$f\big(g(x)\big) = 3g(x) - 2 = 3(2x + p) - 2 \;\rightarrow f\big(g(x)\big) = 6x + 3p - 2$$
Expressing $g\big(f(x)\big)$ by substitute $f(x)$ for x;
$$g\big(f(x)\big) = 2f(x) + p = 2(3x - 2) + p \;\;\rightarrow\;\; g\big(f(x)\big) = 6x - 4 + p$$
Because $f\big(g(x)\big) = g\big(f(x)\big)$,
$$6x + 3p - 2 = 6x - 4 + p \;\;\rightarrow\;\; 3p - 2 = -4 + p \;\;\rightarrow\;\; 2p = -2$$

Thus, the value of p is -1.

39. Answer (**B**)

A horizontal asymptote is $y = \frac{a}{c}$.

A horizontal asymptote is $y = \frac{a}{c}$ for $y = \frac{ax + b}{cx + d}$.

So, horizontal asymptote is
$$y = \frac{1}{2} \text{ for } y = \frac{x - p}{2x + q}$$

Thus, the horizontal asymptote is $y = \frac{1}{2}$.

40. Answer (**C**)

Rearrange the data.

Rearrange the data;
$$120, 140, 150, 180, 240, 280, 320, 320, 360$$

Thus, the correct answer is **C**.

41. Answer (**G**)

The median is the middle number.

Rearrange the data;
$$120, 140, 150, 180, 240, 280, 320, 320, 360$$

Thus, the middle price is 5th number; 240.

42. Answer (**D**)

$210 is a discount price.

The relation between prices and discount rate is;
$$discount\ price = original\ price \times (1 - discount\ rate)$$
Let P be original price;
$$210 = P \times (1 - 0.25) \;\;\rightarrow\;\; 210 = 0.75P$$
Divide both side by 0.75;
$$0.75P = 210 \;\;\rightarrow\;\; P = \frac{210}{0.75} = 280$$

Thus, the original price is $280.

43. Answer (**H**)

The mean of n data is the sum of the data divided by n.

The mean of the data of original prices is;
$$\frac{(\$360, + \$240 + \cdots + \$140)}{9} = \frac{\$2110}{9}$$
Adding 3 additional prices;
$$\frac{\$2110}{9} = \frac{\$2110 + A + B + C}{9 + 3} = \frac{\$2,110 + A + B + C}{12}$$
Thus, the correct answer is **H**.

44. Answer (**D**)

Take square on both sides.

Substitute 16 for b and then take square on both sides;
$$\sqrt{a} = 2b \;\;\rightarrow\;\; \sqrt{a} = 2 \times 16 \;\;\rightarrow\;\; \sqrt{a} = 32 \;\;\rightarrow\;\; (\sqrt{a})^2 = 32^2 = 1,024$$

Thus, the value of a is 1,024.

45. Answer (**J**)

Negative numbers are also data.

The mean of the temperature is;
$$\frac{75 + 4 + (-5) + (-50) + (-10)}{5} = \frac{14}{5} = 2.8°C$$

Thus, the mean temperature is 2.8°C.

46. Answer (**C**)

Finding the common ratio.

The common ratio is; $\frac{12}{8} = \frac{18}{12} = \frac{3}{2}$ so, from the formula of geometric sequence,
$$a_n = a_1 r^{n-1} \;\;\rightarrow\;\; a_5 = 8\left(\frac{3}{2}\right)^{5-1} = 40.5$$

Thus, the 5th term is 40.5.

47. Answer (**H**)

Using the Pythagorean theorem.

'due south' and 'due west' means that
ΔHSW is a right triangle.
So, using the Pythagorean theorem;
$$\overline{HW}^2 = \overline{HS}^2 + \overline{SW}^2$$
$$\rightarrow\;\; \overline{HW} = \sqrt{\overline{HS}^2 + \overline{SW}^2} = \sqrt{12^2 + 5^2} = \sqrt{169} = 13$$
Thus, the distance is 13.0 kilometers.

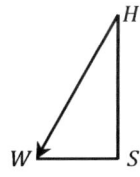

48. Answer (**B**)

The sculpture is a right triangle.

From the formula of triangle area;
$$area = \frac{1}{2} \times base \times height = \frac{1}{2} \times 4 \times 7 = 14$$

Thus, the area is $14\ ft^2$.

49. Answer **(G)**

7% is 0.07.

The total price of these materials is
$$24.5 + 24.5 \times 0.07 + 40 \times (1.2 + 1.2 \times 0.07) + 2 \times (6 + 6 \times 0.07)$$
$$= 90.415$$

Thus, the total cost is $90.415 \approx $90.42.

50. Answer **(C)**

Using the formula of distance.

Let (x, y) be the coordinate of the LED Lighting;
the distance from $(0, 0)$ is $d^2 = (x - 0)^2 + (y - 0)^2 = x^2 + y^2$,
the distance from $(0, 4)$ is $d^2 = (x - 0)^2 + (y - 4)^2 = x^2 + (y - 4)^2$,
the distance from $(7, 0)$ is $d^2 = (x - 7)^2 + (y - 0)^2 = (x - 7)^2 + y^2$.
So,
$$x^2 + (y - 4)^2 = x^2 + y^2 \quad \rightarrow \quad x^2 + y^2 - 8y + 16 = x^2 + y^2$$
$$\rightarrow \quad -8y + 16 = 0 \quad \rightarrow \quad -8y = -16 \quad \rightarrow \quad y = 2$$
And,
$$(x - 7)^2 + y^2 = x^2 + y^2 \quad \rightarrow \quad x^2 - 14x + 49 + y^2 = x^2 + y^2$$
$$\rightarrow \quad -14x + 49 = 0 \quad \rightarrow \quad -14x = -49 \quad \rightarrow \quad x = \frac{7}{2} = 3.5$$

Thus, the coordinate is $(3.5, \ 2)$.

51. Answer **(H)**

Using the Pythagorean theorem.

The length of the hypotenuse, x, of the sculpture is;
$$x^2 = 4^2 + 7^2 \quad \rightarrow \quad x = \sqrt{4^2 + 7^2} = \sqrt{65}$$
Thus, the perimeter is $4 + 7 + \sqrt{65} = 11 + \sqrt{65} \approx 19.0622 \ldots \approx 19.1$.

52. Answer **(C)**

Using the formula of the midpoint.

From the formula of the midpoint;
$$M = \left(\frac{x_1 + x_2}{2}, \frac{y_1 + y_2}{2} \right) = \left(\frac{3 + 7}{2}, \frac{6 + 8}{2} \right) = (5, 7)$$

Thus, the correct answer is **C**.

53. Answer **(C)**

The password is KAY******.

The 3 capital letters are K,A, Y is 1 way so, the number of ways of 6 digits is calculated by counting principle;
$$10 \times 10 \times 10 \times 10 \times 10 \times 10 = 10^6.$$
Therefore, the possible passwords are $1 \times 10^6 = 10^6$

Thus, the correct answer is **C**.

54. Answer **(C)**

Using the trigonometric ratio.

Using the trigonometric ratio;
$$\sin 40° = \frac{O}{H} = \frac{\overline{QT}}{12} \quad \rightarrow \quad \overline{QT} = 12 \times \sin 40° \approx 7.71345 \ldots \approx 7.71$$
$$\cos 40° = \frac{A}{H} = \frac{\overline{ST}}{12} \quad \rightarrow \quad \overline{ST} = 12 \times \cos 40° \approx 9.19253 \ldots \approx 9.19$$
So, the area of $\triangle PQS$ is;
$$area = \frac{1}{2} \times base \times height = \frac{1}{2} \times (\overline{PT} + \overline{TS}) \times \overline{QT}$$
$$= \frac{1}{2} \times (4 + 9.19) \times 7.71 = 50.84745 \approx 50.8$$

Thus, the correct answer is **C**.

55. Answer **(H)**

SOH.

Using the trigonometric ratio;
$$\sin P = \frac{O}{H} = \frac{\overline{QT}}{\overline{PQ}}$$

Thus, the correct answer is **H**.

56. Answer **(E)**

Using the trigonometric ratio.

Let x be the height of the tree and using the trigonometric ratio;
$$\tan 50° = \frac{O}{A} = \frac{x}{35} \quad \rightarrow \quad x = 35 \times \tan 50° \approx 41.71137 \ldots.$$

Thus, the height of the tree is 41.7 feet.

57. Answer **(K)**

360° is 2π radians.

The area of a sector is;
$$sector = circle\ area \times \frac{central\ angle}{2\pi (= 360°)} = \pi r^2 \times \frac{\angle POQ}{2\pi}$$
Using the inverse trigonometric function;
$$\angle POQ = \sin^{-1} \left(\frac{\overline{PR}}{\overline{OP}} \right) = \sin^{-1} \left(\frac{7}{8} \right)$$
So,
$$sector = \pi r^2 \times \frac{\angle POQ}{2\pi} = \pi (8^2) \times \frac{\sin^{-1} \left(\frac{7}{8} \right)}{2\pi} = 32 \sin^{-1} \left(\frac{7}{8} \right)$$

Thus. the correct answer is **K**.

58. Answer **(D)**

$\triangle PQR$ and $\triangle PSR$ are combined to form $\square PQRS$.

In $\square PQRS$, the sum of interior angles is 360°, so
$$90° + 108° + 73° + 29° + \theta + \alpha = 360° \quad \rightarrow \quad 300° + \theta + \alpha = 360°$$
$$\rightarrow \quad \theta + \alpha = 60°$$
Thus,
$$\sin(\theta + \alpha) = \sin 60° = \frac{\sqrt{3}}{2}.$$

59. Answer **(H)**

Finding central angle of each sector.

The circle is divided into 5 sectors;
$$\frac{360°}{5} = 72°$$
Thus, the correct answer is **H**.

60. Answer **(D)**

Multiplication First.

Operating scalar multiplication and then adding;
$$(-2) \begin{bmatrix} 4 & -1 \\ -3 & -5 \end{bmatrix} + 3 \begin{bmatrix} 2 & -2 \\ 0 & 6 \end{bmatrix} = \begin{bmatrix} -8 & 2 \\ 6 & 10 \end{bmatrix} + \begin{bmatrix} 6 & -6 \\ 0 & 18 \end{bmatrix} = \begin{bmatrix} -2 & -4 \\ 6 & 28 \end{bmatrix}$$

Thus, the correct answer is **D**.

Reformed Past Paper ACT MATH TEST 06

60 Questions – 60 Minutes

DIRECTIONS:
Solve each problem, choose the correct answer, and then fill in the corresponding oval on your answer in the grid on the answer sheet.

Do not linger over problems that take too much time. ~~as many as you can; then return to the others in the time you have left for the test.~~

You are permitted to use a calculator on this test.

Note: Unless otherwise stated, all of the following should be assumed.

1. ~~Figures~~ .... are drawn to scale unless ~~otherwise indicated.~~

2. All figures lie in a plane unless otherwise indicated.

3. All variables and expressions used represent real numbers unless otherwise indicated.

01.

A supercomputer is a computer with a high level of computing performance compared to a general-purpose computer. If a certain supercomputer performs 1.62×10^{12} calculations during 1 hour, then what is the calculation speed(calculations per second) of the supercomputer ?

F. 3.5×10^{12}

G. 1.62×10^{11}

H. 1.62×10^{10}

J. 4.5×10^{9}

K. 4.5×10^{8}

02.

If k and $\dfrac{5k}{3}$ are integers, which of the following statements about k must be **true** ?

A.   3 is factor k

B. k is a positive even number

C. k is an odd number

D.   15 is multiple of k

E. k is a prime number.

03.

In figure below, all of the small triangles are equal in area and the area of the large triangle is $\dfrac{1}{4}$. Which of the following expression represents the area of the shaded region ?

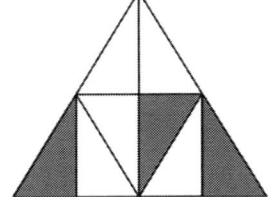

F. $\dfrac{1}{4} \times \dfrac{3}{8}$

G. $\dfrac{1}{4} \times 3$

H. $\dfrac{1}{4} \times \dfrac{1}{8}$

J. $\dfrac{1}{8} \times 3$

K. $\dfrac{3}{4} \times \dfrac{3}{8}$

04.

If $A = x - 4$ and $B = x - 5$, then what is the value of $A - B$?

A. -9

B. -1

C. 1

D. $2x$

E. $2x - 9$

05.

Circles with centers $A, B, C,$ and D, respectively, are mutually tangent, as shown below, and have radii of lengths $a, b, c,$ and d, respectively. The length of $\overline{AB}$ is 15cm, $\overline{BC}$ is 17cm, $\overline{CD}$ is 16cm, and $\overline{AD}$ is 14cm.

What is the sum of radii of four circles?

F. 29

G. 30

H. 31

J. 32

K. 33

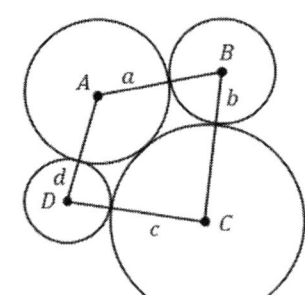

06.

If the width of a rectangle with area 108 square inches is 6 inches, then what is the perimeter of rectangle, in inches ?

A. 24

B. 36

C. 40

D. 48

E. 52

07.

For $\overleftrightarrow{XZ}$ shown above, Y lies on $\overline{XZ}$, the length of $\overline{XY}$ is 6 *inches*, and the length of $\overline{YZ}$ is 8 *inches*. What is the distance between X and the midpoint of $\overline{YZ}$?

F. 7

G. 8

H. 9

J. 10

K. 11

08.

The table below shows the income earned during 3 months from selling tickets in an art museum. Each month was earned the same amount for each ticket sold.

Month	Number of ticket sold	Income earned
January	2,357	$ 28,873.25
February	2,016	$ 24,696.00
March	3,105	$ 38,036.25

In April, the museum earned that same amount for each ticket sold, for an income earned of $ 39,702.25 from selling tickets. How many tickets did the museum sell?

A. 3,124

B. 3,412

C. 3,142

D. 3,241

E. 3,421

09.

For the 4 o'clock hour on Isabella's father clock, the bell is struck 4 times. For the 5 o'clock, the bell is struck 5 times. For every hour, 3 second elapse between consecutive strikes of the bell. If it took 21 seconds between the first and last, what time is it?

A. 9

B. 8

C. 7

D. 6

E. 5

10.

If $\dfrac{5x}{4} + 12 = 7$, then what is the value of x ?

A. 1

B. -2

C. 3

D. -4

E. 5

11.

If a function h is defined as $h(a) = 2a^2 - 3a$, what is the value of $h(-2)$?

F. -20

G. -15

H. 2

J. 14

K. 22

12.

The formula below is a method of measuring the total cholesterol in your blood to see if you are at risk for heart disease.

The formula is $Total\ cholesterol = L + H + \dfrac{T}{5}$ where L is the concentration of low density lipoproteins in mg per deciliter, H is the concentration of high density lipoproteins in mg per deciliter and T is the concentration of triglycerides in mg per deciliter. In John's blood, the amount of high density lipoproteins is 50 mg/dL, triglycerides is 130 mg/dL, and total cholesterols is 151 mg/dL. According to the formula, which of the following value is the concentration of low density lipoprotein in mg/dL ?

A. 65

B. 70

C. 75

D. 80

E. 85

13.

The line $x + 2y = 10$ and the line $3x - 2y = 6$ intersect at $(4, 3)$. The region $\square OABC$ is bounded by these two lines, the x-axis, and y-axis. What is the area of the region $\square OABC$?

F. 11

G. 12

H. 13

J. 14

K. 15

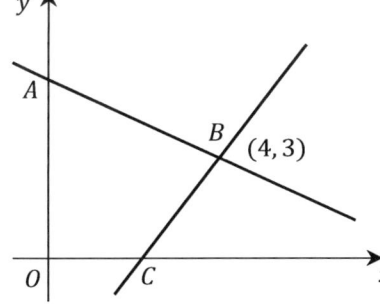

14.

If a line given by the equation is $-2x - 5y = 7$, what is the slope of the line ?

A. $-\dfrac{2}{5}$

B. $\dfrac{2}{5}$

C. -2

D. 2

E. $-\dfrac{7}{5}$

15.

The table below gives the dry weights at sowing and at 2 month for 4 varieties of soybeans. A researcher models these dry weights as a linear function where the dry weight at 2 months is determined by the dry weight at sowing. Which of the following models could be best ?

Variety	Dry weight at sowing (s grams)	Dry weight at 2 months (w grams)
A	0.3	15.2
B	0.7	34.8
C	0.5	25.9
D	0.9	45.4

F. $w = 50s - 13$

G. $w = 5s + 21$

H. $w = 50s$

J. $w = 500s$

K. $w = 500s - 129$

16.

The shaded region in the standard (x, y) coordinate plane below is bounded by a line and a line. Which of the following inequalities are the solution set of the shaded region and its boundary lines ?

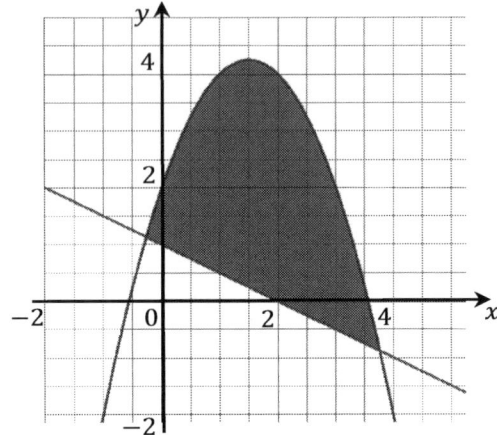

A. $\begin{cases} y < -x^2 + 3x + 2 \\ y > -\dfrac{1}{2}x + 1 \end{cases}$

B. $\begin{cases} y \geq -x^2 + 3x + 2 \\ y \leq -\dfrac{1}{2}x + 1 \end{cases}$

C. $\begin{cases} y \leq -x^2 + 3x + 2 \\ y \geq -\dfrac{1}{2}x + 1 \end{cases}$

D. $\begin{cases} y \leq x^2 - 3x - 2 \\ y \geq \dfrac{1}{2}x - 1 \end{cases}$

E. $\begin{cases} y \geq x^2 - 3x - 2 \\ y \leq \dfrac{1}{2}x - 1 \end{cases}$

Use the following information to answer questions 17 - 19.

The table below shows the number of apples, prunes, and oranges required to make 100 of each of 3 types of fruit cookies sold at Fresh Bakery. Let a represent the price of 1 apple, p the price of 1 prune, and o the price of 1 orange. All prices are in dollars.

Type of cookie	Numbers of apple	Numbers of prune	Numbers of orange
Bargar	78	63	52
Daldal	75	82	66
Macci	42	72	88

17.

How many numbers of apples are required to make 250 daldal cookies?

A. 182

B. 187.5

C. 192

D. 198.5

E. 203

18.

The bakery has 189 apples, 252 prunes, and 352 oranges in stock. What is the maximum number of Macci cookies the bakery could make from the fruits in stock?

A. 200

B. 300

C. 350

D. 400

E. 450

19.

Which of the following expressions gives the price of the apples, prunes, and oranges required to make 100 bargar cookies and 100 daldal cookies?

F. $153a + 145p + 118o$

G. $\dfrac{153}{a} + \dfrac{145}{p} + \dfrac{118}{o}$

H. $\dfrac{a}{153} + \dfrac{p}{145} + \dfrac{o}{118}$

J. $153a^2 + 145p^2 + 118o^2$

K. $(153 + 145 + 118)(a + p + o)$

20.

Which of the following statements must be true, when $|a| = -a$?

A. $a \geq 0$

B. $a < 0$

C. $a \leq 0$

D. $a > 0$

E. $a \neq 0$

21.

Sarah earns her regular salary of $8.50 per hour for the first 36 hours of work in a week. For each hour over 36 hours of work in a week, Sarah is paid $10.25 per hour. Last week Sarah earned $439.25. How many hours did Sarah work last week?

F. 49

G. 50

H. 51

J. 52

K. 53

22.

In a plane, the distinct line segments $\overline{AB}$ and $\overline{CD}$ intersect at a point E, where E is between A and B, and between C and D. If the measure of $\angle BED$ is 62°, then what is the measure of $\angle AED$?

A. 62°

B. $(90 + 62)°$

C. $2 \times 62°$

D. $(180 - 62)°$

E. $(180 + 62)°$

23.

As shown in the figure below, the two lines l and m are intersected by a transversal t. If the following statements are true, which could **not** always be used to prove that the two lines l and m are parallel?

A. $a = e$

B. $c = f$

C. $b = g$

D. $f = g$

E. $d = h$

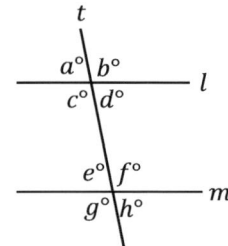

24.

As shown in the figure below, two right triangle ΔOAB and ΔOPQ have sides that are given in centimeters. What is the length, in centimeters, of $\overline{OQ}$?

F. 6

G. 8

H. 9

J. 10

K. 12

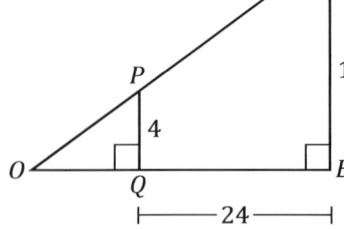

25.

As shown in the figure below, a point O is the center of the circle, $\overline{AC}$ is a diameter, a point B lies on the circumference, a point P is outside the circle, and $\overrightarrow{PD}$ is tangent to the circle at a point D. Which of the following minor arcs or angles has the least degree measure ?

A. arc $\overarc{CD}$

B. arc $\overarc{AD}$

C. $\angle AOD$

D. $\angle PDO$

E. Could not determined from the given information

26.

The side lengths of the flat, trapezoidal backyard of a house are given in the figure below. Miny will lay the entire backyard with artificial grass, the artificial grass that has a price of $32 per box and is sold only by the full box. Each box of artificial grass lays an area of 15 square feet. What is the total price of the artificial grass that Miny needs to buy?

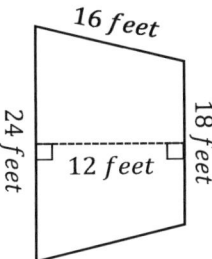

F. $512

G. $544

H. $567

J. $602

K. $632

27.

As shown in the figure below, the vertices B and C of $\triangle BCD$ lie on a line segment $\overline{AE}$, the measure of $\angle ABC$ is 123°, and the measure of $\angle CDE$ is 108°. What is the measure of $\angle BCD$?

A. 81°

B. 72°

C. 57°

D. 51°

E. 42°

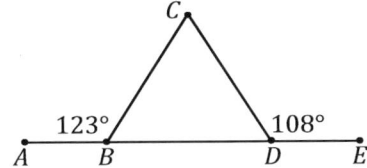

28.

The two legs of a right triangle $\triangle ABC$ are $\overline{AC}$ and $\overline{BC}$. Which of the following statements should be **true** $\triangle ABC$?

F. $m(\overline{AB}) = m(\overline{AC}) + m(\overline{BC})$

G. $m(\overline{AC}) \neq m(\overline{BC})$

H. $\overline{AB} \cong \overline{AC}$

J. The sum of $\angle A$ and $\angle B$ is less than 90°

K. The measure of $\angle C$ is 90°

29.

In $\triangle PQR$, the sum of the measures of $\angle P$ and $\angle Q$ is 78°. What is the measure of $\angle R$?

A. 72°

B. 82°

C. 92°

D. 102°

E. 112°

30.

In the figure below, the dimensions of the triangle are in centimeters. What is the area, in square centimeters, of the triangle?

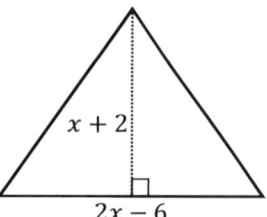

A. $x^2 + 6$

B. $2x^2 - 12$

C. $x^2 - x - 6$

D. $2x^2 - 2x + 12$

E. $2x^2 - 2x - 12$

31.

If $x = 2$ is one solution of a quadratic equation $x^2 + px - 16 = 0$, what is the other solution?

F. -10

G. -8

H. -4

J. 4

K. 8

32.

Which of the following expressions is a linear factor of the polynomial $x^2 + x - 42$?

F. $x + 3$

G. $x - 3$

H. $x - 7$

J. $x + 6$

K. $x + 7$

33.

As shown in the figure below, the graph of $f(x)$, dashed line, and $g(x)$, solid line, are shown in the standard (x, y) coordinate plane. Which of the following expressions represents $g(x)$ in term of $f(x)$?

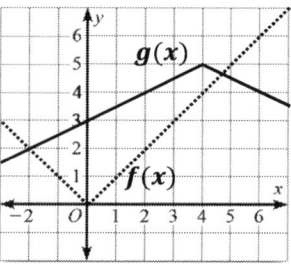

A. $-2f(x + 4) + 5$

B. $-2f(x - 4) + 5$

C. $2f(x - 4) + 5$

D. $-\dfrac{1}{2}f(x + 4) + 5$

E. $-\dfrac{1}{2}f(x - 4) + 5$

34.

As shown in the figure below, a point $(5, 3)$ and a line $x = 2$ are graphed in the standard (x, y) coordinate plane. What are the coordinates of the point's image after the point has been reflected on the line?

F. $(2, 3)$

G. $(-2, 3)$

H. $(-1, 3)$

J. $(-2, 5)$

K. $(3, 5)$

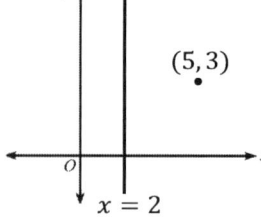

35.

Which of the following polynomial equations has solutions −3 and 2?

A. $(x-3)(x+2)^2 = 0$

B. $(x+3)^2(x-2) = 0$

C. $(x-3)^2(x+2) = 0$

D. $(x+1)^2(x-6) = 0$

E. $(x+1)(x-6)^2 = 0$

36.

Which of the following expressions is equivalent to $\dfrac{\left(\dfrac{x^9}{x^3}\right)}{\left(\dfrac{x^{15}}{x^5}\right)}$, for all positive real numbers x ?

F. $\dfrac{1}{x^4}$

G. $\dfrac{1}{x^3}$

H. 1

J. x^3

K. x^4

37.

What is the solution of the equation $2^{x+6} = 4^{x-1}$?

F. 10

G. 8

H. 6

J. 4

K. 2

38.

A fair colored cube has six sides; one side is white, two sides are black, and three sides are red. A fair coin has two sides; one side is head and another side is tail. The cube and the coin are each tossed once. What is the probability that the side facing up on the cube is black and the side facing up on the coin is head?

A. $\dfrac{1}{12}$

B. $\dfrac{1}{6}$

C. $\dfrac{1}{4}$

D. $\dfrac{1}{3}$

E. $\dfrac{1}{2}$

39.

A school surveyed its students to find the blood type of its 250 students. Each student has only one type of blood. The results of the survey are given in the bar graph below.
When one student from this survey is randomly selected , what is the probability that this student has either Type AB or Type O blood?

A. $\dfrac{60}{250}$

B. $\dfrac{103}{250}$

C. $\dfrac{129}{250}$

D. $\dfrac{238}{250}$

E. $\dfrac{237}{250}$

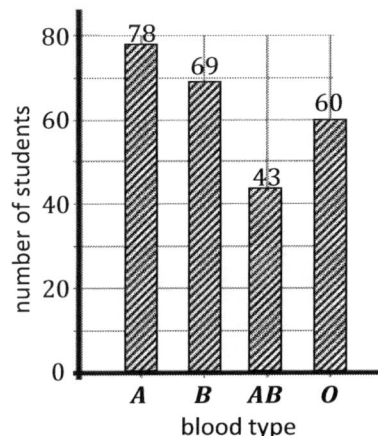

Use the following information to answer questions 40 - 42.

An urban agriculture program is currently offering a special rate to citizens who sign contracts for 5 years or more. According to this special rate, the first year's rent is $10, and for each year after the first year, citizens pay the regular annually rental rate. The table below shows the leased land unit size available and the regular annually rental rate. Assume that the cultivation conditions of all the lands are the same.

Land type	Land dimensions, in yards	Regular annually rental rate
1	2 × 3	$50
2	3 × 4	$90
3	4 × 5	$120
4	5 × 6	$210

40.

Conrad will sign a contract to rent a land type 2 for 6 years at the current special rate. The amount Conrad will pay for 6 years at the current special rate represents what percent decrease from the regular rental rate for 6 years?

A. 14.81%

B. 13.26%

C. 12.67%

D. 11.11%

E. 10.98%

41.

Land type 4 could be subdivided to form other land types. What is the greatest number of land type 1s that could be formed from a single land type 4?

A. 4

B. 5

C. 6

D. 7

E. 8

42.

Edgar, the manger of urban agriculture program, is considering making new types that have land dimensions larger than land type 4. He will use the land area to determine the adjustment of partitions of agricultural land. For this calculation, Edgar will use the same relationship between the land type number and the respective land area for types 1 through 4. Which of the following expressions is the land area, in square yards, of a Land Type n ?

F. $3n + 3$

G. $2n + 4$

H. $n^2 + 2$

J. $n^2 + 3n$

K. $n^2 + 3n + 2$

43.

A box contains 6 white balls, 4 black balls, and 8 blue balls. How many additional black balls must be added to the 18 balls in the box so that the probability of randomly drawing a black ball is $\frac{1}{3}$?

A. 1

B. 2

C. 3

D. 4

E. 5

44.

As shown the figure below, Mr. Sylvester made a bar graph of the 20 scores on the final science project.

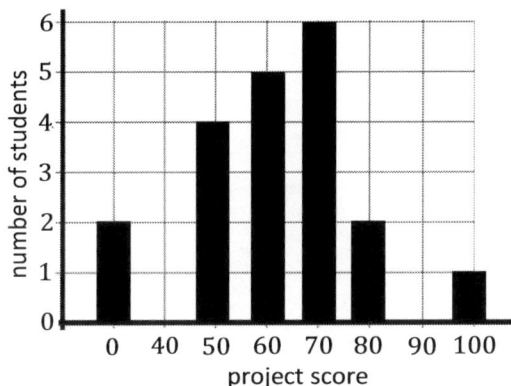

What is the mean of the 20 scores?

F. 77.00

G. 78.25

H. 79.46

J. 83.74

K. 85.56

45.

Doris will be framing a picture and choose frame types, colors, and material. Doris will choose 1 of the 8 frame types, 1 of the 10 colors, and 1 of the 3 materials. How many different ways can she frame the picture?

A. 60

B. 80

C. 120

D. 240

E. 480

46.

What is the sum of the geometric series?

$$\sum_{i=1}^{6} 6(-2)^{i-1}$$

A. 482

B. −510

C. −604

D. 628

E. −720

47.

In the standard (x,y) coordinate plane below, a line passes through the origin $(0,0)$ and a point $(2,3)$. If the acute angle between the line and the x-axis has measures θ, then what is the value of θ?

F. $\tan^{-1}\left(\frac{3}{2}\right)$

G. $\tan^{-1}\left(\frac{2}{3}\right)$

H. $\tan^{-1}\left(\frac{3}{\sqrt{13}}\right)$

J. $\tan^{-1}\left(\frac{3}{5}\right)$

K. $\tan^{-1}\left(\frac{2}{5}\right)$

48.

As shown below, a regular pyramid with a square base is shown in the figure. The slant height is $\sqrt{31}$ inches and the length of the base edge is 4 inches. What is the total length, in inches, of all 8 edges of the pyramid?

A. 36

B. 40

C. $16 + 4\sqrt{31}$

D. $16 + 12\sqrt{7}$

E. $16 + 16\sqrt{3}$

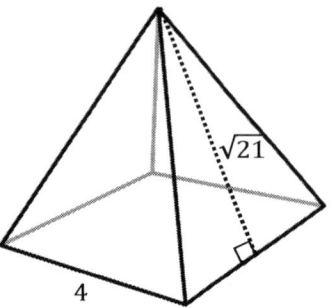

49.

In the standard (x, y) coordinate plane, a circle intersects the y-axis at $(0, 5)$ and $(0, 1)$. The radius of the circle is $\sqrt{20}$ coordinate units. Which of the following coordinates could be the center of the circle?

F. (3, 4) or (−4, 3)

G. (4, 3) or (−4, 3)

H. (3, −4) or (4, 3)

J. (4, 3) only

K. (3, −4) only

50.

Suppose that each side of a square is 4 coordinate units long and in the standard (x, y) coordinate plane, one vertex of the square is $(2, 3)$. Which of the following coordinates can be another vertex of the square ?

A. $(5, 3)$

B. $(6, 3)$

C. $(7, 4)$

D. $(3, 5)$

E. $(3, 6)$

Use the following information to answer questions 51 - 52.

As shown below, rectangle $ABCD$ is a soccer field and point O is midpoint of $\overline{AD}$.

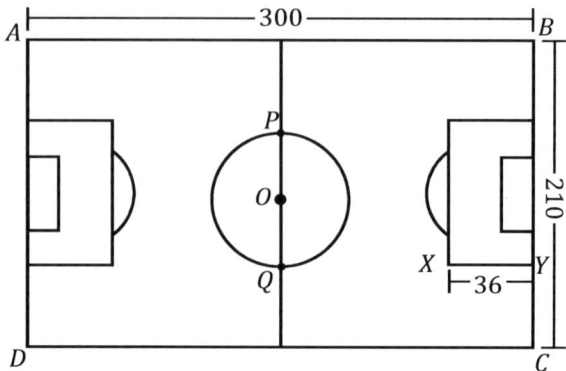

51.

If the diameter of the center circle, O, one third of the length of $\overline{BC}$, what is the length of arc $\widehat{PQ}$?

A. 17.5π

B. 30π

C. 35π

D. 70π

E. 140π

52.

Assume that the figure will be in the standard (x, y) coordinate plane, point O is at the origin, and $\overline{XY}$ is parallel to the x-axis. What is the x-coordinate of point X ?

F. 96

G. 108

H. 114

J. 226

K. 264

53.

The sentences below describe 3 types of phenomena as functions of time.

  I. The height of throwing a ball vertically upwards.
  II. The distance of a bus travels while moving at a constant speed.
  III. The distance of an object whose speed is increased by applying a constant force.

In the figure below, graph $A, B,$ and C each represent one of these functions. For all graphs, the y-axis represents distance or height and x-axis represents time. Which is of which function?

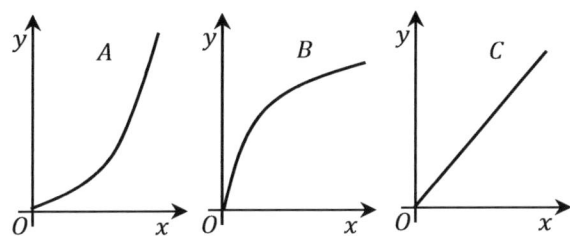

	Sentence I	Sentence II	Sentence II
A.	A	C	B
B.	C	B	A
C.	B	C	A
D.	A	B	C
E.	A	C	B

54.

Assume an angle with measure α at right triangle, $\cos\alpha = \frac{21}{29}$ and $\tan\alpha = \frac{20}{21}$. What is the value of $\sin\alpha$?

F. $\dfrac{\sqrt{70}}{20}$

G. $\dfrac{\sqrt{70}}{21}$

H. $\dfrac{\sqrt{70}}{29}$

J. $\dfrac{20}{29}$

K. $\dfrac{21}{20}$

55.

On the map below, Beatrice is standing on a sailing boat at point B on the north side of the island. As measured by line of sight, she is 60 miles from a light house at W, and 100 miles from another light house at E. Suppose that Beatrice, B, west light house, W, and east light house, E, are all same elevation, and the measure of $\angle W$ is 32°. What is the equation for the measure of $\angle E$?

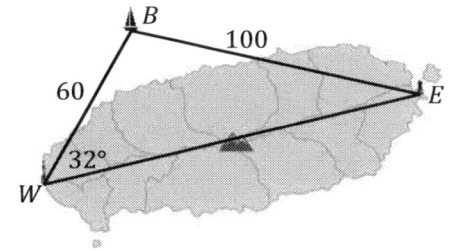

F. $\dfrac{\sin E}{160} = \dfrac{\sin 32°}{40}$

G. $\dfrac{\sin E}{60} = \dfrac{\sin 32°}{100}$

H. $\dfrac{\sin E}{100} = \dfrac{\sin 32°}{60}$

J. $\dfrac{\sin E}{\sin 32°} = \dfrac{60}{100}$

K. $\dfrac{\sin E}{60} = \dfrac{\sin 32°}{40}$

56.

Suppose that $\cos^2 x + \cos x = -\frac{1}{4}$, for $0 \le x \le \pi$, what is the value of $\sin x$?

A. $\frac{1}{2}$ only

B. $\frac{1}{2}$ and $-\frac{1}{2}$

C. $\frac{\sqrt{3}}{2}$ only

D. $\frac{\sqrt{3}}{2}$ and $-\frac{\sqrt{3}}{2}$

E. $\frac{\sqrt{15}}{4}$

57.

In the graphs below, the two trigonometric functions $f(x) = a \cos x$ and $g(x) = b \cos(x + c) + d$ are graphed in the standard (x, y) coordinate plane. Suppose that the two functions have the same maximum and minimum values, what is **true** statement about the constants $a, b, c,$ and d?

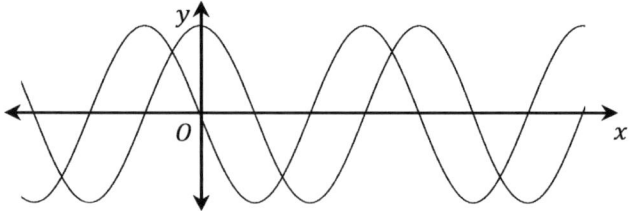

F. $a > b, c = 0$ and $d > 0$

G. $a = b, c < 0$ and $d = 0$

H. $a < b, c < 0$ and $d = 0$

J. $a = b, c > 0$ and $d < 0$

K. $a \ne b, c > 0$ and $d \ne 0$

58.

The lengths of the three sides of an obtuse triangle are 6 inches, 8 inches, and 12 inches. When solved for θ that is the measure of the smallest angle of the triangle, what is the equation for the smallest angle θ?

(Note: sine law,
$$\frac{a}{\sin A} = \frac{b}{\sin B} = \frac{c}{\sin C}$$
cosine law,
$$a^2 = b^2 + c^2 - 2bc \cos A \qquad)$$

A. $8^2 = 6^2 + 12^2 - 2 \times 6 \times 12 \times \cos \theta$

B. $6^2 = 8^2 + 12^2 - 2 \times 8 \times 12 \times \cos \theta$

C. $12^2 = 6^2 + 8^2 - 2 \times 6 \times 8 \times \cos \theta$

D. $\dfrac{6}{\sin \theta} = \dfrac{8}{12}$

E. $\dfrac{6}{\sin \theta} = \dfrac{12}{8}$

59.

Suppose that the side lengths of a right triangle ΔPQR are given in centimeters in the figure below. What is the trigonometric ratio that is equal to $\frac{12}{5}$?

F. $\cos P$

G. $\tan P$

H. $\sin P$

J. $\tan R$

K. $\sin R$

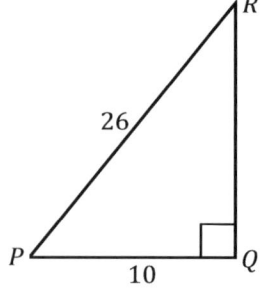

60.

Which of the following augmented matrices expresses the system of linear equations below;

$$-x + 3y = -6$$
$$2x - 7y = 4$$

A. $\begin{bmatrix} -1 & 3 & | & 6 \\ 2 & -7 & | & 4 \end{bmatrix}$

B. $\begin{bmatrix} -1 & 2 & | & 6 \\ 3 & -7 & | & -4 \end{bmatrix}$

C. $\begin{bmatrix} -1 & 3 & | & -6 \\ 2 & -7 & | & 4 \end{bmatrix}$

D. $\begin{bmatrix} -1 & 3 & | & 6 \\ 2 & -7 & | & -4 \end{bmatrix}$

E. $\begin{bmatrix} -1 & 2 & | & -6 \\ 3 & -7 & | & 4 \end{bmatrix}$

BLANK PAGE *by K·DEAN*

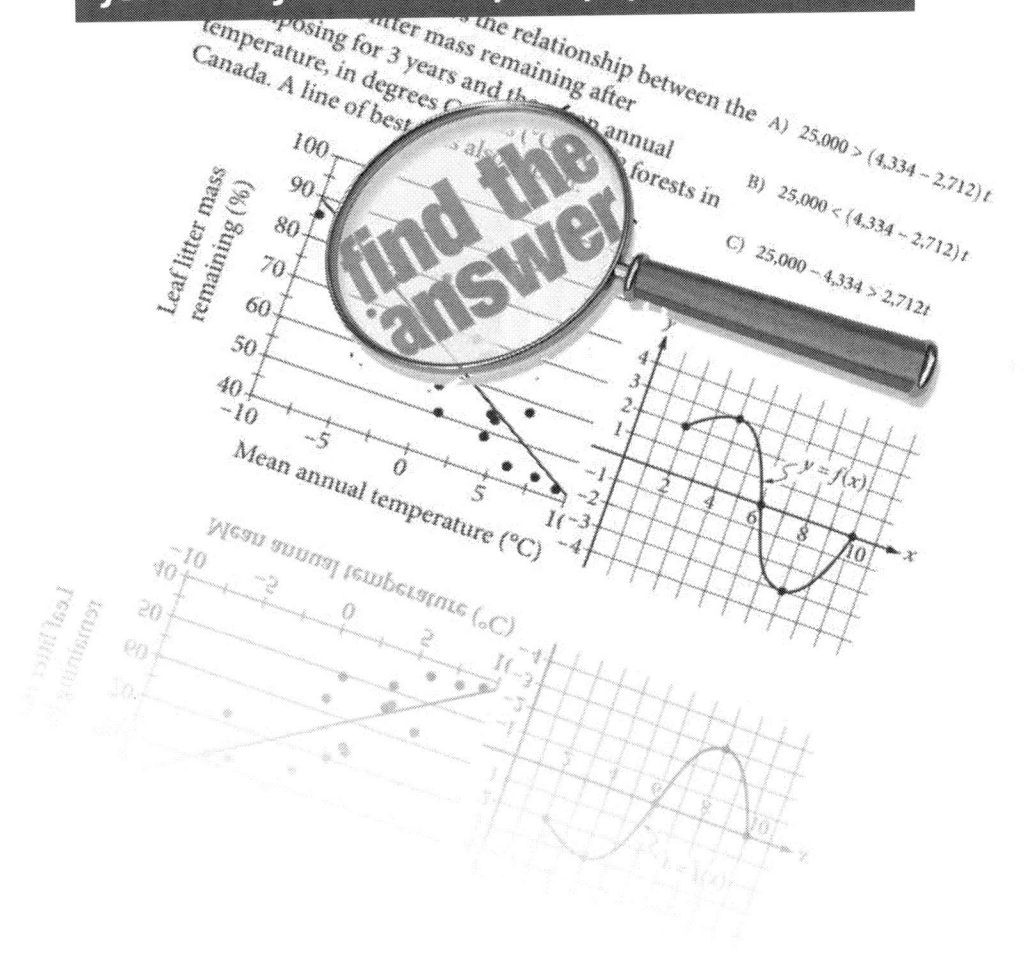

posing for 3 years and the relationship between the
temperature, in degrees C... mass remaining after
Canada. A line of best... annual
... forests in

A) $25{,}000 > (4{,}334 - 2{,}712)\,t$

B) $25{,}000 < (4{,}334 - 2{,}712)\,t$

C) $25{,}000 - 4{,}334 > 2{,}712\,t$

y = f(x)

Obtain Scale Scores from Raw Scores

Scale Score	Raw Score	Scale Score	Raw Score	Scale Score	Raw Score
36	60	24	36-37	12	7
35	58-59	23	34-35	11	5-6
34	57	22	32-33	10	4
33	55-56	21	30-31	9	-
32	54	20	29	8	3
31	52-53	19	27-28	7	-
30	50-51	18	24-26	6	2
29	48-49	17	21-23	5	-
28	45-47	16	17-20	4	1
27	43-44	15	13-16	3	-
26	40-42	14	11-12	2	-
25	38-39	13	8-10	1	0

1. Scoring Key

Key		Question Category	Y/N
01.	K	Number Theory	
02.	A	Number Theory	
03.	F	Number Theory	
04.	C	Expression and Linear Equation	
05.	H	Expression and Linear Equation	
06.	D	Expression and Linear Equation	
07.	J	Expression and Linear Equation	
08.	D	Expression and Linear Equation	
09.	B	Expression and Linear Equation	
10.	D	Expression and Linear Equation	
11.	J	Linear Function inequality	
12.	C	Linear Function inequality	
13.	H	Linear Function inequality	
14.	A	Linear Function inequality	
15.	H	Linear Function inequality	
16.	C	Linear Function inequality	
17.	B	Arithmetic Topic and Ratio	
18.	C	Arithmetic Topic and Ratio	
19.	F	Arithmetic Topic and Ratio	
20.	C	Linear Function inequality	
21.	F	Arithmetic Topic and Ratio	
22.	D	Basic Geometry	
23.	D	Basic Geometry	
24.	G	Basic Geometry	
25.	A	Basic Geometry	
26.	G	Basic Geometry	
27.	D	Basic Geometry	
28.	K	Basic Geometry	
29.	D	Arithmetic Topic and Ratio	
30.	C	Quadratic and Polynomial Function	

Key		Question Category	Y/N
31.	G	Quadratic and Polynomial Function	
32.	K	Quadratic and Polynomial Function	
33.	E	Quadratic and Polynomial Function	
34.	H	Quadratic and Polynomial Function	
35.	B	Quadratic and Polynomial Function	
36.	F	Further Equations and Functions	
37.	G	Further Equations and Functions	
38.	B	Statistics and Probability	
39.	B	Statistics and Probability	
40.	A	Further Equations and Functions	
41.	B	Further Equations and Functions	
42.	K	Further Equations and Functions	
43.	C	Statistics and Probability	
44.	F	Statistics and Probability	
45.	D	Statistics and Probability	
46.	B	Sequence and Series	
47.	F	Analytic Geometry and Conic Section	
48.	A	Analytic Geometry and Conic Section	
49.	G	Analytic Geometry and Conic Section	
50.	B	Analytic Geometry and Conic Section	
51.	C	Analytic Geometry and Conic Section	
52.	H	Analytic Geometry and Conic Section	
53.	C	Analytic Geometry and Conic Section	
54.	J	Trigonometric Functions	
55.	H	Trigonometric Functions	
56.	C	Trigonometric Functions	
57.	G	Trigonometric Functions	
58.	B	Trigonometric Functions	
59.	G	Trigonometric Functions	
60.	C	Intermediate Algebra	

2. Answer Explanations

01. **Answer** (*K*)

The number, which is represented by scientific notation, consists of a integer part and a power part. And speed is the quotient of calculations and time.

Converting to scientific notation;
$$1\ hour = 3600sec = 3.6 \times 10^3 sec$$

Calculating speed;
$$speed = \frac{calculations}{time} = \frac{1.62 \times 10^{12}}{3.6 \times 10^3} = \frac{1.62}{3.6} \times \frac{10^{12}}{10^3} = 0.45 \times 10^9$$
$$= 4.5 \times 10^{-1} \times 10^9 = 4.5 \times 10^8$$

02. **Answer** (*A*)

The integers are the numbers $..., -3, -2, -1, 0, 1, 2, 3, ...$.

In order for $\frac{5k}{3}$ to be an integer, when $5k$ is divided by 3, the remainder is zero. This means that k is multiple of 3 or 3 is factor of k.

03. **Answer** (*F*)

The fractional expression is the quotient of parts and total.

There are 3 shaded triangles. So its fractional expression is;
$$\frac{parts}{total} = \frac{shaded\ triangle}{total} = \frac{3}{8}$$
Thus, the area of shaded region is;
$$\frac{1}{4} \times \frac{3}{8}$$

04. **Answer** (*C*)

$-(a + b)$ *means* $(-1) \times (a + b) = -a - b$.

Substitute $x - 4$ for A and $x - 5$ for B;
$$A - B = (x - 4) - (x - 5)$$
Rewrite the expression;
$$x - 4 - x + 5 = x - x - 4 + 5 = 1$$

05. **Answer** (*H*)

The sum of radii is a+b+c+d.

The sum of the four line segments is;
$$\overline{AB} + \overline{BC} + \overline{CD} + \overline{AD} = 15 + 17 + 16 + 14 = 62,$$
and substituting $a + b$ for $\overline{AB}$, $b + c$ for $\overline{BC}$, $c + d$ for $\overline{CD}$, $a + d$ for $\overline{AD}$;
$$\overline{AB} + \overline{BC} + \overline{CD} + \overline{AD} = 62$$
$$\rightarrow a + b + b + c + c + d + a + d = 62 \rightarrow 2a + 2b + 2c + 2d = 62$$
$$\rightarrow 2(a + b + c + d) = 62$$
Dividing the both sides by 2;
$$a + b + c + d = \frac{62}{2} = 31$$
Thus, the correct answer is *H*.

06. **Answer** (*D*)

The perimeter is twice of the sum of width and length.

The area is the product of width and length and let the length be L ;
$$area = width \times length \rightarrow 108 = 6 \times L$$
Dividing by 6 on both sides;
$$6L = 108 \rightarrow \frac{6L}{6} = \frac{108}{6} \rightarrow L = 18$$
So, the perimeter is;
perimeter$= 2 \times$(width+length) $\rightarrow$ perimeter$= 2 \times (6 + 18) = 48$.
Thus, the perimeter of the rectangle is 48 inches.

07. **Answer** (*J*)

The midpoint is located at half the length of $\overline{YZ}$.

If the midpoint of $\overline{YZ}$ is W, than;

the length of $\overline{YW}$ is 4 inches and the length $\overline{XW}$ is $\overline{XY} + \overline{YW}$.
Thus, $\overline{XW} = \overline{XY} + \overline{YW} = 6 + 4 = 10 inches$.

08. **Answer** (*D*)

The price per ticket is same.

The price per ticket is;
$$\frac{\$28,873.25}{2,357} = \frac{\$24,696.00}{2,016} = \frac{\$38,036.25}{3,105} = \$12.25\ per\ ticket$$
Therefore,
the number of tickets at April is;
$$\frac{\$39,702.25}{\$12.25} = 3,241.$$

09. **Answer** (*B*)

There are three elapsed times at four o'clock and four elapsed times at five o'clock.

If the time is n o'clock, the elapsed time is $(n - 1)$. So, the elapsed time is $3 \times (n - 1)$ seconds.
$$3 \cdot (n - 1) = 21 \rightarrow 3n - 3 = 21$$
Add 3 to both sides;
$$3n - 3 = 21 \rightarrow 3n - 3 + 3 = 21 + 3 \rightarrow 3n = 24$$
Divide by 3 on both sides;
$$3n = 24 \rightarrow \frac{3n}{3} = \frac{24}{3} \rightarrow n = 8$$
Thus, it is 8 o'clock.

10. **Answer** (*D*)

Solve the equation for x by using inverse operation

Subtract 12 from both sides;
$$\frac{5x}{4} + 12 = 7 \rightarrow \frac{5x}{4} + 12 - 12 = 7 - 12 \rightarrow \frac{5x}{4} = -5$$
Multiply by 4 on both sides;
$$\frac{5x}{4} = -5 \rightarrow 4 \times \frac{5x}{4} = -5 \times 4 \rightarrow 5x = -20$$
Divide by 5 on both sides;
$$5x = -20 \rightarrow \frac{5x}{5} = \frac{-20}{5} \rightarrow x = -4$$
Thus, the value of x is -4.

11. **Answer** (*J*)

Substituting -2 for a and then evaluating.

Substituting -2 for a;
$$h(a) = 2a^2 - 3a \rightarrow h(-2) = 2(-2)^2 - 3(-2) \rightarrow h(-2) = 14$$
Thus, the value of $h(-2)$ is 14.

12. **Answer** (*C*)

Substitute each value and then solve the equation.

Substitute 50 for H, 130 for T, and 151 for total cholesterol;
$$Total\ cholesterol = L + H + \frac{T}{5} \rightarrow 151 = L + 50 + \frac{130}{5}$$
$$\rightarrow 151 = L + 76$$
Subtracting 76 from both sides;
$$L + 76 = 151 \rightarrow L + 76 - 76 = 151 - 76 \rightarrow L = 75$$
Thus, the concentration of low density lipoprotein is 75mg/dL.

13. Answer **(H)**

x-intercept is x-value at y=0 and y-intercept is y-value at x=0.

$\overleftrightarrow{AB}$ is $x + 2y = 10$ and its y-intercept is,
substitute 0 for x;
$x + 2y = 10 \rightarrow 0 + 2y = 10 \rightarrow y = 5$
So, A point is $(0, 5)$.
$\overleftrightarrow{BC}$ is $3x - 2y = 6$ and its x-intercept is,
substitute 0 for y;
$3x - 2y = 6 \rightarrow 3x - 2 \cdot 0 = 6 \rightarrow x = 2$
So, C point is $(2, 0)$, and D is $(4, 0)$, E is $(4, 5)$.

$$\text{Area of } \square OABC = \square OAED - \triangle AEB - \triangle BDC$$

Area of $\square OAED = 5 \times 4 = 20$

Area of $\triangle AEB = \frac{1}{2} \times 2 \times 4 = 4$.   Area of $\triangle CBD = \frac{1}{2} \times 2 \times 3 = 3$

Thus $\square OABC = 20 - 4 - 3 = 13$.

14. Answer **(A)**

Convert the equation to the slope intercept form.

Convert the given equation to slope-intercept form by;
  adding $2x$ to both sides;
  $-2x - 5y = 7 \rightarrow -2x - 5y + 2x = 7 + 2x \rightarrow -5y = 7 + 2x$
  dividing both sides by -5;
  $-5y = 2x + 7 \rightarrow \frac{-5y}{-5} = \frac{2x + 7}{-5} \rightarrow y = -\frac{2}{5}x - \frac{7}{5}$

Thus, the slope of the equation is $-\frac{2}{5}$.

15. Answer **(H)**

Let's look at the approximate relationship.

If the dry weights at sowing is input values and the dry weights at 2 months, then we make the relation between the two values, it is,
$\frac{15.2}{0.3} = 50.67, \frac{34.8}{0.7} = 49.71, \frac{25.9}{0.5} = 51.8, \frac{45.4}{0.9} = 50.44$
Approximately, the output values is 50 times the input values.
Thus, the best linear function model is $w = 50s$.

16. Answer **(C)**

The shaded region is above a line and below a parabola.

The y-intercept of the line is 1 and the slope is a negative value.
So, the line equation is $y = -\frac{1}{2}x + 1$. Testing a point $(0, 0)$.
$$y = -\frac{1}{2}x + 1 \rightarrow 0 \cdots -\frac{1}{2} \times 0 + 1 \rightarrow 0 < 1$$
Thus, the linear inequality is;
$$y \geq -\frac{1}{2}x + 1 \leftarrow \because (0,0) \text{ is not solution and solid line}$$

The parabola is a open down parabola so, the quadratic equation is $y = -x^2 + 3x + 2$. Testing a point $(0, 0)$.
$$y = -x^2 + 3x + 2 \rightarrow 0 \cdots -0^2 + 3 \times 0 + 2 \rightarrow 0 < 2$$
Thus, the quadratic inequality is;
$$y \leq -x^2 + 3x + 2 \leftarrow \because (0,0) \text{ is solution and solid line}$$

Therefore, the correct answer is **C**.

17. Answer **(B)**

Using the proportion.

If the number of apples for 250 daldal cookies is n;
$$\frac{75}{100} = \frac{n}{250} \rightarrow 100n = 75 \times 250 \rightarrow n = 187.5$$
Thus, numbers of apple are 187.5.

18. Answer **(C)**

Law of the Minimum states that yield is proportional to the amount of the most limiting factor.

Finding each fruit;
$$apple \rightarrow \frac{189}{42} = 4.5, \quad prune \rightarrow \frac{252}{72} = 3.5, \quad orange \rightarrow \frac{352}{88} = 4$$
So, limiting factor, fruit, is prune and using proportion;
$$\frac{100}{72} = \frac{x}{252} \rightarrow 72x = 100 \times 252 \rightarrow x = 350$$

19. Answer **(F)**

Making algebraic expression and the simplifying.

For 100 bargar cookies;
$$78a + 63p + 52o$$
For 100 daldal cookies;
$$75a + 82p + 66o$$
Thus, the total price is;
$$78a + 63p + 52o + 75a + 82p + 66o$$
$$= 78a + 75a + 63p + 82p + 52o + 66o$$
$$= 153a + 145p + 118o$$

20. Answer **(C)**

Absolute value is never negative.

Absolute value is never negative so, $|a| = -a \geq 0 \rightarrow -a \geq 0$.
Multiplying both sides by -1;
$$-a \geq 0 \rightarrow (-1) \times (-a) \geq (-1) \times 0 \rightarrow a \leq 0$$
The correct answer is **C**.

21. Answer **(F)**

Making a linear equation for over 36 hours working time.

If t is working time over 36 hours, the total earned money is;
$$\$439.25 = \$8.5 \times 36 + \$10.25 \times t \rightarrow 439.25 = 306 + 10.25t$$
Solving for t;
$$10.25t + 306 = 439.25 \rightarrow 10.25t = 133.25 \rightarrow t = 13$$
Thus, the total working time is $36 + t = 36 + 13 = 49$.

22. Answer **(D)**

Let's draw a picture of the situation given in the problem.

$\angle BED$ and $\angle AED$ are a linear pair so, their angle sum is $180°$.
$\angle AED + \angle BED = 180° \rightarrow \angle AED + 62° = 180°$
$\rightarrow \angle AED = (180 - 62)° = 118°$
Thus, the correct answer is **D**.

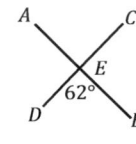

23. Answer **(D)**

Using the angle relationships.

If lines $l \parallel m$ and line t is transversal;
Corresponding angles are same
  $\angle a \cong \angle e, \quad \angle b \cong \angle f, \quad \angle c \cong \angle g, \quad \angle d \cong \angle h$
Alternate interior angles;
  $\angle c \cong \angle f, \quad \angle d \cong \angle e$
Alternate exterior angle;
  $\angle a \cong \angle h, \quad \angle b \cong \angle g$
Thus, the correct answer is **D**.

24. *Answer* **(G)**

Using the property of triangle similarity.

$\angle POQ \cong \angle AOB$ ($\because$ common angle) and $\angle Q = \angle B = 90°$
so, $\triangle OPQ \backsim \triangle OAB$ ($\because$ angle-angle (AA) similarity). Using triangle similarity;
$$\frac{\overline{PQ}}{\overline{AB}} = \frac{\overline{OQ}}{\overline{OB}} = \frac{4}{16} = \frac{1}{4}$$
Let the length of $\overline{OQ}$ be x;
$$\frac{\overline{OQ}}{\overline{OB}} = \frac{x}{x+24} = \frac{1}{4} \quad \rightarrow \quad 4x = x + 24$$
$$\rightarrow \quad 3x = 24 \quad \rightarrow \quad x = 8$$
Thus, the length of $\overline{OQ}$ is 8.

25. *Answer* **(A)**

The central angle could also be expressed in arc length.

Because the point D is tangency, $\angle PDO$ is 90°, $\angle COD$ or arc $\overparen{CD}$ is less than 90°. And $\angle AOD$ or arc $\overparen{AD}$ is greater than 90°. So,
$$\overparen{CD} < \angle PDO < \angle AOD = \overparen{AD}$$
Thus, the least value is $\overparen{CD}$.

26. *Answer* **(G)**

Calculate the number of boxes needed..

The area of the backyard is;
$$area = \frac{1}{2}(b_1 + b_2)h = \frac{1}{2}(18 + 24) \times 12 = 252 \ ft^2$$
The number of boxes that needs to buy is;
$$Nbr\ of\ boxes = area \div area\ per\ box = 252 \div 15 = 16.8$$
So, the number of boxes is 17 and the price of the boxes is;
$$price = unit\ price \times Nbr\ of\ boxes = 32 \times 17 = 544$$
Thus, the total price of the artificial grass is \$544.

27. *Answer* **(D)**

Using linear pair.

Using linear pairs;
$$\angle ABC + \angle CBD = 180° \quad \rightarrow \quad 123° + \angle CBD = 180° \rightarrow \quad \angle CBD = 57°$$
$$\angle CDE + \angle CDB = 180° \quad \rightarrow \quad 108° + \angle CDB = 180° \rightarrow \quad \angle CDB = 72°$$
Using triangle angle sum theorem;
$$\angle BCD + \angle CBD + \angle CDB = 180°$$
$$\rightarrow \quad \angle BCD + 57° + 72° = 180° \quad \rightarrow \quad \angle BCD + 129° = 180°$$
$$\rightarrow \quad \angle BCD = 51°$$
Thus, the measure of angle $\angle BCD$ is 51°.

28. *Answer* **(K)**

Right triangle has exactly 90° angle.

F. $\overline{AB}^2 = \overline{AC}^2 + \overline{BC}^2$
G. If $\triangle ABC$ is an isosceles right,
    it is possible $m(\overline{AC}) = m(\overline{BC})$.
H. $\overline{AB}$ is a hypotenuse so, $m(\overline{AB}) > m(\overline{BC})$.
J. $\angle A + \angle B = 90°$ ($\because \angle A + \angle B + \angle C = 180°$)
K. $\overline{AB}$ is a hypotenuse so, $\angle C = 90°$.

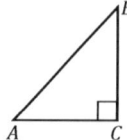

29. *Answer* **(D)**

Using triangle angle sum theorem.

Using triangle angle sum theorem;
$$\angle P + \angle Q + \angle R = 180° \quad \rightarrow \quad 78° + \angle R = 180° \quad \rightarrow \quad \angle R = 102°$$
Thus, the measure of $\angle R$ is 102°.

30. *Answer* **(C)**

Using FOIL pattern.

Using the formula of triangle's area;
$$A = \frac{1}{2} \times b \times h = \frac{1}{2}(2x - 6)(x + 2) = \frac{1}{2}(2x^2 + 4x - 6x - 12)$$
$$= \frac{1}{2}(2x^2 - 2x - 12) = x^2 - x - 6$$
Thus, the area is $x^2 - x - 6$.

31. *Answer* **(G)**

The product of the two roots is -16.

Substitute 2 for x;
$$x^2 + px - 16 = 0 \rightarrow 4 + p(2) - 16 = 0 \rightarrow 2p - 12 = 0 \rightarrow p = 6$$
Rewrite the equation;
$$x^2 + 6x - 16 = 0 \quad \rightarrow \quad (x + 8)(x - 2) = 0$$
So, $x + 8 = 0$ or $x - 2 = 0 \quad \rightarrow \quad x = -8$ or $x = 2$
Or using other method, the product of the two roots is -16 so, the other solution is -8.

Thus, the other solution is -8.

32. *Answer* **(K)**

The product is 42, and the difference is 1.

The product is 42, and the difference is 1. So;
$$x^2 + x - 42 \quad \rightarrow \quad (x + 7)(x - 6)$$
Thus, the linear factors are $x + 7$ and $x - 6$.

33. *Answer* **(E)**

New vertex is parameters of translation.

Compare to $f(x)$, $g(x)$ is reflected, is translated, is compressed vertically.
Let $g(x)$ be $af(x - h) + k$,
the vertex, (0, 0) is moved to (4, 5) so, $h = 4$ and $k = 5$.
$g(x)$ is reflected and compressed vertically so, $a < 0$ and $|a| < 1$.
And a point of $f(x)$, $(1,1)$, is changed to the point of $g(x)$, $(6,4)$, so, $a = -\frac{1}{2}$.

Thus, $g(x) = -\frac{1}{2}(x - 4) + 5$.

34. *Answer* **(H)**

The line is a perpendicular bisector between the point and its image.

If the point $(5,3)$ is A and its image is A',
$x = 2$ is perpendicular bisector of $\overline{AA'}$.
So, $\overline{OA} = \overline{OA'}$, $O = (2,3)$, the coordinates of A' is $(-1,3)$.

Thus, the coordinates is $(-1,3)$.

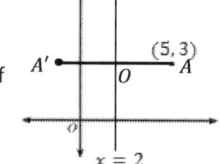

35. *Answer* **(B)**

If x=p is solution (x-p) is a factor.

If the $x = p$ is a x-intercept of a polynomial function graph, then
    $x = p$ is a real solution of the polynomial equation,
    $(x - p)$ is a factor of the polynomial equation, and
    $x = p$ is a zero of function.

So, $x = -3$ and $x = 2$ are solutions of polynomial equation, the factors of the equation are $(x + 3)$ and $(x - 2)$.

Thus, the correct answer is **B**.

36. Answer **(F)**

Using the properties of exponential.

From the properties of exponential;

$$\frac{\left(\frac{x^9}{x^3}\right)}{\left(\frac{x^{15}}{x^5}\right)} = \frac{x^{9-3}}{x^{15-5}} = \frac{x^6}{x^{10}} = x^{6-10} = x^{-4} = \frac{1}{x^4}$$

Thus, the correct answer is **F**.

---

37. Answer **(G)**

The given equation is expressed the same base.

Using $4 = 2^2$;
$$2^{x+6} = 4^{x-1} \rightarrow 2^{x+6} = (2^2)^{x-1} \rightarrow 2^{x+6} = 2^{2x-2}$$
So, $x + 6 = 2x - 2 \rightarrow x + 8 = 2x \rightarrow x = 8$

Thus, the solution of the equation answer is 8.

---

38. Answer **(B)**

The given two events are independent events.

The probability of first event is $\frac{2}{6}$ and the probability of second event is $\frac{1}{2}$. So, the probability is;
$$P = \frac{2}{6} \times \frac{1}{2} = \frac{2}{12} = \frac{1}{6}$$

Thus, the correct answer is **B**.

---

39. Answer **(B)**

"OR" event is "sum".

The number of students either Type AB or Type O blood is $43 + 60 = 103$. So, the probability is;
$$P = \frac{43 + 60}{250} = \frac{103}{250}$$

Thus, the correct answer is **B**.

---

40. Answer **(A)**

Calculating the change of money.

The percent decrease is calculated by;
$$\frac{regular\ rental\ rate - current\ special\ rate}{regular\ rental\ rate} \times 100$$
So,
$$\frac{(6 \times \$90 - (5 \times \$90 + \$10))}{6 \times \$90} \times 100 = 14.81481\ldots.$$

Thus, the percent decrease is 14.81%.

---

41. Answer **(B)**

Finding the quotient of Type 4 and Type 1.

The greatest number of land type 1 is calculated by;
$$\frac{5 \times 6}{2 \times 3} = \frac{30}{6} = 5$$

Thus, the greatest number of type 1 is 5.

---

42. Answer **(K)**

Finding Rule.

Land Type 1; $2 \times 3 \rightarrow (1+1) \times (1+2)$
Land Type 2; $3 \times 4 \rightarrow (2+1) \times (2+2)$
Land Type 3; $4 \times 5 \rightarrow (3+1) \times (3+2)$
Land Type 4; $5 \times 6 \rightarrow (4+1) \times (4+2)$
So,
Land Type n; $(n+1) \times (n+2)$ and the area is;
$$area = width \times length = (n+1)(n+2) = n^2 + 2n + n + 2$$

Thus, the land area of Land Type n is $n^2 + 3n + 2$.

---

43. Answer **(C)**

Increasing the number of black balls and total balls.

Let b be the number of additional black balls, so, the probability is;
$$P = \frac{4+b}{18+b} = \frac{1}{3}$$
Using cross product;
$$3 \times (4+b) = 1 \times (18+b) \rightarrow 12 + 3b = 18 + b$$
Solving equation for b;
$$3b = b + 18 - 12 \rightarrow 3b - b = 6 \rightarrow 2b = 6 \rightarrow b = 3$$

Thus, the correct answer is **C**.

---

44. Answer **(F)**

0 point is also score.

The mean is calculated by;
$$\bar{x} = \frac{0 \times 2 + 40 \times 0 + 50 \times 4 + 60 \times 5 + 70 \times 6 + 80 \times 2 + 90 \times 0 + 100 \times 2}{20}$$
$$= \frac{1540}{20} = 77$$
Or using GDC.

Thus, the mean is 77.00.

---

45. Answer **(D)**

Using fundamental counting principle.

The number of ways for frame types is 8 ways, for colors is 10 ways, for materials is 3 ways. So,
$$8 \times 10 \times 3 = 240\ ways$$

Thus, the number of ways is 240.

---

46. Answer **(B)**

Finding the first term and common ratio.

From the formula of geometric sequence, $a_1(r)^{n-1} = 6(-2)^{i-1}$, the first term is 6 and the common ratio is -2.
From the formula of geometric series;
$$S_n = a_1\left(\frac{1-r^n}{1-r}\right) \rightarrow S_8 = 6 \times \left(\frac{1-(-2)^8}{1-(-2)}\right) = -510$$
Or using GDC.

Thus, the sum is -510.

---

47. Answer **(F)**

Using inverse trigonometric ratio.

Drawing an auxiliary line;
$$\tan\theta = \frac{3}{2} \rightarrow \theta = \arctan\left(\frac{3}{2}\right) = \tan^{-1}\left(\frac{3}{2}\right)$$

Thus, the correct answer is **F**.

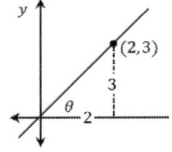

---

48. Answer (A)

Using the Pythagorean theorem.

A lateral face of the pyramid is an isosceles triangle, and let x be the length of the leg of the lateral face. So, using the Pythagorean theorem;

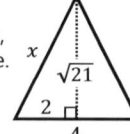

$$x^2 = 2^2 + \left(\sqrt{21}\right)^2 = 25 \quad \rightarrow \quad x = \sqrt{25} = 5.$$

Because there are 4 base edges (4 inches) and there are 4 lateral edges (5 inches), the total length of all 8 edges is $4 \times 4 + 4 \times 5 = 36$ inches.

Thus, the correct answer is **A**.

49. Answer (G)

The intersecting points lie on the circle.

Let (x, y) be the coordinates of the center and the two points lie on the circle. So the distance of between the center and the two points are same ($\because$ it is radius.).
Using the distance formula;

$$\sqrt{(x-0)^2 + (y-5)^2} = \sqrt{(x-0)^2 + (y-1)^2}$$

Take square on both sides;

$$x^2 + (y-5)^2 = x^2 + (y-1)^2 \quad \rightarrow \quad -10y + 25 = -2y + 1$$
$$-8y = -24 \quad \rightarrow \quad y = 3$$

Because the circle has a radius $\sqrt{20}$;

$$\sqrt{(x-0)^2 + (3-1)^2} = \sqrt{20} \rightarrow \sqrt{x^2+4} = \sqrt{20}$$

Take square on both sides;

$$x^2 + 4 = 20 \quad \rightarrow \quad x^2 = 16 \quad \rightarrow \quad x = \pm\sqrt{16} = \pm 4.$$

Thus, the coordinates are (4, 3) or (−4, 3).

50. Answer (B)

A rectangle has 4 right angles.

The square has 4 right angles so, one of the coordinates of $x-$ or y-coordinate is equal to the given coordinate. And the length is 4 coordinate units.

Thus, the correct answer is **B**.

51. Answer (C)

The circumference is $2\pi r$.

The diameter of the circle is $\frac{1}{3} \times 210 = 70$ and the radius, r, is 35. Using the formula of the circumference of circle is $2\pi r$ and the length of arc $\overparen{PQ}$ is;

$$arc\, PQ = 2\pi(35) \times \frac{180°}{360°} = 35\pi$$

Thus, the correct answer is **C**.

52. Answer (H)

Drawing x-y coordinate on the given figure.

Point X is $\frac{1}{2} \times 300 - 36 = 114$ apart in the x-direction from O.

Thus, the x-coordinate of point X is 114.

53. Answer (C)

The slope is a speed of each situation.

The speed is the slope of each graph.
Sentence I: the ball's height is increased and its speed is decreased so, it corresponding to graph B.
Sentence II: the bus's distance is increased and its speed is constant so, it corresponding to graph C.
Sentence III: the object's distance is increased and its speed is increased so, it corresponding to graph A.

Thus, the correct answer is **C**.

54. Answer (J)

Using trigonometric ratio.

Because,

$$\cos\alpha = \frac{A}{H} = \frac{21}{29} \qquad \tan\alpha = \frac{O}{A} = \frac{20}{21}$$

So,

$$\sin\alpha = \frac{O}{H} = \frac{20}{29}.$$

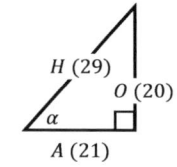

Thus, the correct answer is **J**.

55. Answer (H)

Two side lengths and one opposite angle.

The given values are two sides lengths and one opposite angle, so using sine law;

$$\frac{\sin E}{60} = \frac{\sin 32°}{100}$$

Thus, the correct answer is **H**.

56. Answer (C)

The given problem is a quadratic equation.

Let $\cos x$ be X;

$$\cos^2 x + \cos x = -\frac{1}{4} \;\rightarrow\; X^2 + X = -\frac{1}{4} \;\rightarrow\; X^2 + X + \frac{1}{4} = 0$$

Using the complete square formula:

$$X^2 + X + \frac{1}{4} = 0 \;\rightarrow\; \left(X + \frac{1}{2}\right)^2 = 0 \;\rightarrow\; X = -\frac{1}{2}$$

So,

$$\cos x = -\frac{1}{2} \;\rightarrow\; x = \cos^{-1}\left(-\frac{1}{2}\right) = \frac{2}{3}\pi \;\rightarrow\; \sin\frac{2}{3}\pi = \frac{\sqrt{3}}{2}$$

Thus, the correct answer is **C**.

57. Answer (G)

Cosine function is a periodic function.

The two functions have same amplitude, so $a = b$ and same maximum and minimum value, so $d = 0$. And the value of c does not matter(not only $c \neq 0$) because the shape of cosine function looks the same in any horizontal shift.

Thus, the correct answer is **G**.

58. Answer (B)

The given value are three sides lengths.

Drawing the triangle, the smallest angle is the opposite angle of the smallest side. And because the given values are the lengths of three sides, using the cosine law;

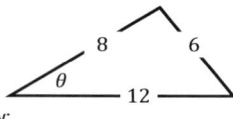

$$a^2 = b^2 + c^2 - 2bc\cos A \;\rightarrow\; 6^2 = 8^2 + 12^2 - 2 \times 8 \times 12 \times \cos\theta$$

Thus, the correct answer is **B**.

59. Answer (G)

Pythagorean theorem always useful.

Using the Pythagorean theorem;

$$\overline{QR} = \sqrt{26^2 - 10^2} = \sqrt{576} = 24$$

$$\tan P = \frac{24}{10} = \frac{12}{5}$$

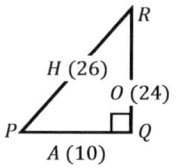

Thus, the correct answer is **G**.

---

60. *Answer* (**C**)

The matrix is composed of coefficients and constant terms.

The matrix is composed of coefficients and constant terms, so;

$$\begin{bmatrix} -1 & 3 & | & -6 \\ 2 & -7 & | & 4 \end{bmatrix}$$

Thus, the correct answer is **C**.

BLANK PAGE   *by K·DEAN*

Reformed Past Paper ACT MATH TEST 07

60 Questions – 60 Minutes

DIRECTIONS:
Solve each problem, choose the correct answer, and then fill in the corresponding oval on your answer in the grid on the answer sheet.

Do not linger over problems that take too much time. as many as you can, then return in the time you have left for this test.

You are permitted to use a calculator on this test.

Note: Unless otherwise stated, all of the following should be assumed.

1. Figures are drawn to scale unless otherwise indicated.

2. All figures lie in a plane unless otherwise indicated.

3. All variables and expressions used represent real numbers unless otherwise indicated.

This test has reformed the REAL ACT Mathematics Test

01.

What is the least common denominator (LCD) of $\frac{8}{9}$, $\frac{3}{16}$, and $\frac{5}{22}$?

- **A.** 3168
- **B.** 198
- **C.** 352
- **D.** 1024
- **E.** 1584

02.

Let following 3 statements be all **true** about any positive integers $p, q,$ and r.

- I. p is a integer between 10 and 13, inclusive.
- II. q is a smallest odd prime number.
- III. r is a cube number such that $10 < r < 50$.

What is the value of integer $\frac{pq^2}{r}$?

- **F.** 4
- **G.** 6
- **H.** 9
- **J.** 12
- **K.** 15

03.

If k is a real number and $\frac{9k^2}{27k^3}$ is a rational number, then which of the following statements about k **must** be true ?

- **F.** $k = 3$
- **G.** $k = \frac{1}{3}$
- **H.** k is a real number.
- **J.** k is a irrational number.
- **K.** k is a rational number.

 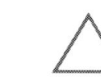
04.

Which of the following expressions is equivalent to $(2x^2 + 3x - 7) - (-3x^2 + 4x - 5)$ for all real values of x ?

A. $5x^2 - x - 2$

B. $-x^2 + 7x - 12$

C. $5x^2 + 7x - 2$

D. $-x^2 + 7x - 2$

E. $5x^2 + 7x - 2$

05.

If $4p - 2(a - 6ny) = 0$, which of the following expressions is equal to a ?

F. $-4p + 12ny$

G. $-4p - 6ny$

H. $4p + 6ny$

J. $-2p - 6ny$

K. $2p + 6ny$

06.

Which of the following values is closet to the distance, in centimeters, the length of a small feather ?

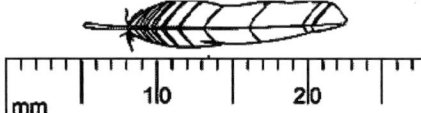

A. $2\frac{3}{4}$

B. $2\frac{1}{4}$

C. $1\frac{9}{10}$

D. $1\frac{3}{4}$

E. $\frac{7}{10}$

07.

On January, Miny and Geouny created different bank accounts with initial deposits of $530 and $250 respectively. Every month after creating the accounts, Miny will withdraw $23.50 to her account and Geouny will deposit $12.00 to his account. Which of the following equations, when solved, gives the number of months (m) after creating the accounts that she and he will have same amount of money in their respective accounts ?

A. $-530m - 23.5 = 250m + 12$

B. $-530m + 23.5 = 250m - 12$

C. $530m + 23.5 = 250m + 12$

D. $530 - 23.5m = 250 + 12m$

E. $530 + 23.5m = 250 - 12m$

08.

What value of n makes $n + \frac{4}{7} = \frac{6}{35}$ true ?

F. $-\frac{2}{7}$

G. $-\frac{2}{5}$

H. $-\frac{2}{35}$

J. $\frac{2}{7}$

K. $\frac{10}{7}$

09.

In the standard (x, y) coordinate plane below, which of the following graphs represents $y = \sqrt{1 - \sin^2 x}$ for $0 \leq x \leq \pi$?

F.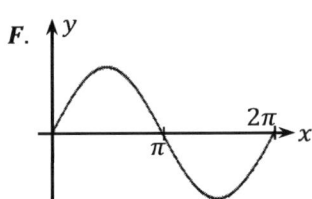

G.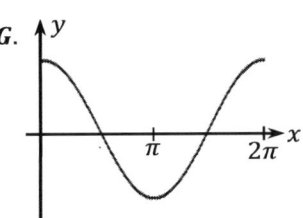

H.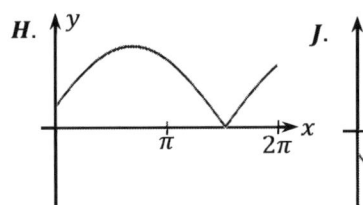

J.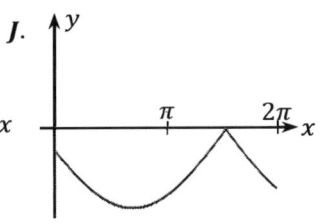

K.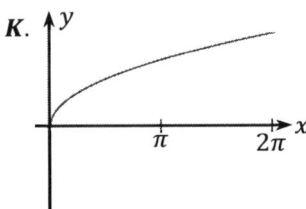

10.

$$3x + y = p$$
$$2x - y = -q$$

What is the value of x in the solution of the system of equations above ?

F. 0

G. $-p + q$

H. $p - q$

J. $\dfrac{p - q}{5}$

K. $\dfrac{q - p}{5}$

11.

The temperature C in degrees Celsius is related to the temperature F in degrees Fahrenheit by the equation $C = \dfrac{5}{9}(F - 32)$. Which of the following temperatures, in degrees Fahrenheit, is to 80 degrees Celsius ?

A. 144

B. 152

C. 164

D. 176

E. 213

12.

The pitch of a roof is the ratio of vertical length, v, to horizontal length, h. Which of the following pitches has the greatest pitch ?

F. $4:11$

G. $5:16$

H. $6:23$

J. $7:22$

K. $8:24$

13.

If $y \geq -2$ and $x + y \leq 5$, what is the **GREATEST** value that x could have ?

A. 9

B. 7

C. 3

D. −3

E. −7

Use the following information to answer questions 14 - 16.

The table below gives the prices for Good Math application.

Type of Membership	Pre-Algebra	Algebra
3-month	$5	$10
6-month	$8	$15

14.

Kelly purchased the app for 6 students and made online payment $36 to have all 6 downloaded Pre-Algebra program. How many 6-months memberships did Kelly have purchased?

A. 1

B. 2

C. 3

D. 4

E. 5

15.

Edwin purchased 3-month membership of Algebra application 4 times. Edwin made online payment full price for the first 3 times download, and received a discount coupon for the fourth download, giving him a 25% discount on the fourth download. How much did he pay for the 4 times download?

A. $30.0

B. $32.5

C. $37.5

D. $40.0

E. $42.5

16.

When the app developer of Good Math App decreases the price of 6 -month membership of Algebra, the number of downloader per day increases. The expression $mx + b$ represents the number of 6-month membership of Algebra per day whenever the price is x dollars per download. The number of 6 -month membership of Algebra downloader per day was 58 when the price in the table was in effect. The number of the downloader per day increases by 6 for every $2 decrease in price. What is the expression, $mx + b$, for the relationship?

F. $2x + 58$

G. $-2x + 58$

H. $\dfrac{3}{2}x + 64$

J. $3x + 103$

K. $-3x + 103$

17.

What is the value of $|5 - 2| - |2 - 7| = ?$

F.   8

G. −8

H. −2

J.   2

K. −11

18.

Lamis current annual salary for working at Wishcet design company is \$38,000. Lamis is told that at the beginning of next year, his new annual salary will be an increase of 8% of his current annual salary. What will be Lamis's new annual salary ?

A. \$39,180

B. \$40,060

C. \$41,040

D. \$42,080

E. \$43,260

19.

The price of a phone increased from \$800 to \$920. The price increased by what percent ?

F. 12%

G. 15%

H. 18%

J. 21%

K. 24%

20.

The sound intensity from a point source of sound will obey the inverse square law. When a noise source generates sound, the intensity of that sound, I, in unit of sound intensity, could be expressed as $\frac{k}{r^2}$, where r is the distance, in meters, the noise source is from an observer, and k is a constant of variation. For one noise source generating sound, $d = 10m$ and $I = 25W/m^2$. If $d = 5m$ for the same noise source generating sound, what is the corresponding value of I?

A.   50

B. 100

C. 150

D. 200

E. 250

21.

What number is $\frac{1}{6}\%$ of $\frac{5}{8}$?

F. $\frac{1}{48}$

G. $\frac{5}{48}$

H. $\frac{5}{480}$

J. $\frac{1}{960}$

K. $\frac{1}{963}$

22.

A circle is inscribed a rectangle that is 8cm wide and 10cm long and is tangent to 3 sides of the rectangle. What is the area, in centimeters, of the inscribed circle?

A. 4π

B. 12π

C. 16π

D. 36π

E. 64π

23.

Humphery wants to paint the one pentagonal wall of the outside of the warehouse shown below. Each quart of paint will cover an area of 40 square feet with 1 coat of paint. The price of the paint is $6 per quart and is sold only by the full quart. What is the total price of the paint that Humphery needs to buy?

F. $24

G. $30

H. $32

J. $36

K. $40

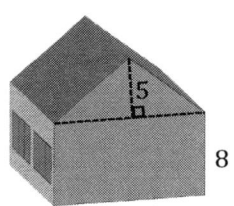

24.

As shown in the figure below, a circle has radius, 12cm, and $\overline{OQ}$ is perpendicular to $\overline{PR}$. If the length of $\overline{OQ}$ is 8cm, how many centimeters is $\overline{PR}$?

A. $4\sqrt{5}$

B. $8\sqrt{5}$

C. $10\sqrt{5}$

D. $12\sqrt{5}$

E. $\sqrt{80}$

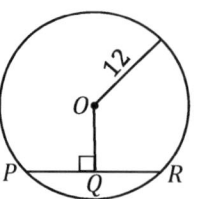

25.

As shown in the figure below, the measures of 4 angles of a pentagon are given. What is the value of x?

F. 98

G. 107

H. 115

J. 122

K. 130

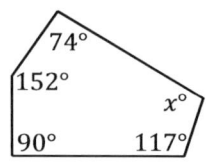

26.

All quadrilaterals in one of the following categories have diagonals that are perpendicular bisected each other. Which category?

A. Trapezoid

B. Parallelogram

C. Rhombus

D. Rectangle

E. Kite

27.

In isosceles triangle $\triangle PQR$, $\overline{PQ}$ is congruent to $\overline{PR}$ and the measure of a base angle is 48°. What is the measure of vertex angle ?

F. 74°

G. 78°

H. 84°

J. 88°

K. 94°

28.

Triangle ΔQRS and point Q that lies on line $\overline{PS}$ are shown in figure below. The measure of $\angle QRS$ is 45°, the measure of $\angle PQR$ is $(3x - 52)°$, and the measure of $\angle RQS$ is $(x + 27)°$. What is the measure of $\angle QSR$?

A. 41°

B. 52°

C. 67°

D. 88°

E. 94°

29.

In the standard (x, y) coordinate plane below, which of the following functions represents the graph?

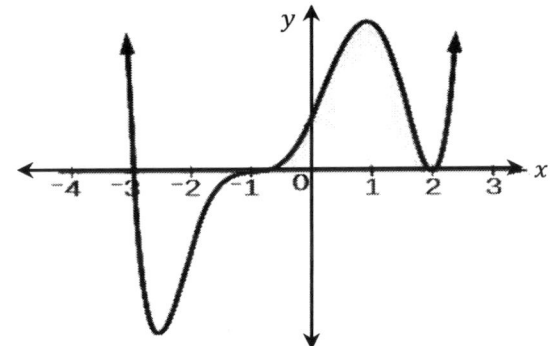

A. $f(x) = (x + 3)(x + 1)(x - 2)$

B. $g(x) = (x + 3)(x + 1)^2(x - 2)^3$

C. $h(x) = (x + 3)^2(x + 1)(x - 2)^3$

D. $r(x) = (x + 3)(x + 1)^2(x - 2)^3(x^2 + 1)$

E. $t(x) = (x + 3)(x + 1)^3(x - 2)^2(x^2 + 1)$

30.

Which of the following is a quadratic equation that has $\dfrac{4}{5}$ as its solution?

A. $5x^2 - 3x + 4 = 0$

B. $5x^2 + 4 = 0$

C. $5x^2 - 4 = 0$

D. $25x^2 - 16 = 0$

E. $25x^2 + 16 = 0$

31.

If the two solutions of an equation $x^2 + px + 11 = 0$ are positive integers, what is the value of p?

F. -8

G. 7

H. -12

J. 12

K. -7

32.

What is the value of i^{2021} ?

F. i

G. $-i$

H. 1

J. -1

K. -2

33.

Which of the following numbers is a zero of the polynomial function $g(x) = 3x^3 + 5x^2 - 12x$?

A. $-\dfrac{2}{3}$

B. $\dfrac{1}{3}$

C. 3

D. $\dfrac{4}{3}$

E. 4

34.

The graph of a quadratic function $y = ax^2 + bx + c$ is shown in the standard (x, y) coordinate plane below for real numbers $a, b,$ and c. Which of following statements is **true** for solution of the quadratic equation $ax^2 + bx + c = 0$?

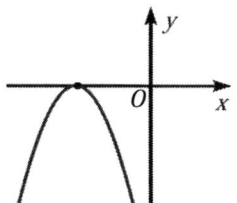

F. 1 real solution and 1 non-real solution.

G. 2 real solutions that are distinct.

H. 2 real solutions that are equal.

J. 2 distinct solutions that are not real.

K. Could not determined from the graph.

35.

In the figure below, the graph of $y = g(x)$ is shown in the standard (x, y) coordinate plane. Which of the following graphs is that of $y = |g(x)|$?

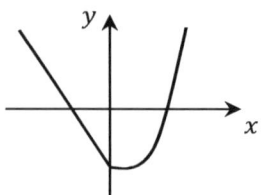

A.
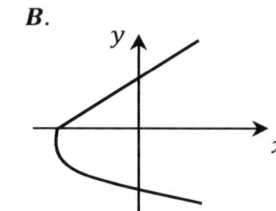

B.

C.

D.

E.
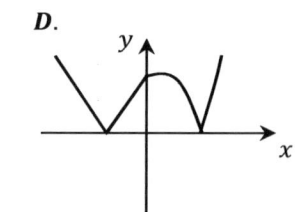

36.

What is the simplest form of $\dfrac{28x^4-21x^3}{7x^3}$,for all nonzero real numbers x ?

A. $4x - 3$

B. $4x^2 - 3$

C. $4x^2 - 3x$

D. $21x - 14$

E. $21x^2 - 14x$

37.

Which of the following expressions is equivalent to $-\dfrac{14x^5y^4}{7x^2y^2}$, for all nonzero real numbers x and y ?

F. $7x^2y^2$

G. $7x^3y$

H. $-2x^2y^2$

J. $-2x^3y$

K. $-2x^3y^2$

38.

Given that $\sqrt{x} = y$ and $y = 4$, $x = $?

A. 64

B. 16

C. $4\sqrt{2}$

D. 2

E. $\dfrac{1}{2}$

39.

What is the horizontal asymptote(s) of a rational function of $f(x) = \dfrac{6x^3-18x+12}{2x^2-x+1}$?

F. $x = 2$

G. $x = 3$

H. $y = 1$

J. $y = 2$

K. $y = 3$

40.

Which of the following is simplified form of $\dfrac{3}{\sqrt{5}} + \dfrac{2}{\sqrt{3}}$?

F. $\dfrac{5}{\sqrt{15}}$

G. $\dfrac{5\sqrt{8}}{8}$

H. $\dfrac{5}{\sqrt{8}}$

J. $\dfrac{3\sqrt{3} + 2\sqrt{5}}{\sqrt{15}}$

K. $\dfrac{3\sqrt{5} + 2\sqrt{3}}{\sqrt{15}}$

Use the following information to answer questions 41 - 44.

A company plant to build their online shopping mall. They have a total budget of $20,000 to pay costs in 5 categories. Not all the budget has been assigned. The budget amounts that have been assigned are shown in the table below.

Cost category	Budget amount
Web-page production	$5,500
Maintaining web-page	?
Renting a server	$9,000
Purchasing domain	$500
Other	?
Total cost	$20,000

41.

The amount budgeted for *Web-page production* is the sum of the 4 process - collecting data, web designing, HTML applying, setting and testing. What is the average cost per process?

A. $1,325

B. $1,350

C. $1,375

D. $1,400

E. $1,425

42.

In a circle graph representing the 5 budget amounts in the table, what should be the measure of the central angle of the *Purchasing domain* sector?

F. 2°

G. 5°

H. 9°

J. 32°

K. 36°

43.

Assume a bar graph will be constructed representing the amounts of the assigned costs. The height of the bar for *Web-page production* should be what fraction of the height of the bar for *Renting a server*?

A. $\frac{5}{9}$

B. $\frac{11}{18}$

C. $\frac{2}{3}$

D. $\frac{13}{18}$

E. $\frac{7}{9}$

44.

Which of the following numbers is closet to the percent of the total budget that remaining to be assigned?

F. 12%

G. 25%

H. 48%

J. 53%

K. 75%

45.

In the figure below, the circle graph is represented a company's quarterly sales. The quarter in which the company's sales were greatest is what percent of their total annual sales, to the nearest 0.1% ?

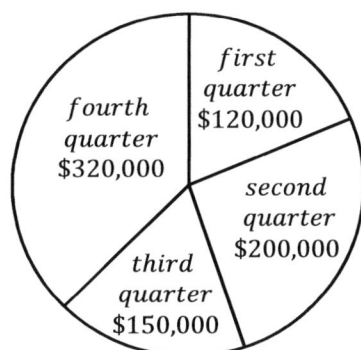

A. 36.41%

B. 38.24%

C. 40.51%

D. 42.17%

E. 44.92%

46.

Assume that the first term is 216 in the geometric sequence $216, 36, 6, ...$. What is the sixth term of the geometric sequence?

F. $\dfrac{1}{36}$

G. $\dfrac{1}{18}$

H. $\dfrac{1}{12}$

J. $\dfrac{1}{6}$

K. $\dfrac{1}{3}$

47.

Sparky is a making a roof for a new garden shed. As shown below, the roof is represented by $\triangle OPR$. The two legs $\overline{OP}$ and $\overline{OR}$ are each 7 feet long and the base side $\overline{PR}$ is 12 feet long. The central column, represented by $\overline{OS}$, is perpendicular to the base side and its length is 15 feet. What is the length, in feet, of $\overline{QS}$?

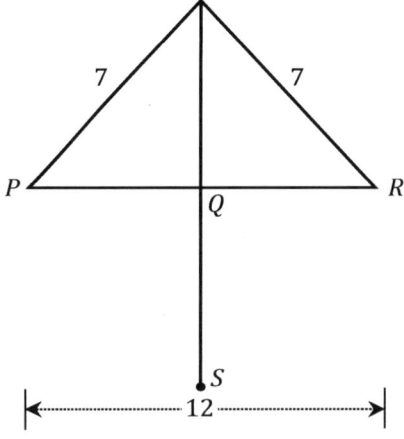

A. $15 - \sqrt{13}$

B. $15 - 2\sqrt{3}$

C. $15 - \sqrt{17}$

D. 14

E. 12

48.

In the standard (x, y) coordinate, the coordinate of point P is $(2, 5)$ and the coordinate of point Q is $(5, -3)$. What is the length, in coordinate units, of $\overline{PQ}$?

F. 5

G. 13

H. 15

J. $\sqrt{73}$

K. $\sqrt{113}$

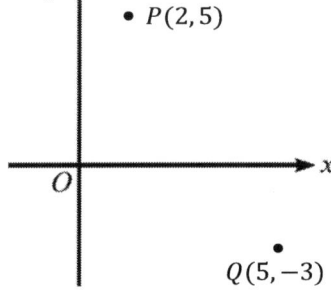

Use the following information to answer questions 49 - 50.

As shown in the figure below, □$PQRS$ is a square and it has side length 16 inches. The square is divided into 16 nonoverlapping congruent squares. Point O is the center of □$PQRS$.

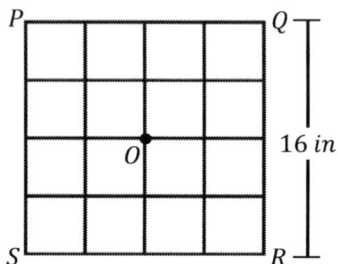

49.

Suppose that point X starts at point P and is rotated clockwise about O a total 630°. What is the final location of point X ?

A. P

B. Q

C. R

D. S

E. O

50.

Assume that □$PQRS$ is placed in standard (x, y) coordinate plane, $\overline{PS}$ is on the y-axis, the midpoint of $\overline{PS}$ is at the origin, and 1 coordinate unit is equal to 1 inch. Which of the followings is the coordinate of point Q?

F. $(2, 4)$

G. $(4, 2)$

H. $(8, 4)$

J. $(16, 8)$

K. $(32, 16)$

51.

As shown figure below, a point P $(4, 0)$ is placed in the standard (x, y) coordinate plane. The set of all points such that each is three times as far from P as from the origin, O, forms a circle. The point $(0, \sqrt{2})$ is one point of the circle. Which of the following coordinates are the center of the circle?

A. $(1, 2)$

B. $\left(1, 1\frac{1}{2}\right)$

C. $\left(\frac{1}{2}, \frac{1}{2}\right)$

D. $\left(-\frac{1}{2}, 0\right)$

E. $\left(-\frac{1}{4}, \frac{1}{2}\right)$

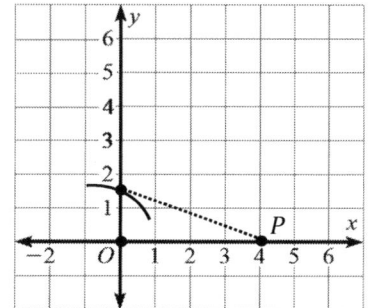

52.

In the figure below, the shaded region represents the solution set of systems of inequalities. What is the systems of inequalities?

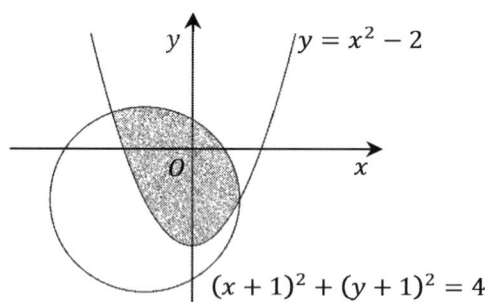

F. $(x + 1)^2 + (y + 1)^2 \geq 4$
   $y \geq x^2 - 2$

G. $(x + 1)^2 + (y + 1)^2 \geq 4$
   $y \leq x^2 - 2$

H. $(x + 1)^2 + (y + 1)^2 \leq 4$
   $y \geq x^2 - 2$

J. $(x + 1)^2 + (y + 1)^2 > 4$
   $y \leq x^2 - 2$

K. $(x + 1)^2 + (y + 1)^2 < 4$
   $y < x^2 - 2$

53.

As shown below, a right triangle with horizontal leg 8 centimeters long and hypotenuse 17 centimeters long is rotated 360° around vertical leg to form a right cone. What is the volume of the cone, in cubic centimeters?

(Note: volume of cone, $V = \frac{1}{3}\pi r^2 h$)

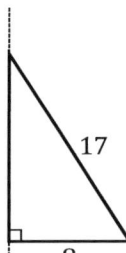

A.　40π

B.　160π

C.　240π

D.　320π

E.　640π

54.

As shown below, Cyma is loading a cargo truck by using a ramp. The ramp connecting the ground to a loading platform 3 feet above the ground. The ramp measures 10 feet from the ground to the top of the loading platform. Which of the following expressions is the angle of elevation formed by the ramp and the ground?

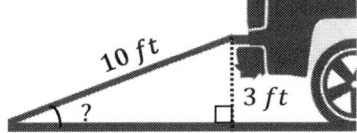

A.　$\arccos\left(\dfrac{10}{3}\right)$

B.　$\arccos\left(\dfrac{3}{10}\right)$

C.　$\arccos\left(\dfrac{7}{10}\right)$

D.　$\arcsin\left(\dfrac{3}{10}\right)$

E.　$\arcsin\left(\dfrac{10}{3}\right)$

Use the following information to answer questions 55 - 56.

In the figure below, the stars of Aquarius is placed standard (x, y) coordinate plane. One coordinate unit is 1 light-year, 1 light-year $\approx 5.88 \times 10^{12}$ miles.

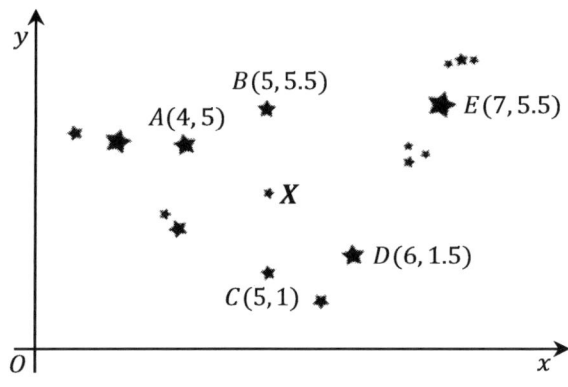

55.

Supposes that the star X is located in the center of stars A, B, C and D. What is the coordinates of the star X?

A.　$(3.5, 4.5)$

B.　$(4.5, 3.5)$

C.　$(3.25, 5)$

D.　$(5, 3.25)$

E.　$(5, 5)$

56.

What is the sine of the angle formed by $\overline{EB}$ and $\overline{EC}$ in the above graph ?

F.　0.785

G.　0.825

H.　0.868

J.　0.914

K.　0.952

57.

Suppose that the side lengths of a right triangle ΔXYZ are given in inches in the figure below. Which of the following expressions has a value that is equal to $\sin X$?

A. $\cos Z$

B. $\sin Z$

C. $\tan Z$

D. $\cos X$

E. $\tan X$

59.

In the circle below, central angle θ measures $30°$, and minor arc $\overset{\frown}{PQ}$ is 2π inches. What is the radius, in inches, of the circle?

A. 6

B. 10

C. 12

D. 15

E. 16

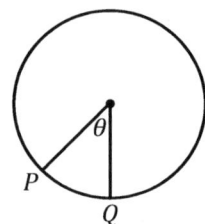

58.

In the triangle ΔABC below, the length of $\overline{XY}$ is 15 inches. When solved for the length, in inches, of $\overline{XZ}$, which of the following equations is the equation for the length of $\overline{XZ}$?

F. $\dfrac{15}{\sin 79°} = \dfrac{\overline{XZ}}{\sin 55°}$

G. $\dfrac{15}{\sin 55°} = \dfrac{\overline{XZ}}{\sin 79°}$

H. $\dfrac{15}{\sin 48°} = \dfrac{\overline{XZ}}{\sin 55°}$

J. $\dfrac{\sin 55°}{\sin 79°} = \dfrac{\overline{XZ}}{15}$

K. $\dfrac{15}{\sin 24°} = \dfrac{\overline{XZ}}{\sin 48°}$

60.

Four matrices are given below;

$$A = \begin{bmatrix} 1 \\ 2 \end{bmatrix} \quad B = \begin{bmatrix} 3 & 4 \end{bmatrix} \quad C = \begin{bmatrix} 5 & 6 \\ 7 & 8 \end{bmatrix} \quad D = \begin{bmatrix} 9 & 10 \\ 11 & 12 \\ 13 & 14 \end{bmatrix}$$

Which of the following matrix products is defined?

F. AB

G. AC

H. AD

J. CB

K. DB

the relationship between the

posing litter mass remaining after
temperature for 3 years and the mean annual
Canada. A line of best ... forests in
temperature, in degrees C...

A) $25,000 > (4,334 - 2,712)t$

B) $25,000 < (4,334 - 2,712)t$

C) $25,000 - 4,334 > 2,712t$

Obtain Scale Scores from Raw Scores					
Scale Score	Raw Score	Scale Score	Raw Score	Scale Score	Raw Score
36	60	24	36-37	12	7
35	58-59	23	34-35	11	5-6
34	57	22	32-33	10	4
33	55-56	21	30-31	9	-
32	54	20	29	8	3
31	52-53	19	27-28	7	-
30	50-51	18	24-26	6	2
29	48-49	17	21-23	5	-
28	45-47	16	17-20	4	1
27	43-44	15	13-16	3	-
26	40-42	14	11-12	2	-
25	38-39	13	8-10	1	0

1. Scoring Key

Key		Question Category	Y/N
01.	E	Number Theory	
02.	F	Number Theory	
03.	K	Number Theory	
04.	A	Expression and Linear Equation	
05.	K	Expression and Linear Equation	
06.	D	Expression and Linear Equation	
07.	D	Expression and Linear Equation	
08.	G	Expression and Linear Equation	
09.	G	Expression and Linear Equation	
10.	J	Expression and Linear Equation	
11.	D	Linear Function inequality	
12.	F	Linear Function inequality	
13.	B	Linear Function inequality	
14.	B	Linear Function inequality	
15.	C	Linear Function inequality	
16.	K	Linear Function inequality	
17.	H	Linear Function inequality	
18.	C	Arithmetic Topic and Ratio	
19.	G	Arithmetic Topic and Ratio	
20.	B	Arithmetic Topic and Ratio	
21.	J	Arithmetic Topic and Ratio	
22.	C	Basic Geometry	
23.	J	Basic Geometry	
24.	B	Basic Geometry	
25.	G	Basic Geometry	
26.	C	Basic Geometry	
27.	H	Basic Geometry	
28.	C	Basic Geometry	
29.	E	Quadratic and Polynomial Function	
30.	D	Quadratic and Polynomial Function	

Key		Question Category	Y/N
31.	H	Quadratic and Polynomial Function	
32.	F	Quadratic and Polynomial Function	
33.	D	Quadratic and Polynomial Function	
34.	H	Quadratic and Polynomial Function	
35.	D	Quadratic and Polynomial Function	
36.	A	Further Equations and Functions	
37.	K	Further Equations and Functions	
38.	B	Further Equations and Functions	
39.	K	Further Equations and Functions	
40.	J	Further Equations and Functions	
41.	C	Statistics and Probability	
42.	H	Statistics and Probability	
43.	B	Statistics and Probability	
44.	G	Statistics and Probability	
45.	C	Statistics and Probability	
46.	F	Sequence and Series	
47.	A	Analytic Geometry and Conic Section	
48.	J	Analytic Geometry and Conic Section	
49.	D	Analytic Geometry and Conic Section	
50.	J	Analytic Geometry and Conic Section	
51.	D	Analytic Geometry and Conic Section	
52.	H	Analytic Geometry and Conic Section	
53.	D	Analytic Geometry and Conic Section	
54.	D	Trigonometric Functions	
55.	D	Trigonometric Functions	
56.	J	Trigonometric Functions	
57.	A	Trigonometric Functions	
58.	G	Trigonometric Functions	
59.	C	Trigonometric Functions	
60.	F	Intermediate Algebra	

2. Answer Explanations

---

01. Answer (**E**)

LCD is the least common multiple (LCM) of denominators.

Prime factorization;
$$9 = 3 \times 3 = 3^2, \qquad 16 = 2 \times 2 \times 2 \times 2 = 2^4, \qquad 22 = 2 \times 11$$

So, LCM of $9, 16$ and 22 is;
$$\text{LCM} = 2 \times 2 \times 2 \times 2 \times 3 \times 3 \times 11 = 2^4 \times 3^2 \times 11 = 1584.$$

Thus, the LCD of the fractions is 1584.

---

02. Answer (**F**)

A cube number is a number which can be expressed as the third power of an integer.

II. q is a smallest odd prime number; $q = 3$.
III. r is a cube number such that $10 < r < 50$; $r = 27 = 3 \times 3 \times 3 = 3^3$

So, $\frac{pq^2}{r} = \frac{p \times 9}{27} = \frac{p}{3}$ and because the value of $\frac{pq^2}{r} = \frac{p}{3}$ is integer, p must be the multiple of 3.

I. p is a integer between 10 and 13; p is 11 or 12 and 12 is a multiple of 3.

Thus, $\frac{pq^2}{r} = \frac{12 \times 3^2}{27} = 4.$

---

03. Answer (**K**)

A rational number is a number that can be written as a quotient of two integers.

Always, the first step is simplifying; $\frac{9k^2}{27k^3} = \frac{1}{3k}$. If $\frac{1}{3k}$ is a rational number, it is written as a quotient of two integers, $\frac{a}{b}$, a and b is an integer.

So, $\frac{1}{3k} = \frac{a}{b} \rightarrow 3ka = b \rightarrow k = \frac{b}{3a}$, thus k is a rational number.

---

04. Answer (**A**)

$-(a+b)$ *means* $(-1) \times (a+b) = -a - b$

Rewrite the expression:
$$(2x^2 + 3x - 7) - (-3x^2 + 4x - 5) = 2x^2 + 3x - 7 + 3x^2 - 4x + 5$$
Combing the like terms;
$$\rightarrow 2x^2 + 3x^2 + 3x - 4x - 7 + 5 = 5x^2 - x - 2$$

---

05. Answer (**K**)

Expanding and then solving for a.

Expanding the expression;
$$4p - 2(a - 6ny) = 0 \rightarrow 4p - 2a + 12ny = 0$$
Adding to $2a$ on both sides;
$$0 = 4p - 2a + 12ny \rightarrow 2a = 4p + 12ny$$
Dividing by 2 on both sides;
$$2a = 4p + 12ny \rightarrow a = 2p + 6ny$$
Thus, a is equal to $2p + 6ny$.

---

06. Answer (**D**)

The length of feather is about 1.75cm.

The length of feather is about 1.75cm.

1.75 convert to fraction; $1.75 = \frac{175}{100} = \frac{7}{4} = 1\frac{3}{4}$.

Thus, the length of feather is about $1\frac{3}{4}$ cm.

---

07. Answer (**D**)

"Deposit" means adding and "withdraw" means subtracting.

After m months,
the amount of money Miny's account is $530 - 23.5m$
and Geouny's account is $250 + 12m$
Thus, the correct equation is
$$530 - 23.5m = 250 + 12m$$

---

08. Answer (**G**)

Solve the equation by using LCD.

Subtract $\frac{4}{7}$ from both sides;
$$n + \frac{4}{7} = \frac{6}{35} \rightarrow n + \frac{4}{7} - \frac{4}{7} = \frac{6}{35} - \frac{4}{7} \rightarrow n = \frac{6}{35} - \frac{20}{35} = -\frac{14}{35}$$
Thus, the value of n is $-\frac{14}{35} = -\frac{2}{5}$.

---

09. Answer (**G**)

Simplifying by trigonometric identities.

Using the Pythagorean identity; $\sin^2 \theta + \cos^2 \theta = 1$.
$$\cos^2 x = 1 - \sin^2 x \rightarrow \sqrt{1 - \sin^2 x} = \cos x$$
So, the graph is $y = \cos x$.

Thus, the correct answer is **G**.

---

10. Answer (**J**)

Add or subtract the equations to eliminate one variable..

Add the two equation ($\because y$ and $-y$);
$$
\begin{array}{r}
3x + y = p \\
2x - y = -q \\
\hline
5x = p - q
\end{array}
$$
Dividing both sides by 5;
$$5x = p - q \rightarrow \frac{5x}{5} = \frac{p-q}{5} \rightarrow x = \frac{p-q}{5}$$
Thus, x value is $\frac{p-q}{5}$.

---

11. Answer (**D**)

Substituting and solving equation.

Substitute 80 for C;
$$C = \frac{5}{9}(F - 32) \rightarrow 80 = \frac{5}{9}(F - 32)$$
Multiply both sides by $\frac{9}{5}$;
$$80 = \frac{5}{9}(F - 32) \rightarrow \frac{9}{5} \times 80 = \frac{5}{9}(F - 32) \times \frac{9}{5} \rightarrow 144 = F - 32$$
Add 32 to both sides;
$$F - 32 = 144 \rightarrow F - 32 + 32 = 144 + 32 \rightarrow F = 176$$
Thus, the temperature is 176°F.

---

12. **Answer** (F)

The decimal form is better when comparing fractions.

The pitch is the slope so, use the formula of slope;
$$\frac{4}{11} = 0.3636\dots, \qquad \frac{5}{16} = 0.3125, \qquad \frac{6}{23} = 0.2608\dots$$
$$\frac{7}{22} = 0.31818\dots, \qquad \frac{8}{24} = 0.3333\dots.$$
Thus, the greatest pitch is $4:11$.

13. **Answer** (B)

Finding the intersecting point.

Finding the intersecting point of the two boundary lines $y = -2$ and $x + y = 5$, substituting $y = -2$ for $x + y = 5$;
$x + y = 5 \;\rightarrow\; x + (-2) = 5 \;\rightarrow\; x = 7$
So, the intersecting point is $(7, -2)$.

Interpreting the intersecting point,
$y \geq -2 \;\rightarrow\;$ the minimum value of y is -2.
$\quad x + y \leq 5 \;\rightarrow\; x + (-2) \leq 5 \;\rightarrow\; x \leq 7$.

Thus, the greatest value of x value is 7.
Or using graphic calculator.

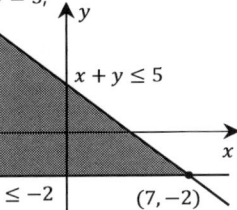

14. **Answer** (B)

Make system of equation.

If t is number of 3-moth memberships and s is the number of 6-month memberships;
The total number of downloaded is 6;
$$t + s = 6 \qquad - \text{①}$$
The total payment is 36;
$$5t + 8s = 36 \qquad - \text{②}$$
Using eliminating method ②$-5\times$①
$$
\begin{array}{r}
5t + 8s = 36 \\
t + s = 6 \quad -\times 5 \rightarrow \quad \underline{5t + 5s = 30} \\
3s = 6 \quad \rightarrow \quad s = 2
\end{array}
$$

Thus, the number of 6-month memberships is 2.

15. **Answer** (C)

25% is 0.25 in number.

"25% discount" is; $\$10 - 0.25 \times \$10 = \$7.5$

Thus, payment for the 4 times download is
$$3 \times \$10 + \$7.5 = \$37.5$$

16. **Answer** (K)

Find two point and then make linear equation.

The relationship between price, x, and number of downloader, y, is linear relationship. At the price is \$15, the downloader is 58 and at the price will be \$13, the downloader will be 64.

So, the two points are $(15, 58)$ and $(13, 64)$.
The slope is;
$$m = \frac{y_2 - y_1}{x_2 - x_1} = \frac{64 - 58}{13 - 15} = \frac{6}{-2} = -3$$
Therefore, the linear equation is;
$$y = mx + b \;\rightarrow\; y = -3x + b$$
Substitute $(13, 64)$ for the equation;
$y = -3x + b \;\rightarrow\; 64 = -3(13) + b \;\rightarrow\; 64 = -39 + b \;\rightarrow\; b = 103$

Thus, the linear equation is $y = -3x + 103$.

17. **Answer** (H)

Absolute value is never negative.

Evaluate;
$$|5 - 2| - |2 - 7| = |3| - |-5| = 3 - 5 = -2$$
Thus, the value is -2.

18. **Answer** (C)

"increase" means that "add"

His new annual salary is;
$$\$38,000 + 0.08 \times \$38,000 = \$38,000 + \$3,040 = \$41,040$$
Thus, the new annual salary is \$41,040.

19. **Answer** (G)

Change of the price is 920-800=120.

The percent of change is;
$$percent\ of\ change = \frac{amount\ of\ change}{original\ amount} \times 100$$
$$= \frac{920 - 800}{800} \times 100 = 15\%$$
Thus, the percent of change is 15%.

20. **Answer** (B)

Using an inverse variation equation.

From the formula, finding the value of k;
$$I = \frac{k}{r^2} \;\rightarrow\; 25 = \frac{k}{10^2} \;\rightarrow\; 25 = \frac{k}{100} \;\rightarrow\; k = 2,500$$
So, for $5m$
$$I = \frac{k}{r^2} \;\rightarrow\; I = \frac{2500}{(5)^2} = 100W/m^2$$

Thus, the corresponding value of I is 100.

21. **Answer** (J)

Using proportion and what number is a part.

"a is p percent of t" is $\rightarrow\; \frac{a}{t} = \frac{p}{100}$.
So, what number is $\frac{1}{6}\%$ of $\frac{5}{8}$ is;
$$\frac{a}{t} = \frac{p}{100} \;\rightarrow\; \frac{a}{\frac{5}{8}} = \frac{\frac{1}{6}}{100} \;\rightarrow\; 100a = \frac{1}{6} \times \frac{5}{8} \;\rightarrow\; 100a = \frac{5}{48}$$
Dividing both sides by 100;
$$100a = \frac{5}{48} \;\rightarrow\; \frac{100a}{100} = \frac{\frac{5}{48}}{100} \;\rightarrow\; a = \frac{1}{960}$$
Thus, the number is $\frac{1}{960}$.

22. **Answer** (C)

Drawing figure for given question.

Because the width of rectangle is 8cm, the radius of circle is 4cm. So,
$$area = \pi(4)^2 = 16\pi$$
Thus, the area of the inscribed circle is 16π.

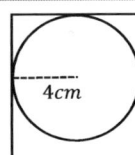

---

23. **Answer** **(J)**

Using the formula of the area of rectangle and triangle.

The area of the wall is;

$$area = rectangle + triangle = 8 \times 20 + \frac{1}{2} \times 20 \times 5 = 210\ ft^2$$

The amount of the paint is;

$$\frac{40\ ft^2}{1\ quart\ paint} = \frac{(210\ ft^2)}{x\ quart} \rightarrow 40x = 210 \rightarrow x = 5.25$$

Because the paint is sold only by the full quart, the amount of the paint is 6 quarts. The price of the paint is $6 \times 6 = \$36$.

Thus, the total price of the paint is $36.

---

24. **Answer** **(B)**

Using Pythagorean theorem.

Because ΔOPQ is a right triangle,

$$\overline{OP}^2 = \overline{OQ}^2 + \overline{PQ}^2 \rightarrow 12^2 = 8^2 + \overline{PQ}^2$$
$$\rightarrow \overline{PQ}^2 = 80 \rightarrow \overline{PQ} = \sqrt{80} = 4\sqrt{5}$$

So, $\overline{PR} = 2\overline{PQ} = 2 \times 4\sqrt{5} = 8\sqrt{5}$.

Thus, the length of $\overline{PR}$ is $8\sqrt{5}$.

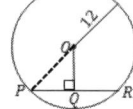

---

25. **Answer** **(G)**

Angles sum of a pentagon is 540°.

Angles sum of a pentagon is 540° so,

$$540 = 74 + 152 + 90 + 117 + x \rightarrow x + 433 = 540 \rightarrow x = 107°$$

Thus, the value of x is 107.

---

26. **Answer** **(C)**

Bisect at 90°.

The following picture is the relation of quadrilaterals and its diagonal.

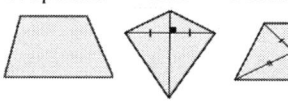

Trapezoid   Kite   Parallelogram

Rhombus   Rectangle   Square

Thus, the answer is rhombus or square.

---

27. **Answer** **(H)**

∠P is vertex angle.

$\overline{PQ} \cong \overline{PR}$

so, ∠Q and ∠R are base angles and ∠P is vertex angle.
Using triangle angle sum theorem;

$$\angle P + 48° + 48° = 180°$$
$$\rightarrow \angle P + 96° = 180 \rightarrow \angle P = 84°$$

Thus, the measure of vertex angle ∠P is 84°.

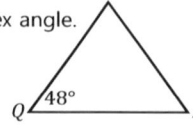

---

28. **Answer** **(C)**

Using linear pair.

Using linear pair;

$$\angle PQR + \angle RQS = 180° \rightarrow 3x - 52 + x + 27 = 180$$
$$\rightarrow 5x - 25 = 180 \rightarrow 5x = 205 \rightarrow x = 41$$

So, $\angle RQS = 68°$ and using triangle angle sum theorem;

$$\angle QSR + \angle RQS + \angle QRS = 180° \rightarrow \angle QSR + 68° + 45° = 180°$$
$$\rightarrow \angle QSR + 113° = 180° \rightarrow \angle QSR = 67°$$

Thus, the measure of ∠QSR is 67°.

---

29. **Answer** **(E)**

Note that only the real zeros appear as x-intercepts..

Only the real zeros appear as x-intercepts($\because x^2 + 1$ is not appear on the x-axis.). And when a factor $x - p$ of a function f is raised to an odd power, the graph of f crosses the x-axis at $x = p$, when a factor $x - p$ of a function f is raised to an even power, the graph of f is tangent to the x-axis at $x = p$.

Thus, the correct answer is **E**.

---

30. **Answer** **(D)**

Solution means $x = \frac{4}{5}$.

Take both sides by square;

$$x = \frac{4}{5} \rightarrow x^2 = \left(\frac{4}{5}\right)^2 \rightarrow x^2 = \frac{16}{25} \rightarrow 25x^2 = 16 \rightarrow 25x^2 - 16 = 0$$

Thus, the quadratic equation is $25x^2 - 16 = 0$.

---

31. **Answer** **(H)**

Using the product and sum of two roots.

Let a and b be the two roots of the equation;

$$(x - a)(x - b) = 0 \rightarrow x^2 - bx - ax + ab = 0$$
$$\rightarrow x^2 - (a + b)x + ab = 0$$

So, $x^2 - (a + b)x + ab = x^2 + px + 11$.
Because 11 is a prime number, $a = 1, b = 11$. The sum of the two roots is 12 so, $p = -12$.

Thus, the value of p is -12.

---

32. **Answer** **(F)**

$i^2 = -1$.

From the definition of i;

$$i^1 = i \qquad i^2 = -1 \qquad i^3 = i^2 i = -i \qquad i^4 = i^2 i^2 = 1$$

So,

$$i^{2021} = i^{2020} i^1 = (i^4)^{505} i = 1 \times i = i$$

Thus, the correct answer is **F**.

---

33. **Answer** **(D)**

Grouping by the common factors.

Grouping by x;
$$3x^3 + 5x^2 - 12x = x(3x^2 + 5x - 12)$$
Factoring by using factors of 3 and 12;
$$x(3x^2 + 5x - 12) = x(x + 4)(3x - 4)$$
So, zero of function $g(x) = 0$ is
$$x = 0\ or\ x + 4 = 0\ or\ 3x - 4 = 0$$
$$\rightarrow x = 0\ or\ x = -4\ or\ x = \frac{4}{3}$$

Or using graphic method:
x-intercepts and zero of function are same value.

Thus, the correct answer is **D**.

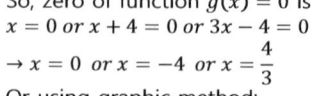

---

34. *Answer* **(H)**

There is one x-intercept.

If the $x = p$ is a x-intercept of a polynomial function graph, then
   $x = p$ is a real solution of the polynomial equation,
   $(x - p)$ is a factor of the polynomial equation, and
   $x = p$ is a zero of function.

The given graph has one x-intercept so, the solution of the quadratic equation has a repeated solution, repeated solution means 2 equal real solutions.

Thus, the correct answer is H.

35. *Answer* **(D)**

Absolute value is never negative.

The value of $|g(x)|$ is never negative,

thus the correct answer is D.

36. *Answer* **(A)**

Factoring and then simplifying.

Factoring and then simplifying;
$$\frac{28x^4 - 21x^3}{7x^3} = \frac{7x^3(4x - 3)}{7x^3} = 4x - 3$$

Thus, the correct answer is A.

37. *Answer* **(K)**

Using the properties of exponential.

Using the properties of exponential;
$$-\frac{14x^5y^4}{7x^2y^2} = -\frac{14}{7} \cdot \frac{x^5}{x^2} \cdot \frac{y^4}{y^2} = -2 \times x^{5-2}y^{4-2} = -2x^3y^2$$

Thus, the correct answer is K.

38. *Answer* **(B)**

For all real x, $\left(\sqrt{x}\right)^2 = |x|$.

Substitute 4 for y;
$$\sqrt{x} = y \quad \rightarrow \quad \sqrt{x} = 4$$
Take square on both sides;
$$(\sqrt{x})^2 = 4^2 \quad \rightarrow \quad x = 16$$

Thus, the value of x is 16.

39. *Answer* **(K)**

The degree of numerator is equal to denominator.

Because the degree of numerator equation is equal to the degree denominator, horizontal asymptote is the ratio of the leading coefficient of numerator equation to the leading coefficient of denominator.

Thus, the horizontal asymptote is $y = \frac{6}{2} = 3$.

40. *Answer* **(J)**

Finding LCD(least common denominator).

The LCD of $\sqrt{5}$ and $\sqrt{3}$ is $\sqrt{15}$ so,
$$\frac{3}{\sqrt{5}} + \frac{2}{\sqrt{3}} = \frac{3}{\sqrt{5}} \times \frac{\sqrt{3}}{\sqrt{3}} + \frac{2}{\sqrt{3}} \times \frac{\sqrt{5}}{\sqrt{5}} \quad \rightarrow \quad \frac{3\sqrt{3}}{\sqrt{15}} + \frac{2\sqrt{5}}{\sqrt{15}} = \frac{3\sqrt{3} + 2\sqrt{5}}{\sqrt{15}}$$

Thus, the correct answer is J.

41. *Answer* **(C)**

The average is the quotient of total cost and the number of process.

The average cost is the quotient of total cost and the number of process. So,
$$average\ cost = \frac{5,500}{4} = \$1,375$$

Thus, the average cost is \$1,375.

42. *Answer* **(H)**

The central angle and ratio of budget vary directly.

The central angle is determined by the ratio of budget amount. So,
$$central\ angle = \frac{500}{20,000} \times 360° = 9°$$

Thus, the measure of central angle is 9°.

43. *Answer* **(B)**

Finding a ratio.

The ratio of the budget of Web-page production to the budget of Renting a server is;
$$\frac{\$5500}{\$9000} = \frac{11}{18}$$

Thus, the correct answer is B.

44. *Answer* **(G)**

Finding the amount of budget that remaining to be assigned.

The amount of budget that remaining to be assigned is calculated by;
$$20,000 - (5,500 + 9,000 + 500) = 5,000$$
So, the percent is
$$\frac{5,000}{20,000} \times 100 = 25\%$$

Thus, the percent is 25%.

45. *Answer* **(C)**

The quarter of greatest sales is 4th quarter.

The total annual sales are;
$$\$120,000 + \$200,000 + \$150,000 + \$320,000 = \$790,000$$
So, the percent is;
$$\frac{\$320,000}{\$790,000} \times 100 = 40.50632911 \dots \%$$

Thus, the percent is 40.51%.

46. *Answer* **(F)**

Finding the common ratio.

The common ratio, r, is;
$$\frac{36}{216} = \frac{6}{36} = \frac{1}{6}$$
From the formula of geometric sequence;
$$a_n = a_1 r^{n-1} \quad \rightarrow \quad a_6 = 216\left(\frac{1}{6}\right)^{6-1} = 216\left(\frac{1}{6}\right)^5 = \frac{1}{36}$$

Thus, the sixth term is $\frac{1}{36}$.

47. Answer (A)

Using the Pythagorean theorem.

ΔOPQ is a right triangle and $\overline{PQ}$ is 6 ($\because \Delta OPR$ is isosceles triangle).
So, using the Pythagorean theorem;
$$\overline{OP}^2 = \overline{OQ}^2 + \overline{PQ}^2 \quad \rightarrow \quad 7^2 = \overline{OQ}^2 + 6^2 \quad \rightarrow \quad \overline{OQ} = \sqrt{7^2 - 6^2} = \sqrt{13}$$
Because $\overline{OS} = \overline{OQ} + \overline{QS} \quad \rightarrow \quad 15 = \sqrt{13} + \overline{QS} \quad \rightarrow \quad \overline{QS} = 15 - \sqrt{13}.$

Thus, the correct answer is **A**.

48. Answer (J)

Using the formula of distance.

Using the formula of distance;
$$d = \sqrt{(x_2 - x_1)^2 + (y_2 - y_1)^2} = \sqrt{(5-2)^2 + (-3-5)^2}$$
$$= \sqrt{3^2 + (-8)^2} = \sqrt{73}$$

Thus, the correct answer is **J**.

49. Answer (D)

$630 = 360 + 180 + 90.$

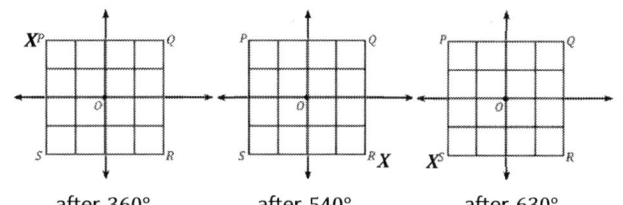

after 360°   after 540°   after 630°

Thus, the final location is same as point S.

50. Answer (J)

Drawing x-y coordinate on the given figure.

The point Q is 4 unit (16in) x-direction and 2 unit (8in) y-direction from the origin.

Because 1 in is equal to 1 coordinate unit, the coordinate is $(16, 8)$.

Thus, the correct answer is **J**.

51. Answer (D)

Using the distance formula.

From the given question's sentence 'all points such that each is three times as far from P as from the origin, O, forms a circle', let (x, y) be the coordinates of a point on the circle circumference.

And using distance formula;
$$3d_{OC} = d_{PC} \quad \rightarrow \quad 3\sqrt{(x-0)^2 + (y-0)^2} = \sqrt{(x-4)^2 + (y-0)^2}$$
Take square on both sides;
$$\left(3\sqrt{x^2 + y^2}\right)^2 = \left(\sqrt{(x-4)^2 + y^2}\right)^2 \quad \rightarrow \quad 9x^2 + 9y^2 = (x-4)^2 + y^2$$
$$\rightarrow \quad 9x^2 + 9y^2 = x^2 - 8x + 16 + y^2 \quad \rightarrow \quad 8x^2 + 8x + 8y^2 = 16$$
$$\rightarrow \quad x^2 + x + y^2 = 2$$
Using the complete square:
$$\rightarrow \quad x^2 + x + \frac{1}{4} + y^2 = 2 + \frac{1}{4} \quad \rightarrow \quad \left(x + \frac{1}{2}\right)^2 + y^2 = \frac{9}{4} = \left(\frac{3}{2}\right)^2$$

Thus, the circle has center $\left(-\frac{1}{2}, 0\right)$ and has radius $\frac{3}{2}$.

52. Answer (H)

Substitute a suitable point.

Point $(0, 0)$ is included in the shaded region so, substitute $(0, 0)$ for x and y;
Circle inequality
$$(x + 1)^2 + (y + 1)^2 = 4 \quad \rightarrow \quad (0 + 1)^2 + (0 + 1)^2 ? \ 4$$
$$\rightarrow \quad 1^2 + 1^2 ? 4 \quad \rightarrow \quad 2 < 4$$
and the boundary line is the solid line therefore,
$$(x + 1)^2 + (y + 1)^2 \leq 4$$
Quadratic inequality
$$y = x^2 - 2 \quad \rightarrow \quad 0 ? 0^2 - 2 \quad \rightarrow \quad 0 > -2$$
and the boundary line is the solid line therefore,
$$y \geq x^2 - 2$$

Thus, the correct answer is **H**.

53. Answer (D)

'h' is the length of vertical leg.

Let h be the length of the vertical leg and then using the Pythagorean theorem;
$$17^2 = h^2 + 8^2 \quad \rightarrow \quad h = \sqrt{17^2 - 8^2} = 15$$
Substitute 8 for r and 15 for h;
$$V = \frac{1}{3}\pi r^2 h \quad \rightarrow \quad V = \frac{1}{3}\pi (8^2)(15) = 320\pi$$

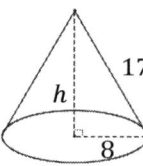

Thus, the correct answer is **D**.

54. Answer (D)

$\sin^{-1}$ and arcsin are the same representation of inverse sine function.

Let θ be the angle of elevation. Because the hypotenuse is $10ft$ and the opposite side is $3ft$.
$$\sin\theta = \frac{O}{H} = \frac{3}{10}$$
Using the definition of inverse trigonometric function;
$$\theta = \sin^{-1}\frac{3}{10} = \arcsin\left(\frac{3}{10}\right)$$

Thus, the correct answer is **D**.

55. Answer (D)

Using the midpoint formula.

The center is the midpoint of $\overline{AD}$ or $\overline{BC}$. let (x, y) be the coordinates of the X;
$$M = \left(\frac{x_1 + x_2}{2}, \frac{y_1 + y_2}{2}\right)$$
$$X = \left(\frac{5 + 5}{2}, \frac{5.5 + 1}{2}\right) = (5, 3.25) \quad or \quad = \left(\frac{4 + 6}{2}, \frac{5 + 1.5}{2}\right) = (5, 3.25)$$

Thus, the correct answer is **D**.

56. Answer (J)

Drawing a right triangle.

ΔEBC is an right triangle,
the length of $\overline{EB} = |7 - 5| = 2$ and
the length of $\overline{CB} = |5.5 - 1| = 4.5$.
Using the Pythagorean theorem;
$$\overline{CE} = \sqrt{4.5^2 + 2^2} = \frac{\sqrt{97}}{2}.$$
Using the trigonometric ratio;
$$\sin\theta = \frac{O}{H} = \frac{4.5}{\frac{\sqrt{97}}{2}} \approx 0.91381154 \ldots .$$

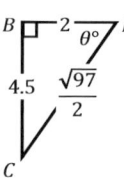

Thus, the correct answer is **J**.

---

57. `Answer` (A)

Using trigonometric ratio.

Using trigonometric ratio;
$$\sin X = \frac{O}{H} = \frac{15}{25} = \frac{3}{5}$$
In view of the angle Z,
$$\cos Z = \frac{A}{H} = \frac{15}{25} = \frac{3}{5}$$

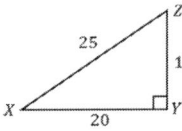

Thus, the correct answer is A.

---

58. `Answer` (G)

One side length and three angles.

The given values are one sides length and three angles, so using sine law;
$$\frac{15}{\sin 55°} = \frac{\overline{XZ}}{\sin 79°}$$

Thus, the correct answer is G.

---

59. `Answer` (C)

The arc length is proportional to the central angle.

Using the formula for arc length;
$$arc\ length = circumference \times \frac{30°}{360°}$$
$$\rightarrow \qquad 2\pi = 2\pi r \times \frac{1}{12} \quad \rightarrow \quad r = 12$$

Thus, the correct answer is C.

---

60. `Answer` (F)

Finding the dimensions of matrices.

The dimensions of four matrices are;
$$A = 2 \times 1 \qquad B = 1 \times 2 \qquad C = 2 \times 2 \qquad D = 2 \times 3$$
The product of two matrices M and N is defined provided the number of columns in M is equal to the number of rows in N.

Thus, only $AB = 2 \times 1 \cdot 1 \times 2 = 2 \times 2$ is defined.

BLANK PAGE _by K·DEAN_

Reformed Past Paper ACT MATH TEST 08

60 Questions – 60 Minutes

DIRECTIONS:
Solve each problem, choose the correct answer, and then fill in the corresponding oval on your answer in the grid on the answer sheet.

Do not linger over problems that take too much time as many as you can, then other in the time you have left for the test.

You are permitted to use a calculator on this test.

Note: Unless otherwise stated, all of the following should be assumed.

1. Figures ~~are drawn~~ to scale unless ~~otherwise indicated~~.

2. All figures lie in a plane unless otherwise indicated.

3. All variables and expressions used represent real numbers unless otherwise indicated.

This test has reformed the REAL ACT Mathematics Test

01.

The least common multiple (LCM) of two positive integers is 72 and the greatest common factor (GCF) of these same two numbers is 12. Which of the following pairs of numbers are the two numbers?

A. 6 and 12

B. 12 and 36

C. 20 and 36

D. 24 and 34

E. 24 and 36

02.

A bell rings every 12 minutes, another every 18 minutes. At 8:00 am the two ring simultaneously. At what time will the bells ring again at the same time?

F. 8:30 am

G. 8:36 am

H. 9:24 am

J. 10:36 am

K. 11:54 am

03.

In all positive real number a, which of following statements are **not** true?

F. $-3a < 0$

G. $a^3 > 0$

H. $-a - a^2 < 0$

J. $|-a| < 0$

K. $a + |-a| > a$

04.

The difference of a polynomial $3x^2 - 3x + 12$ and which of the following is $4x + 8$?

A. $3x^2 + x + 4$

B. $-3x + x - 4$

C. $3x^2 - 7x + 4$

D. $-3x^2 + 7x - 4$

E. $3x^2 - x - 4$

05.

What is the expression equivalent to $(x + 2i)^3$, for all real numbers x and $i = \sqrt{-1}$?

F. $x^3 - 8$

G. $x^3 - 8i$

H. $x^3 + 3ix^2 + 3x - i$

J. $x^3 + 3ix^2 - 3x - i$

K. $x^3 + 3ix^2 - 3x + i$

06.

If $\frac{3}{4}x - 5 = 1$, then what is the value of x ?

A. -10

B. -8

C. 8

D. 10

E. 12

07.

Miny told Geony that if she saved $\$240$ to her saving account, her saving account would have at most $\frac{11}{8}$ as much in it as it has now. From her statement , Geony could induce that the least amount of money that she could have in her savings account now is;

F. $\$480$

G. $\$520$

H. $\$560$

J. $\$600$

K. $\$640$

08.

The Hawaiian volcano Mauna Loa has erupted many times. In 1859, lava from the volcano traveled 52 km to the Pacific Ocean at an average speed of 6.5 km per hour. The lava's distance d (in kilometers) from the ocean t hours after it left the volcano can be approximated by the equation $d = 52 - 6.5t$. How long did it take the lava to reach the ocean ?

F. 6 hours

G. 8 hours

H. 10 hours

J. 12 hours

K. 14 hours

09.

Which of the following ordered pairs is the solution for the system of equations below ?
$$x - 3y = 6$$
$$2x - 3y = 3$$

A. $(-1, 1)$

B. $(1, 1)$

C. $(1, -3)$

D. $(-3, 1)$

E. $(-3, -3)$

10.

In the National Basketball Association (NBA) Eastern Conference that consists of 15 teams requires that every conference team must play each of other conference teams at least once in a season. If a conference consists of n teams, the number of conference games played in a season must then be at least $\dfrac{n^2 - n}{2}$. What is the minimum number of conference games for NBA Eastern Conference ?

F. 30

G. 45

H. 90

J. 100

K. 105

11.

Given the function $h(x) = \dfrac{-4(x^2 - x - 2)}{-12x + 12}$, what is the value of $h(-3)$?

A. $-\dfrac{8}{9}$

B. $-\dfrac{5}{6}$

C. $\dfrac{3}{4}$

D. $\dfrac{5}{6}$

E. $\dfrac{8}{9}$

12.

If $a = bc^2 d^3$, $a = 720$, $c = 3$, and $d = 2$, what is the value of b ?

F. 0.6

G. 8

H. 10

J. 1.2

K. 14

13.

In standard (x, y) coordinate plane, if the equation of line is $y = -\dfrac{1}{3}x + 4$, which of the following is an equation of a line that is perpendicular to the line ?

A. $y = \dfrac{1}{3}x + 4$

B. $y = -\dfrac{1}{3}x - 4$

C. $y = 3x - \dfrac{1}{4}$

D. $y = -3x + 4$

E. $y = -\dfrac{3}{4}x + 1$

14.

The table shows the distance (in feet) of an object moving at a constant rate along a straight line for times (in seconds).

t (time; sec)	0	1	2	3	4
d (distance; ft)	7	10	13	16	19

Which of the following equations is expressed as this relationship between d and t ?

A. $d = t + 7$

B. $d = 3t$

C. $d = -3t + 7$

D. $d = 3t + 7$

E. $d = 7t$

15.

A parking meter only accepts quarters ($0.25) and dimes ($0.1). When the meter was emptied Sunday evening, 387 coins were counted and had a value of $70.95. Which of the following systems of equations, gives the number of quarters, q, and the number of dimes, d ?

F. $25q + 10d = 387$
   $0.25q + 0.1d = 70.95$

G. $q + d = 387$
   $0.25q + 0.1d = 70.95$

H. $q + d = 387$
   $25q + 10d = 70.95$

J. $q + d = 70.95$
   $0.25q + 0.1d = 387$

K. $25q + 10d = 387$
   $q + d = 70.95$

16.

Which of the following graphs represents the solution set for the inequality $3x - 4 \geq 5$?

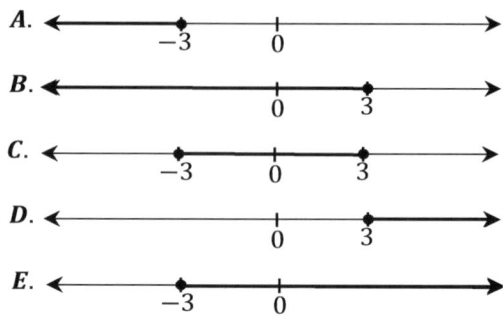

17.

A Fresh Food Market, Jenna paid $16.00 when she bought oranges, apples and eggplants. Jenna paid $0.50 for each orange, $0.75 for each apple, and $0.40 for each eggplant. She knew she had bought 12 oranges and 8 apples. What is the number of eggplants that Jenna bought at the market?

A. 8

B. 9

C. 10

D. 11

E. 12

18.

Squares A, B, and C have the length of sides of s centimeters, $3s$ centimeters, and $5s$ centimeters, respectively. What is the ratio of the length of side of Square B to the perimeter of Square A?

A. 3:2

B. 3:1

C. 1:3

D. 3:4

E. 4:3

19.

Which of the following proportions, when solved for x, gives the correct answer to the problem given below?

25 is 40% of what number, x.

F. $\dfrac{x}{40} = \dfrac{25}{100}$

G. $\dfrac{100}{x} = \dfrac{25}{40}$

H. $\dfrac{25}{x} = \dfrac{40}{100}$

J. $\dfrac{x}{25} = \dfrac{40}{100}$

K. $\dfrac{40}{x} = \dfrac{25}{100}$

20.

Andrea and Bessie started running simultaneously from the same point on a 300-meter circular track. They each ran 20 laps clockwise around the course maintaining constant speeds. Andrea ran at a constant speed 150 meter per minute and Bessie ran at a constant speed 200 meter per minute. How many laps Andrea have left to run when Bessie had completed her run?

A. 3 laps

B. $3\dfrac{1}{2}$ laps

C. $4\dfrac{1}{4}$ laps

D. $4\dfrac{3}{4}$ laps

E. 5 laps

21.

Samuel will have a 300-meter-long electric wire laid on his farm. The Electrical Contractor Company charges a $800.00 fee, plus a set amount per foot of electric wire. The Electrical Contractor Company has given Samuel an estimate of $4,700.00 to lay the electric wire on his farm. What is the set amount per meter of electric wire?

F. $12.33

G. $12.67

H. $13.00

J. $13.33

K. $13.67

22.

In the figure below, the distinct line segments l, m, and n all intersect at a point O. The measures of 2 angles are given. What is the measure of $x°$?

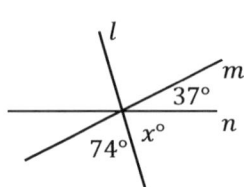

A. 60°

B. 62°

C. 69°

D. 89°

E. 99°

23.

As shown in the figure below, the angle $\angle ABC$ measures 108°, the angle $\angle ACD$ measures 146°, and three points B, C, and D are collinear. What is the measure of the angle $\angle BAC$?

F. 38°

G. 42°

H. 46°

J. 50°

K. 54°

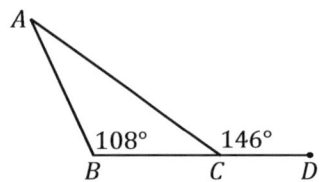

24.

Which of the following numbers is the exact value of $\log_3 \sqrt{27}$?

A. $\dfrac{1}{2}$

B. $\dfrac{3}{2}$

C. $\dfrac{1}{3}$

D. $\dfrac{2}{3}$

E. $3\sqrt{3}$

25.

In the figure below, a points D lies on $\overline{AC}$, and the measure of angle $\angle ABD$ is $(2x)°$. Which of the following inequalities for x is true?

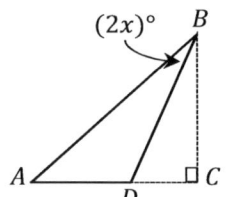

F. $0 < x < 15$

G. $0 < x < 30$

H. $0 < x < 45$

J. $30 < x < 45$

K. $45 < x < 90$

26.

In the figure below, $\triangle PQR$ is similar to $\triangle XYZ$ with $\angle P \cong \angle X$ and $\angle Q \cong \angle Y$. The given lengths are in centimeters. What is the length, in centimeters, of $\overline{YZ}$?

A. $7\dfrac{1}{3}$

B. $7\dfrac{2}{3}$

C. 8

D. $8\dfrac{1}{3}$

E. $8\dfrac{2}{3}$

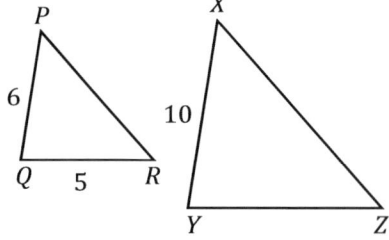

27.

A cube has a total surface area of X square inches. Which of the following expressions is the edge length, in term of X, of the cube?

A. $\dfrac{\sqrt[3]{6X}}{6}$

B. $\dfrac{\sqrt[3]{X}}{6}$

C. $\dfrac{\sqrt{X}}{6}$

D. $\dfrac{\sqrt{6X}}{6}$

E. $\sqrt{6X}$

28.

In the figure below, a right triangular prism has dimensions given in centimeters. What is the prism's total surface area, in square centimeters?

A. 236

B. 248

C. 250

D. 262

E. 274

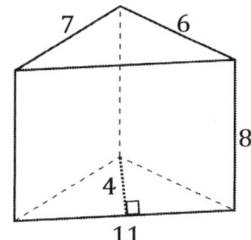

29.

In the figure below, a point O is the center of the circle, and right triangle $\triangle PRO$ intersects the circle at two points S and T. The point S lies on $\frac{2}{3}$ of $\overline{OR}$, which is 18 inches long. If the shaded region inside the circle is 120π square inches, what is the measures of $\angle P$?

F. 60°

G. 45°

H. 40°

J. 30°

K. 20°

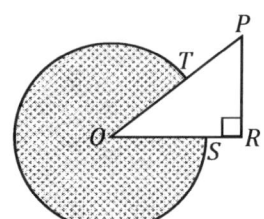

30.

A square and an equilateral triangle have the same area. The base of the triangle is 12 inches, and the height of the triangle is 8 inches. What is the length, in inches, of a side of the square?

A. 4

B. $3\sqrt{4}$

C. $4\sqrt{3}$

D. $2\sqrt{3} + 2$

E. 5

31.

A red kangaroo is jumped from the ground. Its height h feet above the ground, t seconds after it is jumped, is given by $h(t) = -2t^2 + 12t$. How long is the height of the kangaroo's jumping above 10 feet?

F. 1

G. 2

H. 3

J. 4

K. 5

32.

Which of the following complex numbers equals to $(\pi - 2i)(-4 + 5i)$?

A. $9\pi + 18i$

B. $(-4\pi + 10) + (5\pi + 8)i$

C. $(4\pi - 8) + (10\pi - 6)i$

D. $(-5\pi - 8) + (-4\pi - 10)i$

E. $(-5\pi + 10) + (4\pi + 8)i$

33.

What is the least degree of the polynomial function whose graph is shown in the (x, y) coordinate plane below?

F. 1

G. 2

H. 3

J. 4

K. Can not be determined.

34.

As shown in the figure below, a point $(3,1)$ and a line $y = 3$ are graphed in the standard (x, y) coordinate plane. What are the coordinates of the point's image after the point has been reflected on the line?

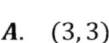

A. $(3,3)$

B. $(3,5)$

C. $(3,-5)$

D. $(5,-3)$

E. $(5,3)$

35.

For all real numbers $x \neq 3$, which of the following expressions is equivalent to $\dfrac{x^2+x-12}{x-3} -x + 4$?

F. x

G. 8

H. $x + 8$

J. $-2x$

K. $-2x + 8$

36.

For what value(s) of x is(are) the rational expression $\dfrac{x}{x^2-9}$ undefined?

A. 0

B. $-3, and\ 3$

C. $0, and\ 3$

D. $-3, and\ 0$

E. $-3, 0, and\ 3$

37.

Let $f(x) = x^2 - 4$ and $g(x) = 2x + 5$. What is the value of $g(f(-1))$?

A. -1

B. 0

C. 1

D. 2

E. 3

38.

Which of the following is the LCD(least common denominator) for $\dfrac{1}{2x^2-18}+\dfrac{1}{5x+15}$?

A. $(x+3)$

B. $10(x+3)$

C. $(x+3)(x-3)$

D. $10(x+3)(x-3)$

E. $10(x+3)^2(x-3)$

40.

If $\log_{(x-2)}(x^2-4)=2$, then what is real value of x?

A. -2

B. 2

C. -4

D. 2

E. 0

39.

Given that $xy^2=-1$ for all real numbers x and y, which of the following equations is y in term of x?

F. $\sqrt{\dfrac{1}{x}}$

G. $-\sqrt{\dfrac{1}{x}}$

H. $\pm\sqrt{\dfrac{-1}{x}}$

J. $\pm\sqrt{\dfrac{1}{x}}\,i$

K. $\pm\sqrt{\dfrac{-1}{x}}\,i$

41.

A graphic designer makes 500-piece jigsaw puzzle and includes 10 extra pieces to more challenging and these 10 extra pieces do not fit anywhere in the puzzle. Suppose that you buy the jigsaw box and pick up a random piece of the puzzle immediately, what is the probability that it would be one of the extra pieces?

F. $\dfrac{1}{51}$

G. $\dfrac{1}{510}$

H. $\dfrac{1}{5}$

J. $\dfrac{11}{510}$

K. $\dfrac{10}{511}$

Use the following information to answer questions
42 - 43.

The school math study group and the school science study group ate lunch together at Ole Noodles Restaurant. An order of noodles comes in 1 of 2 types of sauce, vegetable or meat, and consist of 1 of 5 garnishes and 1 of 3 sizes, small, medium or large. The table below shows the number of vegetable and meat orders of noodles bought by each group, and the price each group paid for their orders of noodles(without tax and tip).

Study group	Number of orders		Price
	Vegetable	Meat	
Math	5	3	$28.20
Science	3	4	$23.30

42.

How many different possible orders of noodles could a student order?

A. 4

B. 6

C. 15

D. 30

E. 60

43.

Regardless of the garnish and the size, assuming that the price is the same for each order of a given sauce, what is the price of a vegetable order of noodles?

F. $3.28

G. $3.60

H. $3.90

J. $3.96

K. $4.02

44.

A set of numbers consist of all the even integers that are greater than 1 and less than 30. What is the probability that a number randomly chosen from the set will be divisible by 4?

A. $\dfrac{1}{28}$

B. $\dfrac{7}{30}$

C. $\dfrac{1}{4}$

D. $\dfrac{6}{29}$

E. $\dfrac{7}{29}$

45.

A bottle contains only 7 white balls, 6 black balls, 2 green balls, and R red balls. The color of each ball is not changed. What is the probability that a ball picked at random from the bottle is green?

F. $\dfrac{2}{15}$

G. $\dfrac{2}{15 + R}$

H. $\dfrac{R - 2}{15 + R}$

J. $\dfrac{R}{15 + R}$

K. $\dfrac{R + 2}{15 + R}$

Use the following information to answer questions 46 - 49.

As shown the figure below, a large circle with center O has a diameter $\overline{PQ}$ and the length of the diameter is 20 inches. A point R is placed on the large circle and the measure of $\angle POR$ is 60°. And the length of a small circle's diameter is equal to the length of $\overline{OQ}$.

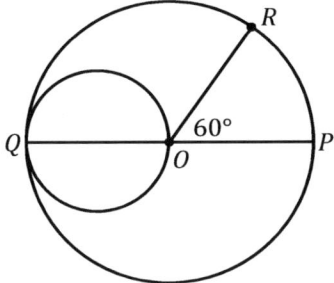

46.

Which of the following values is the area, in square inches, of the large circle?

A. 25π

B. 100π

C. 150π

D. 200π

E. 400π

47.

Which of the following values is the length, in inches, of arc $\overset{\frown}{OQ}$?

A. 5π

B. 10π

C. 15π

D. 20π

E. 40π

48.

Suppose that the figure is placed in standard (x, y) coordinate plane so that point O has coordinates $(0, 0)$ and $\overline{PQ}$ is parallel to x-axis. Which of the following values is the x-coordinate of point R?

F. 5

G. 7

H. 9

J. 11

K. 13

49.

The table below shows sums of consecutive odd numbers and the sum is always a perfect square. One of the sequences described below has a sum of 196 . What is the largest odd number in the sequence?

A. 21

B. 23

C. 25

D. 27

E. 31

n	Sum of first n odd numbers
1	1
2	$1 + 3 = 4$
3	$1 + 3 + 5 = 9$
4	$1 + 3 + 5 + 7 = 16$

50.

In the standard (x, y) coordinate below, the rational function, $f(x) = \frac{x^2 + 2x - 3}{x + 4}$, has two asymptotes. Which of the following points is the intersection of two asymptotes?

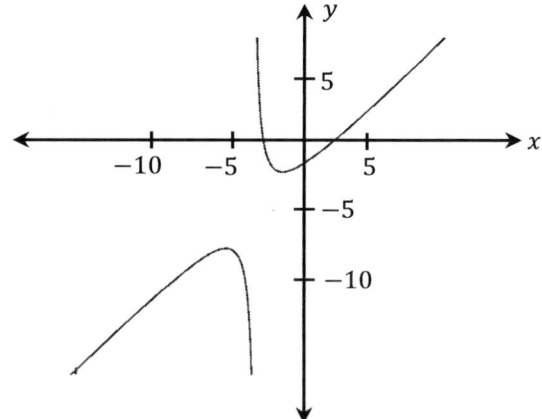

F. $(3, -1)$

G. $(3, -4)$

H. $(-4, 1)$

J. $(-4, -3)$

K. $(-4, -6)$

51.

Which of the following equations is the equation of the ellipse that is graphed in the standard (x, y) coordinate plane below?

A. $\dfrac{(x - 3)^2}{25} - \dfrac{(y - 2)^2}{9} = 1$

B. $\dfrac{(x + 3)^2}{9} - \dfrac{(y + 2)^2}{4} = 1$

C. $\dfrac{(x - 3)^2}{9} + \dfrac{(y - 2)^2}{4} = 1$

D. $\dfrac{(x + 3)^2}{9} + \dfrac{(y + 2)^2}{4} = 1$

E. $\dfrac{(x - 3)^2}{16} + \dfrac{(y - 2)^2}{8} = 1$

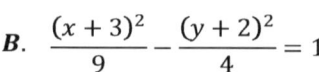

52.

A circle has its center $(2, -3)$ and passes through $(-4, 7)$ in the standard (x, y) coordinate plane. What is the area, in square coordinate units, of the circle?

A. 25π

B. 76π

C. 96π

D. 121π

E. 136π

53.

On the number line, a point A is 2 and another point B is -6. What is the distance between A and B ?

F. -8

G. 8

H. -4

J. 4

K. 2

Use the following information to answer questions
54 - 55.

As shown below, a point A is located at (5, 1), B is
located at (1, 1), and C is located at (1, 6) to form a
right triangle ΔABC in the standard (x, y) coordinate
plane. The given dimensions are in coordinate units.

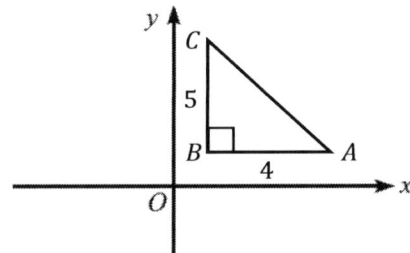

54.

The right triangle ΔABC will be rotated about the
vertical line $x = 1$ to form a right circular cone. What
is the volume, in cubic coordinate units, of the cone?

A. $\dfrac{20}{3}$

B. $\dfrac{20}{3}\pi$

C. 80

D. 80π

E. $\dfrac{80}{3}\pi$

55.

What is the measure of $\angle CAB$?

F. $\cos^{-1}\left(\dfrac{5}{4}\right)$

G. $\cos^{-1}\left(\dfrac{4}{5}\right)$

H. $\tan^{-1}\left(\dfrac{4}{5}\right)$

J. $\tan^{-1}\left(\dfrac{5}{4}\right)$

K. $\sin^{-1}\left(\dfrac{4}{5}\right)$

56.

In the standard (x, y) coordinate plane, the graph of
$f(x) = \tan x$ is reflected about x-axis, translated left
π units, and then translated down 2 units. What is
the image function of the equation, $g(x)$, after the
three transformations?

A. $g(x) = -\tan(x + \pi) + 3$

B. $g(x) = \tan(-x + \pi) + 3$

C. $g(x) = -\tan(x - \pi) - 3$

D. $g(x) = -\tan(x + \pi) - 3$

E. $g(x) = \tan(-x + \pi) - 3$

57.

The trigonometric function $y = 4\tan 0.5(x + \pi)$ is
graphed below. Which of the following values is the
period of the trigonometric function?

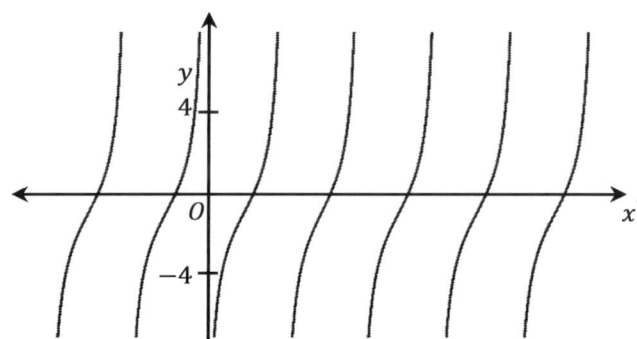

F. 2π

G. $\dfrac{3\pi}{2}$

H. π

J. $\dfrac{\pi}{2}$

K. $\dfrac{\pi}{4}$

58.

In the standard (x, y) coordinate plane, the graph of $f(x) = 2 - 3\cos(x + \pi)$ is shown below. What is the range of $f(x)$?

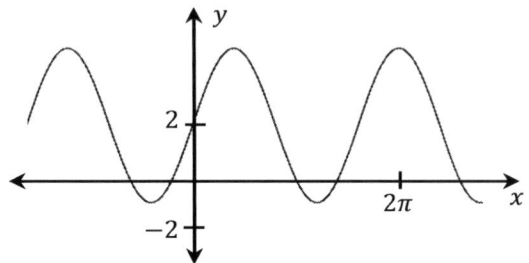

A. $-1 \le y \le 2$

B. $-3 \le y \le 3$

C. $-1 \le y \le 5$

D. $0 \le x \le 2\pi$

E. $0 \le x \le \dfrac{3\pi}{2}$

59.

Suppose that the side lengths of a right triangle ΔXYZ are given in centimeters in the figure below.

What is the trigonometric ratio that is equal to $\dfrac{2\sqrt{2}}{3}$?

F. $\sin X$

G. $\cos X$

H. $\tan X$

J. $\cot X$

K. $\sec X$

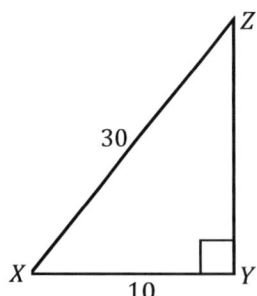

60.

Which of the following matrices is equal to the product of the two matrices:

$$\begin{bmatrix} -1 & 0 \\ 5 & 4 \end{bmatrix} \cdot \begin{bmatrix} 4 \\ -6 \end{bmatrix} = ?$$

A. $\begin{bmatrix} 20 & 16 \\ 6 & 0 \end{bmatrix}$

B. $\begin{bmatrix} 6 & 0 \\ 20 & 16 \end{bmatrix}$

C. $\begin{bmatrix} -4 & 0 \\ -30 & -24 \end{bmatrix}$

D. $\begin{bmatrix} -4 \\ -4 \end{bmatrix}$

E. $\begin{bmatrix} -4 & -4 \end{bmatrix}$

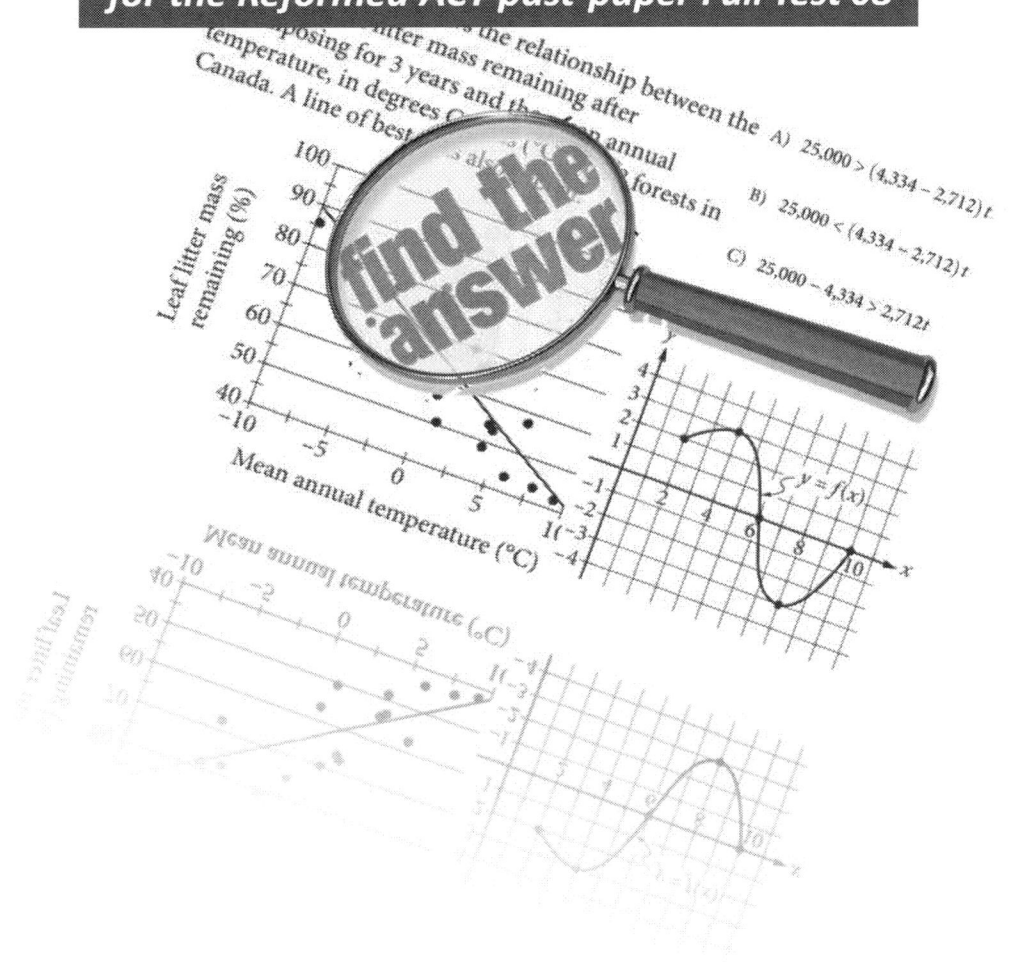

Obtain Scale Scores from Raw Scores					
Scale Score	Raw Score	Scale Score	Raw Score	Scale Score	Raw Score
36	60	24	36-37	12	7
35	58-59	23	34-35	11	5-6
34	57	22	32-33	10	4
33	55-56	21	30-31	9	-
32	54	20	29	8	3
31	52-53	19	27-28	7	-
30	50-51	18	24-26	6	2
29	48-49	17	21-23	5	-
28	45-47	16	17-20	4	1
27	43-44	15	13-16	3	-
26	40-42	14	11-12	2	-
25	38-39	13	8-10	1	0

1. Scoring Key

Key		Question Category	Y/N
01.	E	Number Theory	
02.	G	Number Theory	
03.	J	Number Theory	
04.	C	Expression and Linear Equation	
05.	J	Expression and Linear Equation	
06.	C	Expression and Linear Equation	
07.	K	Expression and Linear Equation	
08.	G	Expression and Linear Equation	
09.	E	Expression and Linear Equation	
10.	K	Expression and Linear Equation	
11.	B	Linear Function inequality	
12.	H	Linear Function inequality	
13.	C	Linear Function inequality	
14.	D	Linear Function inequality	
15.	G	Linear Function inequality	
16.	D	Linear Function inequality	
17.	C	Linear Function inequality	
18.	D	Arithmetic Topic and Ratio	
19.	H	Arithmetic Topic and Ratio	
20.	E	Arithmetic Topic and Ratio	
21.	H	Arithmetic Topic and Ratio	
22.	C	Basic Geometry	
23.	F	Basic Geometry	
24.	B	Basic Geometry	
25.	H	Basic Geometry	
26.	D	Basic Geometry	
27.	D	Basic Geometry	
28.	A	Basic Geometry	
29.	J	Arithmetic Topic and Ratio	
30.	C	Quadratic and Polynomial Function	

Key		Question Category	Y/N
31.	J	Quadratic and Polynomial Function	
32.	B	Quadratic and Polynomial Function	
33.	J	Quadratic and Polynomial Function	
34.	B	Quadratic and Polynomial Function	
35.	G	Quadratic and Polynomial Function	
36.	B	Further Equations and Functions	
37.	A	Further Equations and Functions	
38.	D	Further Equations and Functions	
39.	H	Further Equations and Functions	
40.	B	Further Equations and Functions	
41.	F	Statistics and Probability	
42.	D	Statistics and Probability	
43.	H	Statistics and Probability	
44.	C	Statistics and Probability	
45.	G	Statistics and Probability	
46.	B	Analytic Geometry and Conic Section	
47.	A	Analytic Geometry and Conic Section	
48.	F	Analytic Geometry and Conic Section	
49.	D	Sequence and Series	
50.	K	Analytic Geometry and Conic Section	
51.	D	Analytic Geometry and Conic Section	
52.	E	Analytic Geometry and Conic Section	
53.	G	Analytic Geometry and Conic Section	
54.	E	Trigonometric Functions	
55.	J	Trigonometric Functions	
56.	D	Trigonometric Functions	
57.	F	Trigonometric Functions	
58.	C	Trigonometric Functions	
59.	F	Trigonometric Functions	
60.	D	Intermediate Algebra	

2. Answer Explanations

01. *Answer* (E)

Using prime factorization.

Prime factorizations of 12 and 72;
$$12 = 2^2 \times 3, \qquad 72 = 2^3 \times 3^2 = (2^2 \times 3) \times 2 \times 3$$

From the definitions of LCM and GCF, the two numbers must have factor $2^2(4)$ and 3. And at least one of the two numbers must have 2 and 3 as prime factors.

Thus, the correct answer is E.

02. *Answer* (G)

The two bells ring at the same time after the LCM time.

Prime factorization;
$$12 = 2 \times 2 \times 3 = 2^2 \times 3, \qquad 18 = 2 \times 3 \times 3 = 2 \times 3^2$$

So, LCM of 12 and 18 is;
$$\text{LCM} = 2 \times 2 \times 3 \times 3 = 2^2 \times 3^2 = 36.$$

Thus, the two bells ring simultaneously at $8:36$ am.

03. *Answer* (J)

It is also a good idea to substitute a specific number for a.

a is positive number;
$F. -3a$ is negative so, $-3a < 0$ is true.
$G. \ a^3 = a \times a \times a > 0$ is true.
$H. \ -a$ is negative and a^2 is positive so,
$\quad -a - a^2 (ex: -2 - (2)^2 = -6) < 0$ is true.
$J. \ -a$ is negative and absolute value is always positive so,
$\quad |-a| < 0$ is not true.
$K. \ |-a| = a$ so, $a + |-a| = 2a$ so, $a + |-a| > a$ is true.

04. *Answer* (C)

Suppose that the polynomial is $ax^2 + bx + c$.

If the polynomial is $ax^2 + bx + c$, then the difference is;
$$3x^2 - 3x + 12 - (ax^2 + bx + c) = 3x^2 - 3x + 12 - ax^2 - bx - c$$
Combining the like terms;
$$\rightarrow \ (3 - a)x^2 + (-3 - b)x + (12 - c) = 4x + 8$$
Using the property of identity;
$$3 - a = 0, \qquad -3 - b = 4, \qquad 12 - c = 8$$
Therefore, $a = 3$, $b = -7$, and $c = 4$.
Thus, the polynomial is $3x^2 - 7x + 4$

05. *Answer* (J)

The square of i is -1.

Expanding the given expression;
$$(x + 2i)^3 = x^3 + 3x^2 i + 3xi^2 + i^3$$
By $i^2 = -1$ and $i^3 = -i$,
$$(x + 2i)^3 = x^3 + 3x^2 i + 3xi^2 + i^3 = x^3 + 3ix^2 - 3x - i$$

Thus, the correct answer is J.

06. *Answer* (C)

Solving the equation.

Add 5 to both sides;
$$\frac{3}{4}x - 5 = 1 \ \rightarrow \ \frac{3}{4}x - 5 + 5 = 1 + 5 \ \rightarrow \ \frac{3}{4}x = 6$$
Multiply by 4 on both sides;
$$\frac{3}{4}x = 6 \ \rightarrow \ 4 \cdot \frac{3}{4}x = 6 \cdot 4 \ \rightarrow \ 3x = 24$$
Divide by 3 on both sides;
$$3x = 24 \ \rightarrow \ \frac{3x}{3} = \frac{24}{3} \ \rightarrow \ x = 8$$
Thus, the value of x is 8.

07. *Answer* (K)

"at most" means "less than or equal to"

Let x be the amount of money that she has in her savings account now. The following inequality could be established.
$$x + 240 \le \frac{11}{8}x$$
Subtract x form both sides;
$$\frac{11}{8}x \ge x + 240 \ \rightarrow \ \frac{11}{8}x - x \ge 240 \ \rightarrow \ \frac{3}{8}x \ge 240$$
Multiply by $\frac{8}{3}$ on both sides;
$$\frac{3}{8}x \ge 240 \ \rightarrow \ \frac{8}{3} \times \frac{3}{8}x \ge 240 \times \frac{8}{3} \ \rightarrow \ x \ge 640$$
Thus, the least amount of money is $\$640$.

08. *Answer* (G)

The lava's moving speed is 6.5 km per hour.

If the lava reaches to the ocean, d is zero. So, substitute 0 for d;
$$d = 52 - 6.5t \ \rightarrow \ 0 = 52 - 6.5t$$
Adding $6.5t$ to both sides;
$$0 = 52 - 6.5t \ \rightarrow \ 0 + 6.5t = 52 - 6.5t + 6.5t \ \rightarrow \ 6.5t = 52$$
Divide by 6.5 on both sides;
$$6.5t = 52 \ \rightarrow \ \frac{6.5t}{6.5} = \frac{52}{6.5} \ \rightarrow \ t = 8$$
Thus, after 8 hours, the lava reaches to the ocean.

09. *Answer* (E)

Solve for one variable and then substitute the value for other equation.

At the first equation, adding $3y$ to both sides;
$$x - 3y = 6 \ \rightarrow \ x - 3y + 3y = 6 + 3y \ \rightarrow \ x = 3y + 6$$
Substituting $3y + 6$ for x on the second equation;
$$2x - 3y = 3 \ \rightarrow \ 2(3y + 6) - 3y = 3 \ \rightarrow \ 6y + 12 - 3y = 3$$
$$\rightarrow \ 3y + 12 = 3$$
Subtracting 12 from both sides;
$$3y + 12 = 3 \ \rightarrow \ 3y + 12 - 12 = 3 - 12 \ \rightarrow \ 3y = -9$$
Dividing both sides by 3;
$$3y = -9 \ \rightarrow \ \frac{3y}{3} = \frac{-9}{3} \ \rightarrow \ y = -3$$
Substituting -3 for y on the first equation;
$$x - 3y = 6 \ \rightarrow \ x - 3(-3) = 6 \ \rightarrow \ x + 9 = 6$$
Subtracting 9 from both sides;
$$x + 9 = 6 \ \rightarrow \ x + 9 - 9 = 6 - 9 \ \rightarrow \ x = -3$$
Thus, the ordered pair is $(-3, -3)$.

10. Answer **(K)**

Substitute 15 for n.

Substitute 15 for n;
$$\frac{n^2 - n}{2} = \frac{15^2 - 15}{2} = \frac{225 - 15}{2} = \frac{210}{2} = 105$$
Thus, the minimum number of games is 105.

11. Answer **(B)**

Substitute each value and then evaluate.

Substitute -3 for x;
$$h(x) = \frac{-4(x^2 - x - 2)}{-12x + 12} \rightarrow h(-3) = \frac{-4((-3)^2 - (-3) - 2)}{-12(-3) + 12}$$
$$= \frac{-40}{48} = -\frac{5}{6}$$
Thus, the value of $h(-3)$ is $-\frac{5}{6}$.

12. Answer **(H)**

Substitute each value and then solve the equation.

Substituting 720 for a, 3 for c, and 2 for d;
$$a = bc^2d^3 \rightarrow 720 = b(3)^2(2)^3 \rightarrow 720 = b \times 72$$
Dividing both sides by 72;
$$72b = 720 \rightarrow \frac{72b}{72} = \frac{720}{72} \rightarrow b = 10$$
Thus, the value of b is 10.

13. Answer **(C)**

Two lines are perpendicular if and only if their slopes are negative reciprocals of each other.

Because the slope of the line, m', that is perpendicular to the given line is the negative reciprocal, the value is;
$$m' = -\frac{1}{m} = -\frac{1}{-\frac{1}{3}} = 3$$
In the slope intercept form, $y = mx + b$, the slop is m.
Thus, the line C, $y = 3x - \frac{1}{4}$, is perpendicular to the given line.

14. Answer **(D)**

The initial value is y-intercept and the rate of change is slope.

The distance, d, is output value so, d is y, and the time, t, is input value so t is x.
The initial value(at $t = 0$) is $7ft$ so, y-intercept is 7. The rate of change, slope m, is;
$$m = \frac{y_2 - y_1}{x_2 - x_1} = \frac{10 - 7}{1 - 0} = \frac{3}{1} = 3$$
Thus,
substitute the each value for slope intercept form $y = mx + b$;
$$y = 3x + 7 \rightarrow d = 3t + 7$$

15. Answer **(G)**

The total number of coins is 387 and the total value is $70.95.

The total number of coins is 387, so;
$$q + d = 387$$
The total value of coins is $70.95, therefore;
$$0.25q + 0.1d = 70.95$$
Thus, the correct answer is G.

16. Answer **(D)**

Solving inequality by using inverse operation.

Adding 4 to both sides;
$$3x - 4 \geq 5 \rightarrow 3x - 4 + 4 \geq 5 + 4 \rightarrow 3x \geq 9$$
Dividing both sides by 3;
$$3x \geq 9 \rightarrow \frac{3x}{3} \geq \frac{9}{3} \rightarrow x \geq 3$$
Thus, D.

17. Answer **(C)**

Making a linear equation.

Let x be the number of eggplants;
$$\$0.5 \times 12 + \$0.75 \times 8 + \$0.4 \times x = \$16.00 \rightarrow 0.4x + 12 = 16$$
Subtract 12 from both sides and then divide by 0.4;
$$0.4x + 12 - 12 = 16 - 12 \rightarrow 0.4x = 4 \rightarrow \frac{0.4x}{0.4} = \frac{4}{0.4} \rightarrow x = 10$$
Thus, the number of eggplants is 10.

18. Answer **(D)**

Average is the quotient total money and total students.

The perimeter of Square A is $4s$ and the ratio of a to b is $a:b$.
Thus, the ratio of the length of side of Square B to the perimeter of Square A is $3s:4s = 3:4$.

19. Answer **(H)**

A proportion is an equation that states that two ratios are equivalent..

"a is p percent of b" is expressed as $\frac{a}{b} = \frac{p}{100}$.
So, "25 is 40% of what number, x" is expressed as;
$$\frac{25}{x} = \frac{40}{100}$$
Thus, the correct answer is H.

20. Answer **(E)**

Time the quotient of distance and time.

Bessie's finishing time is;
$$time = \frac{distance}{speed} = \frac{20 \times 300m}{200m/min} = \frac{6,000}{200} = 30min$$
The Andrea's distance for 30 minutes is;
$$distance = speed \times time = 150m/min \times 30 = 4,500 \, meters$$
So, the remaining distance is;
$$6,000m - 4,500m = 1,500 \, meters$$
it is
$$\frac{1,500 \, m}{300m/lap} = 5 \, laps$$

21. Answer **(H)**

The total charge is the sum of fee and set amount.

Let x be set amount, the total charge is calculated by;
$$\$4,700 = \$800 + x \rightarrow x = \$3,900$$
The rate of set amount to length of wire is;
$$\frac{\$3,900}{300 \, meters} = \frac{\$13}{1 \, meter}$$
Thus, the set amount per meter is $13 per meter.

22. Answer **(C)**

Three angles lie on same line.

Three angles lie on same line, m, so;
$$37° + x° + 74° = 180° \rightarrow x + 111° = 180° \rightarrow x = 69°$$
Thus, the measure of $x°$ is 69°.

23. Answer **(F)**

Using exterior angle theorem.

Using exterior angle theorem;
$$\angle ACD = \angle ABC + \angle BAC \rightarrow 146° = 108° + \angle BAC \rightarrow \angle BAC = 38°$$
Thus, the measure of the angle $\angle BAC$ is 38°.

24. Answer **(B)**

Using logarithm property.

$\sqrt{27} = \sqrt{3^3} = 3^{\frac{3}{2}}$ and rewrite; $\log_3 \sqrt{27} = \log_3 3^{\frac{3}{2}}$.
Using logarithm property $\log_b b^N = N$ so, $\log_3 3^{\frac{3}{2}} = \frac{3}{2}$.

Thus, the correct answer is **B**.

25. Answer **(H)**

Using exterior angle theorem.

Using exterior angle theorem;
$$\angle ADB = 90° + \angle DBC \rightarrow \angle ADB \text{ is greater than } 90°$$
$$\rightarrow \angle ADB > 90°$$
Using triangle sum angle theorem;
$$\angle ABD + \angle BAD + \angle ADB = 180° \rightarrow (2x)° + \angle BAD + \angle ADB = 180°$$
Because $\angle ADB > 90°$,
$$0° < (2x)° < 90 \rightarrow 0 < x < 45$$
Thus, the correct answer is **H**.

26. Answer **(D)**

Using proportional equation.

$\Delta PQR \backsim \Delta XYZ$ so,
$$\frac{\overline{PQ}}{\overline{QR}} = \frac{\overline{XY}}{\overline{YZ}} \rightarrow \frac{6}{5} = \frac{10}{\overline{YZ}} \rightarrow 6 \times \overline{YZ} = 5 \times 10$$
$$\rightarrow \overline{YZ} = \frac{50}{6} \rightarrow \overline{YZ} = 8\frac{1}{3}$$
Thus, the length of $\overline{YZ}$ is $8\frac{1}{3}$.

27. Answer **(D)**

In a cube, width=length=height.

Let a be a edge length of the cube, the surface area is $6 \times a^2$. So,
$$X = 6a^2 \rightarrow a^2 = \frac{X}{6} \rightarrow a = \pm\sqrt{\frac{X}{6}} = \pm\frac{\sqrt{6X}}{6}$$

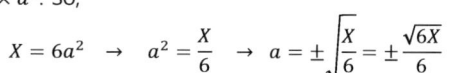

Thus, the edge length of the cube is $\frac{\sqrt{6X}}{6}$ ($\because$ edge length is always positive).

28. Answer **(A)**

Using the net of the given prism.

Area of two triangles;
$$2 \times \frac{1}{2} \times 11 \times 4 = 44 \ cm^2$$
Area of a rectangle;
$$(6 + 11 + 7) \times 8 = 192 \ cm^2$$
Thus, the total surface area is
$192 + 44 = 236 \ cm^2$.

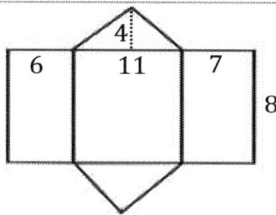

29. Answer **(J)**

Finding the sector area.

The radius of the circle, r, is $\frac{2}{3} \times 18 = 12$.
And using the formula of sector area;
$$sector \ area = circle's \ area \times \frac{central \ angle}{360°} = \pi r^2 \times \frac{\angle O}{360°}$$
$$\rightarrow 120\pi = \pi(12)^2 \times \frac{\angle O}{360°} \rightarrow 120\pi = 144\pi \times \frac{\angle O}{360°}$$
$$\rightarrow \angle O = \frac{120\pi}{144\pi} \times 360° \rightarrow \angle O = 300°$$
From angle sum of triangle,
$$\angle P + (360° - \angle O) + 90° = 180° \rightarrow \angle P + 60° + 90° = 180°$$
$$\rightarrow \angle P = 30°$$
Thus, the measure of $\angle P$ is 30°.

30. Answer **(C)**

Area of a square is s^2.

Calculate the area of the triangle;
$$area = \frac{1}{2} \times b \times h = \frac{1}{2} \times 12 \times 8 = 48.$$
Let the side length of the square be x;
$$area = x^2 \rightarrow 48 = x^2$$
Take both side by square root;
$$\sqrt{x^2} = \pm\sqrt{48} \rightarrow x = 4\sqrt{3} \ (side \ length \ is \ always \ positive)$$
Thus, the length of a side of the square is $4\sqrt{3}$.

31. Answer **(J)**

Making the equation.

The motion of the kangaroo's jumping is a parabola shape so,
$$-2t^2 + 12t = 10 \rightarrow -2t^2 + 12t - 10 = 0 \rightarrow -2(t^2 - 6t + 5) = 0$$
Factoring; the product is 5 and the sum is 6
$-2(t^2 - 6t + 5) = 0$
$$\rightarrow -2(t - 1)(t - 5) = 0$$
$$\rightarrow t - 1 = 0 \ or \ t - 5 = 0$$
$$\rightarrow t = 1 \ or \ t = 5$$
Or using graphic method;
Thus, the time is 4 seconds.

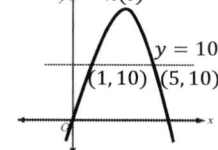

32. Answer **(B)**

Using FOIL pattern.

Expanding by using FOIL pattern;
$$(\pi - 2i)(-4 + 5i) = -4\pi + 5\pi i + 8i - 10i^2$$
$$= -4\pi + (5\pi + 8)i - 10i^2$$
Because $i^2 = -1$;
$$-4\pi + (5\pi + 8)i - 10i^2 = -4\pi + (5\pi + 8)i + 10$$
$$= (-4\pi + 10) + (5\pi + 8)i$$
Thus, the correct answer is **B**.

33. *Answer* **(J)**

There are 4 x-intercept's.

If the number of x-intercept of a polynomial function graph is N, then
    the number of real solution of the polynomial equation is N,
    the least degree of the polynomial function is N.
The given graph has 4 x-intercept's so, the least degree of the polynomial function is 4.

Thus, the correct answer is **J**.

34. *Answer* **(B)**

The line is a perpendicular bisector between the point and its image.

If the point $(3,1)$ is A and its image is A',
$y = 3$ is perpendicular bisector of $\overline{AA'}$.
So, $\overline{OA} = \overline{OA'}$, $O = (3,3)$, the coordinates of
A' is $(3,5)$.

Thus, the coordinates is $(3,5)$.

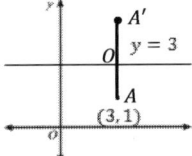

35. *Answer* **(G)**

Factoring and then simplifying

The product is 12 and the difference is 1 so factoring numerator:
$$\frac{x^2 + x - 12}{x - 3} - x + 4 \quad \rightarrow \quad \frac{(x-3)(x+4)}{x-3} - x + 4$$
Simplifying;
$$\frac{(x-3)(x+4)}{x-3} - x + 4 \quad \rightarrow \quad x + 4 - x + 4 = 8$$

Thus, the equivalent to 8.

36. *Answer* **(B)**

At vertical asymptotes, the expression undefined.

The vertical asymptotes are real zeros of denominator equation so,
$$x^2 - 9 = 0 \quad \rightarrow \quad (x+3)(x-3) = 0 \quad \rightarrow \quad x + 3 = 0 \ or \ x - 3 = 0$$
$$\rightarrow \quad x = -3 \ or \ x = 3$$

Thus, the correct answer is **B**.

37. *Answer* **(A)**

Using the concept of composition of function.

1st Method; substituting
    Finding $f(-1)$;
        $f(x) = x^2 - 4 \ \rightarrow \ f(-1) = (-1)^2 - 4 = 1 - 4 = -3.$
    Substituting -3 for $f(-1)$ on $g(f(-1))$;
        $g(f(-1)) = g(-3) \ \rightarrow \ g(-3) = 2(-3) + 5 = -6 + 5 = -1$

2nd Method; composition function
    Finding $g(f(x))$;
        $g(f(x)) = 2f(x) + 5 = 2(x^2 - 4) + 5 \ \rightarrow \ g(f(x)) = 2x^2 - 3$
    Substituting -1 for x;
        $g(f(-1)) = 2(-1)^2 - 3 = 2 - 3 = -1$

Thus, the value of $g(f(-1))$ is -1.

38. *Answer* **(D)**

LCD is least common multiple of denominators.

Factoring the rational expression;
$$\frac{1}{2x^2 - 18} + \frac{1}{5x + 15} \quad \rightarrow \quad \frac{1}{2(x^2 - 9)} + \frac{1}{5(x + 3)}$$
By sum and difference patterns; $a^2 - b^2 = (a+b)(a-b)$
$$\frac{1}{2(x^2 - 9)} + \frac{1}{5(x + 3)} \quad \rightarrow \quad \frac{1}{2(x+3)(x-3)} + \frac{1}{5(x+3)}$$
So, LCM of $2x^2 - 18$ and $5x + 15$ is $2 \times 5 \times (x + 3)(x - 3)$.

Thus, the LCD is $10(x + 3)(x - 3)$.

39. *Answer* **(H)**

x is an negative real number.

Because y^2 is positive x is negative number and solve for y;
$$xy^2 = -1 \quad \rightarrow \quad y^2 = \frac{-1}{x}$$
Take square root on both sides;
$$y = \pm \sqrt{\frac{-1}{x}} \quad \left(\frac{-1}{x} > 0 \ \because x < 0 \right)$$

Thus, the correct answer is **H**.

40. *Answer* **(B)**

Using the properties of logarithm.

Take the power of $(x - 2)$ on both sides;
$$\log_{(x-2)}(x^2 - 4) = 2 \quad \rightarrow \quad (x-2)^{\log_{(x-2)}(x^2-4)} = (x-2)^2$$
So,
$$(x^2 - 4) = (x - 2)^2 \quad \rightarrow \quad x^2 - 4 = x^2 - 4x + 4 \quad \rightarrow \quad -4 = -4x + 4$$
Subtract -4 from both sides;
$$-4x + 4 = -4 \quad \rightarrow \quad -4x = -4 - 4 \quad \rightarrow \quad -4x = -8$$
Divide both sides by -4;
$$-4x = -8 \quad \rightarrow \quad x = \frac{-8}{-4} = 2$$

Thus, the value of x is 2.

41. *Answer* **(F)**

The number of total pieces of puzzle is 510.

The number of total pieces of the puzzle is $500 + 10 = 510$ so, the probability is;
$$P = \frac{extra}{total} = \frac{10}{500 + 10} = \frac{10}{510} = \frac{1}{51}$$

Thus, the correct answer is **F**.

42. *Answer* **(D)**

Using fundamental counting principle.

The total number of possible orders is;
        types of sauce $\times$ kinds of garnishes $\times$ types of sizes
So, possible orders $= 2 \times 5 \times 3 = 30$ orders.

Thus, the correct answer is **D**.

43. **Answer** (**H**)

Make system of linear equation.

Let v be the price of a vegetable noodles and m be the price od a meat vegetable;

$$5v + 3m = 28.20 \quad - \;①$$
$$3v + 4m = 23.30 \quad - \;②$$

Rewrite the two equation by ① × 4 and ② × 3

$$20v + 12m = 112.80 \quad - \;③$$
$$9v + 12m = 69.90 \quad - \;④$$

Operate ③ − ④;

$$20v - 9v + 12m - 12m = 112.8 - 69.9 \quad \rightarrow \quad 11v = 42.9$$

Divide both sides by 11;

$$v = \frac{42.9}{11} = 3.9$$

Thus, the price of a vegetable order of noodles is $3.90.

---

44. **Answer** (**C**)

Find the multiples of 4.

The total number of the set's numbers(element) is 28($\because$ 2~29). And there are 7 multiples of 4 ($\because$ 4, 8, 12, 16, 20, 24, 28). So, the probability is

$$P = \frac{7}{28} = \frac{1}{4}$$

Thus, the correct answer is **C**.

---

45. **Answer** (**G**)

How many total balls in the bottle?

There are 15+R (7+6+2+R) balls in the bottle and 2 green balls. So, the probability is;

$$P = \frac{2}{15 + R}$$

Thus, the correct answer is **G**.

---

46. **Answer** (**B**)

Using the formula of the circle area.

Because the diameter of the large circle is 20 inches, the radius is 10($= 20 \div 2$) inches. Using the formula of the circle area;

$$area = \pi r^2 = \pi(10)^2 = 100\pi$$

Thus, the correct answer is **B**.

---

47. **Answer** (**A**)

Using the formula of the circle circumference.

From the formula of the length of circle arc and the length of $\overline{OQ}$ is 10 inches and it is diameter of the small circle.

$$arc\ length = 2\pi r \times \frac{central\ angle}{360°} = 2\pi(5) \times \frac{180°}{360°} = 5\pi$$

Thys, the correct answer is **A**.

---

48. **Answer** (**J**)

An equilateral triangle is also an isosceles triangle. .

Because $\overline{OR} = \overline{OP} = 10\ in$ and $\angle ROP = 60°$, $\triangle OPR$ is an equilateral triangle.
In $\triangle OPR$, draw perpendicular line from R to the base side and intersecting point is S.
The coordinates of point P are (10, 0) so, the coordinates of S is (5, 0). Because S and R have same x-coordinate, the x-coordinate of point R is 5.

Thus, the correct answer is **F**.

---

49. **Answer** (**D**)

Finding 'n'.

The sum is n^2 so, $n^2 = 196 \quad \rightarrow \quad n = \sqrt{196} = 14$ and the sequence is an arithmetic sequence, first term $a_1 = 1$, common difference $d = 2$. So, from the formula of arithmetic sequence;

$$a_n = a_1 + (n - 1)d \quad \rightarrow \quad a_{14} = 1 + (14 - 1) \times 2 = 27$$

Thus, the largest odd number is 27.

---

50. **Answer** (**K**)

The given function has a vertical asymptote and a slant asymptote.

The vertical asymptote is;
$x + 4 = 0 \quad \rightarrow \quad x = -4$.

And the slant asymptote is;
$$\frac{(x^2 + 2x - 3)}{x + 4} = x - 2 + \frac{5}{x + 4}$$
$$\rightarrow \quad y = x - 2.$$

So, the intersecting point is calculated by substituting -4 for x;
$$y = x - 2 \quad \rightarrow \quad y = (-4) - 2 = -6$$
$$\therefore (-4, -6)$$

Thus, the correct answer is **K**.

---

51. **Answer** (**D**)

Drawing auxiliary lines.

Because the conic section is an ellipse and the major axis is horizontal, the equation has this form;
$$\frac{(x - h)^2}{a^2} + \frac{(y - k)^2}{b^2} = 1 \quad (a > b)$$
The center of the ellipse lies on quadrant IV, $h < 0, k < 0$.

Thus, the correct answer is **D**.

---

52. **Answer** (**E**)

Using circle equation.

From the circle equation;
$$(x - h)^2 + (y - k)^2 = r^2 \quad \rightarrow \quad (x - 2)^2 + (y + 3)^2 = r^2.$$
Substitute -4 for x and 7 for y;
$$(-4 - 2)^2 + (7 + 3)^2 = r^2 \quad \rightarrow \quad r^2 = 136 \quad \rightarrow \quad r = \sqrt{136}.$$
Using the formula of circle area
$$area = \pi r^2 = \pi(136) = 136\pi$$

Thus, the correct answer is **E**.

---

53. **Answer** (**G**)

The distance is never negative.

The distance, d, is;
$$d = |-6 - 2| = |-8| = 8.$$

Thus, the distance is 8.

---

54. **Answer** (**E**)

Finding the radius of the cone's base.

The height, h, of the cone is 5 and the radius, r, is 4.
So, using the formula of circular cone;
$$V = \frac{1}{3}\pi r^2 h = \frac{1}{3}\pi(4)^2(5) = \frac{80}{3}\pi$$

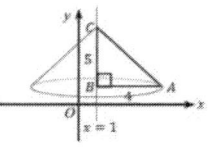

Thus, the correct answer is **E**.

---

55. Answer (J)

Using the inverse trigonometric function.

In view of $\angle CAB$, $\overline{AB}$ is adjacent side and $\overline{BC}$ is opposite side, so

$$\angle CAB = \tan^{-1}\left(\frac{5}{4}\right)$$

Thus, the correct answer is **J**.

56. Answer (D)

Applying the transformations one by one.

Let $y = f(x)$ be before transformation.
Reflected about x-axis;
$$y = f(x) \rightarrow -y = f(x) \rightarrow y = -f(x)$$
Translated left π unit;
$$y = -f(x) \rightarrow y = -f(x - (-\pi)) \rightarrow y = -f(x + \pi)$$
Translated down 3 unit;
$$y = -f(x + \pi) \rightarrow y = -f(x + \pi) - 3$$
So,
$$f(x) = \tan x \rightarrow g(x) = -\tan(x + \pi) - 3$$

Thus, the correct answer is **D**.

57. Answer (F)

Finding b value.

The period of the trigonometric function $y = a \tan b(x - h) + k$ is;
$$period = \frac{\pi}{|b|} = \frac{\pi}{|0.5|} = 2\pi$$

Thus, the correct answer is **F**.

58. Answer (C)

Check amplitude and vertical translation.

From the standard form, $y = a\cos b(x - h) + k$, the range is
$$-a + k \leq y \leq a + k.$$
Rewrite the function;
$$f(x) = -3\cos(x + \pi) + 2.$$
So, the range is;
$$-3 + 2 \leq y \leq 3 + 2 \rightarrow -1 \leq y \leq 5$$

Thus, the correct answer is **C**.

59. Answer (F)

Pythagorean theorem always useful.

Using the Pythagorean theorem;
$$\overline{ZY} = \sqrt{30^2 - 10^2} = \sqrt{800} = 20\sqrt{2}$$
$$\sin X = \frac{O}{H} = \frac{20\sqrt{2}}{30} = \frac{2\sqrt{2}}{3}$$

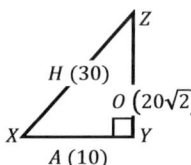

Thus, the correct answer is **F**.

60. Answer (D)

The rule for multiplying matrices.

By multiplying matrices rule;
$$\begin{bmatrix} -1 & 0 \\ 5 & 4 \end{bmatrix} \cdot \begin{bmatrix} 4 \\ -6 \end{bmatrix} = \begin{bmatrix} -1 \times 4 + 0 \times (-6) \\ 5 \times 4 + 4 \times (-6) \end{bmatrix} = \begin{bmatrix} -4 \\ -4 \end{bmatrix}$$

Thus, the correct answer is **D**.

BLANK PAGE *by K·DEAN*

Reformed Past Paper ACT MATH TEST 09

60 Questions – 60 Minutes

DIRECTIONS:
Solve each problem, choose the correct answer, and then fill in the corresponding oval on your answer in the grid on the answer sheet.

Do not linger over problems that take too much time. as many as you can, then other in the time you have left for this test.

You are permitted to use a calculator on this test.

Note: Unless otherwise stated, all of the following should be assumed.

1. Figures are drawn to scale unless otherwise indicated.

2. All figures lie in a plane unless otherwise indicated.

3. All variables and expressions used represent real numbers unless otherwise indicated.

01.

What is the least common denominator (LCD) of $\frac{5}{x^3y^2z}$, and $\frac{7}{x^2yz^3}$?

A. xyz

B. x^2yz

C. $x^3y^2z^3$

D. $x^3y^3z^3$

E. $x^5y^3z^4$

02.

What is the simplified form of $\frac{\sqrt{2}}{3-\sqrt{5}}$?

F. $-\frac{\sqrt{2}}{2}$

G. $\frac{\sqrt{2}}{3+\sqrt{5}}$

H. $\frac{-3\sqrt{2}+10}{2}$

J. $\frac{3\sqrt{2}-10}{4}$

K. $\frac{3\sqrt{2}+10}{4}$

03.

If -0.6798 is between $\frac{A-1}{1000}$ and $\frac{A}{1000}$, then what is the value of A ?

F. -6798

G. -680

H. -679

J. -678

K. -67

04.

$$x^2 - 2x - 2, \quad -x^2 + 3x + 4, \quad 2x^2 - x - 2$$
What is the sum of the 3 trinomial listed above ?

A. 0

B. -8

C. $x - 8$

D. $2x^2 - x - 8$

E. $2x^2$

05.

If $a = 1$, $b = 2$, and $c = -4$, then what is the value of $-2a + b - c$?

A. -5

B. -3

C. 0

D. 2

E. 4

06.

The capacity of one water tank exceeds 5 times the capacity of another fuel tank by 36 gallons. The capacity of smaller fuel tank is g gal. Which of the following expressions is the capacity of the larger fuel tank, in gal.?

F. $g - 36$

G. $g + 36$

H. $5g + 36$

J. $5g - 36$

K. $5g - 180$

07.

Given that $\dfrac{3}{x} = 0.3$, what is the value of x ?

A. 0.1

B. 0.3

C. 6

D. 9

E. 10

08.

What is the solution of the equation $\dfrac{5(x+4)}{2} = 10$?

A. -5

B. -3

C. 0

D. 2

E. 4

09.

A hat contains a combination of colored cards. If $\dfrac{1}{4}$ of the cards are blue, $\dfrac{1}{3}$ are green, $\dfrac{1}{8}$ are black and the remaining 14 cards are red. How many black cards in the hat?

F. 3

G. 4

H. 6

J. 8

K. 12

2 △ △ △ △ △ △ △ △ △ **2**

10.

$$3x - 4y = 7$$
$$3y = -2$$

In the (x, y) solution to the system of above, $x = ?$

A. 3

B. $-\dfrac{9}{11}$

C. $\dfrac{13}{9}$

D. 2

E. $-\dfrac{1}{6}$

11.

If the function $v(t) = -2t^3 + 3t - 7$, what is the value of $v(-2)$?

F. 3

G. -6

H. 12

J. -24

K. 36

12.

The cost, in dollars, to lay bricks a wall that has a surface area to be laid of S square meters is $12.5\,S + 35\,t$, where t is the number of hours it takes to lay the wall. What is the cost of laying a wall that has a surface area to be laid of 180 square meters and takes 4 hours to lay ?

A. 2,390

B. 2,240

C. 2,020

D. 1,860

E. 1,620

13.

In the standard (x, y) coordinate plane, if an equation of line is $y = -3x + 12$, what is the y-intercept and x-intercept of the line ?

F. y-intercept $(12, 0)$, x-intercept $(0, -4)$

G. y-intercept $(0, -12)$, x-intercept $(4, 0)$

H. y-intercept $(0, 12)$, x-intercept $(4, 0)$

J. y-intercept $(0, -12)$, x-intercept $(-4, 0)$

K. y-intercept $(12, 0)$, x-intercept $(0, 4)$

14.

The parallelogram □$ABCD$ is lied on the x, y coordinate plane. What is the equation of $\overleftrightarrow{AB}$?

A. $y = -3x$

B. $y = -x + 3$

C. $y = x + 3$

D. $y = 3$

E. $x = 3$

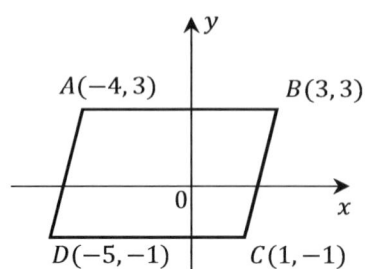

16.

The table shows the distance (in feet) of an object moving at a constant rate along a straight line for times (in seconds).

t (time; sec)	0	1	2	3	4
d (distance; ft)	17	21	25	29	33

Which of the following equations is expressed as this relationship between d and t?

A. $d = 4t$

B. $d = 4t + 17$

C. $d = 17t$

D. $d = 17t + 17$

E. $d = 8.25t + 17$

15.

$$y = 3x + 2$$
$$x + 3y = 4$$
$$-6x - 2y = 1$$

There are three linear equation are given above. In the standard (x, y) coordinate plane, how are the three linear equations in terms of intersecting, being parallel, being perpendicular?

F. Exactly 2 of the lines are parallel.

G. All of the three lines are parallel.

H. All the three lines meet in a point.

J. Exactly 2 of the lines are perpendicular.

K. None of the three lines are perpendicular.

17.

If one of the following inequalities for real number b and c, is graphed in the standard (x, y) coordinate plane below, then which inequality is it?

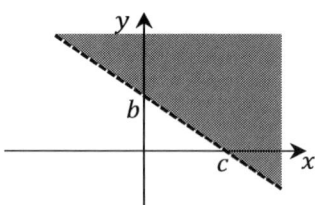

F. $y > -\dfrac{c}{b}x + b$

G. $y < -\dfrac{c}{b}x + b$

H. $y > -cx + b$

J. $y < -\dfrac{b}{c}x + b$

K. $y > -\dfrac{b}{c}x + b$

2   **2**

18.

Astronergy solar panels that produce 9,300 Watts of electrical capacity are needed for a proposed eco farm. If the solar panels are manufactured to produce 15.50 Watts per square foot of surface area, the surface area of each panel needs to be how many square feet?

A. $600.00 ft^2$

B. $625.25 ft^2$

C. $645.50 ft^2$

D. $655.65 ft^2$

E. $672.75 ft^2$

20.

On a map, 2 centimeters represents 50 kilometers. How many centimeters on this map represent 350 kilometers?

A. 11

B. 12

C. 13

D. 14

E. 15

19.

A smart phone was bought 3 years ago for $897.00. The current value of the phone is $228.00. What was the car's average decrease in value per year?

F. $218.00

G. $220.67

H. $222.33

J. $223.00

K. $224.67

21.

Lamis current annual salary for working at Wishcet design company is $42,000. Lamis is told that at the beginning of next year, his new annual salary will be an increase of 9% of his current annual salary. What will be Lamis's new annual salary ?

F. $45,780

G. $45,870

H. $46,720

J. $46,780

K. $46,870

22.

As shown in the figure below, the border of a house and the border of a fence surrounding that the house are similar rectangles each other. The given dimensions are in feet. What is the width of the fence, in feet?

A. 36

B. 39

C. 42

D. 45

E. 48

23.

As shown in the figure below, a circle is drawn two chords, in inches. What is the value of x?
(Note: When two chords intersect each other inside a circle, the products of their segments are equal.)

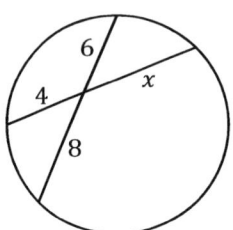

F. 4

G. 6

H. 7

J. 10.5

K. 12

24.

In the standard (x, y) coordinate plane, the three line with equation $y = -2x$, $y = 12$, and $x = 6$ bound a triangular region. What is the area of the triangular region (1 coordinate unit is 1 in.)?

A. $36\ in^2$

B. $72\ in^2$

C. $108\ in^2$

D. $132\ in^2$

E. $144\ in^2$

25.

A smart business office building is 5 stories tall. Each story has 3 identical offices. Each office's working space consists of 4 rectangular room: a conference room 6 feet by 7 feet, a server room 5 feet by 5 feet, a monitoring room 10 feet by 12 feet, and an utility room 4 feet by 5 feet. What is the area, to the nearest 100 square feet, of working space in the 5-story building?

F. 3,000

G. 3,100

H. 3,200

J. 3,300

K. 3,400

26.

Considering the two similar right triangles shown below with dimensions given in centimeters, what is the area of the larger triangle?

A. 7.5

B. 15

C. 30

D. 45

E. 50

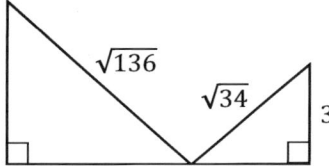

28.

As shown in the figure below, a point O lies $\frac{2}{3}$ of the way from P to S on rectangle $PQRS$. The area of $\triangle POQ$ is what fraction of the area of rectangle $PQRS$?

A. $\frac{1}{6}$

B. $\frac{1}{4}$

C. $\frac{1}{3}$

D. $\frac{2}{3}$

E. $\frac{4}{9}$

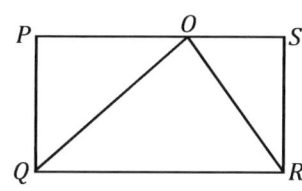

27.

In the standard (x, y) coordinate plane below, a line passes through the origin $(0,0)$ and a point $(2,3)$. If the acute angle between the line and the x-axis has measures θ, then what is the value of θ?

F. $\tan^{-1}\left(\frac{3}{2}\right)$

G. $\tan^{-1}\left(\frac{2}{3}\right)$

H. $\tan^{-1}\left(\frac{3}{\sqrt{13}}\right)$

J. $\tan^{-1}\left(\frac{3}{5}\right)$

K. $\tan^{-1}\left(\frac{2}{5}\right)$

29.

As shown in the figure below, four angle measures are given. The angle marked with a measure of $x°$ is an exterior angle. What is the value of x?

F. 36

G. 42

H. 48

J. 50

K. 60

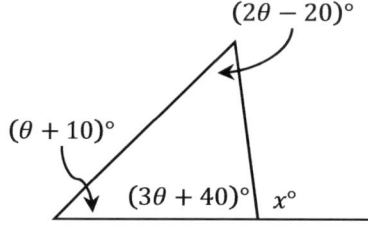

30.

As shown in the standard (x, y) coordinate plane below, $\square PQRS$ will be translated 5 coordinate units right and 7 coordinate units down. What will be the coordinates of P after the translation?

A. $(5, -7)$

B. $(-3, 13)$

C. $(13, -3)$

D. $(7, -1)$

E. $(-7, 1)$

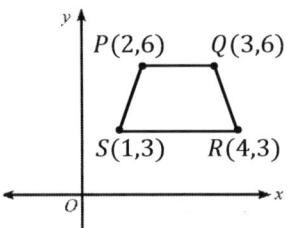

33.

Which of the following expressions is a factoring form of $x^2 - x - 12$?

A. $(x - 3)(x + 4)$

B. $(x + 3)(x - 4)$

C. $(x - 3)(x - 4)$

D. $(x + 3)(x + 4)$

E. $(x - \sqrt{12})(x + \sqrt{12})$

31.

The square root of a number is about 4.58258. The number is between what two numbers?

F. $4 \ and \ 5$

G. $9 \ and \ 16$

H. $15 \ and \ 16$

J. $16 \ and \ 17$

K. $20 \ and \ 22$

34.

All of the following monomials are factors, including integers, of $15x^2y^3 - 30x^2y^2 - 45xy^3$ **Except** :

F. 5

G. 15

H. $3x^2y$

J. $5xy$

K. $15xy^2$

35.

If the product of $(2 - 3i)$ and a complex number is 10, then what is the complex number?

F. $\dfrac{5}{6} - \dfrac{5}{6}i$

G. $\dfrac{5}{6} + \dfrac{5}{6}i$

H. $2 + 3i$

J. $\dfrac{20}{13} - \dfrac{30}{13}i$

K. $\dfrac{20}{13} + \dfrac{30}{13}i$

32.

If two real numbers have a product of -24 and a sum of 0, what is the greater of the two numbers?

F. 4

G. 6

H. 8

J. $2\sqrt{6}$

K. $-2\sqrt{6} + 4$

2   **2**

36.

What is the simplest form of $\dfrac{(9x^4y^2)(16x^3y^{12})}{12x^8y^{10}}$,for all nonzero real numbers x and y ?

A. $\dfrac{4y^4}{x}$

B. $\dfrac{12y^4}{x}$

C. $\dfrac{36y^4}{x}$

D. $\dfrac{12x}{y^4}$

E. $\dfrac{4x}{y^4}$

37.

What is the value of $\dfrac{1}{12^{25}} - \dfrac{1}{12^{26}}$?

F. $\dfrac{11}{12}$

G. $\dfrac{1}{12^{26}}$

H. $\dfrac{11}{12^{26}}$

J. $\dfrac{1}{12^{51}}$

K. $\dfrac{11}{12^{51}}$

38.

A SNS account refers to a social media ID that contains a personal journal. According to a media analyst, over one 24 months period, the number of SNS accounts in existence doubled about every 3 months. The analyst estimated that there were about 200,000 SNS accounts at the beginning of the period. How many SNS accounts were there at the end of the period?

A.   2,160,000

B.   6,480,000

C.   24,600,000

D.   51,200,000

E.   368,000,000

39.

$3a^3 7a^7$ is equivalent to:

A. $10a^4$

B. $10a^{10}$

C. $10a^{21}$

D. $21a^{10}$

E. $21a^{21}$

40.

For what value(s) of x, if any, is there no value of y such that (x, y) is on the rational function graph of $y = \dfrac{(x+4)}{(x-1)(x+1)(x-3)}$ in the standard (x, y) coordinate plane?

A. -4

B. $-4, and\ 3$

C. $-1, and\ 1$

D. $-1, 1, and\ -4$

E. $-1, 1, and\ 3$

Use the following information to answer questions 41 - 43.

The graph below shows the height of seawater at sea level for one day on May 18, 2018. The number near each point is the actual height of seawater for the time corresponding with the point. The curve represents a model equation that comes close to fitting the actual height measured by time.

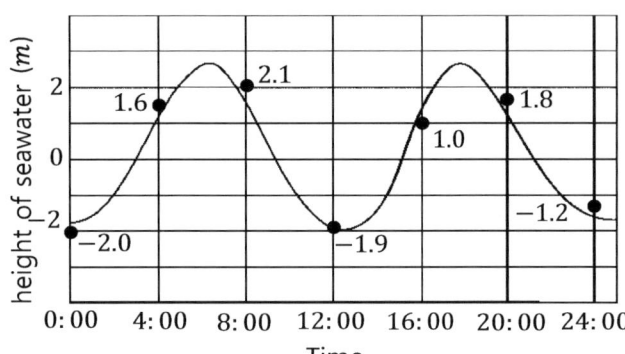

41.

One of the following is the number for 08:00 on the model curve. Which one?

A. 0.0

B. 1.0

C. 2.1

D. 2.0

E. 1.7

42.

What is the average height of seawater actually measured between and including 0:00 and 12:00?

A. 0.4

B. 0.04

C. −0.0167

D. −0.05

E. −0.5

43.

A spring tide is a type of tide just after a new moon or full moon, when there is the greatest difference between the highest and lowest height of seawater. If the height of seawater increases by 12% during that period, what is the predicted maximum height in the spring tide period?

F. 1.8

G. 2.0

H. 2.5

J. 3.0

K. 3.5

44.

Vanessa got scores of 65, 83, 74, and 70 points on the first 4 math tests, and she has 1 more test remaining. What is the minimum point Vanessa needs to get on the 5th test so that the mean of her scores on all 5 tests is at least 3 points more than the mean of the scores she got on the first 4 tests?

A. 86

B. 88

C. 90

D. 92

E. 94

45.

A glass bottle contains 50 candies of which 12 are hard candies, 20 are mint candies, and 18 are jelly candies. One piece of candy will be randomly picked from the glass bottle. What is the probability the candy picked is **not** mint candy?

A. $\dfrac{29}{50}$

B. $\dfrac{2}{5}$

C. $\dfrac{3}{5}$

D. $\dfrac{4}{5}$

E. $\dfrac{21}{25}$

46.

Assume that a arithmetic sequence has 9 terms, and the first term is $\dfrac{4}{5}$. What is the difference of the median and mean of the 9 terms?

A. 5

B. $\dfrac{16}{25}$

C. $\dfrac{8}{5}$

D. $\dfrac{4}{5}$

E. 0

47.

The length of the hypotenuse of a right triangle is 9 inches and one leg of the right triangle is 4 inches. Which of the following lengths, in feet, is closest to the length of the other leg of the right triangle?

F. 8.1

G. 8.4

H. 8.8

J. 9.2

K. 9.5

Use the following information to answer questions 48 - 50.

As shown in the standard (x,y) coordinate plane below, a circle has center $(5.5, 3.5)$ and has radius 4 coordinate units.

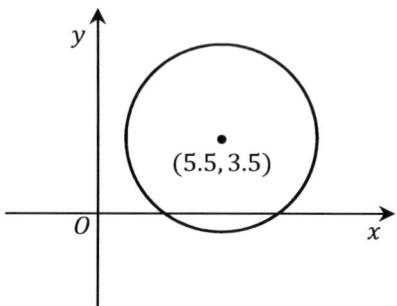

48.

What is the circumference, in coordinate units, of this circle?

A. 4π

B. 8π

C. 10π

D. 16π

E. 25π

49.

What is the equation of this circle?

A. $(x - 5.5)^2 + (y - 3.5)^2 = 2$

B. $(x - 5.5)^2 + (y - 3.5)^2 = 4$

C. $(x - 5.5)^2 + (y - 3.5)^2 = 16$

D. $(x + 5.5)^2 + (y + 3.5)^2 = 4$

E. $(x + 5.5)^2 + (y + 3.5)^2 = 16$

50.

Assume that the circle will be reflected in the x-axis. Which of the following coordinates is the center of the image of the circle?

F. $(3.5, 5.5)$

G. $(5.5, -3.5)$

H. $(-5.5, 3.5)$

J. $(-5.5, -3.5)$

K. $(-3.5, -5.5)$

51.

Suppose that the coordinates of the midpoint of $\overline{CD}$ are $(-4, 2)$ and the coordinates of C are $(6, -6)$. What are the coordinates of D?

A. $(-14, 10)$

B. $(-16, 12)$

C. $(-18, 14)$

D. $(12, -14)$

E. $(14, -16)$

52.

In the standard (x, y) coordinate plane, a rectangle has vertices at $(2, 6), (1, 2), (4, 1),$ and $(5, 5)$. What are the coordinates of the two diagonal's intersecting point?

F. $(2.75, 2.75)$

G. $(2.75, 3)$

H. $(3, 3)$

J. $(3, 3.5)$

K. $(3.5, 3.5)$

53.

In the standard (x, y) coordinate plane, which of the following equations is the equation of the parabola with vertex at $(5, 4)$ and focus at $(-3, 4)$?

A. $(y + 4)^2 = 32(x + 5)$

B. $(y - 4)^2 = 32(x - 5)$

C. $(y - 4)^2 = -32(x - 5)$

D. $(y - 4)^2 = -8(x - 5)$

E. $(y + 4)^2 = 8(x + 5)$

54.

In the figure below, Conrad pushed the wheelchair, and the wheel rotated $\frac{5}{3}\pi$ radians. The distance that the wheel rotated is what fraction of the circumference of the wheel?

A. $\frac{1}{3}$

B. $\frac{5}{6}$

C. $\frac{5}{3}$

D. $\frac{5}{2}$

E. $\frac{10}{3}$

55.

In $\triangle ABC$ shown below, $\sin A$ is $\frac{8}{15}$. What is the value of $\cos B$?

F. $\frac{\sqrt{161}}{8}$

G. $\frac{8}{\sqrt{161}}$

H. $\frac{\sqrt{161}}{15}$

J. $\frac{8}{15}$

K. $\frac{15}{8}$

56.

Suppose that the $\cos\theta = \dfrac{15}{17}$, what is the value of $\csc\theta$ $(0 \le \theta \le \pi)$?

A. $\dfrac{8}{17}$

B. $\dfrac{17}{8}$

C. $\dfrac{17}{15}$

D. $\dfrac{8}{15}$

E. $\dfrac{15}{8}$

58.

An airship is flying 850 meters horizontally from a hangar and 250 meters vertically from the ground level. What is the expression for the angle θ?

A. $\cos^{-1}\left(\dfrac{25}{850}\right)$

B. $\cos^{-1}\left(\dfrac{5}{17}\right)$

C. $\tan^{-1}\left(\dfrac{17}{5}\right)$

D. $\tan^{-1}\left(\dfrac{5}{17}\right)$

E. $\sin^{-1}\left(\dfrac{5}{17}\right)$

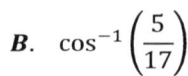

57.

The figure shows a lighthouse on top of cliff. A measuring device in the lighthouse is 75 meters above sea level and indicates an angle of depression of 48° to a boat. What is the approximate horizontal distance, in meters, between the navigational device and the boat?

(Note: $\sin 48° \approx 0.74, \cos 48° \approx 0.67, \tan 48° \approx 1.11$)

F. 61.9

G. 63.8

H. 65.3

J. 67.6

K. 69.2

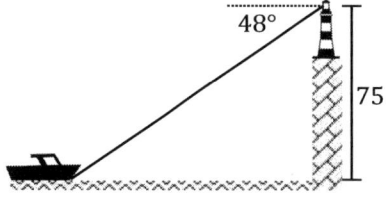

59.

Suppose that $\tan\theta = 1$, for $0 \le \theta \le 2\pi$, what is the value of θ in radians?

F. $\dfrac{1}{4}\pi$ only

G. $\dfrac{1}{4}\pi$ and $\dfrac{3}{4}\pi$

H. $\dfrac{1}{4}\pi$ and $\dfrac{5}{4}\pi$

J. $\dfrac{3}{4}\pi$ only

K. $\dfrac{1}{4}\pi$ and $\dfrac{7}{4}\pi$

60.

What is the sum of x and y that satisfies the matrix equation below?

$$-2\left(\begin{bmatrix} -3x & -1 \\ 4 & y \end{bmatrix} + \begin{bmatrix} 9 & -4 \\ -5 & 3 \end{bmatrix}\right) = \begin{bmatrix} 12 & 10 \\ 2 & -18 \end{bmatrix}$$

A.   3

B.   −5

C.   7

D.   −9

E.   11

BLANK PAGE *by K·DEAN*

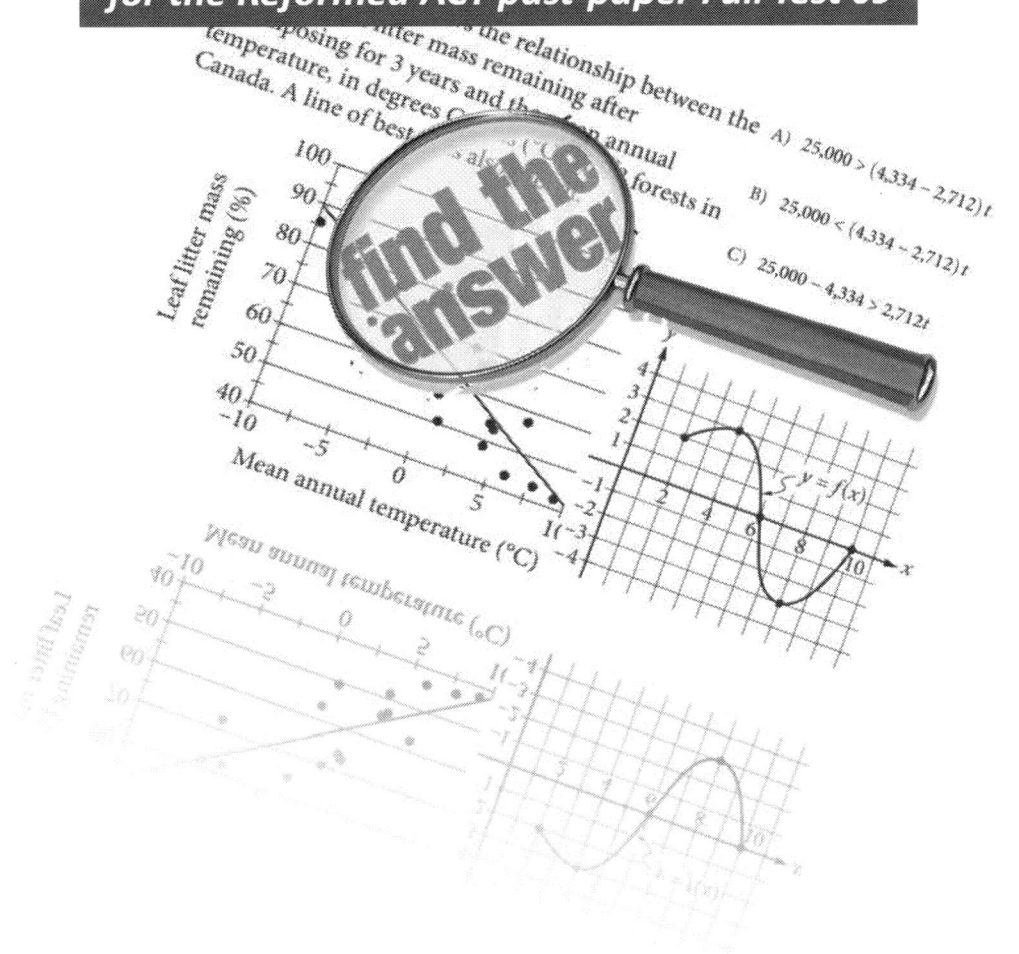

Obtain Scale Scores from Raw Scores

Scale Score	Raw Score	Scale Score	Raw Score	Scale Score	Raw Score
36	60	24	36-37	12	7
35	58-59	23	34-35	11	5-6
34	57	22	32-33	10	4
33	55-56	21	30-31	9	-
32	54	20	29	8	3
31	52-53	19	27-28	7	-
30	50-51	18	24-26	6	2
29	48-49	17	21-23	5	-
28	45-47	16	17-20	4	1
27	43-44	15	13-16	3	-
26	40-42	14	11-12	2	-
25	38-39	13	8-10	1	0

1. Scoring Key

Key		Question Category	Y/N		Key		Question Category	Y/N
01.	C	Number Theory			31.	K	Quadratic and Polynomial Function	
02.	K	Number Theory			32.	J	Quadratic and Polynomial Function	
03.	H	Number Theory			33.	B	Quadratic and Polynomial Function	
04.	E	Expression and Linear Equation			34.	H	Quadratic and Polynomial Function	
05.	E	Expression and Linear Equation			35.	K	Quadratic and Polynomial Function	
06.	H	Expression and Linear Equation			36.	B	Further Equations and Functions	
07.	E	Expression and Linear Equation			37.	H	Further Equations and Functions	
08.	C	Expression and Linear Equation			38.	D	Further Equations and Functions	
09.	H	Expression and Linear Equation			39.	D	Further Equations and Functions	
10.	C	Expression and Linear Equation			40.	E	Further Equations and Functions	
11.	F	Linear Function inequality			41.	E	Statistics and Probability	
12.	A	Linear Function inequality			42.	D	Statistics and Probability	
13.	H	Linear Function inequality			43.	J	Statistics and Probability	
14.	D	Linear Function inequality			44.	B	Statistics and Probability	
15.	J	Linear Function inequality			45.	C	Statistics and Probability	
16.	B	Linear Function inequality			46.	E	Sequence and Series	
17.	K	Linear Function inequality			47.	F	Analytic Geometry and Conic Section	
18.	A	Arithmetic Topic and Ratio			48.	B	Analytic Geometry and Conic Section	
19.	J	Arithmetic Topic and Ratio			49.	C	Analytic Geometry and Conic Section	
20.	D	Arithmetic Topic and Ratio			50.	G	Analytic Geometry and Conic Section	
21.	F	Arithmetic Topic and Ratio			51.	A	Analytic Geometry and Conic Section	
22.	D	Basic Geometry			52.	J	Analytic Geometry and Conic Section	
23.	K	Basic Geometry			53.	C	Analytic Geometry and Conic Section	
24.	E	Basic Geometry			54.	B	Trigonometric Functions	
25.	G	Basic Geometry			55.	J	Trigonometric Functions	
26.	C	Basic Geometry			56.	B	Trigonometric Functions	
27.	F	Trigonometric Functions			57.	J	Trigonometric Functions	
28.	C	Basic Geometry			58.	D	Trigonometric Functions	
29.	J	Arithmetic Topic and Ratio			59.	H	Trigonometric Functions	
30.	D	Quadratic and Polynomial Function			60.	E	Intermediate Algebra	

2. Answer Explanations

01. *Answer* **(C)**

The LCD of monomials is also obtained in the same way as numbers.

A LCM is the product of all factors of two monomials, using each common factor only once.

So, LCD of x^3y^2z and x^2yz^3 is $x^3y^2z^3$.

02. *Answer* **(K)**

No radical in a denominator.

Using conjugate for rationalizing the denominator;
$$\frac{\sqrt{2}}{3-\sqrt{5}}\times\frac{3+\sqrt{5}}{3+\sqrt{5}}=\frac{3\sqrt{2}+\sqrt{10}}{3^2-5}=\frac{3\sqrt{2}+10}{4}$$

Thus, the correct answer is **K**.

03. *Answer* **(H)**

First, convert decimal to fraction.

-0.6798 rewrite fraction form $-\frac{6798}{10000}=\frac{-679.8}{1000}$.

So, $\frac{-680}{1000}<\frac{-679.8}{1000}<\frac{-679}{1000}$. Therefore $\frac{-679-1}{1000}<-0.6798<\frac{-679}{1000}$.

04. *Answer* **(E)**

Combining the like terms .

Rearrange vertically;
$$\begin{array}{r}x^2-2x-2\\-x^2+3x+4\\2x^2-x-2\end{array}$$
And adding
$$+\ \overline{\begin{array}{r}\\2x^2+0x+0\end{array}}$$

Thus, the sum of 3 trinomial is $2x^2$.

05. *Answer* **(E)**

Substitute the value for the variables and then evaluate.

Substitute 1 for a, 2 for b, and 3 for c;
$$-2a+b-c=-2(1)+2-(-4)=-2+2+4=4$$
Thus, the value of $-2a+b-c$ is 4.

06. *Answer* **(H)**

5 times the capacity of another fuel tank by 36 gallons.

"5 times the capacity of another fuel tank by 36 gallons" means that "multiplying 5 and then adding 36".
Thus, if the capacity of smaller tank is g gal, then the capacity of larger tank is $5g+36$.

07. *Answer* **(E)**

Solving the equation.

Multiply by x on both sides;
$$\frac{3}{x}=0.3\ \rightarrow\ x\cdot\frac{3}{x}=0.3x\ \rightarrow\ 3=0.3x$$
Divide by 0.3 on both sides;
$$0.3x=3\ \rightarrow\ \frac{0.3x}{0.3}=\frac{3}{0.3}\ \rightarrow\ x=10$$

08. *Answer* **(C)**

Solving the equation.

Multiply by 2 on both sides;
$$\frac{5(x+4)}{2}=10\ \rightarrow\ 2\cdot\frac{5(x+4)}{2}=2\cdot10\ \rightarrow\ 5(x+4)=20$$
Divide by 5 on both sides;
$$5(x+4)=20\ \rightarrow\ \frac{5(x+4)}{5}=\frac{20}{5}\ \rightarrow\ x+4=4$$
Subtract 4 from both sides;
$$x+4-4=4-4\ \rightarrow\ x=0.$$

09. *Answer* **(H)**

The LCD of 4, 3, and 8 is 24

If the number of total cards in the hat is x;
$$x-\left(\frac{1}{4}x+\frac{1}{3}x+\frac{1}{8}x\right)=14\ \rightarrow\ x-\left(\frac{6}{24}x+\frac{8}{24}x+\frac{3}{24}x\right)=14$$
$$\rightarrow\ \frac{24}{24}x-\frac{17}{24}x=14\ \rightarrow\ \frac{7}{24}x=14$$
Multiply by $\frac{24}{7}$ on both sides;
$$\frac{24}{7}\times\frac{7}{24}x=14\times\frac{24}{7}\ \rightarrow\ x=48$$
So, the number of total cards in the hat is 48.
$\frac{1}{8}$ of the cards are black
$$\frac{1}{8}\times48=6.$$
Thus, the number of black cards is 6 cards.

10. *Answer* **(C)**

Solve for one variable and then substitute the value for other equation.

Dividing the second equation by 3;
$$3y=-2\ \rightarrow\ \frac{3y}{3}=\frac{-2}{3}\ \rightarrow\ y=\frac{-2}{3}$$
Substituting $\frac{-2}{3}$ for y on the first equation;
$$3x-4y=7\ \rightarrow\ 3x-4\left(\frac{-2}{3}\right)=7\ \rightarrow\ 3x+\frac{8}{3}=7$$
Subtracting $\frac{8}{3}$ from both sides;
$$3x+\frac{8}{3}-\frac{8}{3}=7-\frac{8}{3}\ \rightarrow\ 3x=\frac{21}{3}-\frac{8}{3}\ \rightarrow\ 3x=\frac{13}{3}$$
Multiplying both sides by $\frac{1}{3}$;
$$3x=\frac{13}{3}\ \rightarrow\ \frac{1}{3}\times3x=\frac{13}{3}\times\frac{1}{3}\ \rightarrow\ x=\frac{13}{9}$$

11. *Answer* **(F)**

Substitute each value and then solve the equation.

Substituting -2 for t;
$$v(t)=-2t^3+3t-7\ \rightarrow\ v(-2)=-2(-2)^3+3(-2)-7$$
$$\rightarrow\ v(-2)=16-6-7=3$$
Thus, the value of $v(-2)$ is 3.

12. *Answer* **(A)**

Substitute each value and then evaluate.

Substitute 180 for S, and 4 for t;
$$22.5\,S+35t\ \rightarrow\ 22.5\times180+35\times4=2390$$
Thus, the cost is $\$2,390$.

13. `Answer` **(H)**

y-intercept is y-value at x=0 and x-intercept is x-value at y=0.

Substitute 0 for x to find y-intercept;
$$y = -3x + 12 \quad \rightarrow \quad y = -3(0) + 12 \quad \rightarrow \quad y = 12$$
Substitute 0 for y to find x-intercept;
$$y = -3x + 12 \quad \rightarrow \quad 0 = -3x + 12$$
add $3x$ to both sides;
$$0 = -3x + 12 \quad \rightarrow \quad 3x = -3x + 12 + 3x \quad \rightarrow \quad 3x = 12$$
divide both sides by 3;
$$3x = 12 \quad \rightarrow \quad \frac{3x}{3} = \frac{12}{3} \quad \rightarrow \quad x = 4$$
Thus, y-intercept of the line is $(0, 12)$ and x-intercept is $(4, 0)$.

14. `Answer` **(D)**

The line AB is a horizontal line.

The line $\overleftrightarrow{AB}$ is a horizontal line, $y = b$, and passes through the two points $(-4, 3)$ and $(3, 3)$.

Thus, the equation of the line $\overleftrightarrow{AB}$ is $y = 3$.

15. `Answer` **(J)**

Two lines are parallel if and only if they have the same slope and two lines are perpendicular if and only if their slopes are negative reciprocals of each other.

Convert the standard form to the slope intercept form;
subtracting x from both sides;
$$x + 3y = 4 \quad \rightarrow \quad x + 3y - x = 4 - x \quad \rightarrow \quad 3y = 4 - x$$
dividing both sides by 3;
$$3y = -x + 4 \quad \rightarrow \quad \frac{3y}{3} = \frac{-x+4}{3} \quad \rightarrow \quad y = -\frac{1}{3}x + \frac{4}{3}$$
adding $6x$ to both sides;
$$-6x - 2y = 1 \quad \rightarrow \quad -6x - 2y + 6x = 1 + 6x \quad \rightarrow \quad -2y = 1 + 6x$$
dividing both sides to -2;
$$-2y = 6x + 1 \quad \rightarrow \quad \frac{-2y}{-2} = \frac{6x+1}{-2} \quad \rightarrow \quad y = -3x - \frac{1}{2}$$
Therefore, the first equation $(m = 3)$ and the second equation $\left(m = -\frac{1}{3}\right)$ are perpendicular each other and because the three equation have different slopes, the graphs intersect each other.

16. `Answer` **(B)**

The initial value is y-intercept and the rate of change is slope.

The distance, d, is output value so, d is y, and the time, t, is input value so t is x.
The initial value (at $t = 0$) is $17ft$ so, y-intercept is 17. The rate of change, slope m, is;
$$m = \frac{y_2 - y_1}{x_2 - x_1} = \frac{21 - 17}{1 - 0} = \frac{4}{1} = 4$$
Thus,
substitute the each value for slope intercept form $y = mx + b$;
$$y = 4x + 17 \quad \rightarrow \quad d = 4t + 17$$

17. `Answer` **(K)**

The boundary line passes through (0, b) and (c, 0)

Making the slope-intercept form, y-intercept is b and slope m is;
$$m = \frac{y_2 - y_1}{x_2 - x_1} = \frac{b - 0}{0 - c} = \frac{b}{-c} = -\frac{b}{c}$$

The boundary line is $y = -\frac{b}{c}x + b$
Testing a point $(0, 0)$;
$$y = -\frac{b}{c}x + b \quad \rightarrow \quad 0 \cdots -\frac{b}{c} \times 0 + b \quad \rightarrow \quad 0 < b \ (\because b > 0)$$
$(0, 0)$ is not solution and the boundary line is a dashed line.

Thus, the inequality is $y > -\frac{b}{c}x + b$.

18. `Answer` **(A)**

15.50 Watts per square foot is an unit rate.

The total capacity is the product of unit capacity and total area.
So,
$$9,300(W) = 15.50(W/ft^2) \times A(ft^2) \quad \rightarrow \quad A = \frac{9300}{15.5} = 600.$$
Thus, the total area is $600 ft^2$.

19. `Answer` **(J)**

Finding the difference of initial and final value.

The average decrease in value per year is calculated by;
$$\frac{change\ of\ value}{time} = \frac{\$897 - \$228}{3\ years} = \frac{\$669}{3\ years} = \$223/year$$
Thus, the correct value is \$223 per year.

20. `Answer` **(D)**

Using proportion.

Let x be centimeters for 350 km;
$$\frac{2\ cm}{50\ km} = \frac{x\ cm}{350\ km} \quad \rightarrow \quad 50x = 2 \times 350 \quad \rightarrow \quad 50x = 700 \quad \rightarrow \quad x = 14.$$
Thus, the correct answer is 14 cm.

21. `Answer` **(F)**

"increase" means that "add"

His new annual salary is;
$$\$42,000 + 0.09 \times \$42,000 = \$42,000 + \$3,780 = \$45,780$$
Thus, the new annual salary is \$45,780.

22. `Answer` **(D)**

Using proportional equation.

The two rectangles are similar to each other so,
$$\frac{84}{56} = \frac{width\ (w)}{30} \quad \rightarrow \quad 56w = 84 \times 30 \quad \rightarrow \quad w = \frac{84 \times 30}{56} = 45$$
Thus, the width of the fence is 45 feet.

23. `Answer` **(K)**

Using the note.

Using the note;
$$4 \times x = 6 \times 8 \quad \rightarrow \quad 4x = 48 \quad \rightarrow \quad x = 12$$
Thus, the value of x is 12.

24. `Answer` **(E)**

The triangle is a right triangle.

The triangle is a right triangle and the three intersecting points are;
$(-6, 12)$, $(6, 12)$, and $(6, -12)$.

So, the area is
$$\frac{1}{2} \times (6 - (-6)) \times (12 - (12)) = 144\ in^2$$

Thus, the correct answer is **E**.

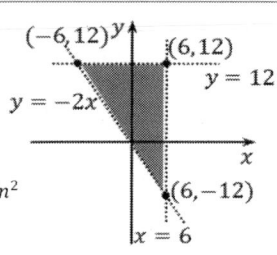

25. Answer (G)

The area of a rectangle is a product of width and length.

The area of each office is;

a conference room's area is $\qquad 6 \times 7 = 42\,ft^2$

a sever room's area is $\qquad 5 \times 5 = 25\,ft^2$

a monitoring room's area is $\qquad 10 \times 12 = 120\,ft^2$

an utility room's area is $\qquad 4 \times 5 = 20\,ft^2$

$$\rightarrow \quad 42 + 25 + 120 + 20 = 207\,ft^2$$

Because the building has $3 \times 5 = 15$ identical offices, the total area of working space is $15 \times 207 = 3,105 ft^2$.

Thus, the area, to the nearest 100 square feet, of working space is $3,100 ft^2$.

26. Answer (C)

The Pythagorean theorem is always useful.

The length of base of the smaller triangle is;

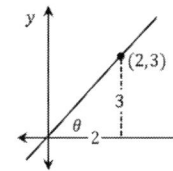

$$\left(\sqrt{34}\right)^2 = 3^2 + x^2 \quad \rightarrow \quad 34 = 9 + x^2$$

$$\rightarrow \quad x^2 = 25 \quad \rightarrow \quad x = 5.$$

And the area od the smaller triangle is;

$$area = \frac{1}{2}bh = \frac{1}{2} \times 3 \times 5 = \frac{15}{2}.$$

Because the two triangle are similar to each other, the ratio of the length of corresponding side is;

$$\frac{\sqrt{134}}{\sqrt{34}} = \frac{2}{1}$$

The ratio of area is;

$$\left(\frac{2}{1}\right)^2 = \frac{4}{1} = \frac{Larger\ triangle}{Smaller\ triangle}$$

So, the area of the larger triangle is 4 times of smaller triangle area;

$$4 \times \frac{15}{2} = 30$$

Thus, the area of the larger triangle is 30.

27. Answer (F)

Using inverse trigonometric ratio.

Drawing an auxiliary line;

$$\tan\theta = \frac{3}{2} \quad \rightarrow \quad \theta = \arctan\left(\frac{3}{2}\right) = \tan^{-1}\left(\frac{3}{2}\right)$$

Thus, the correct answer is **F**.

28. Answer (C)

Using an auxiliary line.

$\overline{PQ} = \frac{2}{3} \times \overline{PS}$ so, area of $\square PQOT = \frac{2}{3} \times \square PQRS$, and area of $\square PQOT = \triangle POQ + \triangle TOQ$, $\triangle POQ = \triangle TOQ$.

Therefore,

$$\square PQOT = \frac{2}{3} \times PQRS = 2\triangle POQ$$

$$\rightarrow \quad \triangle POQ = \frac{1}{3} \times \square PQRS$$

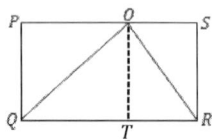

Thus, the fraction is $\frac{1}{3}$.

29. Answer (J)

Using the triangle angle sum theorem.

By the triangle angle sum theorem;

$$\theta + 10 + 2\theta - 20 + 3\theta + 40 = 180 \quad \rightarrow \quad 5\theta + 30 = 180$$

$$\rightarrow \quad 5\theta = 150 \quad \rightarrow \quad \theta = 30$$

By the linear pair;

$$3\theta + 40 + x = 180 \quad \rightarrow \quad 3 \times 30 + 40 + x = 180$$

$$\rightarrow \quad 130 + x = 180 \quad \rightarrow \quad x = 50$$

Thus, the value of x is 50.

30. Answer (D)

Translation; $(x,\ y) \rightarrow (x + h, y + k)$.

"be translated 5 coordinate units right and 7 coordinate units down" means $h = 5$ and $k = -7$. So,

$$(x, y) \rightarrow (x + 5, y - 7), \qquad (2, 6) \rightarrow (2 + 5, 6 - 7) = (7, -1)$$

Thus, translated coordinate is $(7, -1)$.

31. Answer (K)

The square root of a number is $\sqrt{N}$.

Take both side by square;

$$\sqrt{N} = 4.58258 \quad \rightarrow \quad \left(\sqrt{N}\right)^2 = (4.58258)^2 \quad \rightarrow \quad N = 21.000\ ....$$

Thus, the two numbers are 20 and 22.

32. Answer (J)

The sum of two numbers is zero.

If two real numbers are a and b, then $a + b = 0 \quad \rightarrow \quad b = -a$.

So,

$$a \times b = -24 \quad \rightarrow \quad a \times (-a) = -24 \quad \rightarrow \quad -a^2 = -24 \quad \rightarrow \quad a^2 = 24$$

Take both sides by square root;

$$a^2 = 24 \quad \rightarrow \quad \sqrt{a^2} = \pm\sqrt{24} \quad \rightarrow \quad a = \pm 2\sqrt{6}$$

Thus, the greater number is $2\sqrt{6}$.

33. Answer (B)

Factoring form; $ax^2 + bx + c \quad \rightarrow \quad a(x - p)(x - q)$.

Because the product of two root is -12 and the sum of two root is 1;

$$x^2 - x - 12 \quad \rightarrow \quad (x + 3)(x - 4)$$

Thus, the correct answer is **B**.

34. Answer (H)

Grouping the common factors.

The common factor is $15xy^2$ so, grouping;

$$15x^2y^3 - 30x^2y^2 - 45xy^3 = 15xy^2(xy - 2x - 3y)$$

The factors of the expression is the factors of $15xy^2$;

$$15xy^2 = 3 \times 5 \times x \times y \times y$$

35. Answer (K)

Let a+bi be the complex number.

Let $a + bi$ be the complex number;

$$(2 - 3i)(a + bi) = 10 \quad \rightarrow \quad 2a + 2bi - 3ai - 3bi^2 = 10$$

Because $i^2 = -1$;

$$(2a + 3b) + (-3a + 2b)i = 10$$

So, $2a + 3b = 10$ and $-3a + 2b = 0 \quad \rightarrow \quad b = \frac{3}{2}a$

$$2a + 3\left(\frac{3}{2}a\right) = 10 \quad \rightarrow \quad 2a + \frac{9}{2}a = 10 \quad \rightarrow \quad \frac{13}{2}a = 10$$

$$\rightarrow \quad a = \frac{20}{13} \quad \rightarrow \quad b = \frac{3}{2}\left(\frac{20}{13}\right) = \frac{30}{13}$$

Thus, the complex number is $\frac{20}{13} + \frac{30}{13}i$

36. Answer (**B**)

Combining common variables.

Using the properties of exponential;

$$\frac{(9x^4y^2)(16x^3y^{12})}{12x^8y^{10}} = \frac{9 \times 16}{12} \cdot \frac{x^4 \times x^3}{x^8} \cdot \frac{(y^2 \times y^{12})}{y^{10}}$$

$$\rightarrow = \frac{12}{1} \cdot \frac{x^{4+3}}{x^8} \cdot \frac{y^{2+12}}{y^{10}} = \frac{12}{1} \cdot \frac{x^7}{x^8} \cdot \frac{y^{14}}{y^{10}} = 12 \cdot x^{7-8}y^{14-10} = 12x^{-1}y^4$$

Thus, the simplest form is $12x^{-1}y^2 = \frac{12y^4}{x}$.

---

37. Answer (**H**)

Do not use calculator.

Using the common denominator;

$$\frac{1}{12^{25}} - \frac{1}{12^{26}} = \frac{1}{12^{25}} \times \frac{12}{12} - \frac{1}{12^{26}} = \frac{12}{12^{26}} - \frac{1}{12^{26}} = \frac{11}{12^{26}}$$

The correct answer is **H**.

---

38. Answer (**D**)

$24 = 3 \times 8$.

Let S be the number of SNS accounts at the end period, S_0 be the number of SNS accounts at the end period, and t be time, in month. And using exponential growth model;

$$S = S_0(2)^{\frac{t}{3}} = 200,000(2)^{\left(\frac{24}{3}\right)} = 51,200,000$$

Thus, there were 51,200,000 SNS account.

---

39. Answer (**D**)

Using the properties of exponential.

Using the properties of exponential;
$$3a^3 7a^7 = 3 \times 7 \times a^3 \times a^7 = 21 \times a^{3+7} = 21a^{10}$$

Thus, the correct answer is **D**.

---

40. Answer (**E**)

The horizontal asymptotes have not y-value.

The vertical asymptotes are real zeros of denominator expression so,
$(x-1)(x+1)(x-3) = 0$
$\rightarrow x-1 = 0 \ or \ x+1 = 0 \ or \ x-3 = 0 \rightarrow x = 1, x = -1, x = 3$

thus, the correct answer is **E**.

---

41. Answer (**E**)

Just read the model curve not real.

The number is about 1.7.

Thus, the correct answer is **E**.

---

42. Answer (**D**)

Not model curve data but actual measured value.

The average is calculated by;
$$avearage = \frac{(-2.0 + 1.6 + 2.1 + -1.9)}{4} = \frac{-0.2}{4} = -0.05$$

Thus, the average is -0.05.

---

43. Answer (**J**)

The maximum height appears at 6:00 and 18:00.

From the model curve, maximum height is predicted about 2.7. So,

$$2.7 \times (1 + 0.12) = 2.7 \times 1.12 = 3.024$$

Thus, the correct answer is **J**.

---

44. Answer (**B**)

Calculating the mean for the first 4 tests.

The mean of first 4 tests is;
$$\frac{65 + 83 + 74 + 70}{4} = \frac{292}{4} = 73$$
Let x be the score of 5th test and then calculate the mean;
$$\frac{292 + x}{5} \geq 73 + 3 \rightarrow \frac{292 + x}{5} \geq 76$$
Multiply both sides by 5;
$$292 + x \geq 76 \times 5 \rightarrow 292 + x \geq 380$$
Subtract 292 from both sides;
$$292 + x \geq 380 \rightarrow x \geq 380 - 292 \rightarrow x \geq 88$$

Thus, the minimum point is 88.

---

45. Answer (**C**)

There are 20 mint candies.

There are 20 mint candies so, the probability is;
$$P = \frac{50 - 20}{50} = \frac{30}{50} = \frac{3}{5} \quad or$$
$$P = \frac{12 + 18}{50} = \frac{30}{50} = \frac{3}{5}$$

Thus, the correct answer is **C**.

---

46. Answer (**E**)

The median is middle value and the mean is average.

There are 9 terms so, 5th term is the median of the sequence. From the formula of arithmetic sequence,
$$a_n = a_1 + (n-1)d \rightarrow a_5 = a_1 + 4d$$
The mean is the quotient of sum and the number of data so, the sum is, from the formula of arithmetic series;
$$S_n = n\left(\frac{2a_1 + (n-1)d}{2}\right) \rightarrow S_9 = 9\left(\frac{2a_1 + (9-1)d}{2}\right)$$
$$S_9 = 9\left(\frac{2a_1 + 8d}{2}\right) \rightarrow S_9 = 9(a_1 + 4d)$$
Therefore, the mean is:
$$\bar{x} = \frac{S_9}{9} = \frac{9(a_1 + 4d)}{9} = a_1 + 4d$$

Thus, the difference is,
median-mean=$a_5 - \bar{x} = a_1 + 4d - (a_1 + 4d) = 0$.

---

47. Answer (**F**)

Using the Pythagorean theorem.

Let x be the length of the other leg of the right triangle, using the Pythagorean theorem;
$$9^2 = x^2 + 4^2 \rightarrow x^2 = 9^2 - 4^2 \rightarrow x = \sqrt{9^2 - 4^2} = 8.062257\ldots$$

Thus, the length of the other leg is 8.1 inches.

48. Answer (B)

Using the circumference formula.

From the circumference formula;
$$C = 2\pi r \;\to\; C = 2\pi(4) \;\to\; 8\pi$$
Thus, the correct answer is **B**.

49. Answer (C)

Using the circumference formula.

From the circle equation;
$$(x - h)^2 + (y - k)^2 = r^2 \;\to\; (x - 5.5)^2 + (y - 3.5)^2 = 4^2 = 16$$
Thus, the correct answer is **C**.

50. Answer (G)

Reflection in x-axis does not change x-coordinate.

Coordinate notation of reflection in x-axis is;
$$(x, y) \;-reflect\;in\;x\;axis \to\; (x, -y)$$
and the reflection does not change size and shape of pre-image.
So, the image of the circle has center (5.5, -3.5).

Thus, the correct answer is **G**.

51. Answer (A)

Using the formula of the midpoint.

Let (x, y) be the coordinates of D and using the formula of the midpoint;
$$M = \left(\frac{x_1 + x_2}{2}, \frac{y_1 + y_2}{2}\right) = \left(\frac{x + 6}{2}, \frac{y + (-6)}{2}\right) = (-4, 2)$$
So,
$$\frac{x + 6}{2} = -4 \;\to\; x + 6 = -8 \;\to\; x = -14$$
$$\frac{y - 6}{2} = 2 \;\to\; y - 6 = 4 \;\to\; y = 10$$
Thus, the coordinates are $(-14, 10)$.

52. Answer (J)

The two diagonals are congruent and bisect each other.

The two diagonals of a rectangle are congruent and bisect each other.
So, Intersecting point is midpoint of diagonals.(notice: the two points should be opposite vertices.)
$$M = \left(\frac{x_1 + x_2}{2}, \frac{y_2 + y_1}{2}\right) = \left(\frac{2 + 4}{2}, \frac{2 + 5}{2}\right) = (3, 3.5)$$
Thus, the correct answer is **J**.

53. Answer (C)

y-coordinate of vertex and focus is same.

Because y-coordinate of vertex and focus is same, the given parabola has horizontal axis.

From the formula, substitute $(5, 4)$ for (h, k);
$$(y - k)^2 = 4p(x - h) \;\to\; (y - 4)^2 = 4p(x - 5)$$
The vertex $(5, 4)$ and focus $(-3, 4)$ both lie on the line $y = 4$, so the distance between them is $|p| = |-3 - 5| = 8$ and thus $p = \pm 8$. Because the focus $(-3, 4)$ is to the left of the vertex $(5, 4)$, the parabola opens to the left, it follows $p = -8 \;\to\; 4p = -32$.

Thus, the equation of the parabola is $(y - 4)^2 = -32(x - 5)$.

54. Answer (B)

The arc length is proportional to the central angle.

1 rotation, 1 circumference, is 360°, and it is 2π, so let x be the distance and using proportional;
$$\frac{1\;rotation}{2\pi} = \frac{x}{\frac{5}{3}\pi} \;\to\; 2x = \frac{5}{3} \;\to\; x = \frac{5}{6}$$
Thus, the distance is $\frac{5}{6}$ rotation, it is $\frac{5}{6}$ of circumference.

55. Answer (J)

The opposite side and the adjacent side are relative positions according to the angle.

The opposite side and the adjacent side are relative positions according to the angle. In view of the angle B, $\overline{AB}$ is hypotenuse and $\overline{BC}$ is adjacent side, so
$$\cos B = \frac{A}{H} = \frac{8}{15}$$
Thus, the correct answer is **J**.

56. Answer (B)

csc is the reciprocal of sin.

Using the trigonometric ratio and the Pythagorean theorem;
$$\cos\theta = \frac{15}{17} = \frac{A}{H}, \qquad O = \sqrt{H^2 - A^2} = \sqrt{17^2 - 15^2} = 8$$
So,
$$\sin\theta = \frac{O}{H} = \frac{8}{17} \;\to\; \csc\theta = \frac{1}{\sin\theta} = \frac{17}{8}$$
Thus, the correct answer is **B**.

57. Answer (J)

Using the trigonometric ratio.

The angle of elevation is 48°($\because$ alternate interior angle) and let A be the horizontal distance.
So, using the trigonometric ratio;
$$\tan 48° = \frac{O}{A} = 1.11 = \frac{75}{A}$$
$$\to A = \frac{75}{1.11} = 67.56756\ldots$$
Thus, the correct answer is **J**.

58. Answer (D)

Using the inverse trigonometric function.

In view of θ, 850 is adjacent side and 250 is opposite side, so
$$\theta = \tan^{-1}\left(\frac{250}{850}\right) = \tan^{-1}\left(\frac{5}{17}\right)$$
Thus, the correct answer is **D**.

---

59. **Answer** **(H)**

The signs of x and y coordinates are same.

At acute angle (quadrant I);
$$\tan\theta = 1 \quad \rightarrow \quad \theta = \tan^{-1}(1) = 45° = \frac{\pi}{4}$$

Also the value tangent is positive at quadrant III, so
$$\theta = 180° + 45° = 225° = \pi + \frac{\pi}{4} = \frac{5}{4}\pi$$

Thus, the correct answer is **H**.

---

60. **Answer** **(E)**

Addition First.

Operating addition and then scalar multiplication;
$$-2\left(\begin{bmatrix} -3x & -1 \\ 4 & y \end{bmatrix} + \begin{bmatrix} 9 & -4 \\ -5 & 3 \end{bmatrix}\right) = -2\begin{bmatrix} -3x+9 & -5 \\ -1 & y+3 \end{bmatrix}$$
$$= \begin{bmatrix} 6x-18 & 10 \\ 2 & -2y-6 \end{bmatrix} = \begin{bmatrix} 12 & 10 \\ 2 & -18 \end{bmatrix}$$

So,
$$6x - 18 = 12 \quad \rightarrow \quad 6x = 30 \quad \rightarrow \quad x = 5$$
$$-2y - 6 = -18 \quad \rightarrow \quad -2y = -12 \quad \rightarrow \quad y = 6$$

Thus, the sum of $x + y = 5 + 6 = 11$.

BLANK PAGE   *by K·DEAN*

Reformed Past Paper ACT MATH TEST 10

60 Questions – 60 Minutes

DIRECTIONS:
Solve each problem, choose the correct answer, and then fill in the corresponding oval on your answer in the grid on the answer sheet.

Do not linger over problems that take too much time. Do as many as you can, then return to the others in the time you have left for this test.

You are permitted to use a calculator on this test.

Note: Unless otherwise stated, all of the following should be assumed.

1. Figures are not necessarily drawn to scale unless otherwise indicated.

2. All figures lie in a plane unless otherwise indicated.

3. All variables and expressions used represent real numbers unless otherwise indicated.

This test has reformed the REAL ACT Mathematics Test

01.

Let $a < 0 < b$ be true for integer a and b. Which of the following expression have positive value ?

I. $b - a$
II. $|a| + |b|$
III. $-|-a| - |-b|$

A. I only

B. II only

C. III only

D. I and II

E. I, II and III

02.

The complex fraction expression $\dfrac{2}{2+\dfrac{2}{2+\dfrac{2}{3}}}$ is equal to ?

F. $\dfrac{5}{8}$

G. $\dfrac{8}{11}$

H. $\dfrac{11}{12}$

J. $\dfrac{17}{12}$

K. $\dfrac{24}{9}$

03.

The least common multiple (LCM) of two positive integers is 72 and the greatest common factor (GCF) of these same two numbers is 12. Which of the following pairs of numbers are the two numbers?

A. 6 and 12

B. 12 and 36

C. 20 and 36

D. 24 and 34

E. 24 and 36

04.

What is the value of $\dfrac{y}{x}$ when $\dfrac{2x+y}{x-y} = \dfrac{3}{2}$?

F. $-\dfrac{1}{5}$

G. $-\dfrac{1}{3}$

H. -1

J. 1

K. 3

05.

Given that $\frac{3-x}{5-x} = \frac{3}{4}$, then what is the value of $2x$?

A. -4

B. 4

C. -6

D. 8

E. -10

06.

What is the solution of the equation
$2.32x + 5.88 = 0.79 - 0.18x$?

F. -1.364

G. 1.592

H. -2.036

J. 2.724

K. -3.211

07.

$$7x - y = 13$$
$$-21x + py = -39$$

If the system of equations above has infinitely many solutions, then what is the value of p ?

F. 1

G. -2

H. 3

J. -4

K. 5

08.

The perimeter of a triangle is $20\,cm$. The first side of the triangle is $x\,cm$, the second side is 5 less than twice the length of the first side, and the third side is 2 more than one third of the first side. What is the length of the first side, in centimeters, of the triangle ?

A.   4.2

B.   5.8

C.   6.0

D.   6.9

E.   8.4

09.

Which of the following numbers is the exact value of $\log_3 \sqrt{27}$?

A. $\dfrac{1}{2}$

B. $\dfrac{3}{2}$

C. $\dfrac{1}{3}$

D. $\dfrac{2}{3}$

E. $3\sqrt{3}$

10.

Suppose that notebooks sell at $1.32 each or 5 for $5.43, how much is saved, to the nearest cent, on each notebook by buying them 5 at a time ?

A. $1.32

B. $1.29

C. $1.24

D. $1.20

E. $1.17

11.

If the function $g(x) = -2x^2 - 3x + 8$, what is the value of $g(-3)$?

F. 0

G. 1

H. 8

J. 12

K. 24

12.

If a linear equation is $-3x - 5y = -13$, what is the y-intercept of the equation ?

F. -13

G. $-\dfrac{13}{5}$

H. $\dfrac{13}{5}$

J. $-\dfrac{3}{5}$

K. 13

13.

At Everglades Fruit Store, Peggy paid less than $12 for her order of n apples and n oranges. An apple cost c cents, and a orange cost d cents. Which of the following expressions is expressed as the amount of the amount of money, in cents, that Peggy should have received back after she paid for her order with $12 ?

(Note: There is no tax on fruit at the store)

A. $nc + nd$

B. $12 - n(c + d)$

C. $12 - nc + nd$

D. $1200 - n(c + d)$

E. $1200 + n(c - d)$

14.

Which of the following graphs shows the solution set for the inequality 'five more than the product of 4 and x is more than 21.' ?

F.

G.

H.

J.

K.

15.

When the system of inequalities below is graphed in the standard (x, y) coordinate plane, one of the following graphs is that of the solution set of the system. Which one ?

$$-1 \leq x \leq 4$$
$$0 \leq y \leq 5$$
$$y \leq -\frac{1}{2}x + 3$$
$$y \geq -2x + 4$$

A. 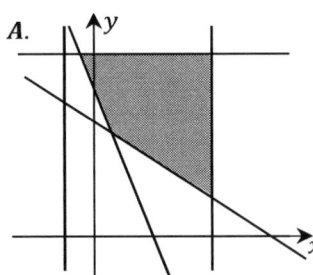   B.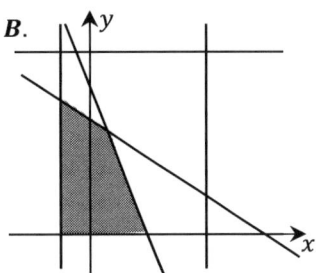

C. 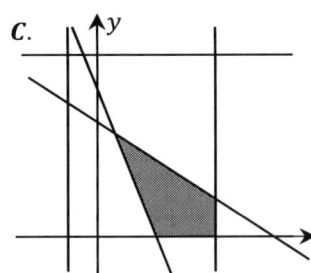   D.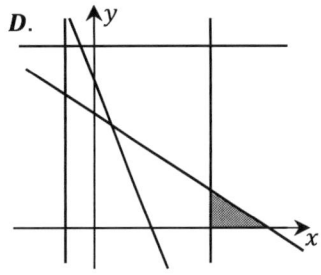

E.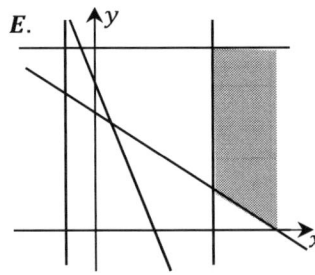

16.

If $|x + 2| + 3 = 1$, then what is the value of x ?

A. All real numbers

B. 4 or 0

C. -4

D. -4 or 0

E. There is no solution

017.

If the value of x is 213, the function $f(x)$ value is 36 less than three times the value of $f(x)$ when $x = 108$. Which of the following equation expresses this relationship ?

F. $f(213) = 36 - 3f(108)$

G. $f(213) = 3f(108) - 36$

H. $f(213) = 3(f(108) - 36)$

J. $f(x) = f(3x) - 36$

K. $f(213) = f(3 \times 108) - 36$

18.

Sarah earns her regular salary of \$8.00 per hour for up to 36 hours of work in a week. For each hour over 36 hours of work in a week, Sarah is paid $1\frac{3}{4}$ times her regular salary. How much does Sarah earn for a week in which she works 45 hours?

A. \$400.75

B. \$408.25

C. \$414.00

D. \$418.50

E. \$420.00

19.

Jonathan wanted to save an average of $8.00 per week for 4 weeks last month. He saved an average of $6.00 per week for the first 3 weeks and saved $10.00 for the last 4th week. On average, how much more should Jonathan have saved each week to reach his purpose?

A. $0.50

B. $1.00

C. $2.00

D. $3.00

E. $4.00

20.

A lawn mower was purchased 5 years ago for $265. The current value of the lawn mower is $55.50. What was the lawn mower's average decrease in value per year?

F. $37.30

G. $39.60

H. $41.90

J. $43.20

K. $45.50

21.

Martin is a real estate agent. He earns 4% of the sale price of every house he intermediates. What is Martin's commission for intermediating a house at the sale price of $180,000 ?

A. $6,000

B. $6,400

C. $6,800

D. $7,200

E. $7,600

22.

As shown in the figure below, the two line segments $\overline{AC}$ and $\overline{BD}$ intersect at a point O and 3 angle measures are given. What is the measure of $\angle ADO$?

F. 38°

G. 50°

H. 64°

J. 86°

K. 92°

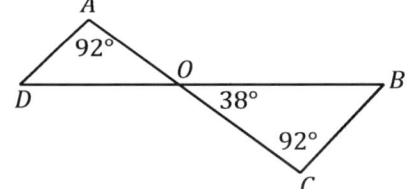

23.

Which of the following angles could not be the value of any angle in an obtuse triangle?

F. 15°

G. 45°

H. 85°

J. 90°

K. 136°

24.

The least common multiple (LCM) of two positive integers is 72 and the greatest common factor (GCF) of these same two numbers is 12. Which of the following pairs of numbers are the two numbers?

A. 6 and 12

B. 12 and 36

C. 20 and 36

D. 24 and 34

E. 24 and 36

25.

The figure below shows 17 congruent line segments, each line segment is determined by a pair of adjacent points. The sum of the length of the 17 line segments is 68 inches. Each intersection of four of the line segments is perpendicular. What is the area, in square inches, of shaded region?

F. 16

G. 20

H. 28

J. 32

K. 36

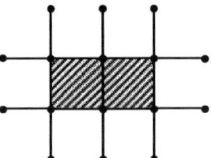

26.

If a function is $f(x) = \dfrac{x^2-1}{x-2}$, then which of the following expressions is equivalent to $f(x+1)$?

A. $\dfrac{x^2 - 2x}{x + 1}$

B. $\dfrac{x^2 + 2x}{x - 1}$

C. $\dfrac{x^2 + x}{x - 2}$

D. $\dfrac{x^2 + x}{x + 2}$

E. $\dfrac{x^2 + 2x}{x - 2}$

27.

An isosceles trapezoid $ABCD$ and a square $AXYZ$ are shown in the figure below. A point X is on $\overline{AB}$, two point Y, Z are on $\overline{CD}$, and the lengths given are in centimeters. What is the ratio of the area of $\square AXYZ$ to the area of $\square ABCD$?

F. $\dfrac{6}{11}$

G. $\dfrac{1}{2}$

H. $\dfrac{7}{13}$

J. $\dfrac{2}{3}$

K. $\dfrac{5}{9}$

28.

Daina plans to construct a circular flower garden with a circumference of 60 meter. Which of the following is closest to the length, in meter, of the decorative road that Diana needs to across the diameter of the flower garden?

A. 13

B. 15

C. 17

D. 19

E. 21

29.

The volume, V, of a right rectangular prism is $V = w \times l \times h$, where w is the width, l is the length of the prism, and h is the height of the prism. What is the height, in inches, of a rectangular prism that has a volume 960 cubic inches and a base that measures 6 inches by 4 inches?

F. 12

G. 16

H. 24

J. 32

K. 40

30.

What is the set of real solutions for $|x|^2 - |x| - 12 = 0$?

A. $\{-3, 3\}$

B. $\{-4, 4\}$

C. $\{-4, -3, 3, 4\}$

D. $\{-2, 2\}$

E. $\{-2, -\sqrt{3}, \sqrt{3}, 2\}$

31.

What is the value of x for $(x + 4)(x - 7) = 0$?

F. $-4 \ or \ 7$

G. $4 \ or -7$

H. $3 \ or -3$

J. $only \ 7$

K. $only -3$

32.

Which of the following transformations translates all points in the standard (x, y) coordinate plane up 3 coordinate units?

A. $(x, y) \rightarrow (x - 3, y + 3)$

B. $(x, y) \rightarrow (x, y - 3)$

C. $(x, y) \rightarrow (x, y + 3)$

D. $(x, y) \rightarrow (x, 3y)$

E. $(x, y) \rightarrow (3x, y)$

33.

What is the value of $(2 + i)^2$, for $i = \sqrt{-1}$?

A. $2 + i$

B. $3 + 4i$

C. $4 + 4i$

D. $5 + 4i$

E. 9

34.

What positive number when divided by its reciprocal, multiplicative inverse, has a result of $\frac{49}{9}$?

F. $\dfrac{7}{4}$

G. $\dfrac{7}{10}$

H. $\dfrac{7}{3}$

J. $\dfrac{3}{7}$

K. $\dfrac{3}{10}$

35.

What is the solution set of the following inequality?
$$(2|x| - 1)^2 \geq 9$$

F. $-2 \leq x \leq 1$

G. $-1 \leq x \leq 2$

H. $1 \leq x \leq 2$

J. $x \leq -1 \ or \ x \geq 1$

K. $x \leq -2 \ or \ x \geq 2$

36.

Which of the following expressions is equivalent to $(2x^4)^5$, for all nonzero real numbers x ?

A. $10x^9$

B. $32x^9$

C. $10x^{20}$

D. $32x^{20}$

E. $64x^{20}$

37.

Let $I = Prt$ be the formula of simple interest , where P is the principal in dollars, I is the simple interest in dollars, r is the annual interest rate in dollars, and t is the time in years the money is deposited. Which of the following expressions gives P when the annual interest rate 8%?

F. $0.8It$

G. $\dfrac{0.08t}{I}$

H. $\dfrac{0.8t}{I}$

J. $\dfrac{I}{0.08t}$

K. $\dfrac{I}{0.8t}$

38.

If $\sqrt{3x} - 6 = 3$, then what is the value of x?

A. 27

B. $9\sqrt{3}$

C. $\sqrt{6}$

D. $\sqrt{3}$

E. 1

39.

If x is a negative integer and y is 5 times x, what is the least common denominator, in term of x, for subtraction of $\frac{1}{x}$ and $\frac{1}{y}$?

F. x

G. xy

H. $5x$

J. $5x^2$

K. $5xy$

40.

If $\frac{2^3 2^x}{(2^3)^2} = \frac{1}{16}$, what is the value of real number x ?

F. 1

G. -1

H. 2

J. -2

K. 3

41.

The data set below gives the waiting times (in minutes) of 10 students waiting for a bus. What is median and mode of the list of data below?

$$4, 8, 12, 15, 3, 2, 6, 9, 8, 7$$

	median	mode
A.	7.5	8
B.	8	7.5
C.	8	8
D.	8.5	8
E.	8	8.5

42.

On average, 5 customers in a bank remain when the bank closes daily. The probability, P, in percent, that exactly c customers remain when the bank closes could be modeled by the relation, $P = \frac{5^c e^{-5}}{(c+1)!} \times 100$. If $e^{-5} \approx 0.07$ then what is the probability that exactly 3 customers remain when the bank closes?

F. 34.03%

G. 36.46%

H. 38.21%

J. 39.38%

K. 40.57%

Use the following information to answer questions
43 - 44.

At agritainment, the 20 members of the part-time farms sold 2 types of processed fruits-orange and grape-in the form of juice and jam. The price of each bottle of fruit juice was $5 and the price of each jar of fruit jam was $6. The table below gives the number of fruit processed foods by types of fruit and processing types.

Fruit type	Processing types	
	Juice	Jam
Orange	144	98
Grape	126	112

The stem-and-leaf plot below shows the number of fruit processed foods, regardless of type, sold by each of the 20 members.

Stem	Leaf
0	9
1	2 4 6 6 7 9
2	0 4 5 7 8 9 9
3	0 1 1 2 5 6

Key: 1 | 2 = 12

43.

Suppose 1 member will picked at random from the 20 members of the part-time farms who sold fruit processed foods to receive a prize. What is the probability a member who sold less than 20 tickets?

A. 0

B. $\dfrac{7}{20}$

C. $\dfrac{3}{10}$

D. $\dfrac{4}{10}$

E. $\dfrac{7}{10}$

44.

For which processing type was the total amount collected for the fruit processed foods, and by how many dollars was it greater?

F. Juice $50

G. Juice $70

H. Juice $90

J. Jam $70

K. Jam $90

45.

In the figure below, the bell-shaped curve represents the normal distribution. The percent of the data that falls within each standard deviation from the mean is given to the nearest 0.1%.

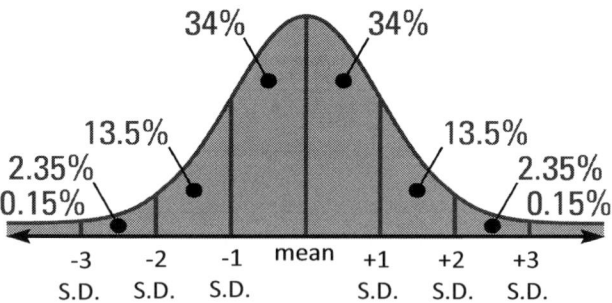

Suppose that the blood cholesterol concentration of men in a certain population are normally distributed with a mean of $170mg/dL$ and a standard deviation of $15mg/dL$. To the nearest 0.1%, what percent of men in the population are at most $185mg/dL$?

F. 2.5%

G. 13.5%

H. 16.0%

J. 34.0%

K. 84.0%

Use the following information to answer questions 46 - 48.

As shown in the standard (x, y) coordinate plane below, a parabola with equation $y - k = a(x - h)^2$ is graphed. The vertex of the parabola is $(0, 4)$ and a point $P (\alpha, \beta)$ lies on the parabola.

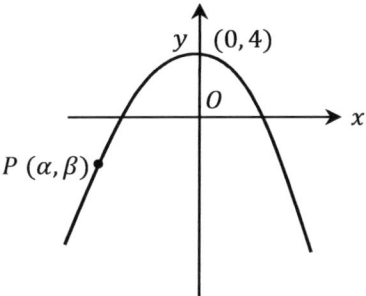

46.

For any point $P (\alpha, \beta)$ on the given parabola, which of the following points must also be on the given parabola?

A. $(-\alpha, \beta)$

B. $(\alpha, -\beta)$

C. $(-\alpha, -\beta)$

D. $(-\alpha^2, \beta)$

E. $(-\alpha, \beta^2)$

47.

Suppose that the coordinates of P are $(-6, -2)$, which of the following values is the value of a?

A. $\dfrac{1}{6}$

B. $-\dfrac{1}{6}$

C. $\dfrac{2}{3}$

D. $-\dfrac{2}{3}$

E. $\dfrac{9}{4}$

48.

Assume that the parabola is rotated anti-clockwise by 90° about the origin. What is the resulting equation from this rotation?

F. $x + 4 = ay^2$

G. $x - 4 = ay^2$

H. $x = a(y - 4)^2$

J. $y = a\sqrt{x - 4}$

K. $y = a(x + 4)^2$

49.

The first three figure in a sequence are shown below. First figure shows an equilateral triangle with sides of length $1cm$, in second figure, there are 4 triangles with sides of length $\frac{1}{2}$ cm, and in third figure, there are 16 triangles with sides of length $\frac{1}{4}$ cm. Which of the following expressions represents length of side of nth figure small triangle?

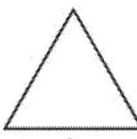 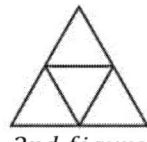 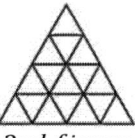

$1st\ figure$	$2nd\ figure$	$3rd\ figure$

A. $\dfrac{1}{2n}$

B. 2^{n-1}

C. 2^n

D. $\dfrac{1}{2^{n-1}}$

E. $\dfrac{1}{2^n}$

50.

As shown in the standard (x, y) coordinate plane below, the three vertices of ΔPQR are $P\ (1,1), Q\ (4,1)$, and $R\ (1,5)$. What are the coordinates of the center of the circle that circumscribes ΔPQR?

A. $(2.5, 2)$

B. $(2.5, 2.5)$

C. $(3, 2.5)$

D. $(2.5, 3)$

E. $(3, 3)$

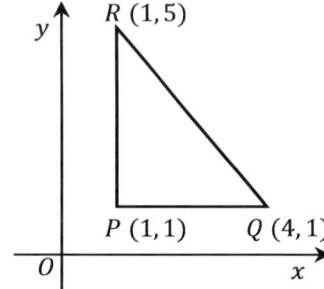

51.

Suppose that a parabola and a circle are drawn in the standard (x, y) coordinate plane. The parabola has vertex $(-3, 2)$, has a horizontal axis of symmetry, and passes through $(-2, 4)$. The circle has center $(0, 2)$ and radius 4. How many intersecting point between the parabola and the circle?

A. 0

B. 1

C. 2

D. 3

E. There are infinitely many points.

52.

Suppose that the two points $P\ (7, -2)$ and $Q\ (3, 14)$ is placed in the standard (x, y) coordinate plane. Which of the following coordinates is the midpoint of $\overline{PQ}$?

F. $(6, 7)$

G. $(5, 6)$

H. $(6, 5)$

J. $(7, 6)$

K. $(8, 7)$

53.

In the standard (x, y) coordinate below, a circle has its center $(-1, 3)$. What is the equation of the circle?

F. $(x + 1)^2 + (y - 3)^2 = 8$

G. $(x + 1)^2 + (y - 3)^2 = 16$

H. $(x - 1)^2 + (y + 3)^2 = 8$

J. $(x - 1)^2 + (y + 3)^2 = 16$

K. $(x - 1)^2 + (y + 3)^2 = 64$

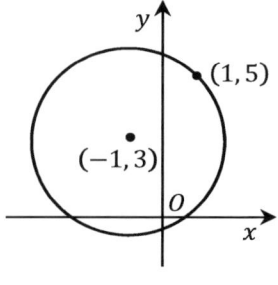

54.

The graph of $y = a \cos b x$ is shown below for $a > 0$, $b > 0$. What is the product of a and b?

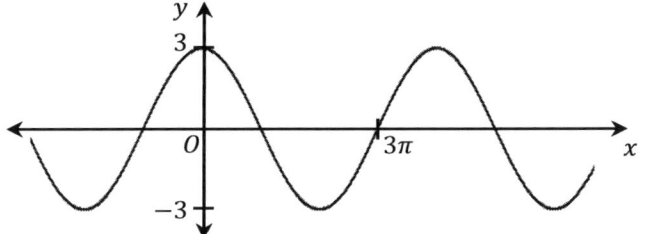

A. 0.5

B. 1

C. 1.5

D. 6

E. 9

55.

Consider a rhombus that has 8 feet side length and two angles of 120°. What is the area, in square feet, of the rhombus?

F. 24

G. $24\sqrt{2}$

H. 32

J. $32\sqrt{3}$

K. 40

56.

In the figure below, a triangle $\triangle ABC$ is a right triangle with the given dimensions in inches. Which of the following values is the length, in inches, of $\overline{BC}$?

A. $\dfrac{120}{\cos 25°}$

B. $120 \cos 25°$

C. $\dfrac{120}{\sin 25°}$

D. $120 \sin 25°$

E. $120 \tan 25°$

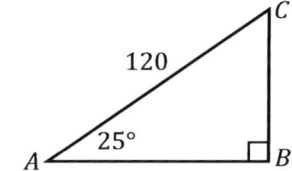

57.

Humphery's computer password consists of 3 capital letters followed by 6 digits. The 3 capital letters must all be different and the followed 6 digits could be any digit 0 through 9, and digits may repeat. Which of the following expressions gives the probability that a randomly selected password contain the word *ACT*, spelled correctly ?

A. $\dfrac{1}{25 \times 24 \times 23 \times 10^6}$

B. $\dfrac{3 \times 2 \times 1}{25 \times 24 \times 23 \times 10^6}$

C. $\dfrac{25 \times 24 \times 23}{25 \times 24 \times 23 \times 10^6}$

D. $\dfrac{10^6}{25 \times 24 \times 23 \times 10^6}$

E. $\dfrac{3 \times 2 \times 1 \times 10^6}{25 \times 24 \times 23 \times 10^6}$

58.

Suppose that $\cos\theta = \dfrac{8}{17}$ for $0° < \theta \le 360°$, what are the all possible value of $\sin\theta$?

A. $-\dfrac{8}{17}$ only

B. $-\dfrac{8}{17}$ and $\dfrac{15}{17}$

C. $\dfrac{15}{17}$ only

D. $\dfrac{15}{17}$ and $-\dfrac{15}{17}$

E. $-\dfrac{8}{17}$ and $-\dfrac{15}{17}$

59.

In the standard (x, y) coordinate plane, the graph of $f(x) = 2 - 3\cos(x + \pi)$ is shown below. What is the range of $f(x)$?

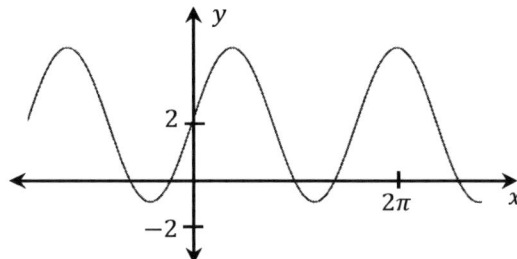

F. $-1 \le y \le 2$

G. $-3 \le y \le 3$

H. $-1 \le y \le 5$

J. $0 \le x \le 2\pi$

K. $0 \le x \le \dfrac{3\pi}{2}$

60.

Mr. Baldy made true statements "At most 20 people in this city have a boat." Which of the following statements must be **false**?

F. There may be 10 people in the city without a ship.

G. There may be 10 people in the city with a ship.

H. At least 21 people in this have a boat.

J. There are people who do not have a ship in the city.

K. In that city, some people have a boat.

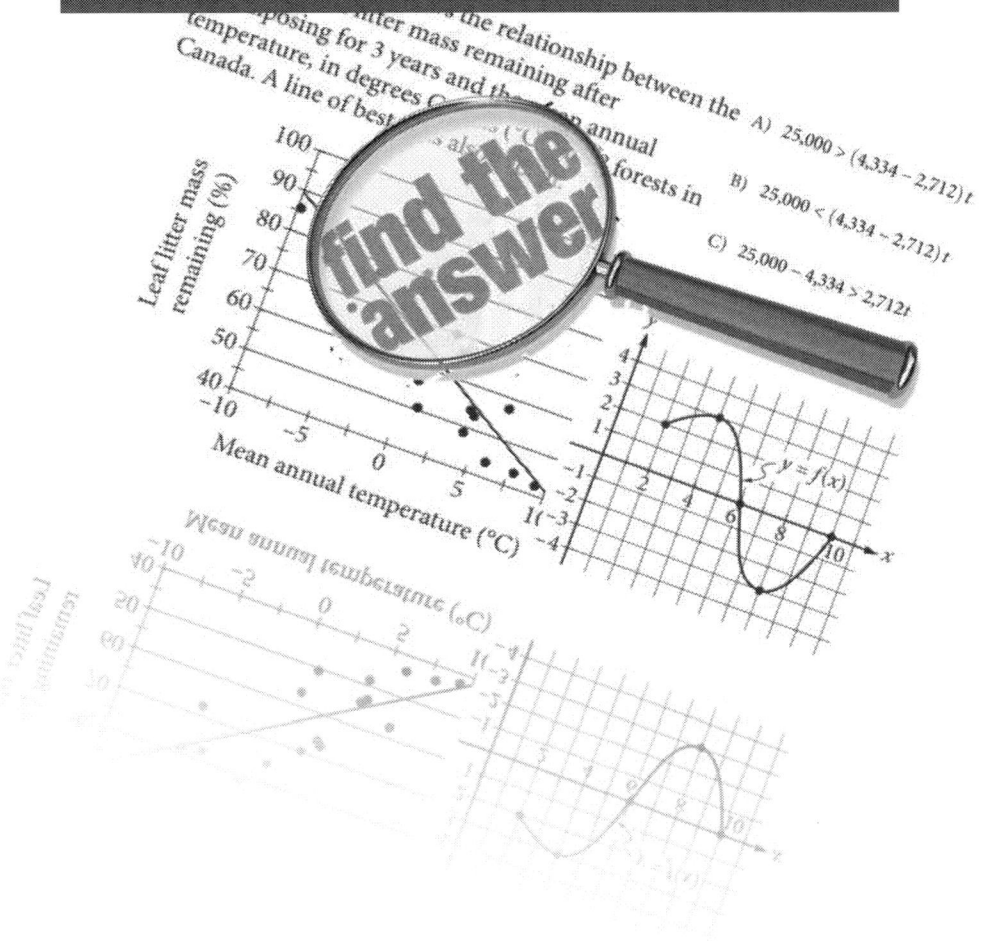

Obtain Scale Scores from Raw Scores

Scale Score	Raw Score	Scale Score	Raw Score	Scale Score	Raw Score
36	60	24	36-37	12	7
35	58-59	23	34-35	11	5-6
34	57	22	32-33	10	4
33	55-56	21	30-31	9	-
32	54	20	29	8	3
31	52-53	19	27-28	7	-
30	50-51	18	24-26	6	2
29	48-49	17	21-23	5	-
28	45-47	16	17-20	4	1
27	43-44	15	13-16	3	-
26	40-42	14	11-12	2	-
25	38-39	13	8-10	1	0

1. Scoring Key

Key		Question Category	Y/N
01.	D	Number Theory	
02.	G	Number Theory	
03.	E	Number Theory	
04.	F	Expression and Linear Equation	
05.	C	Expression and Linear Equation	
06.	H	Expression and Linear Equation	
07.	H	Expression and Linear Equation	
08.	D	Expression and Linear Equation	
09.	B	Further Equations and Functions	
10.	E	Expression and Linear Equation	
11.	G	Linear Function inequality	
12.	H	Linear Function inequality	
13.	D	Linear Function inequality	
14.	H	Linear Function inequality	
15.	C	Linear Function inequality	
16.	E	Linear Function inequality	
17.	G	Linear Function inequality	
18.	C	Arithmetic Topic and Ratio	
19.	B	Arithmetic Topic and Ratio	
20.	H	Arithmetic Topic and Ratio	
21.	D	Arithmetic Topic and Ratio	
22.	G	Basic Geometry	
23.	J	Basic Geometry	
24.	E	Number Theory	
25.	J	Basic Geometry	
26.	B	Further Equations and Functions	
27.	F	Basic Geometry	
28.	D	Basic Geometry	
29.	K	Arithmetic Topic and Ratio	
30.	B	Quadratic and Polynomial Function	

Key		Question Category	Y/N
31.	F	Quadratic and Polynomial Function	
32.	C	Quadratic and Polynomial Function	
33.	B	Quadratic and Polynomial Function	
34.	H	Quadratic and Polynomial Function	
35.	K	Quadratic and Polynomial Function	
36.	D	Further Equations and Functions	
37.	J	Further Equations and Functions	
38.	A	Further Equations and Functions	
39.	H	Further Equations and Functions	
40.	G	Further Equations and Functions	
41.	A	Statistics and Probability	
42.	G	Statistics and Probability	
43.	B	Statistics and Probability	
44.	H	Statistics and Probability	
45.	K	Statistics and Probability	
46.	A	Analytic Geometry and Conic Section	
47.	B	Analytic Geometry and Conic Section	
48.	F	Analytic Geometry and Conic Section	
49.	D	Sequence and Series	
50.	D	Analytic Geometry and Conic Section	
51.	C	Analytic Geometry and Conic Section	
52.	G	Analytic Geometry and Conic Section	
53.	F	Analytic Geometry and Conic Section	
54.	C	Trigonometric Functions	
55.	J	Trigonometric Functions	
56.	D	Trigonometric Functions	
57.	D	Statistics and Probability	
58.	D	Trigonometric Functions	
59.	H	Trigonometric Functions	
60.	H	Intermediate Algebra	

2. Answer Explanations

01. **Answer** **(D)**

It is also a good idea to substitute a specific number for a and b.

For any integer a and $-a$, two numbers are opposites if they have the same absolute value but different signs, for example, 2 and -2.

So, a is negative, its opposite $-a$ is positive, $a < 0$, $-a > 0$ and b is positive, its opposite $-b$ is negative.

I . To subtract an integer, add its opposite.
And positive + positive is always a positive number.
$b - a = b + (-a) > 0$
II. The absolute value of an integer is always positive, thus
$|a| + |b| > 0$.
III. $-|a| - |b| = -(|a| + |b|) < 0$

Or, to substitute a specific number for $a(= -2)$ and $b(= 3)$.

02. **Answer** **(G)**

Calculate the denominator part, and then simplify them..

Calculate the denominator part by using LCD;

$$2 + \frac{2}{3} = \frac{6}{3} + \frac{2}{3} = \frac{8}{3} \quad \rightarrow \quad \frac{2}{2 + \dfrac{2}{2 + \dfrac{2}{3}}} = \frac{2}{2 + \dfrac{2}{\dfrac{8}{3}}}$$

$$\frac{2}{\dfrac{8}{3}} = 2 \div \frac{8}{3} = 2 \times \frac{3}{8} = \frac{3}{4} \quad \rightarrow \quad 2 + \frac{2}{\dfrac{8}{3}} = 2 + \frac{3}{4} = \frac{8}{4} + \frac{3}{4} = \frac{11}{4}$$

Thus,

$$\frac{2}{2 + \dfrac{2}{2 + \dfrac{2}{3}}} = \frac{2}{\dfrac{11}{4}} = 2 \div \frac{11}{4} = 2 \times \frac{4}{11} = \frac{8}{11}$$

03. **Answer** **(E)**

Using prime factorization.

Prime factorizations of 12 and 72;
$$12 = 2^2 \times 3, \qquad 72 = 2^3 \times 3^2 = (2^2 \times 3) \times 2 \times 3$$

From the definitions of LCM and GCF, the two numbers must have factor $2^2(4)$ and 3. And at least one of the two numbers must have 2 and 3 as prime factors.

Thus, the correct answer is **E**.

04. **Answer** **(F)**

Finding the relationship between x and y.

Using the cross product;
$$\frac{2x + y}{x - y} = \frac{3}{2} \quad \rightarrow \quad 2 \times (2x + y) = 3 \times (x - y)$$
$$\rightarrow \quad 4x + 2y = 3x - 3y$$
Solving the equation for x;
$$4x + 2y = 3x - 3y \quad \rightarrow \quad 4x - 3x = -3y - 2y \quad \rightarrow \quad x = -5y$$
Substitute $-5y$ for x;
$$\frac{y}{x} = \frac{y}{-5y} = -\frac{1}{5}$$

Thus, the value of $\frac{y}{x}$ is $-\frac{1}{5}$.

05. **Answer** **(C)**

Solve the equation for x by using cross product.

Cross product and then expanding;
$$\frac{3 - x}{5 - x} = \frac{3}{4} \quad \rightarrow \quad 4(3 - x) = 3(5 - x) \quad \rightarrow \quad 12 - 4x = 15 - 3x$$
Subtract 12 from both sides;
$$12 - 4x - 12 = 15 - 3x - 12 \quad \rightarrow \quad -4x = 3 - 3x$$
Add $3x$ to both sides;
$$-4x + 3x = 3 - 3x + 3x \quad \rightarrow \quad -x = 3$$
Multiply by -1 on both sides;
$$(-1) \cdot (-x) = 3 \cdot (-1) \quad \rightarrow \quad x = -3$$
Thus, the value of $2x$ is $2 \cdot (-3) = -6$.

06. **Answer** **(H)**

Solve the equation for x by using inverse operation

Subtract 5.88 from both sides;
$$2.32x + 5.88 = 0.79 - 0.18x$$
$$\rightarrow \quad 2.32x + 5.88 - 5.88 = 0.79 - 0.18x - 5.88$$
$$\rightarrow \quad 2.32x = -5.09 - 0.18x$$
Add $0.18x$ to both sides;
$$2.32x = -5.09 - 0.18x \quad \rightarrow \quad 2.32x + 0.18x = -5.09 \quad \rightarrow \quad 2.5x = -5.09$$
Divide by 2.5 on both sides;
$$\frac{2.5x}{2.5} = \frac{-5.09}{2.5} \quad \rightarrow \quad x = -2.036$$
Thus, the value of x is -2.036.

07. **Answer** **(H)**

"infinitely many solutions" mean the two lines of the equations are same.

If two line $a_1 x + b_1 y = c_1$ and $a_2 x + b_2 y = c_2$ are same, then;
$$\frac{a_1}{a_2} = \frac{b_1}{b_2} = \frac{c_1}{c_2}.$$
Therefore, for $7x - y = 13$ and $-21x + py = -39$;
$$\frac{a_1}{a_2} = \frac{b_1}{b_2} = \frac{c_1}{c_2} \quad \rightarrow \quad \frac{-21}{7} = \frac{p}{-1} = \frac{-39}{13} = -3$$
Using cross multiplication;
$$\frac{p}{-1} = \frac{-3}{1} \quad \rightarrow \quad p = -3 \times (-1) \quad \rightarrow \quad p = 3$$
Thus, the value of p is 3.

08. **Answer** **(D)**

The perimeter of triangle is the sum of the length of three sides.

By the definition of the perimeter;
$$20 = x + 2x - 5 + \frac{1}{3}x + 2 \quad \rightarrow \quad 20 = \frac{10x}{3} - 3$$
Add 3 to both sides;
$$\frac{10x}{3} - 3 = 20 \quad \rightarrow \quad \frac{10x}{3} - 3 + 3 = 20 + 3 \quad \rightarrow \quad \frac{10x}{3} = 23$$
Multiply by $\frac{3}{10}$ on both sides;
$$\frac{10x}{3} = 23 \quad \rightarrow \quad \frac{3}{10} \times \frac{10x}{3} = 23 \times \frac{3}{10} \quad \rightarrow \quad x = \frac{69}{10} = 6.9$$
Thus, the length of the first side is 6.9 cm,

09. Answer **(B)**

Using logarithm property.

$\sqrt{27} = \sqrt{3^3} = 3^{\frac{3}{2}}$ and rewrite; $\log_3 \sqrt{27} = \log_3 3^{\frac{3}{2}}$.

Using logarithm property $\log_b b^N = N$ so, $\log_3 3^{\frac{3}{2}} = \frac{3}{2}$.

Thus, the correct answer is **B**.

---

10. Answer **(E)**

Comparing two price.

Buying 5 notebook at \$1.32 each → \$1.32 × 5 = \$6.60.
Thus, saving money is \$6.60 − \$5.43 = \$1.17.

---

11. Answer **(G)**

Substitute each value and then evaluate.

Substituting −3 for x;
$g(x) = -2x^2 - 3x + 8$ → $g(-3) = -2(-3)^2 - 3(-3) + 10 = 1$
Thus, the value of $g(-3)$ is 1.

---

12. Answer **(H)**

Convert the equation to slope-intercept form.

Convert the standard form to slope-intercept form by;
  adding $3x$ to both sides;
  $-3x - 5y = -13$ → $-3x - 5y + 3x = -13 + 3x$
  → $-5y = -13 + 3x$
  dividing both sides by −5;
  $-5y = 3x - 13$ → $\frac{-5y}{-5} = \frac{3x - 13}{-5}$ → $y = -\frac{3}{5}x + \frac{13}{5}$
Thus, the y-intercept of the given equation is $\frac{13}{5}$.

---

13. Answer **(D)**

\$12 is 1200 cents and factoring by the distributive property.

The total cost of apples and oranges is;
  $n \times c + n \times d = nc + nd$
The amount of received back is;
  $\$12 - (nc + nd) cents = 1200 \, cents - (nc + nd) cents$
Using the distributive property;
  $1200 cents - (nc + nd) cents = 1200 - n(c + d)$

---

14. Answer **(H)**

Translate the verbal phrase into an algebraic inequality.

Translate the verbal phrase into an inequality and then solve the inequality.
  'five more than the product of 4 and x is more than 21'
  → $4x + 5 > 21$
Subtracting 5 from both sides;
  $4x + 5 > 21$ → $4x + 5 - 5 > 21 - 5$ → $4x > 16$
Dividing both sides by 4;
  $4x > 16$ → $\frac{4x}{4} > 16$ → $x > 4$

Thus, the graph is; H.

---

15. Answer **(C)**

Finding boundary line and then testing a point.

The region is inside part of between $x = -1$, $x = 4$ and between $y = 0$, $y = 5$.
The region of $y \le -\frac{1}{2}x + 3$;
  The boundary line is $y = -\frac{1}{2}x + 3$,
  this line's y-intercept is (0,3) and
  x-intercept is (6,0).
  Test a point (0,0):
  $0 \le -\frac{1}{2} \times 0 + 3 \to 0 \le 3$
  So, the correct region is below
  boundary line.
The region of $y \ge -2x + 4$;
The boundary line is $y = -2x + 4$, this line's y-intercept is (0,4) and x-intercept is (2,0). Test a point (0,0): $0 \ge -2 \times 0 + 4 \to 0 \ge 4$
So, the correct region is above boundary line.

Thus, the correct region is **C**.
Or using graphic calculator.

---

16. Answer **(E)**

Absolute value is never negative.

Subtracting −3 from both sides;
  $|x + 2| + 3 = 1$ → $|x + 2| + 3 - 3 = 1 - 3$ → $|x + 2| = -2$
There is no solution because absolute value is never negative.

---

17. Answer **(G)**

Three times means multiplying 3.

The function value $f(x)$ at $x = 213$ is $f(213)$, and at $x = 108$ is $f(108)$.

Thus, "36 less than three times" means $f(213) = 3f(108) - 36$.

---

18. Answer **(C)**

45 hours = 36 hours + 9 hours.

Salary for 36 hours is; \$8 × 36 = \$288.
Salary for remaining 9 hours is;
  $1\frac{3}{4} \times \$8 \times 9 = \frac{7}{4} \times \$8 \times 9 = \$126.$

Thus, the total salary is \$288 + \$126 = \$414.

---

19. Answer **(B)**

Finding real an average saving rate

His total purposing money is \$8 × 4 = \$32 and his total real saving money is \$6 × 3 + \$10 = \$28. So, he should have saved \$ 4 more to reach his purpose.

This means that
  $\frac{\$4}{4 weeks} = \$1/week$
he should have saved \$1 per week more to reach his purpose.

---

20. Answer **(H)**

Average decrease is an unit rate.

The average decrease per year is;
  $\frac{change\ of\ value}{tine} = \frac{\$55.50 - \$265}{5\ years} = \$ - 41.9\ per\ year$
(−) means decreasing and average decrease is \$41.9 *per year.*

21. Answer *(D)*

To write a decimal as a percent, move the decimal point two places to the right and write a percent sign.

The commission is;
$$0.04 \times \$180{,}000 = \$7{,}200.$$

22. Answer *(G)*

Using converse of Alternate interior angles.

Alternating interior angles $\angle DAO$ and $\angle BCO$ are same so, $\overline{AD} \parallel \overline{BC}$. And using angle sum of triangle;
$$\angle CBO + 92° + 38° = 180° \rightarrow \angle CBO + 130° = 180° \quad \angle CBO = 50°$$
$\angle CBO$ and $\angle ADO$ are also alternating interior angles thus, $\angle ADO$ is 50°.

23. Answer *(J)*

Using the classifying of triangles by angles.

Triangles classified by angles;
① all angles of the acute triangle are less than 90°.
② right triangle has exactly 90° angle.
③ obtuse triangle has exactly a angle that is greater than 90°
→ the given triangle is an obtuse triangle so, one angle is greater than 90°, and other two angles are less than 90°
(∵ angle sum of triangle is 180°)

Thus, the correct answer is *J*.

24. Answer *(E)*

Using prime factorization.

Prime factorizations of 12 and 72;
$$12 = 2^2 \times 3, \qquad 72 = 2^3 \times 3^2 = (2^2 \times 3) \times 2 \times 3$$

From the definitions of LCM and GCF, the two numbers must have factor $2^2(4)$ and 3. And at least one of the two numbers must have 2 and 3 as prime factors.

Thus, the correct answer is *E*.

25. Answer *(J)*

The shaded region is a rectangle.

The length of a line segment is $68 \div 17 = 4$ inches. And the intersecting angle is 90°. So, the shaded region is a rectangle and the area of rectangle is;
$$area = 8 \times 4 = 32 \ in^2$$

Thus, the area of the shaded region is 32.

26. Answer *(B)*

(x+1) substitute for x.

(x+1) substitute for x and then simplifying,
$$f(x+1) = \frac{(x+1)^2 - 1}{(x+1) - 2} = \frac{x^2 + 2x + 1 - 1}{x + 1 - 2} = \frac{x^2 + 2x}{x - 1}$$

Thus, the correct answer is *B*.

27. Answer *(F)*

Drawing a auxiliary lines.

$\square ABCD$ is an isosceles trapezoid so, $\overline{XB}$ is $5 - 2 = 3cm$ and the area of $\square ABCD$ is;
$$area = \frac{1}{2}(b_1 + b_2)h = \frac{1}{2}(13 + 9) \times 6 = 66$$
The area of $\square AXYZ$ is $6 \times 6 = 36$.

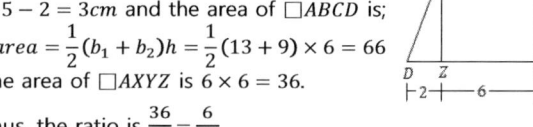

Thus, the ratio is $\dfrac{36}{66} = \dfrac{6}{11}$.

28. Answer *(D)*

The circumference is πd.

From the formula of the circumference of the circle;
$$C = 2\pi r = \pi d \quad \rightarrow \quad 60 = \pi d \quad \rightarrow \quad d = \frac{60}{\pi} \approx 19.09859$$

Thus, the diameter of the flower garden is 19 meter.

29. Answer *(K)*

Using the formula.

The volume of the prism is;
$$V = w \times l \times h \quad \rightarrow \quad 4 \times 6 \times h = 960 \ in^3 \quad \rightarrow \quad h = \frac{960}{24} = 40 \ in$$

Thus, the height of the prism is 40 *in*.

30. Answer *(B)*

Absolute value, $|A|$, is always positive.

Let A be $|x|$;
$$|x|^2 - |x| - 12 = 0 \quad \rightarrow \quad A^2 - A - 12 = 0 \quad \rightarrow \quad (A+3)(A-4) = 0$$
$$\rightarrow \quad A + 3 = 0 \ or \ A - 4 = 0 \quad \rightarrow \quad A = -3 \ or \ A = 4$$
So, $|x| = -3$ (∵ $|x| > 0$, no solution) or $|x| = 4 \rightarrow x = 4 \ or -4$.

Thus, the solutions are 4 or −4.

31. Answer *(F)*

If AB=0, then A=0 or B=0.

If $A \times B = 0$, then $A = 0$ or $B = 0$.
$$(x + 4)(x - 7) = 0 \rightarrow x + 4 = 0 \ or \ x - 7 = 0 \rightarrow \quad x = -4 \ or \ x = 7$$
Thus, the value of x is −4 or 7.

32. Answer *(C)*

Translation; $(x, \ y) \rightarrow (x + h, y + k)$.

"translates ~ up 3 coordinate units" means $h = 0$ and $k = 3$. So,
$$(x, y) \rightarrow (x, y + 3),$$

Thus, the correct answer is *C*.

33. Answer *(B)*

i^2 is -1.

Expanding by using FOIL pattern;
$$(2 + i)^2 = (2 + i)(2 + i) = 2^2 + 2i + 2i + i^2 = 4 + 4i + i^2$$
Because $i^2 = -1$;
$$4 + 4i + i^2 = 4 + 4i - 1 = 3 + 4i$$

Thus, the value is $3 + 4i$.

34. Answer *(H)*

The reciprocal of $\dfrac{a}{b}$ is $\dfrac{b}{a}$.

If x is a number, then its reciprocal is $\dfrac{1}{x}$.
$$x \div \frac{1}{x} = x \times \frac{1}{\frac{1}{x}} = x \times x = x^2 \quad \rightarrow \quad x^2 = \frac{49}{9}$$
Take both sides by square root;
$$\sqrt{x^2} = \pm \sqrt{\frac{49}{9}} \quad \rightarrow \quad x = \pm \frac{7}{3}$$

Thus, the positive number is $\dfrac{7}{3}$.

35. Answer (K)

An absolute value is never negative.

Let A be $(2|x| - 1)$;
$$(2|x| - 1)^2 \geq 9 \quad \rightarrow \quad A^2 \geq 9 \quad \rightarrow \quad A \leq -3 \ or \ A \geq 3$$
So,
First: $A \leq -3 \quad \rightarrow \quad 2|x| - 1 \leq -3 \quad \rightarrow \quad 2|x| \leq -2 \quad \rightarrow \quad |x| \leq -1$
Because the absolute value is never negative it is not solution.

Second: $A \geq 3 \quad \rightarrow \quad 2|x| - 1 \geq 3 \quad \rightarrow \quad 2|x| \geq 4 \quad \rightarrow \quad |x| \geq 2$
$$\rightarrow \quad x \leq -2 \ or \ x \geq 2$$

Thus, the solution set is $x \leq -2 \ or \ x \geq 2$.

36. Answer (D)

Using the properties of exponential.

Using the properties of exponential;
$$(2x^4)^5 = 2^5 x^{4 \times 5} = 32x^{20}$$

Thus, the correct answer is **D**.

37. Answer (J)

Solving for P.

Substituting 0.08 for r and then solving for P;
$$I = Prt \quad \rightarrow \quad I = P(0.08)t \quad \rightarrow \quad 0.08Pt = I \quad \rightarrow \quad P = \frac{I}{0.08t}$$

Thus, the correct answer is **J**.

38. Answer (A)

For all real x, $\left(\sqrt{x}\right)^2 = |x|$.

Add 6 to both sides;
$$\sqrt{3x} - 6 = 3 \quad \rightarrow \quad \sqrt{3x} = 3 + 6 \quad \rightarrow \quad \sqrt{3x} = 9$$
Take square on both sides and then divide by 3;
$$\left(\sqrt{3x}\right)^2 = 9^2 \quad \rightarrow \quad 3x = 81 \quad \rightarrow \quad x = \frac{81}{3} = 27$$

Thus, the value of x is 27.

39. Answer (H)

y=5x.

Because and y is 5 times x ($\leftarrow y = 5x$), the least common multiple of x and $y(= 5x)$ is $5x$.

Thus, the least common denominator is $5x$.

40. Answer (G)

16 is 2^4 .

From the properties of exponential;
$$\frac{2^3 2^x}{(2^3)^2} = \frac{2^{3+x}}{2^6} = 2^{3+x-6} = 2^{x-3}, \qquad \frac{1}{16} = \frac{1}{2^4} = 2^{-4}$$
So,
$$\frac{2^3 2^x}{(2^3)^2} = \frac{1}{16} \quad \rightarrow \quad 2^{x-3} = 2^{-4} \quad \rightarrow \quad x - 3 = -4 \quad \rightarrow \quad x = -1$$

Thus, the value of x is -1.

41. Answer (A)

Rearranging data in order.

Rearrange data in order;
$$2, 3, 4, 6, 7, 8, 8, 9, 12, 15$$
So, the median (middle number) is $\frac{7+8}{2} = 7.5$ and there are two 8, the mode (highest frequency) is 8.

Thus, the correct answer is **A**.

42. Answer (G)

Substitute 3 for c.

Substitute 3 for c;
$$P = \frac{5^c e^{-5}}{(c + 1)!} \times 100 \rightarrow \quad P = \frac{5^3 \times 0.07}{(3 + 1)!} \times 100 \approx 36.45833 \dots \%$$
Thus, the probability is 36.46%.

43. Answer (B)

Finding the number of member who sold less than 20.

The number of member who sold less than 20, (from stem-and-leaf plot; $9, 12, 14, 16, 16, 17, 19$), is 7. So. the probability is
$$P = \frac{7}{20}$$
Thus, the correct answer is **B**.

44. Answer (H)

The price of each juice is \$5, and the price of each jam is \$6.

The total number of juice is $144 + 126 = 270$ and the price of each juice is \$5.
So, the total selling price of juice is $270 \times \$5 = \$1,350$.

The total number of jam is $98 + 112 = 210$ and the price of each jam is \$6.
So, the total selling price of juice is $210 \times \$6 = \$1,260$.

Thus, the correct answer is **H**.

45. Answer (K)

185=170+15.

$185(x) = 170(\bar{x}) + 15(\sigma)$ so, from the curve, $x \leq \bar{x} + \sigma$ is $34 + 34 + + 13.5 + 2.35 + 0.15 = 84\%$

Thus, the percent is 84%.

46. Answer (A)

The parabola is symmetric on y-axis.

The parabola is symmetric, so it has sister points (α, β) and $(-\alpha, \beta)$.

Thus, the correct answer is **A**.

47. Answer (B)

Substitute the coordinates.

Substitute $(0, 4)$ for (h, k);
$$y - k = a(x - h)^2 \rightarrow \quad y - 4 = a(x - 0)^2 \quad \rightarrow \quad y - 4 = ax^2$$
Substitute $(-6, -2)$ for (x, y);
$$y - 4 = ax^2 \quad \rightarrow \quad -2 - 4 = a(-6)^2 \quad \rightarrow \quad -6 = 36a \quad \rightarrow \quad a = -\frac{1}{6}$$
Thus, the value of a is $-\frac{1}{6}$.

48. **Answer** **(F)**

The coordinates of image for anti clockwise 90° are (-y, x)

Rotation of point through 90° about the origin in anti-clockwise direction when point (a, b) is rotated about the origin O through 90° in anticlockwise direction. The new position of point (a, b) will become $(-b, a)$.

So, the vertex $(0, 4)$ will become $(-4, 0)$.
The image of the parabola open right but dose not change the shape;

Therefore,
$$x - h = a(y - k)^2 \rightarrow x + 4 = ay^2$$

Thus, the correct answer is **F**.

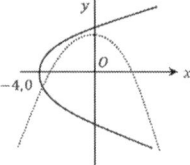

49. **Answer** **(D)**

Finding a general pattern.

The side length of small triangle each figures is a half of previous triangle. $\left(1 \rightarrow \frac{1}{2} \rightarrow \frac{1}{4} \rightarrow \frac{1}{8}....\right)$. And The numbers $1, 2, 4, 8....$are the power of 2. So, finding a pattern of small triangle side length and position number;

$$1st\ figure \rightarrow 1cm \rightarrow \frac{1}{2^0} \rightarrow \frac{1}{2^{(1-1)}}$$
$$2nd\ figure \rightarrow \frac{1}{2}cm \rightarrow \frac{1}{2^1} \rightarrow \frac{1}{2^{(2-1)}}$$
$$3rd\ figure \rightarrow \frac{1}{4}cm \rightarrow \frac{1}{2^2} \rightarrow \frac{1}{2^{(3-1)}}$$
$$4th\ figure \rightarrow \frac{1}{8}cm \rightarrow \frac{1}{2^3} \rightarrow \frac{1}{2^{(4-1)}}$$

Thus, the nth figure's side length is $\frac{1}{2^{n-1}}$.

50. **Answer** **(D)**

The center is a circumcenter.

Let O (x, y) be the center of the circle and the center is circumcenter so, $\overline{OP} = \overline{OQ} = \overline{OR}$.
$$d_{OP} = \sqrt{(x-1)^2 + (y-1)^2}$$
$$d_{OQ} = \sqrt{(x-4)^2 + (y-1)^2}$$
$$d_{OR} = \sqrt{(x-1)^2 + (y-5)^2}$$
$$d_{OP} = d_{OQ} \rightarrow \left(\sqrt{(x-1)^2 + (y-1)^2}\right)^2 = \left(\sqrt{(x-4)^2 + (y-1)^2}\right)^2$$
$$\rightarrow (x-1)^2 + (y-1)^2 = (x-4)^2 + (y-1)^2$$
$$\rightarrow (x-1)^2 = (x-4)^2 \rightarrow x^2 - 2x + 1 = x^2 - 8x + 16$$
$$\rightarrow 6x = 15 \rightarrow x = \frac{15}{6} \rightarrow x = \frac{5}{2} \rightarrow x = 2.5$$
$$d_{OP} = d_{OR} \rightarrow \left(\sqrt{(x-1)^2 + (y-1)^2}\right)^2 = \left(\sqrt{(x-1)^2 + (y-5)^2}\right)^2$$
$$\rightarrow (x-1)^2 + (y-1)^2 = (x-1)^2 + (y-5)^2$$
$$\rightarrow (y-1)^2 = (y-5)^2 \rightarrow y^2 - 2y + 1 = y^2 - 10y + 25$$
$$\rightarrow 8y = 24 \rightarrow y = 3$$
Thus, the coordinates of center are $(2.5, 3)$.

Alternative method;
Because ΔPQR is a right triangle, the circumcenter is the midpoint of the hypotenuse. Using the midpoint formula;
$$M = \left(\frac{x_1 + x_2}{2}, \frac{y_1 + y_2}{2}\right) \rightarrow \left(\frac{4+1}{2}, \frac{1+5}{2}\right) = (2.5, 3)$$

51. **Answer** **(C)**

The intersecting point is the solution of system of equation.

Because the parabola has a horizontal axis of symmetry, the equation is;
$$(y - k)^2 = 4p(x - h) \rightarrow (y - 2)^2 = 4p(x + 3).$$
Substitute $(-2, 4)$ for (x, y);
$$(4 - 2)^2 = 4p(-2 + 3) \rightarrow (2)^2 = 4p(1) \rightarrow 4 = 4p \rightarrow p = 1$$
So, the equation is; $(y - 2)^2 = 4(x + 3)$ — ①

Because the circle has center $(0, 2)$ and radius 4, the equation is;
$$x^2 + (y - 2)^2 = 4^2 = 16 \rightarrow (y - 2)^2 = 16 - x^2$$ — ②

Substitute ② for ① and then making quadratic equation for x;
$$(y - 2)^2 = 4(x + 3) \rightarrow 16 - x^2 = 4(x + 3) \rightarrow 16 - x^2 = 4x + 12$$
$$\rightarrow -x^2 - 4x + 4 = 0 \rightarrow x^2 + 4x - 4 = 0$$

Using quadratic discriminant, D, for $x^2 + 4x - 4 = 0$
$$D = b^2 - 4ac = (4)^2 - 4(1)(-4) = 32 > 0.$$
So, the equation, $x^2 + 4x - 4 = 0$, has two real solutions.

Thus, the number of intersecting points is 2, or using GDC.

52. **Answer** **(G)**

Using the formula of the midpoint.

Using the formula of the midpoint;
$$M = \left(\frac{x_1 + x_2}{2}, \frac{y_1 + y_2}{2}\right) = \left(\frac{7 + 3}{2}, \frac{-2 + 14}{2}\right) = \left(\frac{10}{2}, \frac{12}{2}\right) = (5, 6)$$

Thus, the midpoint is $(5, 6)$.

53. **Answer** **(F)**

Substitute (1,5) for (x, y).

From the circle equation;
$$(x - h)^2 + (y - k)^2 = r^2 \rightarrow (x + 1)^2 + (y - 3)^2 = r^2.$$
Substitute 1 for x and 5 for y;
$$(1 + 1)^2 + (5 - 3)^2 = r^2 \rightarrow r^2 = 8 \rightarrow r = 2\sqrt{2}.$$
Thus, the equation is $(x + 1)^2 + (y - 3)^2 = 8$.

54. **Answer** **(C)**

Finding a and b values.

The amplitude of the function is 3, so $a = 3$. And $\frac{3}{4}$ of the period of the function is 3π, so the period is 4π.
Using the formula of period;
$$period = \frac{2\pi}{|b|} \rightarrow 4\pi = \frac{2\pi}{b} \rightarrow b = \frac{1}{2}$$

Thus, the product of a and b is $a \times b = 3 \times \frac{1}{2} = \frac{3}{2} = 1.5$.

55. **Answer** **(J)**

Drawing the figure for given question.

A rhombus is also a parallelogram so,
$$\angle BAO = \frac{1}{2} \times 120° = 60°$$
And using trigonometric ratio;
$$\sin 60° = \frac{\overline{BO}}{8} \rightarrow \overline{BO} = 8 \times \sin 60° \rightarrow 4\sqrt{3}$$
$$\cos 60° = \frac{\overline{AO}}{8} \rightarrow \overline{AO} = 8 \times \cos 60° \rightarrow 4$$
The area of ΔABC is;
$$area = \frac{1}{2} \times \overline{AC} \times \overline{BO} = \frac{1}{2} \times 2\overline{AO} \times \overline{BO} = \frac{1}{2} \times 2 \times 4 \times 4\sqrt{3} = 16\sqrt{3}$$

Thus, the area of the rhombus is twice of area of ΔABC; $\rightarrow 32\sqrt{3}$.

---

56. Answer (*D*)

Using the Pythagorean theorem.

Let x the length of the $\overline{BC}$ and using the Pythagorean theorem;
$$\sin 25° = \frac{O}{H} = \frac{x}{120} \quad \to \quad x = 120\sin 25°$$

Thus, the correct answer is **D**.

---

57. Answer (*D*)

Using the counting principle.

The total number of ways are;
  3 capital letters; $26 \times 25 \times 24$ ($\because$ must be different)
  6 digits; $10 \times 10 \times 10 \times 10 \times 10 \times 10$($\because$ may repeat)
  so, $25 \times 24 \times 23 \times 10^6$ ways.

The number of ways that contain the word ACT is;
  $1(\because$ ACT- 1way!$)\times 10^6 = 10^6$ ways.

So, the probability is;
$$\frac{10^6}{25 \times 24 \times 23 \times 10^6}$$

Thus, the correct answer is **D**.

---

58. Answer (*D*)

In quadrant I and IV, cosine value is positive.

Using the Pythagorean theorem;
$$r^2 = x^2 + y^2 \quad \to \quad y = \sqrt{17^2 - 8^2} = 15.$$
In quadrant I and IV, cosine value is positive,
so the possible points are A and B.
At point A;
$$\sin\theta = \frac{y}{r} = \frac{15}{17}$$
At point B;
$$\sin\theta = \frac{y}{r} = \frac{-15}{17} = -\frac{15}{17}$$
Thus, the correct answer is **D**.

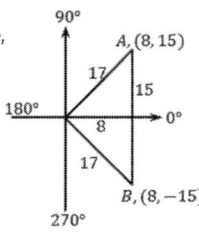

---

59. Answer (*H*)

Check amplitude and vertical translation.

From the standard form, $y = a\cos b(x - h) + k$, the range is
$$-a + k \le y \le a + k.$$
Rewrite the function;
$$f(x) = -3\cos(x + \pi) + 2.$$
So, the range is;
$$-3 + 2 \le y \le 3 + 2 \quad \to \quad -1 \le y \le 5$$

Thus, the correct answer is **H**.

---

60. Answer (*H*)

"at most" is maximum.

'at most' means maximum and 'at least' means minimum.

Thus, the correct answer is **H**.

BLANK PAGE   *by K·DEAN*

Reformed Past Paper ACT MATH TEST 11

60 Questions – 60 Minutes

DIRECTIONS:
Solve each problem, choose the correct answer, and then fill in the corresponding oval on your answer in the grid on the answer sheet.

Do not linger over problems that take too much time as many as you can; then retest in the time you have left for the test.

You are permitted to use a calculator on this test.

Note: Unless otherwise stated, all of the following should be assumed.

1. Figures are drawn to scale unless otherwise indicated.

2. All figures lie in a plane unless otherwise indicated.

3. All variables and expressions used represent real numbers unless otherwise indicated.

~~This test has reformed the REAL ACT Mathematics Test~~

01.

Alexa claims, " If a number is in set N, then it is not multiples of 3." But, Thomas discovers that a number X is a counterexample proving this claim false. Which of the following statements must be true about the number X?

F. It is not multiples of 3 and in another set.

G. It is multiples of 3 and in another set.

H. It is multiples of 3 and in set N.

J. It is not multiples of 3 and in set N.

K. It is factors of 3 and in set N.

02.

The per capita GDP is a measure of the total output of a country that takes gross domestic product (GDP) and divides it by the number of people in the country. In a certain country, last year's GDP was estimated to be 1.463×10^{12} dollars, and last year's population was about 7×10^7 people. Based on this definition, what was last year's per capita GDP in this country ?

F. $2.09

G. $20.9

H. $209

J. $2,090

K. $20,900

03.

Let p be a integer less than or equal to zero. $|x| = |y| = p$ has how many (x, y) solution(s) ?

F. 0

G. 1

H. 2

J. 3

K. Infinitely many solutions.

04.

Let an equation be $3y - 4 = y + k$. Which of the following expressions is equal to y ?

A. $k - 4$

B. $k + 4$

C. $-\dfrac{k}{2} - 2$

D. $\dfrac{k}{2} - 2$

E. $\dfrac{k}{2} + 2$

05.

Elsa co-manages a hotel that currently has 64 employees, which 38 less than three times the number of employees the hotel had 1 year ago. How many employees did the company have 1 year ago ?

F. 21

G. 27

H. 30

J. 34

K. 42

06.

What value of n makes the equation $2(5x + 3) = 5x + 1$ true ?

F. -1

G. $-\dfrac{1}{2}$

H. 0

J. $\dfrac{3}{2}$

K. 2

07.

The sum of two numbers is 72. The smaller number is 46 less than the larger number. What is the larger number ?

F. 59

G. 58

H. 56

J. 54

K. 53

08.

What is the value of b in the solution of the system of equation below ?

$$10a - 5b = -10$$
$$-3a + b = 5$$

A. -3

B. 4

C. -4

D. 5

E. -5

09.

Amos purchased 2,000 shares of stock at $30.50 per share. If a share decreased $0.50 the first week, increased $1.20 the second week, and increased $0.80 the third month, what is the value of the his shares of stock ?

F. $63,000

G. $63,500

H. $64,000

J. $64,500

K. $65,000

10.

Good Teaching Academy receives shipments of only 2 kinds of math practice books: Algebra and Geometry. Today's shipment contains 108 books with three times as many Algebra as Geometry. How many of these 108 are Algebra ?

A.   27

B.   54

C.   81

D.   87

E.   90

11.

In the complex plane, what is the distance, in coordinate unit, between $-3 + 4i$ and $3 - 2i$?

F.   2

G.   12

H. $6\sqrt{2}$

J. $12\sqrt{5}$

K. $\sqrt{21}$

12.

If a line in the coordinate plane is parallel y-axis and it is 3 coordinate unit left apart from y-axis, Which of the following is an equation of the line ?

F. $x = 3$

G. $x = -3$

H. $y = 3$

J. $y = -3$

K. $y = x - 3$

13.

What is the slope of a line that is perpendicular to $-3x + 4y = -12$ in the standard (x, y) coordinate plane ?

A. $\dfrac{1}{4}$

B. $-\dfrac{4}{3}$

C. $\dfrac{4}{3}$

D. $-\dfrac{3}{4}$

E. $\dfrac{3}{4}$

14.

Last Sunday, William jogged the 1.5 mile road from his home to Urban Park. He then jogged 4 times around the Urban Park and returned home by the 1.5-mile road. At the end of his jogging, the smart pedometer showed that he had jogged 12 miles. Which of the following equation, when solved, gives the distance William jogged *once* around the Urban Park, x miles?

F. $4x + 3 = 12$

G. $x - 3 = 12$

H. $4x - 3 = 12$

J. $4x + 1.5 = 12$

K. $x + 1.5 = 12$

15.

If $-2 \leq x \leq 4$ and $-3 \leq y \leq 2$, the smallest possible value for $\dfrac{3}{x-y}$ is:

A. $\dfrac{3}{7}$

B. -3

C. $\dfrac{1}{2}$

D. -1

E. $-\dfrac{4}{3}$

16.

What is the value of $|4 - 6| - |3 - 5| = ?$

F. 3

G. -3

H. -6

J. 8

K. -8

17.

A line passes through the two points $(3, -5)$ and $(7, -10)$ in the standard (x, y) coordinate plane. What is the slope of the line?

A. 2

B. $-\dfrac{4}{5}$

C. $-\dfrac{5}{4}$

D. $\dfrac{5}{4}$

E. -5

18.

Disregarding sales tax, how much will you save when you buy an electronic organizer that is on sale for 25% off the original price of $16.00 ?

F. $0.40

G. $0.56

H. $4.00

J. $6.00

K. $8.20

19.

Helen ordered tablet from "Bimazon Digital Services". She was charged $48.00 for her tablet and was charged 6% of that amount for shipping. How much was Helen charged for her shipping ?

A. $2.68

B. $2.78

C. $2.88

D. $2.98

E. $3.08

20.

Wendy earns her regular salary of $10.50 per hour for the first 42 hours of work in a week. For each hour over 42 hours of work in a week, Wendy is paid twice her regular salary per hour. Wendy worked 48 hours this week. What is her pay for this week?

A. $566.50

B. $567.00

C. $567.50

D. $1,008.00

E. $1,008.50

22.

As shown in the figure below, the line l is parallel to m, and the line t intersects l and m at A and B. Which of the following equations of α and θ must be **true**?

A. $\alpha - \theta = 180$

B. $\alpha + \theta = 180$

C. $\alpha = \theta$

D. $\dfrac{1}{2}(\alpha + \theta) = 180$

E. $\dfrac{1}{2}(\alpha - \theta) = 180$

21.

Jessie purchased a sweater that had an original price of $35.00. The retail store offered a 15% discount on the original price of the sweater, and Jessie paid 8% sales tax on the sale price of the sweater. How much did Jessie pay for the sweater, including sales tax?

F. $32.13

G. $32.86

H. $33.14

J. $33.96

K. $34.15

23.

As shown in the figure below, vertices B and D of $\triangle BCD$ lie on $\overline{AE}$, the measure of angle $\angle ABC$ is 136°, and the measure of angle $\angle CDE$ is 128°. What is the measure of angle $\angle BCD$?

F. 80°

G. 84°

H. 88°

J. 92°

K. 96°

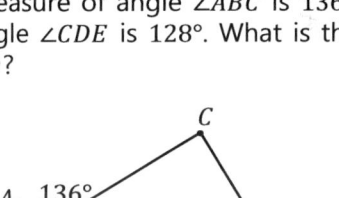

24.

In ΔPQR, the measure of angle $\angle P$ is 58° and the measure of angle $\angle Q$ is 102°. Which of the following inequalities involving length of the sides of ΔPQR could be true?

A. $\overline{PR} > \overline{QR} + \overline{PQ}$

B. $\overline{PR} < \overline{QR}$

C. $\overline{QR} < \overline{PQ}$

D. $\overline{PR} < \overline{QR} < \overline{PQ}$

E. $\overline{PR} > \overline{QR} > \overline{PQ}$

26.

In the figure below, a circle has diameter $\overline{PR}$, and two points Q and S lie on the circle. If the measure of $\angle QPR$ is 20°, what is the measure of minor arc $\widehat{PQ}$, in degrees?

A. 160°

B. 140°

C. 120°

D. 100°

E. 80°

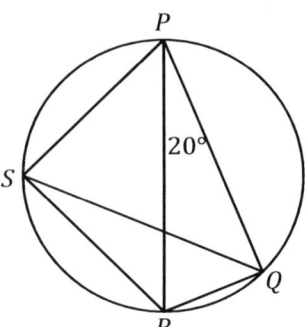

25.

The length of the shorter leg of right triangle ABC is 3 cm less than the length of the hypotenuse , h. The length of the hypotenuse of right triangle PQR, which is similar to ΔABC, is $5h$. In term of h, what is the length of the shorter leg of ΔPQR ?

F. $h - 15$

G. $5h - 3$

H. $5h + 3$

J. $5h - 15$

K. $5h + 15$

27.

A right triangular prism composed two congruent right triangular bases and three rectangular lateral faces is shown 'net' in the standard (x, y) coordinate plane below. Coordinates are vertices of one of the prism. What is the total surface area, in square coordinate units, of the prism?

F. 72

G. 84

H. 96

J. 108

K. 112

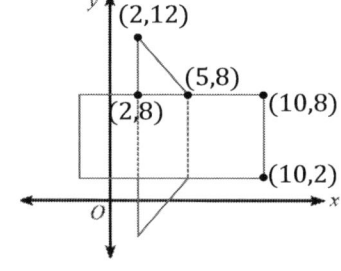

28.

As shown in the figure below, the height and radius of the right cylinder are given in inches. Which of the following is the volume, in cubic inches, of the cylinder?

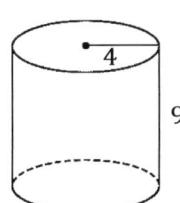

A. 36

B. 36π

C. 144

D. 144π

E. 288π

29.

What is the maximum value of
$$y = -|a\ln(x - b) + c| + d$$ for each set of real numbers $a, b, c,$ and d ?

F. 0

G. d

H. $c + d$

J. $ac - d$

K. $ac + d$

30.

Conrad sells Samsam smart phones. The number of phones, n, that Conrad sells in 1 year depends on the price he sells them for that year, d dollars per phone. The equation $n = 288 - 3d$, where $0 < d \le 96$, gives the relationship between n and d. Conrad's revenue is the money calculated by selling, n, phones. The maximum revenue Conrad could make from the sale of Samsam smart phones in 1 year occurs at what price per phone ?

F. $96

G. $84

H. $62

J. $48

K. $30

31.

What is the length, in centimeters, of a side of a square whose area, in square centimeters, is equal to the area of a 12cm to 14cm rectangle?

F. $\sqrt{14}$

G. $2\sqrt{3}$

H. $2\sqrt{42}$

J. $42\sqrt{2}$

K. $42\sqrt{3}$

32.

What are the 2 roots of an equation $3 - 5x^2 = -10x$?

(Note: The quadratic formula $x = \dfrac{-b \pm \sqrt{b^2 - 4ac}}{2a}$ for the quadratic equation $ax^2 + bx + c = 0$.)

  A. $15\ only$

  B. $\dfrac{1}{2}\ or\ -\dfrac{3}{5}$

  C. $\dfrac{5 \pm 2\sqrt{10}}{5}$

  D. $\dfrac{-5 \pm 10\sqrt{2}}{3}$

  E. $\dfrac{-5 \pm 2\sqrt{10}}{3}$

33.

The number of nonzero terms of a polynomial in x is p and the number of nonzero terms of another polynomial in x is q. These two polynomials are multiplied and all like terms are combined. What is the maximum number of nonzero terms in resulting polynomial in x?

  F. $p + q - 1$

  G. $p + q$

  H. $\dfrac{pq}{2}$

  J. $pq - 1$

  K. pq

34.

The ratio of width to length of a certain rectangle is 2 to 3. If the area of rectangle is 294 square centimeters, what is the length, in centimeters, of the shorter side?

  A. 12

  B. 14

  C. 16

  D. 18

  E. 20

35.

For all $p \neq 0$, what is the simplified form of the rational expression $\dfrac{\left(-2p^3\right)^2 - 6p^4 + \left(2p^2\right)^2}{-2p} = ?$

  A. $-2p^4$

  B. $-2p^4 + p^2$

  C. $4p^4 - 2p^3$

  D. $-2p^5 + p^3$

  E. $4p^5 - 2p^3$

36.

$2a^6 5a^2$ is equivalent to:

A. $7a^8$

B. $7a^{12}$

C. $10a^8$

D. $10a^{10}$

E. $10a^{12}$

37.

If $\left(\sqrt{5}\right)^a = 125^b$, for all positive real number a and b, then what is the value of $\dfrac{b}{a}$?

F. $\dfrac{2}{3}$

G. $\dfrac{1}{6}$

H. 1

J. 2

K. 4

38.

In the standard (x, y) coordinate plane, which of the following linear equations is the vertical asymptote for the rational function graph of $y = \dfrac{12x+25}{11x-23}$?

F. $x = -\dfrac{25}{12}$

G. $x = \dfrac{12}{11}$

H. $x = \dfrac{23}{11}$

J. $y = -\dfrac{25}{23}$

K. $y = -\dfrac{23}{12}$

39.

What is the domain of the function of $y = \dfrac{x+3}{5-|x|}$?

A. $x < -5$

B. $-5 < x < 5 \ or \ x > 5$

C. $x < -5 \ or \ x > 5$

D. $x < -5 \ or \ -5 < x < 5 \ or \ x > 5$

E. All real numbers

40.

A electrical lawnmower costs $250 and the value of the electrical lawnmower decreases by 15% each year. Which of the following numbers is closest to the value of the electrical lawnmower after 5 years?

F. $130

G. $128

H. $111

J. $107

K. $96

41.

In a language art course, Andrea's test average score is exactly 82. She received 88 score one test, 96 on another test, and 78 on each of the other tests. If each test is weighted equally, what is the total number of tests that Andrea has taken in the course?

A. 5

B. 7

C. 9

D. 11

E. 13

42.

The data set below gives the numbers of passing touchdowns for the 10 quarterbacks who threw the most touchdowns during the 2017 NFL regular season.

$$42, 36, 30, 33, 25, 38, 22, 29, 25, 20$$

Which of the following numbers is closest to the mean touchdowns of the 10 quarterbacks ?

F. 29.5

G. 30.0

H. 30.5

J. 31.0

K. 31.5

43.

Gertrude has 4 shits, 3 pairs of pants, 5 pairs of socks and 2 belts, which could be worn in any combination. He needs to choose a outfits combination to wear to the job interview. How many different combinations using 1 of her 4 shirts, 1 of her 3 pairs of pants, 1 of her 5 pairs of socks, and 1 of her 2 belts are possible for Gertrude to wear to the job interview?

A. 14

B. 28

C. 60

D. 120

E. 240

44.

A glass bottle contains 4 red balls, 6 white balls, and a number of yellow balls. There are no other balls in the glass bottle. The probability of randomly choosing a red ball from the glass bottle from the glass bottle is $\frac{1}{5}$. How many yellow balls are in the glass bottle?

A. 2

B. 4

C. 6

D. 8

E. 10

45.

A jar contains 5 white, 3 yellow, and 2 green balls, each of ball's color is not changed. Annie will random pick 1 ball from the jar, record the color of the ball, and put the ball back to the jar. Annie will complete process 70 times. How many times should she expect to record a ball color that is yellow?

A. 17

B. 18

C. 19

D. 20

E. 21

46.

A circular opera house where The Nutcracker will be performed has 20 seats in the 1st row. Each row behind the 1st row has 3 more seats than does the row in front of it.

How many seats are in the 5th row of the circular opera house?

A. 26

B. 29

C. 32

D. 35

E. 38

47.

Umberto is designing a 8-inch-by-10-in rectangular wooden photo frame for his wedding photo. He will attach two wooden sticks along both diagonals of the frame to make it tighter. Which of the following numbers is closest to the total length, in inches, of the two wooden sticks Umberto will need for the wooden photo frame?

A. 24

B. 26

C. 28

D. 30

E. 32

48.

A sailing boat is located 4 kilometers south and 5 kilometers west of Jeju Harbor. There is an island 10 kilometers north and 12 kilometers east of Jeju Harbor. Which of the following numbers is closest to the distance, in kilometers, between the sailing boat and the island?

F. 18.9

G. 20.1

H. 22.0

J. 24.8

K. 26.2

49.

A circle has a radius, r coordinate units and pass through the origin, O, in the standard (x,y) coordinate plane below. The circle has diameter $\overline{OA}$, where point A is placed in the negative x-axis. Which of the following coordinates is the coordinates of A, in term of r?

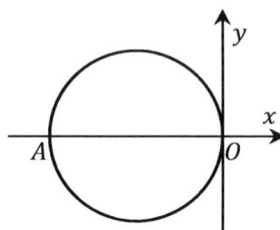

A. $(0, 2\pi r)$

B. $(0, 2r)$

C. $(-r, 0)$

D. $(-2r, 0)$

E. $(-2\pi r, 0)$

50.

Suppose that the two points $P\,(8, -6)$ and $Q\,(2, 12)$ is placed in the standard (x,y) coordinate plane. Which of the following coordinates is the midpoint of $\overline{PQ}$?

F. $(5, 3)$

G. $(4, 2)$

H. $(3, 1)$

J. $(-2, 4)$

K. $(-5, 3)$

51.

In the standard (x, y) coordinate plane, which of the following coordinates are the center of the circle with equation $(x - 2)^2 + (y + \sqrt{3})^2 = 3$?

A. $(\sqrt{3}, -2)$

B. $(\sqrt{3}, 2)$

C. $(2, \sqrt{3})$

D. $(-2, \sqrt{3})$

E. $(2, -\sqrt{3})$

52.

Assume that a right triangle $\triangle ABC$ has its right angle at vertex B. The length of $\overline{AB}$ is 5 inches and the length of $\overline{BC}$ is 7.5 inches. Which of the following numbers is closest to the length, in inches, of $\overline{AC}$?

F. 8.0

G. 8.5

H. 9.0

J. 9.5

K. 10.0

53.

Suppose that the two points $A\,(-8, 5)$ and $B\,(6, 7)$ is placed in the standard (x,y) coordinate plane. Which of the following coordinates is the midpoint of $\overline{AB}$?

A. $(-2, 4)$

B. $(-1, 6)$

C. $(0, -2)$

D. $(2, -4)$

E. $(4, -6)$

54.

For a right triangle ΔXYZ below, $\sin X = \frac{3}{4}$ and the length of $\overline{YZ}$ is 8 inches. Which of the following values is the length, in inches, of $\overline{XZ}$?

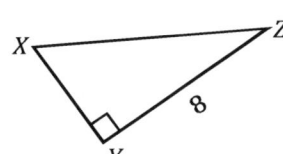

A. 6

B. 12

C. $\dfrac{\sqrt{34}}{4}$

D. $\dfrac{\sqrt{34}}{8}$

E. $\dfrac{32}{3}$

55.

During the last half-century, the use of steel pole structures for electrical transmission lines has increased very rapidly. A support wire is attached to the top of a vertical steel pole that is 80 feet tall height and makes an angle of 45° with level ground. What is the length, in feet, of the support wire?

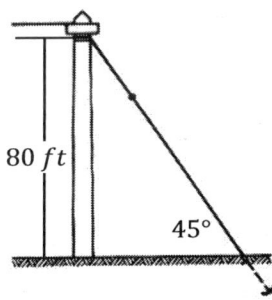

F. $40\sqrt{2}$

G. 80

H. $80\sqrt{2}$

J. 96

K. $96\sqrt{2}$

56.

An airplane is descending at a constant speed for landing. The altitude of the airplane is 1,200 meter and the straight distance between the airplane and the end of runway is 4 kilometers. What is the measure of the angle of descent?

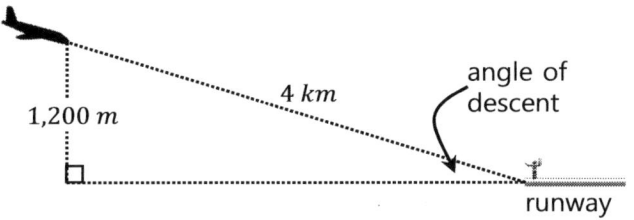

A. $\arcsin\left(\dfrac{1200}{4}\right)$

B. $\arcsin\left(\dfrac{3}{10}\right)$

C. $\arccos\left(\dfrac{1200}{4}\right)$

D. $\arccos\left(\dfrac{3}{10}\right)$

E. $\arctan\left(\dfrac{7}{10}\right)$

57.

Suppose that angle α measures 780° degrees from its initial side to its terminal side and angle β has the same initial side and terminal side as angle α. Which of the following radians could be that of the angle β?

F. $\dfrac{1}{6}\pi$

G. $\dfrac{1}{3}\pi$

H. $\dfrac{2}{3}\pi$

J. $\dfrac{5}{6}\pi$

K. $\dfrac{4}{3}\pi$

58.

For a triangle $\triangle ABC$ shown below, the three sides of the triangle are given in feet. What is the equation for the degree θ?

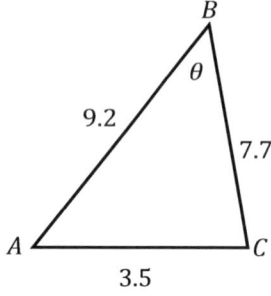

A. $9.2^2 = 7.7^2 + 3.5^2 - 2 \times 7.7 \times 3.5 \times \cos\theta$

B. $7.7^2 = 3.5^2 + 9.2^2 - 2 \times 3.5 \times 9.2 \times \cos\theta$

C. $3.5^2 = 7.7^2 + 9.2^2 - 2 \times 7.7 \times 9.2 \times \cos\theta$

D. $7.7^2 = 3.5^2 - 9.2^2 + 2 \times 3.5 \times 9.2 \times \cos\theta$

E. $3.5^2 = \dfrac{3.5^2 + 9.2^2}{2 \times 3.5 \times 9.2 \times \cos\theta}$

59.

Which of the following polar coordinates represents the same position as $(4,\ 60°)$?

A. $(3,\ -60°)$

B. $(-3,\ -60°)$

C. $(3,\ 120°)$

D. $(-3,\ 300°)$

E. $(3,\ -300°)$

60.

Suppose that the determinant of $\begin{bmatrix} -4 & (x+4) \\ (x-5) & 2 \end{bmatrix}$ is equal to 6, what is all possible values of a?

(Note: Determinant of 2×2 matrix $\begin{bmatrix} a & b \\ c & d \end{bmatrix}$ is $ad - bc$.)

F. $1\ or\ -2$

G. $-2\ or\ 3$

H. $3\ or\ -4$

J. $-4\ or\ 5$

K. $5\ or\ -6$

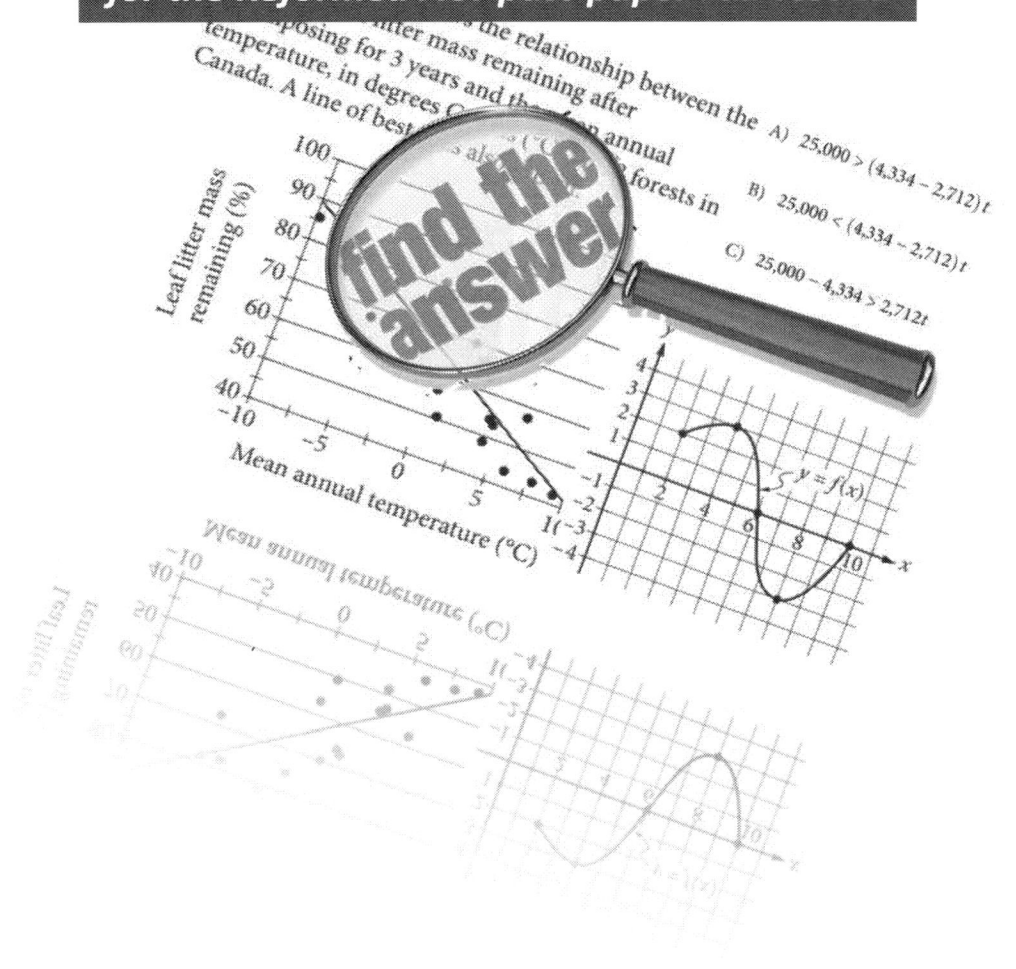

Obtain Scale Scores from Raw Scores					
Scale Score	Raw Score	Scale Score	Raw Score	Scale Score	Raw Score
36	60	24	36-37	12	7
35	58-59	23	34-35	11	5-6
34	57	22	32-33	10	4
33	55-56	21	30-31	9	-
32	54	20	29	8	3
31	52-53	19	27-28	7	-
30	50-51	18	24-26	6	2
29	48-49	17	21-23	5	-
28	45-47	16	17-20	4	1
27	43-44	15	13-16	3	-
26	40-42	14	11-12	2	-
25	38-39	13	8-10	1	0

1. Scoring Key

Key		Question Category	Y/N
01.	H	Number Theory	
02.	K	Number Theory	
03.	G	Number Theory	
04.	E	Expression and Linear Equation	
05.	J	Expression and Linear Equation	
06.	F	Expression and Linear Equation	
07.	F	Expression and Linear Equation	
08.	C	Expression and Linear Equation	
09.	H	Expression and Linear Equation	
10.	C	Expression and Linear Equation	
11.	H	Linear Function inequality	
12.	G	Linear Function inequality	
13.	B	Linear Function inequality	
14.	F	Linear Function inequality	
15.	A	Linear Function inequality	
16.	G	Linear Function inequality	
17.	C	Linear Function inequality	
18.	H	Arithmetic Topic and Ratio	
19.	C	Arithmetic Topic and Ratio	
20.	B	Arithmetic Topic and Ratio	
21.	F	Arithmetic Topic and Ratio	
22.	B	Basic Geometry	
23.	G	Basic Geometry	
24.	E	Basic Geometry	
25.	J	Basic Geometry	
26.	B	Basic Geometry	
27.	G	Basic Geometry	
28.	D	Basic Geometry	
29.	G	Further Equations and Functions	
30.	J	Quadratic and Polynomial Function	

Key		Question Category	Y/N
31.	H	Quadratic and Polynomial Function	
32.	C	Quadratic and Polynomial Function	
33.	K	Quadratic and Polynomial Function	
34.	B	Quadratic and Polynomial Function	
35.	D	Quadratic and Polynomial Function	
36.	C	Further Equations and Functions	
37.	G	Further Equations and Functions	
38.	H	Further Equations and Functions	
39.	D	Further Equations and Functions	
40.	H	Further Equations and Functions	
41.	B	Statistics and Probability	
42.	G	Statistics and Probability	
43.	D	Statistics and Probability	
44.	E	Statistics and Probability	
45.	E	Statistics and Probability	
46.	C	Sequence and Series	
47.	B	Analytic Geometry and Conic Section	
48.	H	Analytic Geometry and Conic Section	
49.	D	Analytic Geometry and Conic Section	
50.	F	Analytic Geometry and Conic Section	
51.	E	Analytic Geometry and Conic Section	
52.	H	Analytic Geometry and Conic Section	
53.	B	Analytic Geometry and Conic Section	
54.	E	Trigonometric Functions	
55.	H	Trigonometric Functions	
56.	B	Trigonometric Functions	
57.	G	Trigonometric Functions	
58.	C	Trigonometric Functions	
59.	E	Trigonometric Functions	
60.	G	Intermediate Algebra	

2. Answer Explanations

01. Answer (H)

A counterexample is used to refute an assertion.

An example of counter example for the given claim is 6 in set N.

Thus, the correct answer is **H**.

02. Answer (K)

The number, which is represented by scientific notation, consists of a integer part and a power part.

By definition;
$$per\ capita\ GDP = \frac{GDP}{population} = \frac{1.463 \times 10^{12}}{7 \times 10^7} = \frac{1.463}{7} \times \frac{10^{12}}{10^7}$$
Using exponent rule;
$$\frac{1.463}{7} \times \frac{10^{12}}{10^7} = 0.209 \times 10^5 = 2.09 \times 10^{-1} \times 10^5 = 2.09 \times 10^4$$
$$= 20,900$$

03. Answer (G)

The absolute value is never negative.

The value of p is less than or equal to zero, $p \leq 0$, and the absolute value of $|x|$ or $|y| \geq 0$.
So, it is $|x| = |y| = 0$ that satisfied both conditions.
Thus, $(x, y) = (0, 0)$ is only solution for given equation.

04. Answer (E)

Solving for y.

Adding to 4 on both sides;
$$3y - 4 = y + k \quad \rightarrow \quad 3y = y + k + 4$$
Subtract y on both sides;
$$3y = y + k + 4 \quad \rightarrow \quad 2y = k + 4$$
Divide by 2 on both sides;
$$2y = k + 4 \quad \rightarrow \quad y = \frac{k}{2} + 2$$
Thus, y is equal to $\frac{k}{2} + 2$.

05. Answer (J)

Let the number of employees 1 year ago is n.

If the number of employees 1 year ago is n, the following relation is established.
$$64 = 3n - 38$$
Add 38 to both sides;
$$3n - 38 = 64 \quad \rightarrow \quad 3n - 38 + 38 = 64 + 38 \quad \rightarrow \quad 3n = 102$$
Divide by 3 on both sides;
$$3n = 102 \quad \rightarrow \quad \frac{3n}{3} = \frac{102}{3} \quad \rightarrow \quad n = 34$$
Thus, the number of employees 1 year ago is 34.

06. Answer (F)

Solve the equation by using distributive property.

Expand the equation by using distributive property;
$$2(5x + 3) = 5x + 1 \quad \rightarrow \quad 10x + 6 = 5x + 1$$
Subtract 6 from both sides;
$$10x + 6 = 5x + 1 \quad \rightarrow \quad 10x + 6 - 6 = 5x + 1 - 6 \quad \rightarrow \quad 10x = 5x - 5$$
Subtract $5x$ from both sides;
$$10x = 5x - 5 \quad \rightarrow \quad 10x - 5x = 5x - 5 - 5x \quad \rightarrow \quad 5x = -5$$
Divide by 5 on both sides;
$$5x = -5 \quad \rightarrow \quad \frac{5x}{5} = -\frac{5}{5} \quad \rightarrow \quad x = -1$$
Thus, the value of x is -1.

07. Answer (F)

Let x be the larger number.

If the larger number is x, than the smaller number is $x - 46$ and the sum is;
$$x + x - 46 = 72 \quad \rightarrow \quad 2x - 46 = 72$$
Add 46 to both sides;
$$2x - 46 = 72 \quad \rightarrow \quad 2x - 46 + 46 = 72 + 46 \quad \rightarrow \quad 2x = 118$$
Divide by 2 on both sides;
$$2x = 118 \quad \rightarrow \quad \frac{2x}{2} = \frac{118}{2} \quad \rightarrow \quad x = 59$$
Thus, the larger number is 59.

08. Answer (C)

Multiply one or both of the equations by a constant so that adding or subtracting the equation will eliminate one variable.

Multiply the 2nd equation by 5 and then add two equation;
$$10a - 5b = -10$$
$$-3a + b = 5 \quad \rightarrow \quad -15a + 5b = 25$$
$$\overline{\qquad\qquad -5a \qquad = 15}$$
Dividing both sides by -5;
$$-5a = 15 \quad \rightarrow \quad \frac{-5a}{-5} = \frac{15}{-5} \quad \rightarrow \quad a = -3$$
Substituting $a = -3$ for $-3a + b = 5$;
$$-3a + b = 5 \quad \rightarrow \quad -3(-3) + b = 5 \quad \rightarrow \quad 9 + b = 5$$
Subtracting 9 from both sides;
$$9 + b - 9 = 5 - 9 \quad \rightarrow \quad b = -4$$
Thus, the value of b is -4.

09. Answer (H)

'increase' means 'adding' and 'decrease' means 'subtracting'.

Calculating the change of the value of the his shares of stock;
decreased \$0.50;
$$\$30.50 - \$0.50 = \$30.00 \quad \rightarrow \quad 2,000 \times \$30.00 = \$60,000$$
increased \$1.20;
$$\$30.00 + \$1.20 = \$31.20 \quad \rightarrow \quad 2,000 \times \$31.20 = \$62,400$$
increased \$0.80;
$$\$31.20 + \$0.80 = \$32.00 \quad \rightarrow \quad 2,000 \times \$32.00 = \$64,000$$
Or other method;
$$2,000 \times \$(30.50 - 0.50 + 1.20 + 0.80) = \$64,000$$

10. Answer (C)

Let x be the smaller one.

If the number of Geometry is x, than Algebra is $3x$ and total is;
$$x + 3x = 108 \quad \rightarrow \quad 4x = 108$$
Divide by 4 on both sides;
$$4x = 108 \quad \rightarrow \quad \frac{4x}{4} = \frac{108}{4} \quad \rightarrow \quad x = 27$$
Thus, the number of Algebra book is $3x = 81$.

11. Answer (H)

Using the Pythagorean theorem.

Using the formula of two points distance;

$$d = \sqrt{(3 - (-3))^2 + (-2 - 4)^2}$$
$$= 6\sqrt{2}$$

Thus, the correct answer is **H**.

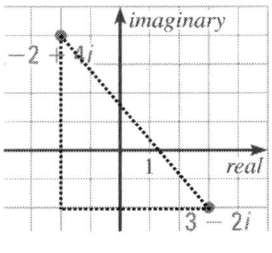

12. Answer **(G)**

The line that is parallel to y-axis is vertical line(x=a).

The line that is parallel to y-axis is a vertical line, $x = a$.
And let's draw a graph of the situation;

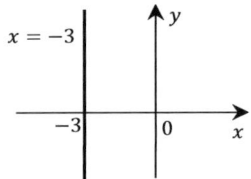

Because the line is a vertical line, the standard form of the line is $x = a$ and passes through $(-3, 0)$.

Thus, the equation of the line is $x = -3$.

13. Answer **(B)**

Two lines are perpendicular if and only if their slopes are negative reciprocals of each other.

Convert the equation to slope-intercept form;
add $3x$ to both sides;
$$-3x + 4y = -12 \rightarrow -3x + 4y + 3x = -12 + 3x \rightarrow 4y = -12 + 3x$$
divide both sides by 4;
$$4y = 3x - 12 \rightarrow \frac{4y}{4} = \frac{3x - 12}{4} \rightarrow y = \frac{3}{4}x - 3$$
So, the slope, m', of the perpendicular line is;
$$m' = -\frac{1}{\frac{3}{4}} = -\frac{4}{3}$$
Thus, the slope is $-\frac{4}{3}$.

14. Answer **(F)**

The total his jogged distance is 12 miles.

Let x be the distance of around the Park, his total distance, 12 is;
1.5(go to park)+4x(four times around the Park)+1.5(back to home)
So,
$$12 = 1.5 + 4x + 1.5 \rightarrow 4x + 3 = 12$$

15. Answer **(A)**

In a fraction, the greater the denominator, the smaller the value of the fraction.

The denominator, $x - y$, has the greatest value, when x is the largest value, 4, and y is the smallest value, -3.
So, $x - y = 4 - (-3) = 7$.

Thus, the smallest possible value is $\frac{3}{7}$.

16. Answer **(G)**

Absolute value is never negative.

Evaluate;
$$|4 - 6| - |3 - 8| = |-2| - |-5| = 2 - 5 = -3$$
Thus, the value is -3.

17. Answer **(C)**

Using the slope formula.

Using slope formula;
$$m = \frac{y_2 - y_1}{x_2 - x_1} = \frac{-10 - (-5)}{7 - 3} = \frac{-5}{4} = -\frac{5}{4}$$
The slope of the line is $-\frac{5}{4}$.

18. Answer **(H)**

The saving money is equal to the discount.

The discount is $0.25 \times \$16 = \$4$. Thus, the saving money is \$4.

19. Answer **(C)**

6% is 0.06 in number.

The cost of shipping is;
$$0.06 \times \$48 = \$2.88.$$

20. Answer **(B)**

Twice is 2×\$10.50.

Her pay considering overtime is;
$$\$10.50 \times 42 + (2 \times \$10.50) \times (48 - 42) = \$441 + \$126 = \$567.00$$
Thus, her pay for this week is \$567.00

21. Answer **(F)**

Sale price =Original price -Discount.

The sale price is calculated by;
$$sale\ price = original\ price - discount$$
$$= \$35 - 0.15 \times \$35 = \$35 - \$5.25 = \$29.75$$
The sales tax is $0.08 \times \$29.75 = \$2.38$.

Thus, the amount of Jessie pay for the sweater is
$$\$29.75 + \$2.38 = \$32.13.$$

22. Answer **(B)**

Using the angle relationships.

If an angle is marked X;
θ and X are corresponding angles. So, $\theta = X$
Because α and X are linear pair, $\alpha + X = 180$.
Substitute θ for X.

Thus, $\alpha + \theta = 180$

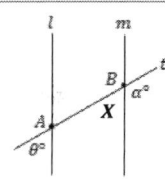

23. Answer **(G)**

Using a linear pair

Using linear pairs;
$$\angle ABC + \angle CBD = 180° \rightarrow 136° + \angle CBD = 180° \rightarrow \angle CBD = 44°$$
$$\angle CDE + \angle CDB = 180° \rightarrow 128° + \angle CDB = 180° \rightarrow \angle CDB = 52°$$
Using triangle angle sum theorem;
$$\angle BCD + \angle CBD + \angle CDB = 180°$$
$$\rightarrow \angle BCD + 44° + 52° = 180° \rightarrow \angle BCD + 96° = 180°$$
$$\rightarrow \angle BCD = 84°$$

Thus, the measure of angle $\angle BCD$ is 84°.

24. Answer **(E)**

Drawing the given triangle.

Using triangle angle sum theorem;
$$\angle P + \angle Q + \angle R = 180°$$
$$\rightarrow 58° + 102° + \angle R = 180°$$
$$\rightarrow 160° + \angle R = 180° \rightarrow \angle R = 20°$$

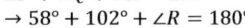
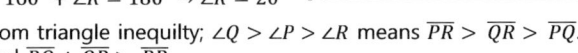

From triangle inequilty; $\angle Q > \angle P > \angle R$ means $\overline{PR} > \overline{QR} > \overline{PQ}$.
And $\overline{PQ} + \overline{QR} > \overline{PR}$.

Thus, the correct answer is E.

---

25. Answer **(J)**

Drawing picture for the given question.

$\triangle ABC \backsim \triangle PQR$ so,

$$\frac{h-3}{x} = \frac{h}{5h} = \frac{1}{5} \quad \rightarrow \quad x = 5(h-3) = 5h - 15$$

Thus, the length of the shorter leg of $\triangle PQR$ is $5h - 15$.

---

26. Answer **(B)**

The central angle could also be expressed in arc length.

Because $\angle QPR$ is $20°$, the central angle or minor arc $\overarc{QR}$ is $40°$.
And $\overline{PR}$ is the diameter so, arc $\overarc{PQR}$ is $180°$.

Therefore, the minor arc $\overarc{PQ} = 180° - 40° = 140°$.

---

27. Answer **(G)**

Finding each side length.

The side length;
$h = (8-2) = 6, \qquad a = (10-5) = 5$
$b = (5-2) = 3, \qquad c = (12-8) = 4$

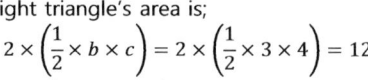

Therefore, the surface area is;
two right triangle's area is;

$$2 \times \left(\frac{1}{2} \times b \times c\right) = 2 \times \left(\frac{1}{2} \times 3 \times 4\right) = 12$$

the area of rectangle is;
$$(a + b + c) \times h = (5 + 4 + 3) \times 6 = 72$$

Thus, the total surface area is $12 + 72 = 84$.

---

28. Answer **(D)**

Using the formula.

From the formula of the cylinder's volume;
$$V = \pi r^2 h = \pi (4)^2 (9) = 144\pi$$

Thus, the volume of the cylinder is 144π.

---

29. Answer **(G)**

Considering absolute function.

The maximum value of $-|a\ln(x-b)+c|$ is zero and
$-|a\ln(x-b)+c|+d$ is translated d units vertically. So, maximum value is d.

Thus, the correct answer is **B**.

---

30. Answer **(J)**

The revenue is the product of the unit price and the number of selling phone.

Because the revenue is function of the unit price, d;
Revenue(R) = the unit price(d) × the number of selling phone(n)
Substitute $288 - 3d$ for n;
$$R = d \times n \quad \rightarrow \quad R = d(288 - 3d) \quad \rightarrow \quad R = 288d - 3d^2$$

From $y = ax^2 + bx + c$, maximum point is $y = c - \frac{b^2}{4a}$ at $x = -\frac{b}{2a}$.

So, from $R = 288d - 3d^2 \quad \rightarrow \quad R = -3d^2 + 288d$:

maximum revenue is $y = c - \frac{b^2}{4a} \rightarrow -\frac{288^2}{4 \times (-3)} = 6912$

at unit price $x = -\frac{b}{2a} \quad \rightarrow \quad -\frac{288}{2 \times (-3)} = 48$

Thus, the unit price, price per phone, is $48.

---

31. Answer **(H)**

Area of a square is s^2.

Calculating the area of the rectangle;
$$area = width \times length = 12 \times 14 = 168 \; cm^2$$
Let the side length of the square be x;
$$area = x^2 \quad \rightarrow \quad 168 = x^2$$
Take both side by square root;
$$\sqrt{x^2} = \pm\sqrt{168} \quad \rightarrow \quad x = 2\sqrt{42} \; (side \; length \; is \; always \; positive)$$

Thus, the length of a side of the square is $2\sqrt{42}$.

---

32. Answer **(C)**

Using the quadratic formula.

Rewriting the equation;
$$3 - 5x^2 = -10x \quad \rightarrow \quad -5x^2 + 10x + 3 = 0$$
Using the quadratic formula;

$$x = \frac{-b \pm \sqrt{b^2 - 4ac}}{2a} = \frac{-10 \pm \sqrt{(10)^2 - 4(-5)(3)}}{2(-5)} = \frac{-10 \pm \sqrt{160}}{-10}$$

$$= \frac{5 \pm 2\sqrt{10}}{5}$$

Thus, the 2 roots of the equation is $\frac{5 \pm 2\sqrt{10}}{5}$.

---

33. Answer **(K)**

Think about ; the resulting polynomial has no like term.

If the resulting polynomial has not any like terms, then resulting polynomial has $p \times q$ nonzero terms. For example,
$$(x + x^2)(x^4 + x^7) = x^5 + x^8 + x^6 + x^9$$

Thus, the correct answer is **K**.

---

34. Answer **(B)**

The shorter side is width.

If the width of the rectangle is $2x$, then the length of the rectangle is $3x$. So,
$$A = width \times length \quad \rightarrow \quad 294 = 2x \times 3x \quad \rightarrow \quad 6x^2 = 294$$
Dividing both sides by 6 and then take square root;
$$6x^2 = 294 \quad \rightarrow \quad \frac{6x^2}{6} = \frac{294}{6} \quad \rightarrow \quad x^2 = 49 \quad \rightarrow \quad x = \pm 7$$

Thus, the length of the shorter side is $2x = 2 \times 7 = 14$

---

35. Answer **(D)**

Grouping by the common factors.

Expanding by using the exponent's rule;
$$\frac{(-2p^3)^2 - 6p^4 + (2p^2)^2}{-2p} = \frac{4p^6 - 6p^4 + 4p^4}{-2p} = \frac{4p^6 - 2p^4}{-2p}$$
Grouping by the common factor and then simplifying;
$$\frac{4p^6 - 2p^4}{-2p} = \frac{2p^4(2p^2 - 1)}{-2p} = -p^3(2p^2 - 1) = -2p^5 + p^3$$

---

36. Answer **(C)**

Using the properties of exponential.

Using the properties of exponential;
$$2a^6 5a^2 = 2 \times 5 \times a^6 \times a^2 = 10 \times a^{6+2} = 10a^8$$

Thus, the correct answer is **C**.

---

37. **Answer** **(G)**

The terms are expressed the form of 5^n.

Because $\sqrt{5} = 5^{\frac{1}{2}}$ and $125 = 5^3$,
$$\left(\sqrt{5}\right)^a = 125^b \rightarrow \left(5^{\frac{1}{2}}\right)^a = (5^3)^b \rightarrow 5^{\frac{1}{2}a} = 5^{3b}$$
The two terms have same base, 5, so,
$$5^{\frac{1}{2}a} = 5^{3b} \rightarrow \frac{1}{2}a = 3b \rightarrow a = 6b$$
Substitute $a = 6b$ for $\frac{b}{a}$;
$$\frac{b}{a} = \frac{b}{6b} = \frac{1}{6}$$
Thus, the correct answer is **G**.

---

38. **Answer** **(H)**

The vertical asymptote is $x = -\frac{d}{c}$.

A vertical asymptote is $x = -\frac{d}{c}$ for $y = \frac{ax+b}{cx+d}$.
So, horizontal asymptote is
$$x = \frac{23}{11} \text{ for } y = \frac{12x+25}{11x-23}$$
Or using GDC.

Thus, the horizontal asymptote is $x = \frac{23}{11}$.

---

39. **Answer** **(D)**

The domain does not contain vertical asymptotes.

The vertical asymptotes are real zeros of denominator expression so,
$$5 - |x| = 0 \rightarrow -|x| = -5 \rightarrow |x| = 5 \rightarrow x = 5 \text{ or } x = -5$$
Thus, the domain is $x < -5$ or $-5 < x < 5$ or $x > 5$.

---

40. **Answer** **(H)**

Using exponential decay model.

Using the exponential decay model;
$$y = a(1-r)^t$$
Substituting 250 for a, 0.15 for r, and 5 for t;
$$y = 250(1-0.15)^5 \approx 110.9263 \dots$$

Thus, the correct answer is **H**.

---

41. **Answer** **(B)**

Make a rational equation.

Let n be the number of the other test, the average is;
$$\frac{(88 + 96 + 78 \times n)}{2 + n} = 82 \rightarrow \frac{78n + 184}{n + 2} = 82$$
Multiply both sides by $(n + 2)$;
$$78n + 184 = 82 \times (n + 2) \rightarrow 78n + 184 = 82n + 164$$
Subtract 164 and $78n$ from both sides;
$$78n + 184 - 164 = 82n \rightarrow 78n + 20 = 82n$$
$$\rightarrow 20 = 82n - 78n \rightarrow 4n = 20$$
Divide both sides by 4;
$$4n = 20 \rightarrow n = \frac{20}{4} = 5$$

Thus, the total number of tests is $n + 2 = 7$.

---

42. **Answer** **(G)**

Adding all numbers and then divide by 10.

The mean is;
$$\frac{42 + 36 + 30 + 33 + 25 + 38 + 22 + 29 + 25 + 20}{10} = \frac{300}{10} = 30$$

Thus, the mean is 30.

---

43. **Answer** **(D)**

Using counting principle.

The total number of possible outfits is;
$$4(shirts) \times 3(pants) \times 5(socks) \times 2(belts) = 120 \text{ possible outfits}$$
Thus, the correct answer is **D**.

---

44. **Answer** **(E)**

Finding the total number of balls.

Let x be the total number of balls in the glass bottle. The probability of red balls is
$$P(red) = \frac{1}{5} = \frac{4}{x}$$
Using cross product;
$$1 \times x = 4 \times 5 \rightarrow x = 20$$
The total number of ball in the glass bottle is 20 so, the number of yellow balls is $10(\because 4 + 6 + yellow = 20)$.

Thus, the correct answer is **E**.

---

45. **Answer** **(E)**

This question about probability.

The probability of yellow balls is;
$$P = \frac{3}{10}$$
So,
$$\frac{3}{10} \times 70 = 21$$
Thus, the correct answer is **E**.

---

46. **Answer** **(C)**

Using Arithmetic sequence rule

The first term, a_0, is 20 and the common difference, d, is 3. So,
$$a_n = a_0 + (n-1)d \rightarrow a_5 = 20 + (5-1) \times 3 = 20 + 4 \times 3 = 32$$
Thus, the number of seats is 32.

---

47. **Answer** **(B)**

Drawing for given question.

Let x be the length of the diagonal of the wooden photo frame, and then using the Pythagorean theorem;
$$x^2 = 10^2 + 8^2 \rightarrow x = \sqrt{10^2 + 8^2} = 2\sqrt{41}$$

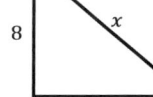

Thus, the total length is $2x = 4\sqrt{41} \approx 25.612 \dots \approx 26$.

---

48. **Answer** **(H)**

Drawing the given question.

Drawing the given question, and let a and b be the length of the two legs and c be the distance.
Using the Pythagorean theorem;
$$c^2 = a^2 + b^2$$
$$\rightarrow c^2 = (5 + 12)^2 + (4 + 10)^2$$
$$\rightarrow c = \sqrt{17^2 + 14^2} \approx 22.022271 \dots$$

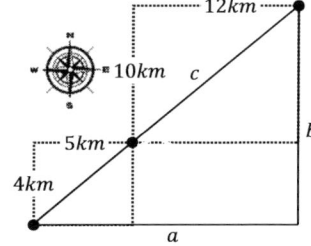

Thus correct answer is **H**.

---

49. **Answer** *(D)*

The diameter of two times of the radius.

Let d be the diameter of the circle and A lies on negative x-axis.
So, the coordinates of A are $(-d, 0)$.
The diameter of two times of the radius, $d = 2r$.

thus, the coordinates of A are $(-2r, 0)$.

---

50. **Answer** *(F)*

Using the formula of the midpoint.

Using the formula of the midpoint;
$$M = \left(\frac{x_1 + x_2}{2}, \frac{y_1 + y_2}{2}\right) = \left(\frac{8 + 2}{2}, \frac{-6 + 12}{2}\right) = \left(\frac{10}{2}, \frac{6}{2}\right) = (5, 3)$$

Thus, the midpoint is $(5, 3)$.

---

51. **Answer** *(E)*

Using the circle equation.

A circle has center (h, k) and has radius r, its equation is;
$$(x - h)^2 + (y - k)^2 = r^2$$

Thus, the coordinates of center is $(2, -\sqrt{3})$.

---

52. **Answer** *(H)*

Drawing the given question.

Drawing the given question, and then using
the Pythagorean theorem;

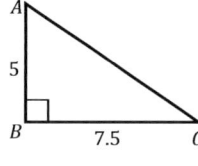

$$\overline{AC}^2 = \overline{AB}^2 + \overline{BC}^2 \rightarrow \overline{AC}^2 = 5^2 + 7.5^2$$
$$\rightarrow \overline{AC} = \sqrt{5^2 + 7.5^2} = \frac{5\sqrt{13}}{2} \approx 9.0138\ldots \approx 9.0.$$

Thys, the correct answer is **H**.

---

53. **Answer** *(B)*

Using the formula of the midpoint.

Using the formula of the midpoint;
$$M = \left(\frac{x_1 + x_2}{2}, \frac{y_1 + y_2}{2}\right) = \left(\frac{-8 + 6}{2}, \frac{5 + 7}{2}\right) = \left(\frac{-2}{2}, \frac{12}{2}\right) = (-1, 6)$$

Thus, the midpoint is $(-1, 6)$.

---

54. **Answer** *(E)*

Trigonometric ratio is set of the ratios of side length.

In view of the angle X, $\overline{XZ}$ is a hypotenuse and $\overline{YZ}$ is an opposite side so,
$$\sin X = \frac{O}{H} = \frac{3}{4} = \frac{\overline{YZ}}{\overline{XZ}} \rightarrow \frac{3}{4} = \frac{8}{\overline{XZ}}$$

Using cross multiply;
$$3 \times \overline{XZ} = 4 \times 8 \rightarrow \overline{XZ} = \frac{32}{3}$$

Thus, the correct answer is **E**.

---

55. **Answer** *(H)*

Using the trigonometric ratio.

Let x be the length of the wire and using trigonometric ratio;
$$\sin 45° = \frac{O}{H} = \frac{1}{\sqrt{2}} = \frac{80}{x} \rightarrow x = 80\sqrt{2}$$

Thus, the length of the wire is $80\sqrt{2}$.

---

56. **Answer** *(B)*

Using the same unit

Let θ be the angle of descent;
$$\theta = \sin^{-1}\left(\frac{1200m}{4km}\right) = \sin^{-1}\left(\frac{1.2}{4}\right) = \sin^{-1}\left(\frac{3}{10}\right) = \arcsin\left(\frac{3}{10}\right)$$

Thus, the correct answer is **B**.

---

57. **Answer** *(G)*

Finding coterminal angle.

Convert 780° to radians;
$$780° \times \frac{\pi}{180°} = \frac{13}{3}\pi \rightarrow \frac{12}{3}\pi + \frac{1}{3}\pi \rightarrow 4\pi + \frac{1}{3}\pi \rightarrow 2(2\pi) + \frac{1}{3}\pi$$

This means that 780° and $\frac{13}{3}\pi$ are same angles, $\frac{13}{3}\pi$ and $\frac{1}{3}\pi$ are coterminal angles, so are same angles.

Thus, the correct answer is **G**.

---

58. **Answer** *(C)*

The given value are three sides lengths.

Because the given values are the lengths of three sides, using the cosine law;
$$b^2 = a^2 + c^2 - 2ac\cos B$$
$$\rightarrow 3.5^2 = 7.7^2 + 9.2^2 - 2 \times 7.7 \times 9.2 \times \cos\theta$$

Thus, the correct answer is **C**.

---

59. **Answer** *(E)*

Finding coterminal angle.

The point P position is $(3, 60°)$ in the counter-clockwise direction and $(3, -300°)$ in the clockwise direction.

Thus, the correct answer is **E**.

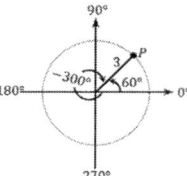

---

60. **Answer** *(G)*

Using the formula of determinant of matrix.

Using the formula of determinant of matrix;
$$\begin{bmatrix} -4 & (x+4) \\ (x-5) & 2 \end{bmatrix} = -8 - (x+4)(x-5) = -x^2 + x + 12$$

Because the determinant is 6;
$$-x^2 + x + 12 = 6 \rightarrow -x^2 + x + 6 = 0 \rightarrow x^2 - x - 6 = 0$$

Solving quadratic equation by factoring;
$$x^2 - x - 6 = 0 \rightarrow (x + 2)(x - 3) = 0 \rightarrow x = -2 \text{ or } x = 3$$

Thus, the correct answer is **G**.

Reformed Past Paper ACT MATH TEST 12

60 Questions – 60 Minutes

DIRECTIONS:
Solve each problem, choose the correct answer, and then fill in the corresponding oval on your answer in the grid on the answer sheet.

Do not linger over problems that take too much time as many as you can; then return to the others in the time you have left for the test.

You are permitted to use a calculator on this test.

Note: Unless otherwise stated, all of the following should be assumed.

1. Figures are drawn to scale unless otherwise indicated.

2. All figures lie in a plane unless otherwise indicated.

3. All variables and expressions used represent real numbers unless otherwise indicated.

01.

What fraction of a 4-inch-radius waffle contains the same amount of waffle as 1 part of a 16-inch-radius of the same thickness cut into 8 equal parts?

A. $\dfrac{1}{8}$

B. $\dfrac{1}{4}$

C. $\dfrac{1}{2}$

D. $\dfrac{3}{4}$

E. 1

02.

A farm sold a cargo of carrots to a wholesale mart for \$320 at the rate of \$0.05 per kilogram. Suppose that their cargo averaged 24 carrots per kilogram, which of the following is approximately to the total number of carrots in the cargo ?

F. 169,000

G. 154,000

H. 143,000

J. 136,000

K. 127,000

03.

Let A be a perfect square. If $A = 24x$, then what is the value of x ?

A. 2

B. 3

C. 4

D. 5

E. 6

04.

If $a = 2$ and $b = 3$ then what is the value of $30 - 2(a - b^2)^2 + a$?

F. -132

G. -66

H. -33

J. 33

K. 66

05.

The sum of between two numbers is 21. Let x be the smaller number. Which of the following expressions is the difference of two numbers ?

A. $21 - x$

B. $21 + x$

C. $x - 10.5$

D. $2x - 21$

E. $21 - 2x$

06.

Newton's law of gravitation, statement that any particle of matter in the universe attracts any other with a force varying directly as the product of the masses and inversely as the square of the distance between them. If k is the constant of variation , which following expressions represents the force of two objects which have mass m_1 and m_2 each and have distance D ?

F. $\dfrac{m_1 m_2}{kD^2}$

G. $k\dfrac{m_1 m_2}{D}$

H. $k\dfrac{m_1 m_2}{D^2}$

J. $k\dfrac{m_1 m_2}{\sqrt{D}}$

K. $k\dfrac{\sqrt{D}}{m_1 m_2}$

07.

Miny had already read 10 books this year before joining a school book club, and she plans to read 2 book every month now that she has joined. After belonging to the book club for 6 months, how many books will Miny have read in all ?

A. 20

B. 22

C. 24

D. 26

E. 28

08.

Mrs. Sofia wants to plant trees at the same 4 meters intervals along a straight 200 meters fence, with 1 of the trees at each end of the fence. How many trees does she need to plant on the above conditions?

F. 49

G. 50

H. 51

J. 52

K. 53

09.

$$6x - 2y = 1$$
$$-2x + 3y = -5$$

The system of above has 1 solution (p, q). What is the value of q ?

F. 4

G. 2

H. $-\dfrac{1}{2}$

J. -2

K. -4

10.

If $\dfrac{x+3y}{2x-y} = \dfrac{3}{5}$, then what is the value of $\dfrac{x}{y}$?

F. 18

G. −9

H. 1

J. $\dfrac{5}{3}$

K. $\dfrac{9}{7}$

11.

Which of the following sentences shows the solution set for the inequality $\dfrac{4+2x}{3} - 2 > 0$?

F. $x > 0$

G. $x > 1$

H. $x > 2$

J. $x > 3$

K. $x > 4$

12.

At Tyler's Handmade Shoes Factory, the total production cost to produce shoes is the sum of an operational cost of \$272 per day, and a material cost of \$120 per pair of shoes produced. For a day in which p pairs of shoes are produced, which of the following expressions gives that day's total production cost, in dollars, to produce p pairs of shoes?

A. $151p$

B. $392p$

C. $272 - 120p$

D. $120p - 272$

E. $272 + 120p$

13.

In standard (x, y) coordinate plane, if the slope of line L is $\dfrac{2}{5}$, which of the following is an equation of a line that is perpendicular to the line L ?

F. $-2x + 5y = 7$

G. $2x - 5y = -7$

H. $5x + 2y = -7$

J. $-5x + 2y = 7$

K. $5x - 2y = -7$

14.

Ella bought five candles for \$ 7.23 which included sale tax of \$ 1.18. At the same cost per candle, what is the cost before the sales tax is added for eight of the same candles ?

F. \$ 9.23

G. \$ 9.56

H. \$ 9.68

J. \$ 9.88

K. \$ 9.96

15.

What is the expression equivalent to $(x + 2i)^3$, for all real numbers x and $i = \sqrt{-1}$?

A. $x^3 - 8$

B. $x^3 - 8i$

C. $x^3 + 3ix^2 + 3x - i$

D. $x^3 + 3ix^2 - 3x - i$

E. $x^3 + 3ix^2 - 3x + i$

17.

The two lines A and B all have an y-intercept of 3. The slope of line A is $-\frac{4}{3}$, and the slope of line B is a half of the slope of A.
What is the x-intercept of line B ?

A. 3

B. 3.5

C. 4

D. 4.5

E. 5

16.

A line passes through the two points $(-2, 5)$ and $(-2, -5)$ in the standard (x, y) coordinate plane. What is the slope of the line ?

F. zero

G. undefined

H. negative

J. positive

K. could not be determined

18.

Given that the solution of $ax = -b$ is $x = 2$ and the solution of $ax + 3 = b$ is $x = 5$. What is the value of $a + b$?

A. $-\dfrac{2}{7}$

B. $\dfrac{3}{7}$

C. $-\dfrac{5}{7}$

D. $\dfrac{9}{7}$

E. $-\dfrac{11}{7}$

2 △ △ △ △ △ △ △ △ △ **2**

19.

In the standard (x, y) coordinate plane, what is the y-intercept of the line with equation $7x + 3y = -10$?

F. -10

G. $-\dfrac{7}{3}$

H. $\dfrac{7}{3}$

J. $-\dfrac{10}{3}$

K. $\dfrac{10}{3}$

20.

What is the property that the statement illustrates below ?

$$(x \cdot 2y) \cdot 5z = x \cdot (2y \cdot 5z)$$

F. Commutative property of addition

G. Identity property of addition

H. Identity property of multiplication

J. Associative property of multiplication

K. Distributive property

21.

Which of the following inequalities is equivalent to the statements below ?

　3 more than the product of 2 and a number n is less than to or equal to 5

F. $2n + 3 \leq 5$

G. $5 \leq 2n + 3$

H. $2n \leq 5 + 3$

J. $2n \leq 3n + 5$

K. $2n + 5 < 3$

22.

A carton of milk has the shape of a right rectangular prism with an inside height of 8 inches, an inside length of 6 inches and an inside width of 5 inches. When you pour the milk from the full carton into a cylindrical glasses with an inside height of 4 inches and an inside diameter of 3 inches, what is the maximum number of cups filled with milk?

F. 14

G. 12

H. 10

J. 8

K. 6

23.

As shown in the figure below, a track is composed of a rectangle and two semicircles. Four points $X, Y, Z,$ and W are four vertices of the rectangle. $\overline{XW}$ and $\overline{YZ}$ are diameters of the two semicircles. What is the perimeter, in yards, of the track?

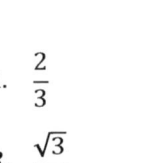

X 120yd Y

100yd

W   Z

A. $50\pi + 440$

B. $100\pi + 120$

C. $100\pi + 240$

D. $200\pi + 240$

E. $200\pi + 440$

24.

As shown in the figure below, the two lines l and m are intersected by a transversal t. If the two lines l and m are parallel, then which of the following statements should **not** always true?

F. $\angle 6 \cong \angle 7$

G. $\angle 1 \cong \angle 5$

H. $\angle 3 \cong \angle 6$

J. $\angle 2 \cong \angle 8$

K. $\angle 2 \cong \angle 7$

$$t$$
$$\begin{array}{cc} 1 & 2 \\ 3 & 4 \end{array}\ l$$
$$\begin{array}{cc} 5 & 6 \\ 7 & 8 \end{array}\ m$$

25.

The two cubes shown below have diagonal $\overline{AC}$, 3 inches, and $\overline{DF}$, 4 inches. What is the ratio of the length of $\overline{AB}$ to $\overline{DE}$?

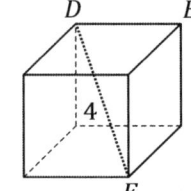

A. $\dfrac{2}{3}$

B. $\dfrac{\sqrt{3}}{2}$

C. $\dfrac{3}{4}$

D. $\dfrac{6}{12}$

E. $\dfrac{9}{16}$

26.

In the rectangle $PQRS$ shown below, a point X lies on $\overline{PS}$ and a point Y lies on $\overline{QR}$ such that rectangle $PQRS$ and rectangle $QYXP$ ($\square PQRS \backsim \square QYXP$), the length of $\overline{PQ}$ is 5 inches, and the length of $\overline{QY}$ is 3 inches. What is the area, in square inches, of $PQRS$?

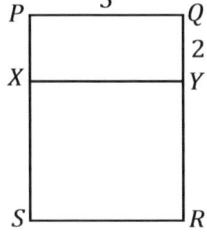

F. 58.5

G. 60.5

H. 62.5

J. 64.5

K. 66.5

27.

If Camilla uses 1 quart of green paint per 60 square to be painted, how many quarts of green paint will she use to paint the region shown below?

A. $2\frac{1}{3}$

B. $2\frac{2}{3}$

C. 3

D. $3\frac{1}{3}$

E. $3\frac{2}{3}$

10 feet

15 feet

5 feet

20 feet

28.

The width of a rectangle is 3 cm shorter than the length. The perimeter of the rectangle is 34 cm. What is the length of the rectangle, in centimeters ?

F. 7

G. 8

H. 10

J. 12

K. 14

29.

The perimeter of parallelogram $\square XYWZ$ is 88 inches. The ratio of the side lengths of $\overline{XY}$ to $\overline{YW}$ is 4 to 7. What is the length, in inches, of $\overline{XY}$?

A. 12

B. 14

C. 16

D. 24

E. 28

30.

The product of two positive integers is 24. The lesser integer is 2 less than the greater integer. What is the lesser integer?

F. 3

G. 4

H. 6

J. 8

K. 12

31.

A neighborhood park is a rectangle 100 feet long by 50 feet wide. The neighboring residents want to triple the area of the park by adding the same amount to the width and the length. What is the width, in feet, of the new neighborhood park?

A. 70

B. 80

C. 90

D. 100

E. 110

32.

An online book store makes a profit of $(375b - b^2)$ dollars from selling b digital books. What is the greatest number of digital books the online book store can sell to make a profit of at least $22,500?

F. 250

G. 300

H. 350

J. 400

K. 450

33.

The top surface area of a rectangular box is 180 square centimeters. The length of the surface is 3 cm more its width. What is the length, in centimeters, of the top surface area of the box?

A. 11

B. 12

C. 13

D. 14

E. 15

34.

Suppose that a quadratic equation $3x^2 + 18x + p = 0$ and the equation has exactly one real solution, what is the value of p ?

F. −27

G. 27

H. −36

J. 36

K. −9

35.

If a and b are positive real numbers and $a - b = 2$, $ab = 35$, then what is the value of a?

A. 7

B. 5

C. 8

D. 4

E. 6

36.

Which of the following expressions is equivalent to $\log\left(\dfrac{x}{3}\right)^{\frac{2}{3}}$ for all positive real numbers, x ?

A. $\log\dfrac{2x}{9}$

B. $\dfrac{2}{3}\log x - 2$

C. $\dfrac{2}{3}\log x - \dfrac{2}{3}\log 3$

D. $\dfrac{2}{3}\log x + \dfrac{2}{3}\log 3$

E. $\dfrac{2\log x}{3\log 3}$

37.

The population of Jeju city is modeled by the exponential growth model $P = 735{,}000(1.0625)^t$, where t is the number of years after January 1, 2017. From the model, which of the following numbers is closest to the population of the city on January 1, 2020 ?

A. 882,000

B. 894,000

C. 902,000

D. 915,000

E. 937,000

38.

Camilla invested $4,000 at 8% interest compounded quarterly. Which of the following expressions represents the balance after 5 years?

A. $4{,}000(1 + 0.08)^{20}$

B. $4{,}000\left(1 + \dfrac{0.08}{4}\right)^{20}$

C. $4{,}000\left(1 + \dfrac{0.08}{4}\right)^{5}$

D. $4{,}000\left(\dfrac{1.08}{4}\right)^{20}$

E. $4{,}000e^{1.6}$

39.

For what value of x is the equation
$$\sqrt[3]{4x + 8} - 6 = -10 \text{ true?}$$

F. -14

G. 14

H. $18i$

J. 18

K. -18

40.

If $3^{a+2} = 3x$, for nonzero real numbers a and x, which of the following is an expression for 3^{a+4} in term of x ?

F. x^4

G. $3x^3$

H. $9x^2$

J. $27x$

K. 81

41.

Twenty cars containing a total 80 people passed through expressway entrance. Each of the twenty cars contained at least 1 people but no more than 5 people. At most how many cars contained exactly 2 people ?

F. 2

G. 4

H. 6

J. 12

K. 19

42.

The average of 5 number is 54. If the first 4 of the numbers are $36, 56, 58$, and 48, what is the 5 th number?

A. 58

B. 62

C. 68

D. 72

E. 78

43.

Assume that X will be randomly selected from a set $\{-2, -1, 0, 1, 2\}$ and that Y will be randomly selected from another set $\{-3, 0, 3\}$. What is the probability of the product of X and Y is less than or equal to 0 ?

F. $\dfrac{7}{15}$

G. $\dfrac{3}{5}$

H. $\dfrac{2}{3}$

J. $\dfrac{11}{15}$

K. $\dfrac{3}{4}$

44.

A multiple choice test contains five answer choice $(A, B, C, D$, and $E)$ for each question. A test consists of 3 question and exactly 1 answer must be chosen. The test has how many possible combinations of answers?

F. 15

G. 25

H. 75

J. 100

K. 125

45.

For 20 batteries were tested to see how long they lasted. The results (in hours) are shown in the table below. Which time interval contains the median of the results?

Time(h)	Frequency
$0 \leq h < 3$	2
$3 \leq h < 6$	3
$6 \leq h < 9$	2
$9 \leq h < 12$	5
$12 \leq h < 15$	8

A. $0 \leq h < 3$

B. $3 \leq h < 6$

C. $6 \leq h < 9$

D. $9 \leq h < 12$

E. $12 \leq h < 15$

46.

Suppose that consecutive terms of a certain arithmetic sequence have a positive common difference. The sum of first 5 terms of the sequence is 25. Which of following values could be the first term of the arithmetic sequence?

F. 25

G. 15

H. 13

J. 6

K. 0

47.

When a certain map is drawn in the standard (x, y) coordinate plane, an island has coordinates $(4, 8)$ and another island has coordinates $(9, 3)$. Assume that 1 coordinate unit corresponding 15 miles, what is the distance, in miles, between the two islands?

A. $5\sqrt{2}$

B. 75

C. $75\sqrt{2}$

D. 125

E. $125\sqrt{2}$

48.

In the figure below, the two points $A\,(11, 1)$ and $B\,(-1, 19)$ lies in the standard (x, y) coordinate plane. Another point C lies on $\overline{AB}$ between A and B such that the length of $\overline{AB}$ is 6 times the length of $\overline{AC}$. What coordinates give the position of the point C ?

A. $(6, 6)$

B. $(7, 6)$

C. $(8, 5)$

D. $(9, 4)$

E. $(10, 3)$

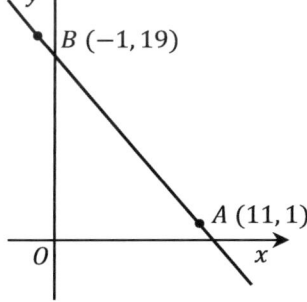

49.

If second term of a geometric sequence is 12 and fifth term of the sequence is −768, then what is the seventh term of the geometric sequence?

A. 14,466

B. −12,288

C. −10,232

D. 9,646

E. −9,208

50.

A glass bottle contains 15 candies; 6 hard candies, 4 mint candies, 3 caramel candies, and 2 jelly candies. One piece of candy will be randomly picked from the glass bottle. What is the probability the candy picked is **not** caramel candy?

A. $\dfrac{1}{5}$

B. $\dfrac{2}{5}$

C. $\dfrac{4}{15}$

D. $\dfrac{3}{4}$

E. $\dfrac{13}{15}$

51.

Which of the following data sets has the least standard deviation ?

F. $3,3,3,3,3,3,3,3,3$

G. $1,2,3,4,5$

H. $6,7,8,9,10,11$

J. $-5,-2,0,2,5$

K. $-3,-1,0,1,3$

52.

In the standard (x, y) coordinate plane, the graph of $f(x) = 2 - 3\cos(x + \pi)$ is shown below. What is the range of $f(x)$?

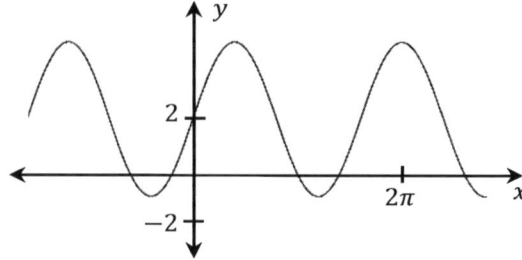

A. $-1 \le y \le 2$

B. $-3 \le y \le 3$

C. $-1 \le y \le 5$

D. $0 \le x \le 2\pi$

E. $0 \le x \le \dfrac{3\pi}{2}$

53.

Suppose that the first term is −4 in the geometric sequence $-4, 12, -36 \ldots$. What is the seventh term of the geometric sequence?

F. 2,916

G. −2,916

H. 8,748

J. −8,748

K. 2160

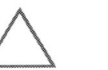  
54.

Suppose that $3\cos(\pi + \alpha) = 3$ and $4\sin\left(\frac{\beta}{6}\right) = 2$, what is the value of $\alpha + \beta$?

A. $-\dfrac{\pi}{5}$

B. $-\dfrac{\pi}{4}$

C. 0

D. $\dfrac{\pi}{2}$

E. π

56.

In the sets of three numbers given below, what is the set that is composed of the length of the sides of the acute triangle?

A. $\{1, 2, 3\}$

B. $\{2, 3, 4\}$

C. $\{3, 4, 5\}$

D. $\{4, 5, 6\}$

E. $\{6, 7, 10\}$

55.

In the figure below, $\overline{QS}$ divides parallelogram $PRST$ into one trapezoid and one right triangle. The measure of $\angle SRQ$ is 60° and the lengths $\overline{PQ}$ and $\overline{RS}$ are given in inches. Which of the following values is the area, in square inches, of parallelogram $PRST$?

F. 65

G. $65\sqrt{3}$

H. 72

J. $72\sqrt{3}$

K. 84

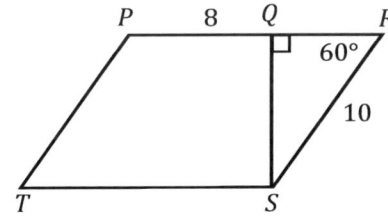

57.

Suppose that $\cos\theta = \dfrac{3}{4}$, for $0 \leq \theta \leq \dfrac{1}{2}\pi$, what is the quotient of $\sin\theta$ and $\tan\theta$, $\dfrac{\sin\theta}{\tan\theta}$?

F. $\dfrac{1}{4}$

G. $\dfrac{3}{4}$

H. $\dfrac{\sqrt{7}}{4}$

J. $\dfrac{\sqrt{7}}{3}$

K. 0

58.

As shown below, the slant height of the right circular cone is 10 centimeters, and the radius of the base of the cone is 6 centimeters. What is the equation for measure, α, of the angle formed by a height of the cone and the slant height?

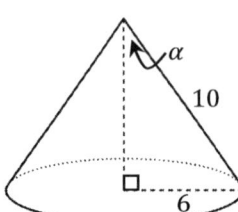

A. $\sin \alpha = \dfrac{2}{5}$

B. $\cos \alpha = \dfrac{4}{5}$

C. $\tan \alpha = \dfrac{3}{5}$

D. $\sin \alpha = \dfrac{3}{5}$

E. $\cos \alpha = \dfrac{3}{5}$

59.

Which of the following is simplified form of $\sqrt{12} + \sqrt{48}$?

A. $3\sqrt{5}$

B. $6\sqrt{10}$

C. $2\sqrt{5}$

D. $2\sqrt{15}$

E. $6\sqrt{3}$

60.

In the standard (x, y) coordinate plane, the three line with equation $y = -2x$, $y = 12$, and $x = 6$ bound a triangular region. What is the area of the triangular region (1 coordinate unit is 1 in.)?

F. $36 \ in^2$

G. $72 \ in^2$

H. $108 \ in^2$

J. $132 \ in^2$

K. $144 \ in^2$

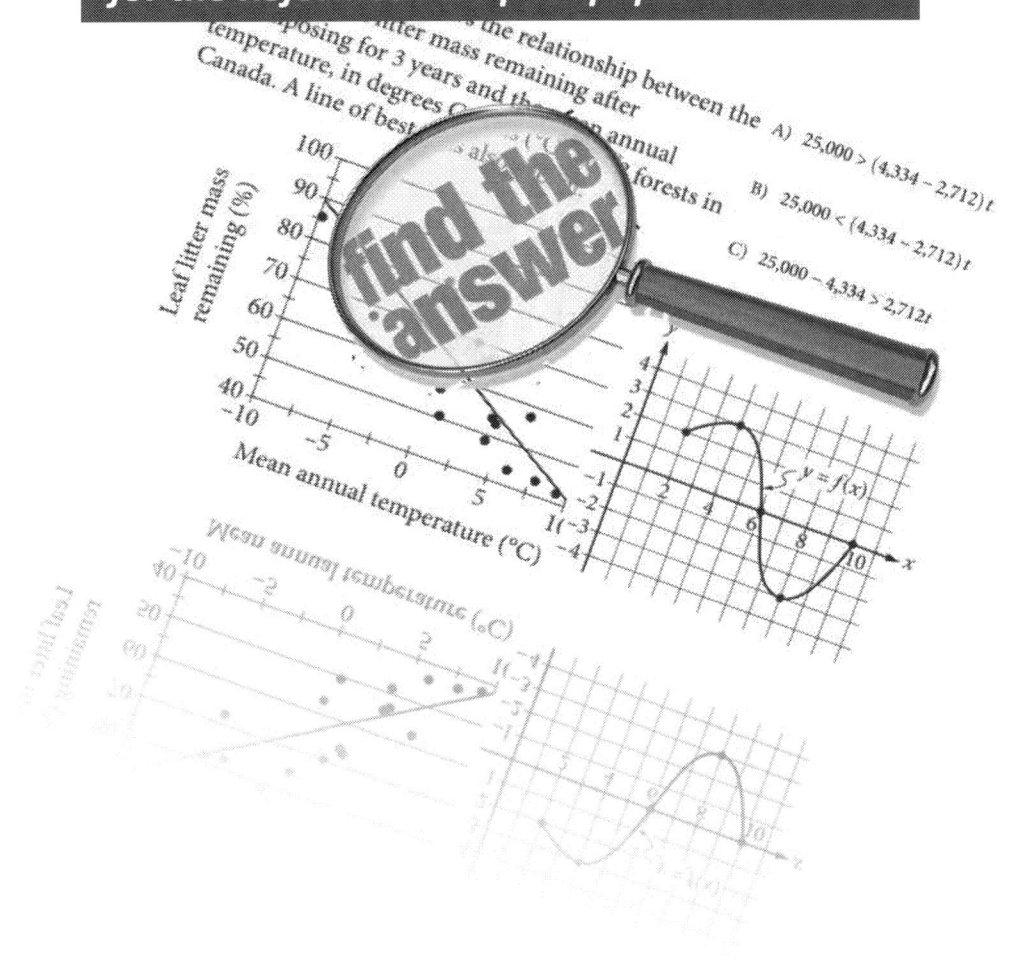

Obtain Scale Scores from Raw Scores

Scale Score	Raw Score	Scale Score	Raw Score	Scale Score	Raw Score
36	60	24	36-37	12	7
35	58-59	23	34-35	11	5-6
34	57	22	32-33	10	4
33	55-56	21	30-31	9	-
32	54	20	29	8	3
31	52-53	19	27-28	7	-
30	50-51	18	24-26	6	2
29	48-49	17	21-23	5	-
28	45-47	16	17-20	4	1
27	43-44	15	13-16	3	-
26	40-42	14	11-12	2	-
25	38-39	13	8-10	1	0

1. Scoring Key

Key		Question Category	Y/N
01.	C	Number Theory	
02.	G	Number Theory	
03.	E	Number Theory	
04.	G	Expression and Linear Equation	
05.	E	Expression and Linear Equation	
06.	H	Expression and Linear Equation	
07.	B	Expression and Linear Equation	
08.	H	Expression and Linear Equation	
09.	J	Expression and Linear Equation	
10.	F	Expression and Linear Equation	
11.	G	Linear Function inequality	
12.	E	Linear Function inequality	
13.	H	Linear Function inequality	
14.	H	Linear Function inequality	
15.	D	Further Equations and Functions	
16.	G	Linear Function inequality	
17.	D	Linear Function inequality	
18.	B	Arithmetic Topic and Ratio	
19.	J	Arithmetic Topic and Ratio	
20.	J	Arithmetic Topic and Ratio	
21.	F	Arithmetic Topic and Ratio	
22.	J	Basic Geometry	
23.	C	Basic Geometry	
24.	J	Basic Geometry	
25.	C	Basic Geometry	
26.	H	Basic Geometry	
27.	D	Basic Geometry	
28.	H	Basic Geometry	
29.	C	Arithmetic Topic and Ratio	
30.	G	Quadratic and Polynomial Function	

Key		Question Category	Y/N
31.	D	Quadratic and Polynomial Function	
32.	G	Quadratic and Polynomial Function	
33.	E	Quadratic and Polynomial Function	
34.	G	Quadratic and Polynomial Function	
35.	A	Quadratic and Polynomial Function	
36.	C	Further Equations and Functions	
37.	A	Further Equations and Functions	
38.	B	Further Equations and Functions	
39.	K	Further Equations and Functions	
40.	J	Further Equations and Functions	
41.	H	Statistics and Probability	
42.	D	Statistics and Probability	
43.	J	Statistics and Probability	
44.	K	Statistics and Probability	
45.	D	Statistics and Probability	
46.	K	Sequence and Series	
47.	C	Analytic Geometry and Conic Section	
48.	D	Analytic Geometry and Conic Section	
49.	B	Sequence and Series	
50.	D	Statistics and Probability	
51.	F	Statistics and Probability	
52.	C	Trigonometric Functions	
53.	G	Sequence and Series	
54.	C	Trigonometric Functions	
55.	G	Trigonometric Functions	
56.	D	Trigonometric Functions	
57.	G	Trigonometric Functions	
58.	B	Trigonometric Functions	
59.	E	Further Equations and Functions	
60.	K	Basic Geometry	

2. Answer Explanations

01. **Answer** **(C)**

The formula of circle area is πr^2 (r is radius).

The area of 1 part of the large waffle;
$$\frac{1}{8} \times \pi \times 16^2 = 32\pi$$
The area of the small waffle;
$$\pi \times 4^2 = 16\pi$$
So, the fractional expression is;
$$\frac{16\pi}{32\pi} = \frac{1}{2}$$

02. **Answer** **(G)**

A unit rate is a rate that has a denominator of 1 when expressed in fraction form.

Converting the cost(money) to the weight(kg);
$$\$320 \div \frac{\$0.05}{1kg} = \$320 \times \frac{1kg}{\$0.05} = 6400kg$$
Converting the weight(kg) to the number of carrots;
$$6,400kg \times \frac{24 carrots}{1kg} = 153,600 \; carrots$$
Thus, the total number of carrots is approximately 154,000.

03. **Answer** **(E)**

The prime factorization form of all perfect square is $a^{even} b^{even} c^{even} \ldots$.

First, prime factorizing A;
$$A = 24x = 2 \times 2 \times 2 \times 3 \times x = 2^3 \times 3 \times x$$
So, x must be included "2 to the **odd** power(2^{odd})" and "3 to the odd power(3^{odd})".
And x may be contained "any other prime number to the even power".

Therefore, **E**, if x is 6 $(= 2 \times 3)$,
$24x = 2^3 \times 3 \times 2 \times 3 = 2^4 \times 3^2 = (2^2 \times 3)^2 = (12)^2 = 144$
144 is a perfect square number.

04. **Answer** **(G)**

Substitute the value for each variable then evaluate. .

Substitute 2 for a and 3 for b;
$$30 - 2(a - b^2)^2 + a = 30 - 2(2 - 3^2)^2 + 2$$
$$= 30 - 2(7)^2 + 2 = 30 - 98 + 2 = -66$$
Thus, the value of $30 - 2(a - b^2)^2 + a$ is -66.

05. **Answer** **(E)**

Larger number is represented in term of the smaller number, x.

If the larger number is y, then
$$x + y = 21 \;(\because \text{ sum of two numbers is 21}).$$
Subtracting x on both sides;
$$x + y = 21 \;\rightarrow\; y = 21 - x$$
Thus, the difference is;
$$y - x = (21 - x) - x = 21 - 2x$$
The difference is $21 - 2x$.

06. **Answer** **(H)**

"varying directly " is above and "inversely" is below.

Convert to algebraic expressions;
"varying directly as the product of the masses "; $\rightarrow \;\; \propto m_1 m_2$
"inversely as the square of the distance "; $\rightarrow \;\; \propto \frac{1}{D^2}$

Thus, the expression of the force is;
$$k\frac{m_1 m_2}{D^2}$$

07. **Answer** **(B)**

An amount is the product of rate and time.

The number of reading books for 6 months;
$$Rate \times Time = \frac{2 \; books}{month} \times 6 months = 12 \; books$$
Total number of reading books is $10 + 12 = 22$ books.

08. **Answer** **(H)**

It is also a good idea to draw a figure.

There are 50 intervals of 4m and each interval is planted one tree.
And don't forget 1 tree at last end of the fence.
Thus, 51 trees is need to plant.

09. **Answer** **(J)**

Substitute p for x and q for y in each equation.

Rewrite the equation by substituting p for x and q for y;
$6p - 2q = 1$ and $-2p + 3q = -5$.
Multiplying the second equation by 3 and then adding the two equations;
$$-2p + 3q = -5 \;\rightarrow\; \begin{array}{r} 6p - 2q = 1 \\ -6p + 9q = -15 \\ \hline 7q = -14 \end{array}$$
Dividing by 2;
$$7q = -14 \;\rightarrow\; q = -2$$
Thus, the value of q is -2.

10. **Answer** **(F)**

Finding the relationship between x and y.

Using the cross product;
$$\frac{x + 3y}{2x - y} = \frac{3}{5} \;\rightarrow\; 5 \times (x + 3y) = 3 \times (2x - y)$$
$$\rightarrow\; 5x + 15y = 6x - 3y$$
Solving the equation for x;
$$5x + 15y = 6x - 3y \;\rightarrow\; 5x - 6x = -3y - 15y$$
$$\rightarrow\; -x = -18y \;\rightarrow\; x = 18y$$
Substitute $18y$ for x;
$$\frac{x}{y} = \frac{18y}{y} = 18$$
Thus, the value of $\frac{x}{y}$ is 18.

11. Answer (G)

Solving inequality by using inverse operation.

Adding 2 to both sides;
$$\frac{4+2x}{3} - 2 > 0 \quad \rightarrow \quad \frac{4+2x}{3} - 2 + 2 > 0 + 2 \quad \rightarrow \quad \frac{4+2x}{3} > 2$$
Multiplying both sides by 3;
$$\frac{4+2x}{3} > 2 \quad \rightarrow \quad 3 \times \frac{4+2x}{3} > 2 \times 3 \quad \rightarrow \quad 4 + 2x > 6$$
Subtracting 4 from both sides;
$$4 + 2x > 6 \quad \rightarrow \quad 4 + 2x - 4 > 6 - 4 \quad \rightarrow \quad 2x > 2$$
Dividing both sides by 2;
$$2x > 2 \quad \rightarrow \quad \frac{2x}{2} > \frac{2}{2} \quad \rightarrow \quad x > 1$$
Thus, the correct answer is $x > 1$.

12. Answer (E)

The operational cost is the same regardless of pairs of shoes produced.

The cost of material cost of p pairs of shoes is; $p \times 120$.
Thus, the total production cost of that day is;
total cost=operational cost + material cost of p pairs of shoes
$$\rightarrow \quad 272 + 120p$$

13. Answer (H)

Two lines are perpendicular if and only if their slopes are negative reciprocals of each other.

Because the slope of the line, m', that is perpendicular to the given line L is the negative reciprocal, the value is;
$$m' = -\frac{1}{m} = -\frac{1}{\frac{2}{5}} = -\frac{5}{2}$$
Convert the each standard form to the slope intercept form;
$$F: -2x + 5y = 7 \quad \rightarrow \quad 5y = 2x + 7 \quad \rightarrow \quad y = \frac{2}{5}x + \frac{7}{5} \quad \rightarrow \quad m' = \frac{2}{5}$$
$$G: 2x - 5y = -7 \quad \rightarrow \quad -5y = -2x - 7 \quad \rightarrow \quad y = -\frac{2}{5}x - \frac{7}{5} \quad \rightarrow \quad m' = -\frac{2}{5}$$
$$H: 5x + 2y = -7 \quad \rightarrow \quad 2y = -5x - 7 \quad \rightarrow \quad y = -\frac{5}{2}x - \frac{7}{2} \quad \rightarrow \quad m' = -\frac{5}{2}$$
$$J: -5x + 2y = 7 \quad \rightarrow \quad 2y = 5x + 7 \quad \rightarrow \quad y = \frac{5}{2}x + \frac{7}{2} \quad \rightarrow \quad m' = \frac{5}{2}$$
$$K: 5x - 2y = -7 \quad \rightarrow \quad -2y = -5x - 7 \quad \rightarrow \quad y = \frac{5}{2}x + \frac{7}{2} \quad \rightarrow \quad m' = \frac{5}{2}$$
Thus, the line G $\left(m' = -\frac{5}{2}\right)$ is perpendicular to the line L.

14. Answer (H)

First, let's calculate the cost per candle.

Calculating the cost per candle without sales tax;
$$7.23 - 1.18 = 6.05 \quad \rightarrow \quad \frac{6.05}{5} = 1.21 \quad \rightarrow \quad \$1.21$$
Thus, the cost of 8 candles is $8 \times \$1.21 = \$9.68$.

15. Answer (D)

The square of i is -1.

Expanding the given expression;
$$(x + 2i)^3 = x^3 + 3x^2 i + 3xi^2 + i^3$$
By $i^2 = -1$ and $i^3 = -i$,
$$(x + 2i)^3 = x^3 + 3x^2 i + 3xi^2 + i^3 = x^3 + 3ix^2 - 3x - i$$
Thus, the correct answer is **D**.

16. Answer (G)

Using the slope formula.

Using slope formula;
$$m = \frac{y_2 - y_1}{x_2 - x_1} = \frac{-5 - 5}{-2 - (-2)} = \frac{-10}{0}$$
The denominator of fraction is never zero, so the slope is undefined.

17. Answer (D)

The y-intercept is (0, y) and x-intercept is (x, 0).

"the slope of line B is a half of the slope of A" so the slope of line B is $-\frac{4}{3} \times \frac{1}{2} = -\frac{2}{3}$. And if x-intercept of line B is $(x, 0)$;
By using slope formula;
$$m = \frac{y_2 - y_1}{x_2 - x_1} \quad \rightarrow \quad -\frac{2}{3} = \frac{0 - 3}{x - 0} \quad \rightarrow \quad \frac{-2}{3} = \frac{-3}{x}$$
Cross multiplication;
$$\frac{-2}{3} = \frac{-3}{x} \quad \rightarrow \quad -2x = -9$$
Dividing both sides by -2;
$$-2x = -9 \quad \rightarrow \quad \frac{-2x}{-2} = \frac{-9}{-2} \quad \rightarrow \quad x = 4.5$$
Thus, the x-intercept of line B is $(4.5, 0)$.

18. Answer (B)

Substitute x value for each the equation.

1st Equation
substitute 2 for x; $ax = -b \quad \rightarrow \quad 2a = -b$ or $b = -2a$

2nd Equation
substitute 5 for x and $-2a$ for b; $ax + 3 = b \quad \rightarrow \quad 5a + 3 = -2a$
subtract $5a$ to both sides; $5a + 3 - 5a = -2a - 5a \quad \rightarrow \quad 3 = -7a$
divide by -7 on both sides; $-7a = 3 \quad \rightarrow \quad a = -\frac{3}{7}$
$b = -2a$ so, $b = -2\left(-\frac{3}{7}\right) = \frac{6}{7}$
Thus, $a + b$ is;
$$a + b = -\frac{3}{7} + \frac{6}{7} = \frac{3}{7}$$

19. Answer (J)

Convert the equation to slope-intercept form.

Convert the standard form to slope-intercept form by;
subtracting $7x$ from both sides;
$$7x + 3y = -10 \quad \rightarrow \quad 7x + 3y - 7x = -10 - 7x \quad \rightarrow \quad 3y = -10 - 7x$$
dividing both sides by 3;
$$3y = -7x - 10 \quad \rightarrow \quad \frac{3y}{3} = \frac{-7x - 10}{3} \quad \rightarrow \quad y = -\frac{7}{3}x - \frac{10}{3}$$
Thus, the y-intercept of the given equation is $-\frac{10}{3}$.

20. Answer (J)

Focusing on the grouping symbol.

Commutative property; $a + b = b + a$ or $a \cdot b = b \cdot a$
Identity property of addition; $a + 0 = a$
Identity property of multiplication; $a \times 1 = a$
Associative property;
$a + (b + c) = (a + b) + c$ or $a \cdot (b \cdot c) = (a \cdot b) \cdot c$
Distributive property; $a \cdot (b + c) = a \cdot b + a \cdot c$
Thus,
the statements is illustrated associative property of multiplication.

21. Answer (F)

" less than or equal to" means ≤.

Convert to algebraic expressions;
"3 more than the product of 2 and a number n; → $2n + 3$
"less than or equal to 5; → ≤ 5

Thus, the inequality is $2n + 3 \leq 5$.

22. Answer (J)

Volume of the prism divided by volume of the glass.

The volume of the prism is;
$$V = w \times l \times h = 8 \times 6 \times 5 = 240 \ in^3$$
The volume of the glass is;
$$V = \pi r^2 h = \pi \left(\frac{1}{2} \times 3\right)^2 \times 4 = 9\pi$$

Thus, the number of cups is $\frac{240}{9\pi} \approx 8.4882 .... \to 8$.

23. Answer (C)

Two semicircles are one circle.

The diameter of semicircle is $100 \ yd$ so, circumference of two semicircle is;
$$2 \times \frac{1}{2} \times 2\pi r = 2 \times \frac{1}{2} \times \pi d = \pi(100) = 100\pi$$
And the track has two $120 \ yd$ length so, $240 \ yd$.

Thus, the perimeter of the track is $(100\pi + 240) \ yd$.

24. Answer (J)

Using the angle relationships.

Vertical angles are always same;
$$\angle 1 \cong \angle 4, \quad \angle 2 \cong \angle 4, \quad \angle 5 \cong \angle 8, \quad \angle 6 \cong \angle 7$$

Because lines $l \parallel m$ and line t is transversal;
Corresponding angles;
$$\angle 1 \cong \angle 5, \quad \angle 2 \cong \angle 6, \quad \angle 3 \cong \angle 7, \quad \angle 4 \cong \angle 8$$
Alternate interior angles;
$$\angle 3 \cong \angle 6, \quad \angle 4 \cong \angle 5$$
Alternate exterior angle;
$$\angle 1 \cong \angle 8, \quad \angle 2 \cong \angle 7$$

Thus, the correct answer is J.

25. Answer (C)

All cubes are similar to each other.

All cubes are similar to each other and the diagonals are also side. So, the ratio of
$$\frac{\overline{AB}}{\overline{DE}} = \frac{\overline{AC}}{\overline{DF}} = \frac{3}{4}$$

Thus, the ratio of the length of $\overline{AB}$ to $\overline{DE}$ is $\frac{3}{4}$.

26. Answer (H)

If the ratio of side lengths is $a:b$, the area ratio is $a^2:b^2$.

$\square PQRS \backsim \square QYXP$ so, the ratio of lengths of side is;
$$\frac{\overline{QY}}{\overline{PQ}} = \frac{2}{5}$$
And the area of $\square QYXP$ is $5 \times 2 = 10 \ in^2$.
Using proportional equation;
$$\frac{area \ of \ QYXP}{area \ of \ PQRS} = \frac{2^2}{5^2} \to \frac{10}{A} = \frac{4}{25} \to 4A = 10 \times 25 \to A = \frac{250}{4}$$
$$\to A = 62.5$$

Thus, the area of $\square PQRS$ is 62.5.

27. Answer (D)

drawing two auxiliary lines.

Drawing two auxiliary lines;
The area is difference of total area and shaded region so,
$$20 \times 15 - 10 \times 10 = 200 ft^2$$
The number of quarts is
$$Nbr \ of \ quart = 200 \ ft^2 \times \frac{1 \ quart \ of \ paint}{60 \ ft^2} = \frac{10}{3} = 3\frac{1}{3} \ quart$$

Thus, the number of quart of the paint is $3\frac{1}{3}$.

28. Answer (H)

Perimeter = $2 \times$ width $+ 2 \times$ length.

Let the length of the rectangle be x, the width is $x - 3$. So, the perimeter is;
$$34 = 2 \times (x - 3) + 2 \times x \to 2x - 6 + 2x = 34$$
$$\to 4x - 6 = 34 \to 4x = 40 \to x = 10$$

Thus the length is 10cm and the width is 7cm.

29. Answer (C)

In parallelogram, opposite sides are parallel and equal.

Drawing the parallelogram $\square XYWZ$;
$$4x + 7x + 4x + 7x = 88 \to 22x = 88$$
$$\to x = 4$$
So, $\overline{XY} = 16$

Thus, the length of $\overline{XY}$ is 16.

30. Answer (G)

The two integers are x and $x - 2$.

If the greater integer is x, then the lesser integer is $x - 2$. So,
$$x(x - 2) = 24 \to x^2 - 2x = -24 \to x^2 - 2x - 24 = 0$$
By factoring;
$$x^2 - 2x - 24 = 0 \to (x - 6)(x + 4) = 0$$
Therefore, $x - 6 = 0$ or $x + 4 = 0 \to x = 6$ or $x = -4$
So, the two positive integers are 6 and 4.

Thus, the lesser integer is 4.

31. Answer (D)

The area of rectangle is product of width and length.

The area of original park is $100 \times 50 = 5000 \ ft^2$. Let x be the adding amount;
$$(100 + x)(50 + x) = 3 \times 5000 \to 5000 + 150x + x^2 = 15000$$
$$\to x^2 + 150x - 10000 = 0 \to (x - 50)(x + 200) = 0$$
So, $x - 50 = 0$ or $x + 200 = 0$
$$\to x = 50 \ or \ x = -200 \ (not \ solution \ x \ is \ always \ positive)$$

Thus, the length is 150 feet and the width is 100 feet.

32. Answer (G)

Making a quadratic inequality.

Making the quadratic inequality; "a profit of at least \$22,500"
$$\to 375b - b^2 \geq 22500 \to -b^2 + 375b - 22500 \geq 0$$
Multiply both side by -1;
$$-b^2 + 375b - 22500 \geq 0 \to b^2 - 375b + 22500 \leq 0$$
Factoring;
$$\to (b - 75)(b - 300) \leq 0 \to 75 \leq b \leq 300$$

Thus, the greatest number of digital books is 300.

---

33. **Answer** (*E*)

The area of rectangle is product of width and length.

If the width of the surface is x, and the area of the surface is;
$$area = width \times length = x(x + 3) = 180$$
Expanding the expression;
$$x(x + 3) = 180 \rightarrow x^2 + 3x - 180 = 0$$
Because the product is 180 and the difference is 3, factoring;
$$x^2 + 3x - 180 = 0 \rightarrow (x + 15)(x - 12) = 0$$
$$\rightarrow x + 15 = 0 \ or \ x - 12 = 0 \rightarrow x = -15 \ or \ x = 12$$

Thus, the width is 12 and the length is $12 + 3 = 15$.

---

34. **Answer** (*G*)

Using the discriminant D=0.

From the discriminant;
$$b^2 - 4ac = 0 \rightarrow (18)^2 - 4(3)p = 0 \rightarrow 324 - 12p = 0$$
$$\rightarrow 12p = 324 \rightarrow p = \frac{324}{12} \rightarrow p = 27$$

Thus, the value of p is 27.

---

35. **Answer** (*A*)

Make a quadratic equation for b.

$$a - b = 2 \rightarrow a = b + 2, \text{ substitute } b + 2 \text{ for } a;$$
$$ab = 35 \rightarrow (b + 2)b = 35 \rightarrow b^2 + 2b = 35 \rightarrow b^2 + 2b - 35 = 0$$
By factoring;
$$b^2 + 2b - 35 = 0 \rightarrow (b + 7)(b - 5) = 0$$
So, $b + 7 = 0$ or $b - 5 = 0 \rightarrow b = -7$ or $b = 5$.

Thus, the value of a is $a = b + 2 = 5 + 2 = 7$.

---

36. **Answer** (*C*)

Using the properties of logarithm.

Using the properties of logarithm;
$$\log_b \frac{m}{n} = \log_b m - \log_b n \ \ and \ \ \log_b m^n = n \log_b m$$
So,
$$\log \left(\frac{x}{3}\right)^{\frac{2}{3}} = \frac{2}{3} \log \left(\frac{x}{3}\right) = \frac{2}{3}(\log x - \log 3) = \frac{2}{3} \log x - \frac{2}{3} \log 3$$
Thus, the correct answer is *C*.

---

37. **Answer** (*A*)

The time, in year, form 2017 to 2020 is 3years.

The time, in year, form 2017 to 2020 is 3 years. So, substituting 3 for t;
$$P = 735,000(1.0625)^t \rightarrow P = 735,000(1.0625)^3 = 881,605.2246$$
Thus, the correct answer is *A*.

---

38. **Answer** (*B*)

There are 4 quarters in a year.

Using the formula of compound interest;
$$A = P\left(1 + \frac{r}{n}\right)^{nt}$$
Substituting 4,000 for P, 0.08 for r, 4 for n, 5 for t;
$$A = 4,000\left(1 + \frac{0.08}{4}\right)^{20}$$
Thus, the correct answer is *B*.

---

39. **Answer** (*K*)

Using inverse operation.

Adding 6 to both sides;
$$\sqrt[3]{4x + 8} - 6 = -10 \rightarrow \sqrt[3]{4x + 8} = -4$$
Taking cube on both sides;
$$\left(\sqrt[3]{4x + 8}\right)^3 = (-4)^3 \rightarrow 4x + 8 = -64$$
Subtracting 8 from both sides and dividing by 4;
$$4x = -64 - 8 \rightarrow 4x = -72 \rightarrow x = \frac{-72}{4} = -18$$

Thus, the value of x is -18.

---

40. **Answer** (*J*)

The given all terms are 3^n.

Using the properties of exponential;
$$3^{a+2} = 3^a \times 3^2 \rightarrow 3^a \times 3^2 = 3^a \times 3 \times 3 = 3x$$
So, $x = 3^a \times 3 = 3^{a+1}$, and;
$$3^{a+4} = 3^{a+1+3} = 3^{a+1} \times 3^3 = x \times 3^3 = 27x$$

Thus, the correct answer is *J*.

---

41. **Answer** (*H*)

The more the cars contained 5 is, the more contained 2 is.

'at most' means maximum value, suppose that the cars are 'contained 2' and 'contained 5'. If the number of the car contained 2 is x and other cars are 'contained 5' then;
$$2x + (20 - x)5 = 80 \rightarrow 2x + 100 - 5x = 80 \rightarrow -3x = -20$$
$$\rightarrow x = 6.666 \dots.$$
If x is 6, the remaining cars are $80 - 12 = 68$.
$$68 = 65 + 3, \text{ so } 65 \text{ is } 5 \times 13 \text{ and } 1 \times 3.$$

Thus, the maximum number of the car contained exactly 2 people is 6 cars, contained 5 is 13 cars and contained 3 is 1 car.

---

42. **Answer** (*D*)

Make a linear equation.

Let N be the 5th number;
$$\frac{36 + 56 + 58 + 48 + N}{5} = 54 \rightarrow \frac{198 + N}{5} = 54$$
Multiply both sides by 5;
$$198 + N = 54 \times 5 \rightarrow N + 198 = 270$$
Subtract 198 from both sides;
$$N = 270 - 198 = 72$$

Thus, the 5th number is 72.

---

43. **Answer** (*J*)

Finding the total case of product.

The total case of products;
① $X = -2$;   **6, 0, -6**   ② $X = -1$;   **3, 0, -3**   ③ $X = 0$;   **0, 0, 0**
④ $X = 1$;   **-3, 0, 3**   ⑤ $X = 2$;   **-6, 0, 6**

The total number of ways is 15 ways and the number of ways that the product is less than or equal to zero(bold numbers) is 11 ways. So, the probability is
$$P(XY \leq 0) = \frac{11}{15}$$

Thus, the correct answer is *J*.

---

44. **Answer** (*K*)

Using counting principle.

The total number of possible combinations of answers is;
$$5 \times 5 \times 5 = 125 \ combinations$$
Thus, the correct answer is *K*.

45. **Answer** **(D)**

The median is the middle of data set.

Because the number of total data is 20, the middle is between 10th and 11th. So, the interval that contains median is $9 \le h < 12$. Or using cumulative frequency;

Time(h)	Frequency	Cumulative frequency
$0 \le h < 3$	2	2
$3 \le h < 6$	3	5
$6 \le h < 9$	2	7
$9 \le h < 12$	5	12
$12 \le h < 15$	8	20

Thus the correct answer is **D**.

46. **Answer** **(K)**

Using the formula of arithmetic series.

From the formula of arithmetic series;
$$S_n = n\left(\frac{2a_1 + (n-1)d}{2}\right) \rightarrow 25 = 5\left(\frac{2a_1 + (5-1)d}{2}\right)$$
$$\rightarrow 25 = 5\left(\frac{2a_1 + 4d}{2}\right) \rightarrow 5 = \frac{2a_1 + 4d}{2} \rightarrow 10 = 2a_1 + 4d$$

Divide both sides by 2 and then solving for a_1;
$$\rightarrow 5 = a_1 + 2d \rightarrow a_1 = 5 - 2d$$
Because $d > 0$, $-2d < 0$, $a_1 = 5 - 2d = 5 + (-2d) < 5$.

Thus, the first term of the sequence, a_1 is less than 5.

47. **Answer** **(C)**

Using the distance formula.

Using the formula of distance;
$$d = \sqrt{(x_2 - x_1)^2 + (y_2 - y_1)^2} = \sqrt{(9-4)^2 + (3-8)^2} = 5\sqrt{2}.$$
Because 1 coordinate unit is 15 miles, the distance is;
$$5\sqrt{2} \times 15 = 75\sqrt{2} \text{ miles.}$$

Thus, the correct answer is **C**.

48. **Answer** **(D)**

Consider x- and y-coordinate separately.

Taking the coordinates into account, display points $D(-1,1)$, E, and F.

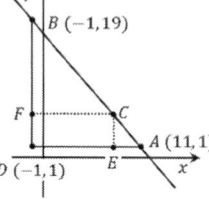

Point E is $\frac{1}{6}$ of $\overline{AD}$ and has same y-coordinate of A. The length of $\overline{AD}$ is 12 and $\overline{AE}$ is 2, so the coordinate of E is $(9,1)$.

Point F is $\frac{1}{6}$ of $\overline{BD}$ and has same x-coordinate of B. The length of $\overline{BD}$ is 18 and $\overline{FD}$ is 3, so the coordinate of F is $(-1,4)$.

The x-coordinate of C is equal to E, and y-coordinate of C is equal to F so, the coordinates of C is $(9,4)$.

Thus, the correct answer is **D**.

49. **Answer** **(B)**

Finding the first term and common ratio.

From the formula of geometric sequence; $a_n = a_1(r)^{n-1}$
$$a_2 = a_1(r)^{2-1} \rightarrow a_1 r = 12$$
$$a_5 = a_1(r)^{5-1} \rightarrow a_1 r^4 = -768$$

Rewrite a_5;
$$a_1 r^4 = a_1 r \times r^3 \rightarrow 12 \times r^3 = -768 \rightarrow r^3 = -\frac{768}{12} = -64$$
Take cubic root on both sides;
$$\sqrt[3]{r^3} = \sqrt[3]{-64} \rightarrow r = -4$$
Substitute -4 for r of a_2;
$$a_2 = a_1 r = 12 \rightarrow a_1(-4) = 12 \rightarrow a_1 = -3$$
So,
$$a_7 = a_1 r^{7-1} = (-3)(-4)^6 = -12,288$$

Thus, the seventh term is $-12,288$.

50. **Answer** **(D)**

There are 3 caramel candies.

There are 3 caramel candies so, the probability is;
$$P = \frac{15 - 3}{15} = \frac{12}{15} = \frac{3}{4} \quad or$$
$$P = \frac{6 + 4 + 2}{15} = \frac{12}{15} = \frac{3}{4}$$

Thus, the correct answer is **D**.

51. **Answer** **(F)**

Do not calculate.

The standard deviation is measure of distance between mean and each data. So, at F, the distance is zero.

Thus, the correct answer is **F**.

52. **Answer** **(C)**

Check amplitude and vertical translation.

From the standard form, $y = a\cos b(x - h) + k$, the range is
$$-a + k \le y \le a + k.$$
Rewrite the function;
$$f(x) = -3\cos(x + \pi) + 2.$$
So, the range is;
$$-3 + 2 \le y \le 3 + 2 \rightarrow -1 \le y \le 5$$

Thus, the correct answer is **C**.

53. **Answer** **(G)**

Finding the common ratio.

The common ratio, r, is;
$$\frac{12}{-4} = \frac{-36}{12} = -3$$
From the formula of geometric sequence;
$$a_n = a_1 r^{n-1} \rightarrow a_7 = -4(-3)^{7-1} = -4(-3)^6 = -2,916$$

Thus, the eighth term is $-2,916$.

54. **Answer** **(C)**

$180°$ is π radians.

Rewrite the given equation;
$$3\cos(\pi + \alpha) = 3 \rightarrow \cos(\pi + \alpha) = 1 \rightarrow \pi + \alpha = 0 \rightarrow \alpha = -\pi$$
$$4\sin\left(\frac{\beta}{6}\right) = 2 \rightarrow \sin\left(\frac{\beta}{6}\right) = \frac{1}{2} \rightarrow \frac{\beta}{6} = \frac{\pi}{6} \rightarrow \beta = \pi$$

Thus, the value of $\alpha + \beta = -\pi + \pi = 0$.

---

55. `Answer` **(G)**

The area of parallelogram is the product of base and height.

Using the trigonometric ratio;

$$\sin 60° = \frac{\sqrt{3}}{2} = \frac{\overline{QS}}{10} \;\rightarrow\; 2 \times \overline{QS} = 10\sqrt{3} \;\rightarrow\; \overline{QS} = 5\sqrt{3}.$$

$$\cos 60° = \frac{1}{2} = \frac{\overline{QR}}{10} \;\rightarrow\; 2 \times \overline{QR} = 10 \;\rightarrow\; \overline{QR} = 5.$$

So, the area is;
$$area = height \times base = \overline{QS} \times (\overline{PQ} + \overline{QR}) = 5\sqrt{3} \times 13 = 65\sqrt{3}.$$

Thus, the area is $65\sqrt{3}$.

---

56. `Answer` **(D)**

Using the Pythagorean theorem and the triangle inequality.

Using the triangle inequality;
for any triangle, the sum of the lengths of any two sides must be greater than or equal to the length of the remaining side.
So, **A.B.** are not triangle sides.

Using the Pythagorean theorem;

C. $3^2 + 4^2 = 5^2$ right triangle.

D. $4^2 + 5^2 = 41 > 6^2$ acute triangle.

E. $6^2 + 7^2 = 85 < 10^2$ obtuse triangle.

Thus, the correct answer is **D**.

---

57. `Answer` **(G)**

Using trigonometric identities.

Using tangent identity;

$$\tan\theta = \frac{\sin\theta}{\cos\theta} \;,so\quad \frac{\sin\theta}{\tan\theta} = \frac{\dfrac{\sin\theta}{1}}{\dfrac{\sin\theta}{\cos\theta}} = \frac{\cos\theta \times \sin\theta}{1 \times \sin\theta} = \cos\theta = \frac{3}{4}$$

Thus, the value is $\dfrac{3}{4}$.

---

58. `Answer` **(B)**

Considering in view of α.

Suppose that the height of cone is x;
$$x = \sqrt{10^2 - 6^2} = 8$$
In view of the angle, α;
$$\cos\alpha = \frac{A}{H} = \frac{x}{10} = \frac{8}{10} = \frac{4}{5}$$

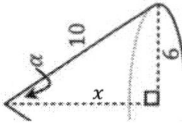

Thus, the correct answer is **B**.

---

59. `Answer` **(E)**

Combining like radicand.

Simplifying the radical expression;
$$\sqrt{12} + \sqrt{48} = \sqrt{4 \times 3} + \sqrt{16 \times 3} = \sqrt{4} \times \sqrt{3} + \sqrt{16} \times \sqrt{3} = 2\sqrt{3} + 4\sqrt{3}$$
So,
$$\sqrt{12} + \sqrt{48} = 2\sqrt{3} + 4\sqrt{3} = 6\sqrt{3}$$

Thus, the correct answer is **E**.

---

60. `Answer` **(K)**

The triangle is a right triangle.

The triangle is a right triangle and the three intersecting points are;
(-6, 12), (6, 12), and (6, -12).

So, the area is

$$\frac{1}{2} \times \big(6 - (-6)\big) \times \big(12 - (12)\big) = 144 \; in^2$$

Thus, the correct answer is **K**.

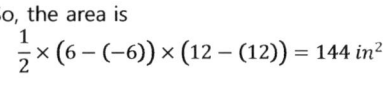
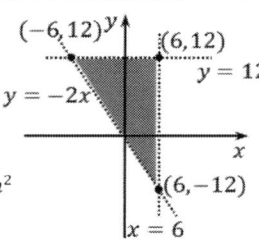

BLANK PAGE   *by K·DEAN*

25106110R00174

Printed in Great Britain
by Amazon